Modern Methods in
Secondary Education

Modern
Methods
in Secondary
Education
FOURTH EDITION

Jean Dresden Grambs and
John C. Carr
University of Maryland

**Holt,
Rinehart
and Winston**
New York   Chicago   San Francisco
Dallas   Montreal   Toronto   London   Sydney

Library of Congress Cataloging in Publication Data

Grambs, Jean Dresden, 1919–
  Modern methods in secondary education.

  Includes bibliographies and index.
  1. Education, Secondary—1945–   I. Carr,
John Charles, 1929–   joint author.   II. Title.
LB1607.G66 1979   373   78–26995
ISBN 0–03–022391–1

preface

"Efficiency" is one of the catchwords of our time. We place strong emphasis on the use of time, on the ordering of space, and on the perfection of operational systems—all with concern for doing things the "right way." As technology has permitted us to gain increased control over our environment, we have become preoccupied with the efficiency of mechanics. Indeed, the machine may be seen as a metaphor for life in the latter part of the twentieth century.

Inevitably, there has been an effort to transfer the lessons of technology —direct and indirect—to the task of teaching. Computers, films, video and sound recording devices, and other machinery are now taken for granted in most schools. Programmed textbooks, individualized learning packages, behavioral objectives, and other forms of competency based instruction are affecting the structure of curriculums and the behavior of teachers.

While technology itself—and its pedagogical offspring—offer exciting opportunities for educational enrichment, a genuine danger exists that in the pursuit of learning efficiency the more important quality of human individuality may be lost. The question is one of means and ends. It is the conviction of the authors of *Modern Methods in Secondary Education* that educational efficiency is merely a means to the greater end of intellectual exploration and self-knowledge. The purpose of this book is to provide educators with approaches to the act of teaching that combine the science and art of education. Earlier editions of *Modern Methods* stressed approaches to learning that make the human being central, approaches that encourage joint participation of students and teachers, utilization of the resources of the total community, and concern with the interests, problems, and talents of young people. The present edition continues that twenty-six-year tradition.

Ways in which the fourth edition is new will be found largely in some emphasis reflecting significant current changes in the schools and in the social world of youth. In addition, social references have been updated; many new authentic anecdotes—long a popular and unique feature of this work—have been added. A structural reorganization allows for better grouping of major topics. Introductory material has been provided for the five sections into which the book is now divided and also for the individual chapters. Of particular note is Chapter 9, "Three Processes for Learning: Creativity, Inquiry-Discovery, Values Clarification," which presents specific classroom approaches to areas increasingly significant in modern education.

There are four appendices, all of which provide annotated resources for students and in-service teachers.

Those aspects of earlier editions which long ago proved their relevancy and are now widely imitated have been maintained and updated—educational games and simulations, group procedures, sociometrics, counseling techniques for the teacher, and theory and practice of democratic discipline.

Once again we want to express our appreciation and thanks to our many students who shared their griefs and triumphs, their failures and achievements, in the often painful and, many times, ecstatic journey between student and teacher. We have benefited from their candid critique of the third edition of *Modern Methods*; many of our students' suggestions have guided this revision. Similarly, our colleagues have shared with us their experiences in using the book with their classes and have suggested changes and additions.

One comment that we have heard needs a response: "You paint too ideal a picture of the school; you don't talk enough about how grim and difficult secondary school teaching is. You preach an ideal which few of us can reach." We emphatically disagree with this comment. We know—from our own knowledge of schools and close partnership in the training of teachers —that most schools are good; that most teachers are performing daily miracles of education; that any teacher can create an inspiring and creative classroom.

JEAN D. GRAMBS
JOHN C. CARR

overview

Across the surface of a highly creative, abstract bulletin board they had assembled, a group of ninth graders wrote, "Beauty is in the eye/aye/I of the beholder." Their insightful comment applies to education as well as to beauty. When applied to education it is insightful in several ways, but principally because 1) it indicates an understanding that learning is multidimensional and 2) it states succinctly the fact that true education is that which requires the active participation of the learner. The learner must "do"; the learner must say "aye" to what is found or experienced; the learner must integrate what is learned into his or her experience.

The kind of learning that motivates, encourages, and challenges the eye/aye/I of students is what this book is about. The seventeen chapters which follow spring logically from intertwined theory and practice which seek to attract the eye/aye/I of students.

The six-part organization places chapters of related concern together so that readings and discussions may be more easily focused on the theoretical and experiential aspects of their content.

Part I is composed of three chapters which deal with fundamental concerns of all who teach: finding one's own teaching style, understanding the environment in which one teaches, and recognizing individual differences in students in order to make appropriate decisions about all aspects of the teaching act.

Part II includes two chapters which deal with sharing: democratic procedures for teaching and learning, and the components of effective communication.

Part III contains three chapters which concern the teacher as an arranger of environment for learning: managing the day-to-day operation of the classroom, organizing and planning for teaching, and determining appropriate resources for teaching.

Part IV groups four chapters dealing with teaching methodology which encourage problem solving and active participation. Specifically, the chapters are concerned with three processes for learning (creativity, inquiry-discovery, values clarification), groups and group processes, role playing and simulation, and reinforcement and retention.

Part V brings together concepts about various kinds of testing and grading.

Part VI links three chapters concerned with interaction in teaching: discipline and counseling.

For those who wish to read the chapters in a different order, no difficulty should be encountered. Each chapter possesses its own internal structure; throughout, the reader is referred to other parts of the text for additional appropriate information. Footnotes and the selected bibliographies at the end of each chapter should be useful whatever order is employed.

Each chapter of *Modern Methods* is preceded by a Focus page which centers attention on the overall concerns of that segment and on certain specific ideas which follow.

Four appendices follow the text proper: Bibliography of Teachers in Literature: Fact and Fiction; Bibliography of Adolescents in Literature: Fact and Fiction; Selected Filmography: Teaching and Learning; Bibliography of Fun and Games for Learning.

In the interest of readability, fewer footnotes appear in this edition than in earlier ones. What is discussed and suggested here is the result of the best research available as well as the experience of countless successful teachers. The annotated references which appear at the ends of chapters are among the many sources used in the writing of this edition.

contents

Understanding of Student Behavior 452; A Word of Caution 453; Counseling in Action 454; Errors to Avoid 461; Learning the Nondirective Approach 461; Extracurricular Activities and the Counseling Function 466; Career Education: Vocational Guidance 467; Parents Can Be Allies 468; "How Do You Talk with Parents?" 472; Summary 475; Selected Readings 475

part I

PEOPLE: realities and myths

PEOPLE, not facts, are the principal ingredients of education. Knowing those aspects of personality and behavior that are effective in the act of teaching will enable one to know the kind of teacher one may be able to become. Knowledge of one's role as a student teacher, as well as understanding of the role of the professionals who will provide assistance during that time, is essential to success in that experience. The nature of teaching requires the presence of students. A knowledge of them—and their individual differences—makes it possible to encourage interaction that promotes learning.

FOCUS ON CHAPTER 1

Chapter 1, "People and Places: Many Teachers, Many Schools," demonstrates that there are many kinds of "good" teachers. The reader is encouraged to reflect on real and vicarious contacts with teachers in order to analyze qualities which either facilitate or hinder learning. Five "case studies" of good teachers are examined. The various settings in which formal education occur are briefly considered.

Significant ideas presented in this chapter include:
- Teaching is still one of the time-honored professions.
- It is difficult to establish a behavior pattern for good teachers.
- All good teachers must know their subject and how to present it.
- The concept of the "ideal teacher" is a myth.
- Good teaching does not depend upon the building in which it occurs.

chapter 1

People and Places: many teachers and many schools

You should revere the teacher more than your father.
The father brought you into this world; your
teacher, who taught you wisdom, brings you to the
life of the world to come.—*The Talmud*
A teacher affects eternity; he can ever tell where
his influence stops.—*Henry Adams*

Although the observations were made centuries apart,
they indicate the degree of respect with which the
teacher has been regarded in Western society. Even now, when questions
are raised about many of our traditions, the importance of the teacher—for
the individual and society—is clearly recognized. In an affluent society that
places great value on outward signs of success, the teaching profession,
whose success cannot be measured immediately or tangibly, is still credited
as among the most admired professions.[1]

Perhaps your encounter with teachers has led you to agree with the
Talmud and Henry Adams and to wish to become a member of the time-
honored profession of teaching. In some way you have concluded that
teaching is a vital and interesting career and that working with adolescents
can be important and exciting as well. You have come to know that there
is both thrill and satisfaction in helping others to know, to clarify, to create,
and to appreciate.

While it may not be possible to determine all the influences which led
you to your decision to teach, certainly it is fair to speculate that your
decision stems partly from the kinds of teachers to whom you have been
exposed. Perhaps some individual teacher helped to illuminate your own

---

[1] Stanley Elam (ed.), *The Gallup Polls of Attitudes toward Education, 1969–1973.*
(Bloomington, Ind.: Phi Delta Kappa, Inc., 1973), pp. 15–16.

existence, or perhaps the reverse is true, and your experiences have been such that you are determined to be better than some (or all) of the teachers you have known.

Whatever influences prevail, your decision to teach indicates your recognition that teaching—metaphorically and actually—is the most powerful force humans have for solving the problems of society. From your recognition has come commitment; from commitment has come the desire to be the kind of teacher who "makes a difference."

Your understanding of what permits a teacher to make a difference may be influenced not only by your real experiences but also by vicarious ones, from reading books such as *Up the Down Staircase, Goodby Mr. Chips, The Prime of Miss Jean Brodie, The Thread That Runs So True,* or *Good Morning, Miss Dove,* or seeing films such as *Charly, To Sir, with Love,* or *The Blackboard Jungle.* Perhaps, too, you admire Annie Sullivan's "miracle working" with Helen Keller or Sylvia Ashton-Warner's work among the Maoris. Or maybe you have read of the challenges and successes encountered by Herbert Kohl, Jonathan Kozol, and James Herndon in their efforts to educate young people of the ghetto. The teachers you look to for comparison—whether they be real or fictional—are all different, and each emerges as uniquely successful.

It is hard to find a pattern among successful teachers, but probably their common characteristics are that they are humane and interesting people, although they may manifest these qualities in many different ways.

KNOWLEDGE VERSUS METHOD

For generations, arguments have raged over whether a teacher is "good" because of proficiency in knowledge of subject matter or because of expertise in the practice of pedagogy. Some critics of education have contended that being a good scholar is sufficient qualification for being a good teacher. But everyone has known teachers who were fine scholars and poor teachers. Likewise, everyone has known adroit teaching technicians who fumbled when depth of knowledge was required. Obviously, the best teachers are those who not only know what they are talking about but who employ the most appropriate techniques for teaching. They are facilitators, individuals who arrange an environment in which others can teach themselves. What experiences of your own schooling do you recall that most facilitated your learning? Which do you recall most hindered you?

A revealing activity (one which can help to clarify feelings about schooling experiences and to establish goals for individual growth) is to write descriptions of your "best" and "worst" teachers. The brief paragraphs should be specific, indicating personality attributes and behaviors which cause those teachers to be as good or poor as you can recall. An analysis of individual as well as group composite profiles can provide valuable insights into teaching that has helped or hindered learning. A graphic depiction of attributes and behaviors can be obtained by dividing a chalkboard in half, listing "best" and "worst" qualities side by side. A discussion might: (a) analyze patterns which exist between and among the attributes and behaviors; (b) determine specific effects on students; and (c) compare and contrast ways in which the profiles coincide with research about teacher effectiveness.[2] The discussion should conclude with the formulation of individual resolutions about those behaviors and attributes one wishes to develop as a teacher as well as those one is determined to avoid.

Following the resolve to perfect qualities that will contribute to good teaching, one faces the questions: How can I become a humane and interesting teacher? How can I become a good teacher?

MANY PEOPLE, MANY TEACHERS

Vicarious visits with several teachers in their classrooms at a typical secondary school and a consideration of what students, parents, and principal think of them will help to isolate their good qualities.

First on the list is a teacher of biology.

DANIEL KEARNS

Mr. Kearns appears to be an amiable person. He does not seem concerned about the noisy way his students enter the classroom. As the bell rings, he is rifling through some papers. With the ringing of the bell the class becomes quiet and attentive as he switches on the overhead projector, which shows the cell of a carrot. After a discussion concerning the process of cloning from a carrot cell, there is a scuffling of chairs as six students move to the front of the room and present ideas for organization of the cloning experiment. After the reports, the discussion gets a bit noisy since some students are adamant in their views. Mr. Kearns occasionally serves as parliamentarian, but makes no other comments. With about five minutes remaining in the period, he calls on two of the students who give reports to summarize the procedure finally agreed upon.

The Classroom

Mr. Kearns' classroom is filled with charts, mock-ups of the human body, and a good many student-constructed projects. Along one wall is a row of cabinets with fish tanks and several cages containing rats, guinea pigs, and

[2] A helpful, concise reference concerning this topic is Don Hamachek, "Characteristics of Good Teachers and Implications for Teacher Education," *Phi Delta Kappan* 50:6 (February 1969), pp. 341–345.

gerbils. A large bookcase is filled with standard reference works and paper-back editions on a wide variety of subjects. Some titles, such as *Inherit the Wind, To Kill a Mockingbird,* and *Karen Ann: The Quinlans Tell Their Story,* seem only distantly related to biology. The bulletin board across the rear wall deals with cloning, but appears to be a bit jumbled.

The Teacher

After class Mr. Kearns explains that he is in his seventh year of teaching.

The first year I taught I lectured far too much. I realized during my student teaching that I really didn't know enough biology, so I spent my first year reading and preparing detailed lecture notes. I remember thinking that if I prepared period-long lectures the student couldn't ask questions that I couldn't answer. As I look back I remember a lot of inattention and talking in my class; it must have been pretty boring. Anyway, after my first year I began to experiment with different teaching techniques. I belong to several professional organizations and get a good many practical teaching tips from their periodicals and conferences. If they seem promising I try them.

Today's class was actually rather routine. Sometimes I try something and it turns out to be a complete fiasco, and I have to drop it and try something else. I think I reach most of the students in one way or another. Take today, for example: I don't imagine too many students will be able to talk intelligently at this point about cloning, but I'll bet most of them are excited about the experiment we are going to do. And I think eventually they'll appreciate the value of scientific data in helping to decide social issues.

The Student

You can't help but be interested in Mr. Kearns' class. He really upsets the sponges—you know, those kids who take down everything the teacher says to get ready for the test. I've seen whole days when Mr. Kearns didn't open his mouth. Sometimes we get off on a tangent, and he has to pull us back. Just knowing the facts isn't enough in his class.

He also has a terrific sense of humor. I don't mean he's a clown or anything; it's just that he usually has something funny to say and somehow or other it always has to do with the lesson. Besides being able to make jokes, he also knows how to take them. Mr. Kearns says that if you don't know how to laugh, you don't know how to live.

The Parent

I remember biology as a lot of things to memorize and diagram. But Ray comes home talking about things that I have to do some checking about myself. Some parents got upset when the class was studying reproduction, but when the principal backed up Mr. Kearns and they found out it was handled tastefully and sensibly, they shut up. Ray tells me they're studying cloning now. I guess there will be more complaints.

The Principal

Mr. Kearns is one of the best teachers in the school. From what I hear of student scuttlebutt, it seems he keeps up to date and provides challenges. Sometimes his classes get a bit noisy, and some of the nearby teachers complain. The one thing that bothers me, however, is that he handles some pretty controversial topics without checking with me first. I had three sets of parents on my neck last year because of topics discussed in his classes. I've learned that he handles things fairly, but I guess I have to say that I'm glad I don't have too many like him on the question of controversial subjects.

TINA LOPEZ

Ms. Lopez is young and stands barely over five feet in height. She teaches a geography class, and the topic is Latin America. As the class enters the room Ms. Lopez is focusing a slide projector. When the bell rings she walks briskly to the front of the room where, from behind a podium which almost hides her, she begins to lecture on the physiographical features of South America. Ms. Lopez's voice is surprisingly strong, although she does not sound particularly confident. Some members of the class appear to be taking notes, but others are peering out the window. After forty minutes of lecture, with an occasional reference to the map or a specific question to the class, Ms. Lopez announces, "I want to show you some slides of life in Colombia." As she shows the slides and describes the contrasting living conditions of the various people of the country, she seems more relaxed and confident, and the students exhibit greater interest. Before the slides are finished, however, the bell rings and the students depart noisily. The lesson is not completed.

The Classroom

The classroom is rather bare. A bulletin board on one wall has a few newspaper clippings about Latin American politics, but there is no theme or organization about them. There are a few books to be seen along with a rolled-down map.

The Teacher

I guess it's obvious that I'm unsure of myself. I've only been teaching for two years and, besides, I was hired to teach psychology. There were cutbacks last year and I was asked if I would be willing to switch to another field.

Well, I had one college course in geography and the principal liked me—so here I am. After I finished college I was a social worker for two years. I enjoyed that but I think this is a better way to work with people. I'd had some education course work in college, but frankly I didn't take it seriously. I was lucky to get a job in this school system. I agreed to take additional education course work and, now, I'm also engaged in completing additional social studies requirements. The other teachers have been terrific to me— offering ideas and lending me materials, but, as you saw I'm still nervous about the newness of what I'm doing. It's going to take a while to "get it together."

The Student

Ms. Lopez gets a bit rattled at times. Some days she runs short of material and other days, like today, she forgets to stop in time to give us the home-work assignment. She tells us some really interesting stories about her experiences as a social worker in Chicago, though. She gets mad at us sometimes and says we don't appreciate our chance to get an education. She's okay; she'll learn.

The Parent

Ms. Lopez is something of an idol to my daughter and some of her friends. I guess it's because she's a person who has practiced what she preaches by doing social work. I think Ms. Lopez has caused Anne, my daughter, to think more about the future and what she'll do with it.

The Principal

I hired Ms. Lopez on what I call "educated impulse." She has a quality of personality that struck me as "right." It was a gamble switching her from psychology to geography this year, but I don't regret it. She's trading on her experiences a lot to get through the year. She'll go to summer school to do some catch-up work. By the time the new year begins she'll be on the right track. I think she has what it takes: interest in her profession, a desire to learn all she can, and a spirit of adventure.

SUZI WILLHOFT

Mrs. Willhoft (she insists on "Mrs.") is a reserved, middle-aged woman who stands quietly behind her desk as the students noiselessly file in and take their seats. There is little noise or talking before the bell. The class is reading *Romeo and Juliet* aloud, with interspersed comments on the passages by Mrs. Willhoft. Most of the class is reasonably attentive, but two students in the back are passing notes. Toward the end of the hour

Mrs. Willhoft distributes a duplicated article from a magazine which discusses the debate over whether Shakespeare or Bacon actually wrote the plays attributed to Shakespeare. The article is homework reading for class discussion the next day. During the last ten minutes of class the students begin the homework assignment.

The Classroom

Mrs. Willhoft's classroom is a model of order. Her bulletin boards are neat; she does them herself. She files the material for each bulletin board topic in manila envelopes for reuse. Among the potted geraniums and African violets on the window ledge are dictionaries and collected works of the authors her class studies throughout the year. A cabinet in the rear of the room holds copies of the mimeographed material that is distributed as it becomes appropriate.

The Teacher

I've been teaching for twenty years now, and I've found that students work better when they know exactly what is expected of them. My students know that the classroom is a place for serious business. It's my job to plan and execute the lessons, and it's their job to do the assigned work and learn. We all know our jobs and we do them.

The Student

Mrs. Willhoft is nice, but she won't put up with any nonsense. Sometimes a new student gets it in the neck before he learns. She just sort of stares you down. Her classes are pretty good and I guess we learn, but I wish she'd smile more.

The Parent

Mrs. Willhoft is solid. She is cut from the old mold. Some of the new teachers are too lax and easygoing. Not Mrs. Willhoft, she makes kids toe the line. Our Karl had a tendency to get out of hand until he got into her class.

The Principal

Mrs. Willhoft is a fixture. She was here when I came, and I have the feeling she'll be here when I'm gone. She does a solid job of teaching and her reports are always on time and models of accuracy. One interesting thing I've noticed: On those rare days when Mrs. Willhoft is out sick and we have to get a substitute, the substitutes always comment that the classes can tell her just what the lesson will be and are concerned that they do not fall behind on the plans Mrs. Willhoft has made. Her discipline seems to become part of the students after a while.

LARRY GLASER

Mr. Glaser is a recently discharged career Navy veteran who teaches industrial arts. His students are currently engaged in a unit on electricity; several are working on their own radio receiver sets, and others are doing research in a separate reference room to one side of the main shop area. Mr. Glaser moves among the students commenting on their work and occasionally helping out with a soldering job. Before long, however, he is talking to a student in his office. As soon as one student departs, another goes in. By the end of the period four students have made the trek to the office.

The Classroom

The equipment in the shop is relatively new and well kept, but there is no attempt on his part to add anything to make the room more than just a workroom. About five minutes before the end of the period, the students begin putting away their projects and replacing tools and equipment. As the bell rings all is in order.

The Teacher

Mr. Glaser explains that somehow he has become father–confessor to his students. He doesn't quite know how it happened. He guesses it may be because he is about the age of many of their fathers and, unlike many of their fathers, he is willing to listen:

> Students often come in after school. One or two of those boys I talked to during class will be in this afternoon. After that I have to do my planning for the next day. I seldom go home before 6 PM, but I don't mind. These boys are usually the ones who won't go on to college and, unfortunately, our school doesn't take as great an interest in them as it does in the college-bound. I suppose I'm infringing on the work of the counselors, but they don't seem to mind.

The Student

> Mr. Glaser is tops. He's the only person in this school who'll listen to us and help us to get jobs when we graduate. A few of us were thinking of quitting school, but he talked us out of it.

The Parent

I resented Mr. Glaser at first. My boy was always talking "Mr. Glaser this" and "Mr. Glaser that." I even went to the school to tell him to mind his own business, but he was so glad to see me I couldn't complain. We talked about my boy for a long time and I think I learned a few things.

The Principal

I suppose Mr. Glaser is right. I guess somehow we are less sensitive to the needs of the boys in shop classes. We're a comprehensive high school but the majority of our students go to college. Mr. Glaser may not be the best shop teacher, but he does help his students by listening to their problems and working with them.

MARGARET CHIN

The preciseness of Ms. Chin's subject is not shown in her rapidly scrawled and explained solutions to the algebra problems on which the class is laboring. While she is a competent teacher, Ms. Chin's main asset is her contribution to school morale. She has a cheerful good morning for everyone—even on Mondays. She is especially well informed about school affairs and spends a few minutes of almost every period discussing the latest school activities with her students. She is present at all school functions and voluntarily chaperones school dances. Ms. Chin was the first Asian-American teacher assigned to this school, and for the first few months was a source of curiosity. However, due to her charm, vivacity, and competence in her subject, she has long since been accepted by everyone.

The Classroom

Ms. Chin's classroom is friendly in a "homey" way. A certain casualness of arrangement is present—along with flowers and a wide variety of magazines. Her bulletin boards do not show great imagination, but they are used to instruct and they interest her students. Always on view are the latest activities posters; and there is a photograph of the school mascot as well as the school emblem, which was presented to Ms. Chin by last year's graduating class.

The Teacher

I enjoy teaching algebra, but I think what I enjoy most is simply working in the school and with the students. I've been here only four years now, but I am student government advisor and on the faculty policy committee. We have one of the best student governments in the state—we even let the students run it! And we have good teacher morale because the teachers also know they can have their just grievances heard without a lot of fuss being kicked up.

The Student

Ms. Chin is all right as a teacher. She sometimes makes mistakes in the problems we're working on, but she doesn't get mad when we correct her— and we do learn our math. As a person, she's terrific! The thing we like best is her interest in school activities. She attends everything and tells kids how well they do in school plays or football games. She even said something nice about the basketball team after we lost by forty points. I guess we sometimes abuse her willingness to help with things we're doing, but she never complains.

The Parent

Our daughter is a junior this year and is pretty excited about the junior banquet and dance. This is a new event instituted by the student government with Ms. Chin's advice. The junior class undertakes various projects to pay for the whole affair. Ms. Chin puts in many Saturdays in the fall organizing and helping the juniors.

The Principal

Ms. Chin gets things done that I would balk at trying—like the time she appeared before the school board and requested more funds for school activities. The school board complimented her on the case she presented, and she got the money. It irked me at the time because I felt that that was my job, but we talked about it and I've gotten over my annoyance.

THE MYTH OF THE IDEAL TEACHER

All of the teachers discussed here are good in different ways. Discuss with fellow students the qualities they possess which make them helpers of learning. What qualities mentioned in the anecdotes indicate ways in which they may hinder learning? Some of the teachers concentrate on subject matter while others are more people-oriented. Their personalities are as varied as their teaching styles. How can you compare these teachers with the ones you recall as "best" and "worst"? Considering the full array of teachers here and in your class discussion, what subject areas are represented? What grade levels? To what degree do individual expectations and values cause us to determine a teacher's competence? In what ways do these considerations make it difficult to "nail down" a definition of good teaching?

All the teachers described in the preceding pages have strengths and weaknesses. They share with all teachers the fact that no one is ideal. Indeed, the ideal teacher—one without faults—is a myth. To concentrate one's efforts on becoming ideal is to lose the opportunity of realistically developing one's potentialities; to concentrate on improving one's knowledge of subject matter and one's expertise in the practice of teaching is essential to personal worth and professional responsibility; to pursue the notion of becoming perfect is to jeopardize one's competence in both.

THE TEACHING–LEARNING PROCESS

The debate about what constitutes good teaching has, at times, generated more heat than light. Theorists and practitioners have sometimes been forced into more extreme positions than they really espouse. In the end, an analysis of the teaching–learning process comes down to "know what," "know why," and "know how." The "what" places emphasis on subject-matter knowledge. The "why" is concerned more with broad values, purposes, and continuity of culture. The "how" is concerned with the practical skills of teaching.

Persons who wish to become effective secondary school teachers must achieve a balance among "why," "what," and "how." Failure to know "why" results in aimless, disorganized teaching that inevitably stresses the acquisition of information for its own sake. Teachers who do not know subject matter cannot determine "why" they are teaching or "what" they should teach; the use of the latest audiovisual equipment cannot disguise the fact the teacher simply does not know what he or she is talking about. Similarly, merely knowing a subject without being able to communicate it to students is of no value.

Two additional aspects of the teaching–learning process should be acknowledged: Know the students and know how well the students are learning.

Considering students as the objects of the learning process suggests the importance of knowing the students themselves. Familiarity with the research of adolescent psychology and learning theory should be coupled with close and concerned observations of adolescent behavior. Good teachers pay close attention to factors affecting students' ability to learn.

An important part of every teacher's job is evaluation; therefore a teacher is always concerned with how well students progress. Daily feedback in a variety of formal and informal ways contributes to the larger assessments of how well goals set for and by students are being met. Chapter 14 deals with this topic.

This book is designed to offer you the opportunity to crystallize what you already know, to explore and learn skills you do not have, and to snythesize for yourself those attributes which will allow you to become that most needed and admirable human being: a good teacher.

MANY BUILDINGS, MANY SCHOOLS

Until the 1950s, the typical American school could be thought of as a series of boxes inside one large box. Rectangular rooms of varying sizes were lined side by side facing one another across a narrow strip of corridor lined with metal lockers. The regular pattern of the classrooms positioned throughout the school was broken occasionally by a cafeteria, the administrative offices, storage rooms, the gymnasium, home economics and science labs, or an art room. Within the classrooms themselves another predictable pattern occurred. Students' ·desks were positioned in rows facing a blackboard and the teacher's desk. Windows—with shades pulled to an exact position—lined one side of the room, while wooden floors and schoolhouse green and beige walls provided a physical conformity and drabness that too often matched the kind and quality of instruction which occurred within the space.

As efforts to create alternative ways of learning manifested themselves in the 1960s and early 1970s, architects conceived new forms and shapes to accommodate the varied ways in which teaching and learning might be achieved. Flexible classroom space—with folding doors, tiled floors, soft colors, and functional furniture—was the hallmark of change. Multipurpose rooms, expanded home economics and science facilities, along with a greater use of open space, contributed to a sense of newness, a sense of "the learning workshop."

As suburban living increased, which created a need for new schools, some schools with new shapes appeared. While most were still boxes within boxes, a wholly new physical appearance came to be associated with all levels of schooling: large areas of open space, carpeted floors, bright colors, comfortable furniture, and equipment undreamed of a generation before, including sophisticated industrial education machinery, television studios, computers, professional stage lighting, individualized learning "hardware and software."

Because school buildings last a long time, it is possible that you as a student teacher, or as a beginning teacher, may work in any kind of setting, from nineteenth-century rectangle to the latest, open "learning space." What are the considerations one needs to make for working within varying kinds of space and with varying kinds of facilities? What are the effects of the differing spaces and facilities on students? How do confined and open spaces, dull and bright colors, constraining and comfortable furniture, silence and noise affect learners and teachers?

As the American people continue to relocate themselves, causing shifts in affluence and poverty, a great variety of school buildings is likely to exist in almost all places. Terms such as city, inner-city, suburban, and rural are still appropriate, as are notions of teaching such as traditional and nontraditional, but buildings themselves can no longer be predicted for form, appearance, or facilities.

The last several years have seen a major change for some areas of the country in designating the beginning of the secondary school level. The emergence of the middle school, which replaces junior high school as a bridge between the upper years of elementary school and senior high school, is an effort to align the needs of young people in a rapidly changing society with the circumstance in which their schooling occurs.

Teaching that makes a difference, in the humane sense discussed in this chapter, knows no time or place, whether it takes place in a self-contained, traditional classroom or in the pod of a chic learning park.

The teacher who makes a difference recognizes that all students and teachers who grow are people who use knowledge to understand themselves and others and thus work toward solving the problems of society and the enrichment of the human spirit.

SUMMARY

Reflecting on the qualities and behaviors of successful teachers causes one to recognize that there is no such thing as an ideal teacher. Many qualities and behaviors allow teachers to guide young people in the learning process; the important task for beginning teachers is to understand and develop their strengths while minimizing their weaknesses. Teachers must achieve a balance among the "why," "what," and "how" of teaching in order to be effective.

SELECTED READINGS

Calisch, Richard W., "So You Want To Be a Real Teacher?" *Today's Education*, 58 (November 1969), pp. 49–51.

Featherstone, Joseph, and Helen Featherstone, "Teaching: An Impossible Profession," *American Educator*, 1:1 (January–February 1977), p. 39. Also recommended is a review of Lortie, Dan C. *School-Teacher: A Sociological Study*. Chicago: The University of Chicago Press, 1975.

Holt, John, *How Children Learn*. New York: Pitman, 1967. Examples of how children employ a natural style of learning and what teachers can do to encourage it.

————, *How Children Fail.* New York: Pitman, 1964. A straightforward, fascinating argument for why students fail with interesting solutions recommended.

Hunter, Elizabeth, and Edmund Amidon, *Student Teaching: Cases and Comments.* New York: Holt, Rinehart and Winston, 1964. A collection of problem situations with accompanying discussion of relevant issues and questions intended to lead the reader to alternate courses of action. Some of the cases presented are concerned with discrimination, creativity, special privileges, loyalties, jealousy, and diplomacy.

Peddiwell, Abner, *The Saber-Tooth Curriculum.* New York: McGraw-Hill, 1939. Classic satire on progressive education, which reveals both its strengths and weaknesses.

Perrodin, Alex F., *The Student Teacher's Reader.* Skokie, Ill.: Rand McNally, 1966. The extensive number of articles included in this collection is intended to parallel the student teacher's gradual induction into teaching; intended to accommodate individuals as they feel the need for information or assistance.

The Real World of the Beginning Teacher. Report of the Nineteenth National Teacher Education and Profession Conference. Washington, D.C.: National Commission on Teacher Education and Professional Standards, 1966. "What it's really like" through the eyes of a variety of writers; contains suggestions about changes needed to make the job of beginning and established teachers a more effective and happy one.

FOCUS ON CHAPTER 2

Chapter 2, "Transition: Student Teaching and Success," provides background discussion and information which can enable student teachers to understand their roles and responsibilities better and to gather information about their students and the school in which they are to work. The "shadow study" and a guide for school and classroom observation are suggested. The relationship among student teacher, resident teacher, and college supervisor is explored with consideration given to the expectations and performances of each. Establishing rapport with students is presented as a major priority for teaching; some specific details of student–teacher relationships are examined.

Significant ideas presented in this chapter include:
- The more information one has about the student teaching experience, the more one can alleviate anxiety and begin to work productively.
- Gathering information quickly about the school and the students will facilitate all aspects of the student teacher's work.
- The relationship among student teacher, resident teacher, and college supervisor is complicated, but it can produce feedback and assistance of quantity and quality which may not be available again in one's career.
- Among the important attributes in student–teacher rapport is a sense of humor.
- Success in student teaching is a good predictor of later success in teaching.

chapter 2

Transition: student teaching and success

It's a different world on the teacher's side of the desk—a world you can't really know about until you're there.[1]

The above remark from a student teacher's end-of-semester report succinctly captures the reaction of most people as they engage in the student teaching experience. What one sees from behind the teacher's desk is entirely different from what one sees from behind the student's desk. It is fortunate that college students have the opportunity to learn about the real world of teaching gradually, through a guided induction that allows them to experiment, reflect, and adjust to that "different world."

Although student teaching is not strictly speaking an aspect of "methods," the rationale behind including a consideration of it here is that most readers of this book soon will be, if they are not already, engaged in teaching or a teaching internship. From their contact with such students, the authors know that many fears and anxieties exist about that experience. Some of the problems are endemic to any new situation. Others are uniquely associated with the peculiar nature of student teaching when one is part student, part teacher.

The discussion in this chapter will focus on "normal" student teaching; that is, one in which the student is placed in a secondary school for a whole day or several periods a day, with one or more resident teachers, and is periodically visited by a college or university special subject supervisor. Nontraditional student teaching settings, such as teacher-education centers, remain in the minority. Although the concepts expressed here hold

[1] Unless otherwise cited, anecdotal material comes from written reports by students and student teachers and from the authors' observations. All anecdotes are authentic.

true for any student teaching experience, the specific items relate to the traditional experience which is typical throughout the country.

A consideration of some initial student teaching experiences and concerns can help to make the transition from student to professional smoother and happier. Those who have had other teaching experiences—in private schools, in military service, as a substitute, as a teacher's aide, or as a teacher at another level in the educational hierarchy—should also find this material instructive. Experienced teachers may find in this chapter insights into the role of supervising teacher and the subtler interpersonal problems involved.

The student teaching experience is organized so that teacher candidates:

- are gradually inducted into teaching
- begin to learn about, and to know, the adolescents they teach
- experiment with a variety of teaching techniques
- employ the resources of the school and community
- are observed and evaluated by the resident teacher and the college supervisor[2] (and perhaps by others)
- are helped to evaluate their own strengths and weaknesses.

In the following sections these and other aspects of the student teaching experience will be discussed and illustrated.

"AM I WELCOME?"

It is natural to have some anxiety and apprehensiveness about moving to the teacher's side of the desk. Questions such as:

- "Does my cooperating teacher really want me?"
- "Will the faculty and staff accept me?"
- "Will my students respect and like me?"
- "Will I do a good job?"
- "Is teaching really the profession for me?" arise.

All of these are reasonable concerns; some thoughtful "mind-setting" can help to alleviate fears and to allow a strong and positive beginning to student teaching. Five basic "mind-sets" are essential:

1. Believe in yourself and your ability to work with adolescents.
2. Realize that all good teachers continue to learn both subject matter and teaching methodology; you *do* know enough about both to become a student teacher.

---

[2] There is some variation in the terminology used to identify various people with whom students work during student teaching. The teacher in the school may be called "resident teacher," "cooperating teacher," "critic teacher," or some equivalent. College and university supervisors are usually referred to as such. Student teachers are sometimes called "intern teachers."

3. Expect a warm, friendly, interested welcome from faculty, staff, and students.
4. Recognize that you will work hard and under pressure.
5. Prepare to change; you will not be the same, personally or professionally, after student teaching.

Here are one student teacher's comments about her first day:

After looking forward to it for so long, I started my student teaching. What a change from the University. These kids are awake and jumping at 8:00 AM —and on Monday morning, no less! . . . Mr. Bogar met me at the office and we went to the classroom together. When I met him two weeks ago, I felt sure we'd hit it off. I feel that way again, today. Mr. Bogar introduced me to all his classes. I'm worried about having to learn 137 names. I carried the seating charts around all day, hoping the names will sink in eventually.
 At lunch I was introduced to several members of the faculty. Everyone was interested in my reactions to the school. During the afternoon I received two added bonuses(?) for a first day. I felt I was getting into the routine of things when a bell sounded in the middle of the fifth period. I sat looking startled until someone yelled "fire drill." I got out with everybody else. After school I saw another school operation—faculty meeting. It wasn't at all like I had pictured. With 150 faculty members it was more like a convention. I found it difficult to take it all in. I was introduced to the whole faculty. At the end of the meeting I met the other career education teachers. Everyone was friendly and offered help. . . . I was so exhausted when I got home that I took a two-hour nap.

Student teaching is a unique experience. Assignment to a classroom means more than just reporting to a particular school and resident teacher, it means becoming part of a school and a school system. Indeed, it means becoming a colleague in a time-honored profession where quality is always welcome.

APPEARANCES MAKE A DIFFERENCE

Some college and graduate students about to embark on student teaching are insulted when college or public school personnel raise issues about personal appearance. Long experience, however, indicates that many beginning teachers require assistance in developing this aspect of self-awareness. This is the first time in the majority of student teachers' lives that they have been on public display for most of the day—the object of careful scrutiny by 150 or more observant, critical, curious adolescents.
 This means that a student teacher must be alert to those aspects of dress, manner, and style, which indicate that one is at ease with oneself as an adult. Such dress should also be acceptable to the school community. It is

possible to dress tastefully without going to the extremes of either looking like "an old maid schoolteacher" or a slave to conformity. The exotic and avant-garde, or the relaxed, at-home, appearance have their places, but not in the classroom, any more than they belong in other professional settings.

> One of the fascinating things we've found with our student teachers is that after they've seen themselves on videotape, their grooming improves immediately. Seeing themselves working with students in a teaching situation seems to enhance their realization of how much appearance makes a difference.

Many student teachers are self-conscious about their age, since perhaps only three or four years separate them from the students they are instructing. Appearance which accentuates maturity and competence is invaluable to the beginning teacher. Useful guidelines concerning the appropriateness of appearance in the community where you will student teach should be considered with your classmates. If possible, ask a teacher or administrator in the community to act as consultant in your discussion.

GETTING TO KNOW YOUR SCHOOL

Most student teachers will be given a quick tour of the building or instructions to help orient them to their new environment. In a few instances student teachers are trapped in the room, or rooms, in which they teach, emerging only when their tours of duty are over. This is unfortunate and one should be careful to avoid such entrapment. The school not only houses resources teachers will need to use, it is also an important part of the world of students. It is important for student teachers to know what students are exposed to daily, as one way of knowing what experiences, attitudes, and opportunities influence what is to be taught. Is the building old, with obsolete staircases and dingy, noisy corridors? Is it modern? Or is it a monstrosity with the look and layout of a particularly efficient and antiseptic prison? How long will it take to get from one corner of the school to another? Where do people congregate to socialize?

An excellent way to get a quick, yet impressive, insight into how a school functions is to do a "Shadow Study." As the name indicates, one becomes a shadow for a day. A student, preferably picked at random from one of the classes to which the student teacher is assigned, is chosen. The day's program for this student is procured. Then the student teacher "shadows" the student throughout the day, sitting, in a sense, in that student's chair for a whole school day, seeing the school as the student sees it, and responding to teachers and peers as the student does. A simple form helps in making observations:

Subject _____   Grade Level _____

Period: General description of classroom or setting (for example, the cafeteria)

Time: Recorded at 5-minute intervals   What subject was doing   What class and teacher were doing

Overview: (At the end of the period) An evaluation of how students seem to have been involved, what seems to have been learned, how teacher and students seem to feel about the class.

One should not let the subject know that he or she is being shadowed, but often students realize what is happening. Avoid behavior and discussions which will cause a student to feel like a subject under a microscope. If possible, the observer should talk with the shadow subject the same day, asking about perceptions of school, congenial teachers and subjects, life goals, and other pertinent questions without prying.

As others have found,[3] shadow studies are revealing both to observers and to readers. They can provide an excellent introduction to the school in which one will teach, providing a rare "student's eye" view of the school.

OBSERVING STUDENTS

At first the role of the student teacher is that of an observer. One doesn't have to wait with "fear and trembling" that at any moment the resident teacher will suddenly say, "Here, Mr. Jones, take over the rest of the lesson while I go to the office." This could happen, of course, but it is unlikely and not recommended.

The resident teacher has a stake in seeing that the student teacher is gradually eased into the full responsibility of the classroom. When instructions are confusing or the class becomes chaotic because the student teacher has had to assume responsibility that he or she is unprepared for, a resident teacher suffers the consequences also. So it is mutually advantageous for the student teacher to spend some time in learning about the classroom, the course, and the students, before taking on independent responsibility.

Observing a room full of adolescents is no easy task. Fortunately, many education students have the opportunity to observe in schools prior to

---

[3] John A. Lonnsbury and Jean V. Marani, *The Junior High School We Saw* (Washington, D.C.: Association for Supervision and Curriculum Development, 1964).

student teaching. The usual observation experience in a "typical" teacher education program emphasizes learning about students. In observations at the beginning of student teaching, though, the student teacher should not only observe to learn about students but also to learn about how the teacher works with a particular class. One must also learn how the unit of work is developed, how order is maintained, how roll is taken, as well as how all the other innumerable details of teaching are carried out.

During this observation period, the student teacher should work consciously to think and feel as a professional teacher. Sit in an inconspicuous place in the classroom, working to gather lucid ideas about some important and practical details of teaching. Several things the student teacher should note are:

GENERAL APPROACH TAKEN BY THE TEACHER. Each teacher's "style" of teaching is individual. Since the student teacher will be continuing where the regular teacher left off, it is important to know what kinds of learning expectations have been built up in the students. Do they expect to be quizzed on details? Are they encouraged to think about broad generalizations? Are certain skills emphasized—spelling, reading, orderliness—or are they ignored in favor of other kinds of learning?

CLASSROOM ROUTINES. The details of classroom management are considered in Chapter 6. However, early in student teaching, the student teacher will want to be crystal clear about basic procedures that simplify classroom routine. For example: How is roll taken? Is an absence list sent to the office? How is it sent? What records of attendance must be kept? How are previous absences, if excused, noted by the teacher? What happens with unexcused absences? How are supplies distributed? Who checks supplies? How much time must be allowed for these routines?

CLASSROOM RULES. Some teachers have strict rules about certain behavior. Gum-chewing, for example, may be forbidden. Other teachers may refuse to permit students to sharpen pencils once class has begun, or they may not permit students to go to hall lockers for forgotten work or materials. The student teacher will want to know precisely which rules have been stressed by this teacher in this class.

Student teachers may also face the problem of wanting to establish rules which the resident teacher does not employ. This is an area about which there should be a thoughtful discussion with the resident teacher. It is possible that the new rules will only confuse or alienate students, create complications for classroom management that are not worth the effort, or offend the resident teacher. Under no circumstances should the student teacher tell students something like, "I'm in charge now. Do what I say."

ESTABLISHING AND MAINTAINING ORDER. If student teachers are fortunate enough to begin classroom observations from the beginning of newly formed classes, they will be able to see in what ways resident teachers establish codes of behavior for individual classes. Considerations for the observer include: How is the behavior code established—solely by the teacher or by teacher and students together? How do students react to the code in general? What happens when there is a behavior infraction? Is the teacher consistent in treating the infraction? How do students react when they are reprimanded or punished? Do the reprimands and punishments seem fair? In what way does the behavior code seem to help the learning process? In what way does the code seem to interfere with individual or group processes?

When student teachers begin their observation period after classes have been formed, it is important to discuss with resident teachers the whats, hows, and whys, of class behavior. Some students will attempt to "test" the observer/student teacher to see if a similar code of behavior is expected when the resident teacher is not present. When students perceive an incongruence in the expectations of the two, student teachers can almost always expect trouble.

It is, of course, important for student teachers to have a copy of any texts that are used as well as any accompanying course of study. They should also know what other instructional materials are available and how they are organized and distributed.

These details may seem obvious. But it is one thing to observe obvious details and quite another to take care of them easily and efficiently. Uncared for, small details effectively disrupt the finest teaching. For this reason, resident teachers often ask for the student teacher to undertake some routine tasks very early in student teaching. Taking roll, for example, is an invaluable "first task." Not only does this acquaint the student teacher with the procedures of taking attendance, it is also an opportunity for associating names with faces.

A second task the student teacher may undertake early is the distribution and handling of supplies, equipment, and other instructional materials. It may look simple to get ten library books to ten different students or to distribute test papers or collect assignments, but unless one knows just what to do and what to say, the student teacher will generate confusion quickly.

OBSERVATION OF DAILY LESSONS. The student teacher comes nearer to the heart of teaching by observing the general approach to subject matter taken by the resident teacher. From texts or other teaching materials, from the nature of the syllabus when one is available, from the type of past examinations, from the nature of current assignments, one will get a partial picture of what is being taught, how the teaching is organized, and how the effectiveness of the teaching is appraised. But the resident teacher at work remains the best resource.

During the first several days of observation there will be many questions about the details of teaching in this class. Ask the resident teacher diplomatically, at a judicious moment—but ask! Why was this aspect of the material emphasized while another was ignored? Why did the teacher spend so much time on one diagram but skip lightly over another? Why was Jim told his answer was good, when it apparently left much to be desired? Why was Mae cross-examined when her answer seemed quite acceptable?

Observation during the first days of student teaching should be accompanied by taking many notes. An observation guide may be provided to direct note taking. Student teachers may consider this recordkeeping an unprofitable exercise, which indeed it is, when the data are not used to develop insight. The activity of writing down the experiences is an important discipline. Instead of having vague "feelings" about teaching, it is important to make concrete statements about what is seen and heard. One must record actual behavior rather than shadowy impressions unsupported by evidence. Careful attention to detail about student behavior and teacher performance will lead to a more realistic understanding and appraisal of teaching. Early in student teaching, make an appointment with the resident teacher to discuss your observation log. It is wise not to leave such interviews to chance. A regular, scheduled appointment with the resident teacher —before school, at lunch, during the free period, after school—should be arranged and adhered to. In addition, it may be profitable to share this log with the college supervisor.

GETTING STARTED

One student teacher described her initial teaching experience this way:

Taught my first class, drama, at 1:05 today, just after lunch. This morning I helped Mr. Garzero with a rehearsal for the one-act play to be given for the PTA tomorrow evening; it was hectic and I was nervous thinking about my "debut" at 1:05. Fortunately, I calmed down by lunch time. My lesson was well organized and the time went quickly but not quite as fast as I went through my lesson. I finished up all the material I had planned to cover before the period was over. However, I had expected a better response from the class. What I gave them today was supposedly not entirely new material, but they acted as if they had never heard it before.

They did cooperate though—they paid attention and they tried. Things don't come out as they do when you plan them on paper . . . maybe I was overconfident.

The typical student teacher becomes impatient and eager to accept responsibility as confidence builds. At the same time, the resident teacher is making judgments about the student teacher's readiness. Some resident teachers are more cautious than others. Some willingly let go of the class; others hold back for a longer time. Sometimes the resident teacher feels that the student teacher is not yet oriented to the classroom and this is always difficult to accept. But, finally, the first teaching day does come, and it probably involves only a part of the full teaching responsibility: "Tomorrow, why don't you prepare to give the assignment we have planned just before study period?" Or, "You can read out the quiz questions in third period and check the answers with the class."

The resident teacher may urge caution and a slow pace in initial teaching plans. "Stay with what you know and use techniques with which you feel full security," is good standard advice. A motion picture is valuable, but can the student teacher use the projector without mishap? What if the resource visitor turns out to be a poor speaker, or does not turn up at all? The student and resident teacher may decide to forego the more dramatic activities at first for those in which they both feel confident. The simple and the unpretentious will build skill surely and steadily.

The resident teacher will probably remain in the room during the first stages of student teaching. Eventually, though, the student teacher is left alone with the class: thirty-plus individual, unpredictable adolescents! Gradually assurance comes, and by the time several weeks have passed the student teacher will have full responsibility in at least one of the classes assigned. By the end of student teaching, one may well be teaching full time in an additional class or classes.

BEING SUPERVISED

Highly important in the student teaching experience is the relationship among the student teacher, the resident teacher, and the college supervisor. The most successful student teaching experience develops when these three people work together for common ends.

In many institutions the relationship between college and high school is a close one. The student teaching experience is a product of joint planning and effort. Some colleges have regular meetings with resident teachers to work out the steps in the induction of student teachers. In other institutions the contact between college and classroom is more formal and less intensive. Whatever the arrangement, student teachers soon realize that their positions under dual supervision are unique.

THE RESIDENT TEACHER

For a moment, look at the relationship between resident and student teacher from the viewpoint of the resident teacher. One of the most trying emotional burdens of teaching is the feeling that no matter how well teaching is done, it can always be better. Some students have been reached only slightly by the best teaching efforts. Others do not seem to respond at all. Some are constant sources of puzzlement and worry. At heart, teachers must have humble views of their successes. Satisfactions are always tempered by the knowledge that teaching is never completely finished, never accomplished to perfection.

Resident teachers are selected because they are experienced and competent, and have achieved skill and poise worth emulating. But even the most assured, experienced teachers have moments of concern and self-doubt. So while they welcome the student teacher, they also often feel defensive under a fresh, critical eye. Resident teachers know that the neophyte usually brings high aspirations to teaching. From their own experiences, resident teachers may believe that such aspirations can only be achieved after long years of hard work. In this sense, then, student teachers may pose a threat to some resident teachers. But there is another threat facing some resident teachers, who may honestly feel that they are not really abreast of the latest educational practices or in touch with the newest scholarship. Such individuals may feel that student teachers actually know more than they do in some areas.

Student teachers sometimes feel that their resident teachers are reluctant to have them try newer classroom techniques. In such cases the resident teacher may be sincerely motivated by a genuine belief that it is better for a student teacher to gain confidence through tried and tested approaches before venturing into the new and unpredictable. But it is also possible that some resident teachers are motivated by defensiveness and uncertainty and may regard proposed innovations as a reminder of personal compromise. Rejecting a beginner's enthusiasm may enhance the resident's own sense of status and security.

On the other hand, many student teachers will find their resident teachers eager to observe a new approach to content or method. Indeed, some teachers testify that supervising student teachers is refreshing and contributes in an important measure to their own stimulation and renewed zest for teaching.

Student teachers often go to assigned classes with definite ideas about how to coach tennis, or teach "The Concept of Genetics," or "The Elements of a Balanced Diet." It is possible that conflicts will arise over such "definite" ideas. Thoughtful discussions with resident teachers about planning will help to avoid disagreements and disappointments.

Whether plans materialize or not will depend not only on the competence of the student teacher but also on the feelings and attitudes of the resident teacher.

The complications of the relationship go further, of course. Student teachers spend many hours observing resident teachers; they will be favorably impressed by some incidents in the classroom and disturbed by others. Since they are, after all, novices, they may find it difficult to understand why teachers ignore certain kinds of behavior.

Student Teacher: "When Bill fell asleep in class for the third time, I began to get nervous. Surely Mrs. Northway would notice this time! It was touch and go whether Bill would even stay in his seat as his six-foot frame relaxed in all directions. But nothing happened. Just before the bell rang Bill woke up. He picked up his books as though nothing were amiss, got the assignment from the girl across the aisle, and sauntered out. I could hardly restrain myself."

Resident Teacher: "Yes, I saw Bill asleep. I guess this is the third time this week, isn't it? Well, when you have taught as long as I have, you learn what to notice and what not to notice. Bill grew awfully fast during the last ten months—something like eight inches in all—and he's just exhausted trying to keep up with himself! I'm pretty sure that in a little while, when he gets enough food in him and learns how to maneuver all that new length, he'll wake up!"

The problem posed by this particular student teacher is pertinent to those with little or no experience in teaching. The experienced teacher can justifiably ignore what may superficially seem to be a gross breach of classroom etiquette. But can a student teacher do the same thing?

Student teachers sometimes feel "caught" in a personality conflict with their resident teachers. What should student teachers do if they find themselves at variance with their resident teachers? The following excerpts are taken from the log of a student teacher with such a problem:

November 9
After two weeks of student teaching, my nerves are really beginning to show. I feel like I am beginning to crack. I am physically sick. I have lost eight pounds, my eyes are bloodshot and have dark circles around them. I don't want to finish my student teaching. I know definitely that I will not teach as a career.

I think my problem may be that I hate my cooperating teacher. There is something about her professionalism that makes me feel inferior. I feel she expects too much from me. I know I've tried my hardest for her and I have learned a vast amount about teaching from her. The grade I get in student teaching doesn't matter.

November 29
I have resigned myself to the rest of student teaching without much resistance. One reason, I think, is the fact that half the battle is won; student teaching is half over, and I feel satisfied to the extent that I can live happily with myself. I still feel that each day I have something to learn, an impression that I haven't gotten before. But most of the tension that I experienced the second week has been relieved. I feel that my analysis of my teacher and the entire situation has helped me to feel this release. I am still tired and still work very hard, but I feel it is worthwhile, and that there is an end.

January 15—Final Evaluation

. . . after being extremely upset for the entire weekend, I made my decision. I would go every day, do the things she wanted me to do, and come home. I would pretend to like her. I would not be nice to her. I never did feel any hostility toward the students. Probably that is the one thing that kept me going; I enjoyed them so much. After I no longer perceived my teacher as so threatening to me that I actually feared the outcome, I realized she knew I could get out of the hole. She simply was going to make me work up to my ability to get out. I feel relieved that the whole experience is over, and my grade truly doesn't matter as long as I didn't fail. I do not agree with all her methods, but I see that her methods and practices are congruent with her personality, and they are successful for her because they are congruent.

Clearly this is an extreme case; such incompatibility of personality and teaching approach may be corrected if discovered sufficiently early in the student teaching experience. It is instructive to consider the summary evaluation comments for this student teacher as filled in by the resident teacher and the college supervisor.

The resident teacher wrote:

She has worked dependably as a student teacher and is qualified to teach. Her subject matter background is adequate for a beginner. She has been most receptive to suggestions for organization and planning. She likes students and is noticeably aware of their problems and anxieties. As is expected at this stage of her inexperience, she has yet to show an enthusiasm that results in a challenging atmosphere in her classroom. She needs to develop more originality of presentation as well as a more dynamic approach.

The college supervisor wrote:

My estimate of her ability and personality are based on an acquaintanceship of approximately three years. During that time I have instructed her in a class in methods, served as her advisor, and had an opportunity to observe her student teaching. She is attractive, has a good scholastic record at the university, is friendly, dependable, and cooperative. Her voice is somewhat low in volume, and she does not appear as dynamic in the classroom as she does outside of it. This may partly be because she was somewhat restricted in what she was able to try out in the school situation in which she was placed. In my judgment she should become a successful teacher.

THE COLLEGE SUPERVISOR

The relationships between student teacher and resident teacher are complicated enough, but there is usually a third figure—the college supervisor—to consider. While some student teaching is entirely supervised by the resident classroom teacher, more often a member of the college staff also visits the student teacher at regular intervals. Many times the college supervisor has taught, or is currently teaching, the student in courses on curriculum and on methods of instruction in the student's subject area. Whether or not the college supervisor has taught the student teacher, he or she represents the college in its effort to keep its teacher-education program in touch with the problems of beginners. Fellow staff members at the college rely on the college supervisor heavily for data on strengths and weaknesses in the preparation of student teachers. So the college supervisor will respect the candor of student teachers who confide, without fear of reprisal, their satisfactions and anxieties about the preparation they have received for teaching.

At the same time the college supervisor is a "resource person," for the student teacher, who knows adolescents, curriculum trends in a given subject, teaching methods, instructional materials, and evaluation procedures. Of course, not all that the college supervisor knows will be useful in any classroom. Ability to help will depend, in part, on the kind of teaching and learning encouraged by the resident teacher; it will also vary with the ability of the student teacher to adapt suggestions to an emerging style of teaching.

Certainly, the frequency of the college supervisor's visits affects the ability to be helpful. More specific recommendations can be made when one knows the day-by-day progress of the student teacher's class. When visits cannot be frequent, the college supervisor may supplement information with reports from the student teacher or the resident teacher or with regular conferences with both. In addition, it may be possible to retain video- or audiotapes of classroom teaching which the supervisor can play and critique at more convenient times.

As suggested earlier, a log book or student diary of experiences, maintained on a daily basis, can help inform the university supervisor about what has gone on between visits. Often university supervisors will want to see previous lesson plans, which help them evaluate the present lesson in the context of previous work. It is also helpful to have a duplicate lesson plan of the day's work for the supervisor. By means of the lesson plan the supervisor can judge how well the student is achieving what he or she states as objectives. Specific expectations of the supervisor will probably have been made clear before the student teachers have left campus.

The student teacher contributes to self-growth when every effort is made to keep the college supervisor well informed about all aspects of the student teaching experience.

It is only realistic to recognize that the college supervisor comes to appraise as well as to help the student teacher. From the beginning, the student teacher must be clear about what that appraisal includes. One must prepare for the visits, be aware of what evaluation entails, and must be sure that the resident teacher is also aware of the way in which judgments will be made.

It can now be seen more clearly that the student teacher is often the servant of two masters: the resident teacher and the college supervisor. The best insurance of support from both is clear and systematic exchange of information among all. Most of this communication can be assumed to be the responsibility of the two supervisors. But a wise student teacher will plan diplomatic checks to see that the communication continues to be regular and ungarbled.

At its best, the system of providing support from a college supervisor as well as from a resident teacher gives the student more direct assistance than he or she is likely ever to have again as a secondary school teacher. Admittedly, the relationships are complex; but they need not be obstructive. On the contrary, student teachers who do their part to make relationships cordial and constructive will benefit immensely by the guidance they receive.

SCHOOL AND COMMUNITY RESOURCES

As one part of the induction process, student teachers will be made acquainted with the services available through their schools. Learning how these services function and how they are used by teachers and students is an important part of student teaching.

Student teachers, because they *are* student teachers and because of their relatively brief stays in schools, may not be able to use all the services. They must learn quickly which services are available to them and how to obtain them. It is necessary to settle such practical concerns as how supplies are ordered, what rules govern student use of the library, how audiovisual materials are obtained and scheduled, what appropriate student information is available from counselors.

It may be useful to prepare a checklist of such practical items during the first few weeks of student teaching. While a standard list might be suggested, each school and each subject has problems peculiar to itself. For example, some schools have audiovisual coordinators who order all materials, whereas in other schools this is the responsibility of the individual. Repair of sewing machines is of no concern to a social studies teacher, nor are the problems of transporting a band of any importance to a typing teacher. The student teacher's own list, developed with the help of the resident teacher and college supervisor, will serve better.

What should student teachers know about the community? A student teacher often makes little use of community resources. Use of these resources may involve long-range planning and a knowledge of the community that the student teacher may not have been able to obtain in so short a time. The student teacher should, however, gauge how much might be done, given the time and the opportunity. It is useful to know, for example, that the local museum has some Indian artifacts that would be the source of a stimulating project for the bored genius in third period. Likewise, the budding scientist might have been assigned the task of interviewing the consulting chemist at the sewage-disposal plant. Knowing community possibilities and making some use of them, if only in a very small way, helps build resources for later use in full-time teaching.

Likewise, the influence in the classroom of the general character of the community should not be overlooked. Student teachers may be so overwhelmed by the new tasks and problems within the classroom that they forget the significance of the outside world in their students' lives. Do they come from a stable and clearly defined community, or are they gathered together from mushrooming suburbs where no sense of "community" has yet been developed? If it is a city school, do many students come from apartment-house or rooming-house areas? Is the school in an economically deprived or slum area? If it is a rural school, are students from a prospering or a marginal farming area? The community setting makes a marked difference in the classroom approaches that can be profitably attempted.

GETTING TO KNOW YOUR STUDENTS

For many prospective teachers, the student teaching situation is the first real opportunity to be an adult leader with a group of adolescents. The questions of first priority are: Can I get along with them? Will they like me?

The adolescents will be equally curious about the student teacher. Contrary to popular report, students usually do not strive to make life miserable for student teachers. Most student teachers find that adolescents are more ready to help, give support, and make the initial teaching experience successful.

Occasionally a class may make the student teacher a handy target for aggressions built up in other parts of the school day. It is only honest to state that some student teachers have difficulty in establishing rapport with adolescents, however much they are assisted; others never do build any secure competence in any part of teaching. This, of course, is one of the reasons for student teaching: It provides an excellent test of whether teaching is a wise vocational choice. Nevertheless, student teachers frequently report how the class "helped them out" when their college supervisor observed them. Incidentally, the same is true of the first year on the job. If a teacher is able to establish any initial rapport with students, the students will be patient as the teacher learns, through mistakes, how to increase his or her skills. They are more likely to be with, rather than against, the teacher.

STUDENT ADVICE TO A BEGINNING TEACHER

Horse racing tips are allegedly better when they come from the "horse's mouth." The following are some tips that one resident teacher collected from her classes and presented to her student teacher:

Student A

1. Do not be really strict.
2. Give tests which are not hard and not easy.
3. Beware of some of my classmates.
4. When you lecture, do it slowly, so that the class can take good and complete notes.
5. Beware of a person's handicap, like me. (Guess who wrote this!)
6. Let us change our seats in class (permanently).

Student B

Get out while you can. Teaching is surely one of the best ways to lose friends and influence people.

Student C

1. Don't be "overeager"—don't try to be too domineering, trying to catch everybody.
2. Don't come in and start antagonizing everyone; start out with a smile.
3. Don't think this class is an all-important subject and that we are all enthusiastic about it. To us it's just another subject that requires study—although we do like it at times.
4. Don't give tests when we're loaded up with them, taking the attitude that all the others will just have to retract their tests. 'Cause they won't.
5. We're human beings, not machines! We can do just so much and no more though we should be challenged and working hard.
6. Be informal and allow for mistakes, exceptions, and so forth (all those human fallacies).
7. There are some who want to learn even though others may not. Judge the group by those who want to learn, not by those who don't.
8. Give a guy a break.
9. Make the subject interesting; use discussions and arguments—and debates because those always get everyone in the discussion.
10. Enforce the rules and keep discipline, but don't overdo it!
11. Don't try to trick us—teach us!

Student D

Student teachers often come into a school with a real strict, stern attitude. They come into a high school with a lot of college ideas. But remember we're in eleventh grade, not in college, yet. So often student teachers try to make us work like they had to in college. Or if not that, they tell us how easy we have it and how it was for them—don't do that, please!

Student E

Be flexible; be able to discuss another subject, or an interesting facet instead of being confined by the subject you planned to discuss. Smile. Do not speak to the blackboard.

Student F

Advice to a Student Teacher—VERY IMPORTANT: Go over the quizzes and tests after they're graded so we'll know what we did wrong. Sometimes we get the same questions on one test that we had on a preceding one and still don't know if the answers are right or wrong. Let us go early to lunch. The lines get real long down in the cafeteria, and I like to have a lot of time to eat.

Student G

It seems to me that the best asset a student teacher (or any teacher, for that matter) could possibly possess is a sense of humor, and a technique of presenting the material in an interesting fashion. Since either you have a sense of humor or you don't that takes care of that. Either you're interesting or you're not, that takes care of that, also. So I imagine that your success as a teacher has been predetermined at the time of your birth—what God gave you to work with. Therefore, if you are a flop, it isn't your fault directly, but the good Lord's.

STUDENT–TEACHER RELATIONSHIPS

Students are curious about the student teacher as a person. They may ply the student teacher with personal questions, some of which may be embarrassing. These questions should be answered judiciously. Students usually want to know about college or university life, why the student teacher chose teaching as a career, or something about the student teacher's life away from school.

Such curiosity is usually friendly and natural rather than malicious. Adolescents, like the children they have so recently been, find security in the knowledge of familiar things about strangers who invade their environment. Since the student teacher is often closer to them in age than the resident teacher, they may also feel freer to ask questions reflecting their own immediate concerns about the future.

Some reserve must be maintained in answering students' questions. One does not, either as a student teacher or as a certified teacher, speak with the same freedom employed with adult friends. Personal life should be kept private, but not so private that the outlines of a human being are obscured by a textbook and a flinty manner. Keep firmly in mind that students' interest in teachers is not hostile, and answers should be given in the proper spirit.

Rapport, of course, includes far more than skill in answering questions. It is a manner, a way of looking at people and speaking to them, a tone of voice, an attitude of genuine interest in others. Adolescents seek, from student teachers, as well as from any teacher, an indication of sincere regard for them as individuals. Being ready to smile, saying hello in the hall, using students' names, remembering what gives them trouble or in what they do well, will aid immeasurably in establishing rapport.

Student teachers sometimes find it difficult to establish rapport with adolescents because they are honestly frightened of them. It is not easy to approach those who create fear with an easy and relaxed smile. But an effort must be made. Casual conversations in the corridor, on the school grounds, or at sports events will help. Helping with extracurricular activities also provides opportunities to know students more informally. This is not to say that student teachers should try to be "buddies" with their students. Students are not seeking an adult "buddy," but an adult friend, a mature individual who has successfully weathered adolescence and who shows an understanding and caring for those going through the process.

REQUIRED: A SENSE OF HUMOR

"A teacher who doesn't have a sense of humor is really a drag, man." Short and to the point, this view of a teacher's ability to laugh is perhaps one that should be framed on every teacher's wall. Students who are asked to identify those qualities they most seek in teachers repeatedly place "sense of humor" high on their lists.

Honest laughter that springs from a source of mutual student–teacher recognition can help establish, or cement, classroom rapport. Of course a teacher must know when it is appropriate to demonstrate a sense of humor: To laugh at people is never acceptable; to laugh with them is not only healthy, but desirable. Laughter that finds its cue in embarrassment, ridicule, or vulgarity is destructive to individual values as well as to the climate of the classroom. On the other hand, laughter that says "This is the human condition and we're all human" is a positive force between students and teachers.

Obviously, though, teachers must be able to make the transition from the humorous to the serious, so that learning continues and nonsense or chaos does not supplant it.

Teachers who never smile . . . lose an opportunity to gain status as human beings, for the thought that after all "Old So-and-So" has a sense of humor or "knows how to take a joke" is one which makes students less inimical and teacher domination less unbearable.[4]

At a deeper, more personal level, teachers need to develop a sense of proportion regarding daily difficulties. The frustrations of working with so many varied human beings in the typical school day demands the ability to laugh.

MAINTAINING PROFESSIONAL SILENCE

One additional and highly significant caution should be mentioned regarding efforts to achieve rapport: This may be the first time the student teacher has been taken behind the scenes in the lives of other people without their being aware of it. Consultations with other teachers and counselors about individual students will sometimes be necessary; however, all inquiries and comments should be made for the sake of gaining insight and understanding in order to work better with adolescents, not merely to indulge in idle gossip. From these teacher conferences and from the cumulative record cards maintained as guidance files, it may be learned that Rona's mother is institutionalized, that Bob's father is an alcoholic, that Jose's family is in serious financial difficulty. Temptation to gossip about any information gleaned about students' personal family backgrounds should absolutely be avoided. It is imperative that student teachers adhere to professional ethics. Extreme circumspection must be observed in places where teachers talk about any part of their teaching. Conversation carried on in supposed privacy may be overheard by some students whose presence escapes your attention. Remember: a teacher may recognize at sight about one hundred students, but there may be three or four hundred who know who the teacher is.

SUCCESS OR FAILURE?

One student teacher phoned his supervisor at home the last week of his fieldwork: "You'll never guess what happened Friday," he said. "My classes got three hundred signatures on a petition and gave it to the principal asking that he hire me next year."

Probably not many student teachers will have such dramatic incidents to clarify their feelings about teaching. But throughout this trial period, all

[4] Willard Waller, *The Sociology of Teaching* (New York: Wiley, 1932), pp. 229–230.

student teachers should be engaged in taking a sharp look at themselves, asking such questions as, "How do I feel about what I am doing?" "How do others perceive my work?" "Can I be happy working—and living—this way?"

Sometimes individuals may expect too much from student teaching. Although success in that experience is the best predictor of future success in teaching, some students who performed at a barely acceptable level have matured into good teachers. They are the "slow starters." On the whole, however, a student who cannot perform satisfactorily in student teaching rarely develops the requisite skills.

One assumption of this book is that teachers are individuals who like, and are interested in, young people. It is possible, however, for a teacher to have these qualities and to exhibit behavior that contradicts intentions. A teacher who makes most of the classroom decisions, who does most of the talking, and who tends to be punitive toward students will have difficulty in creating close rapport with them. Consequently, opportunities for teaching and learning that go beyond facts will be limited. Students will probably go through the mechanical process of mastering information but they will not be interested in seeing how that information relates to their values, their interests, and their goals.

On the other hand, a teacher who is open, rather than distant, who discusses classroom experience with students and treats them with sensitivity will have extensive opportunities to affect positively the attitudes, understanding, and habits of students.

SUMMARY

Moving from the student's side to the teacher's side of the desk is a unique experience which requires many adjustments in thinking and behavior. The better able one is to assess aspects of self, to observe closely teachers, students, and the school setting, the more likely one is to begin a successful student teaching experience. Working well with the resident teacher and the college supervisor is essential; through these two supervisors, one can have the opportunity for more direct assistance than may ever be available again. Central to one's success or failure in student teaching is the ability to work humanely and professionally with students.

SELECTED READINGS

Conforti, Joseph M., "The Socialization of Teachers: A Case Study, *Theory into Practice*, 20 (December 1976), pp. 352–359. What happens when two radical student teachers are assigned to a conservative junior high school.

Filbin, Robert L., and Stefan Vogel, *So You're Going To Be a Teacher.* Woodbury, N.Y.: Barron's Educational Series, 1967 (paperback). A short and simple introduction to teaching.

Friedenberg, Edgar Z., *Coming of Age in America.* New York: Random House, 1965. See Chapter 2, "The Cradle of Liberty," which discusses the impact of school rules and regulations on student attitudes.

Glasser, William, *Schools without Failure.* New York: Harper & Row, 1969. Straightforward, practical presentation of ways in which involvement, relevance, and critical thinking strategies can help to remedy schools' failures. Chapters 10 and 12 can be particularly helpful to classroom teachers.

Greenberg, Herbert M., *Teaching with Feeling.* New York: Crowell, 1969. Practical and readable presentation of the emotional aspects of teaching.

Henry, Jules, *Culture against Man.* New York: Random House, 1963. See Chapter 7, "Rome High School and Its Students." An anthropologist examines the high-school scene and shows how school culture exists around classrooms rather than in them.

Hunter, Elizabeth, and Edmund Amidon, *Student Teaching: Cases and Comments.* New York: Holt, Rinehart and Winston, 1964 (paperback). Case material and comments help to clarify some specific and practical problems typical of the student teacher's peculiar situation. Well done.

Jersild, Arthur T., *When Teachers Face Themselves.* New York: Teachers College, 1955. An enduring classic that should be pondered carefully by all who want to become teachers.

Otty, Nicholas, *Learner Teacher.* Baltimore: Penguin Books, 1972. While this book recounts the experiences of an Englishman engaged in student teaching in an English school, the concerns it expresses are equally appropriate to Americans. Written in diary form, the commentary is alternately humorous and sad, as well as human and real.

FOCUS ON CHAPTER 3

A prized value in American society is individuality. At the same time, there is pressure toward conformity; it is all right to be different, our culture tells us, but not too different. In the classrooms of our schools it is clear that no matter what the cultural message may be, students come in a wide—if not wild—variety of shapes, sizes, aptitudes, abilities, interests, and backgrounds. Teachers may, in many instances, find that the group to which they belong—white, middle class, Protestant, above-average in intelligence—is actually a minority group when compared to the kinds of students in the school. Differences in background and aptitude influence attitudes toward self and learning. Such differences enrich the culture, but they may cause problems for the teacher who is insensitive or unaware of the significance of these differences.

Significant ideas presented in this chapter include:
- Teachers and students come from different generations, and this generational gap may cause differences in values and motivations which interfere with teaching and learning.
- It is important for teachers to recognize areas of prejudice in themselves, and work toward eliminating these, since prejudice and democratic teaching are in obvious conflict.
- The major difference with which the school must cope is that between slow and fast learners. Some policies for dealing with these differences may be questioned; in any event, the teacher needs to understand how such learners approach educational tasks, and how to differentiate instruction so that each may learn at optimum levels.

chapter 3

Adolescents
and the School:
individual
differences
and what they mean

Teaching in the secondary school means teaching adolescents. Just as each of us has "come through" adolescence in his or her own way, the young people of each succeeding generation will have to face this critical and complex period of growth somewhat differently. With each generation the social scene shifts, as does the meaning of social events when viewed from the perspective of any single individual.

Decisions about what to teach, how and when to teach it, are related to what we know about the students in our classrooms. All students are unique, but some are more so than others. While no person is exactly like anyone else, there are some individuals who exhibit greater differences than others. The study of adolescents typically focuses on major generalities about this period of growth. However, the classroom teacher needs to be particularly sensitive to the ways in which any given student differs from the generalizations. For this reason, this chapter focuses particular attention on the significant ways in which adolescents *differ* from each other. When these differences are accommodated adequately in the classroom, there is considerable likelihood that all students will be able to learn to the utmost of their potential.

SHOWDOWN AT GENERATION GAP

Before considering the physical or intellectual differences that students bring to school, it is wise to look at the major difference between students and teachers, which is age. The teacher is always older than the students. The beginning teacher may be a mere four years older than the oldest student, but what a four years! Students view the college student as a being from another world—exciting, glamorous, perhaps unattainable, and certainly different.

In any event, the older one gets, the less one is in touch with the significant events and pressures of adolescence. You may recall the events of your own growing up with pleasure or distress. If you are the product of a typical middle-class suburban upbringing, dilemmas you faced in adolescence may seem childish and trivial compared to those which are the daily threat to an inner-city adolescent.

Within a very few years one drops the attitudes of adolescence. Teachers rarely read the comic books or paperbacks popular with youth; they may prefer public broadcasting, and symphony or ballet to the fare of drive-in movies. It does not take too many years for one to lose touch with the community of the adolescent, and with each passing year the contacts become more tenuous.[1]

While teaching has traditionally been a pathway for upward mobility, there are relatively few who enter the profession from the lower depths of poverty, from inner-city ghettos, from isolated marginal rural wastelands. Typically, the teacher represents solid middle-class values, manners, language, and goals. Students do not all come with values congruent to the teacher's. There are many millions of young people who are impoverished and deprived in every sense of the word. As a result, their values and outlooks on life may be quite different from those of the teacher. The whole system of rewards and punishments a teacher uses may be so removed from the world of these adolescents that they have no power to motivate at all.

Such social differences, coupled with the generational difference, means that teachers may find that an extra effort is needed to get through to adolescents. Awareness that the world of adult–teacher and adolescent–student are not necessarily congruent is a first step toward being able to achieve communication with students and to allow teaching and learning to occur.

[1] "Youth Generations, and Social Change, Parts I and II," *Journal of Social Issues*, 30:2 and 3, 1974.

RACIAL, SOCIAL CLASS, AND ETHNIC DIFFERENCES

After facing the problem of the generation gap, you must examine another pervasive and divisive difference—racial and ethnic identity.

The truism that all kinds of people come to school means exactly that: black, white, yellow, Polish, German, Mexican, Lithuanian. Teachers, like most other Americans, have usually been isolated from persons unlike themselves. Few people have known at all well individuals of other racial or ethnic groups. As a teacher, you will have no say in selecting your students. Your classes will be filled with youth representing all the kinds of people in the community. As metropolitan areas have grown—and most schools are in metropolitan areas today—people have tended to live in enclaves of similar people. This is sometimes due to overt and covert real estate selling policies, and sometimes to economic imperatives. Thus a given school may be overwhelmingly black, while not too far away there may be large numbers of Italian, Jewish, or Appalachian white families. How will you feel about teaching these diverse groups?

Feelings are important, since a teacher instructs in accordance with his or her feelings. Studies show clearly that teachers, however well meaning, tend to pay more attention to students with whom they feel comfortable—students most like themselves. You can diagnose your own feelings about teaching different groups by filling out the questionnaire below and on the following page. Fill out each part independently. Then compare the responses of the two. If there is a marked discrepancy between the responses to Parts I and II, implications might be examined. It has been found that many students entering teaching report that they felt relatively unemotional about members of minority groups as students in their classes, but have strong feelings about such groups when it comes to living arrangements. The question to ask here is, "If I couldn't visit with a feeling of ease in the homes of these people, how can I believe that my classroom attitudes toward their children will be similar to those I have for other youth?"

Part I

Place before each of the groups named below the number of the statement that most nearly expresses the way you feel about having students from any of those groups in your classes. Regard these students as representing an average socioeconomic status (not the highest you have known, nor the lowest). Do not leave any blanks.

1. I would go out of my way to ask for classes consisting of a large number of these students.
2. I would welcome students from this group in my classes.

3. I wouldn't care if students from this group were in my classes.
4. I'd rather not have any students from this group in my classes—at least not more than one or two.
5. If I had a class made up mostly of students from this group, I would request a transfer or resign.

Number	Group	Number	Group
_____	1. Italian	_____	10. Cuban
_____	2. English	_____	11. Protestant
_____	3. Jewish	_____	12. Nigerian
_____	4. Black	_____	13. Canadian
_____	5. Scandinavian	_____	14. Japanese
_____	6. Polish	_____	15. Mexican
_____	7. German	_____	16. Chinese
_____	8. Catholic	_____	17. Hindu
_____	9. French	_____	18. Baptist

Part II

You are going to be a teacher in a community new to you. You have to find a place to live; you are also going to be called upon to have home contact with the parents of the students in your class. Place before each of the groups listed below the statement that would most nearly express your feelings. Again, consider the groups as representing an average socio-economic status. Do not leave any blanks.

1. If I needed a roommate I would be happy to share an apartment with a person of this group.
2. I would be glad to have people of this group as neighbors.
3. I don't have strong feelings one way or another about social contacts with people in this group.
4. I would accept a dinner invitation from people in this group, but I would prefer not to live in the same neighborhood with them.
5. I would be willing to discuss school affairs with people in this group, but I would not be interested in any other contact.

Number	Group	Number	Group
_____	1. Jewish	_____	10. Italian
_____	2. German	_____	11. Nigerian
_____	3. Polish	_____	12. Japanese
_____	4. Baptist	_____	13. Canadian
_____	5. Black	_____	14. Hindu
_____	6. Scandinavian	_____	15. Protestant
_____	7. Mexican	_____	16. Cuban
_____	8. English	_____	17. French
_____	9. Chinese	_____	18. Catholic

Prejudice has no place in the classroom. It is incumbent upon anyone wishing to teach to diagnose his or her own possible areas of bias, and to do some soul searching in an effort to eliminate those feelings. Admittedly, it is not easy to be completely neutral when interacting with groups who have been outside one's own experience, but it is essential to monitor one's behavior in order to eliminate the influence of prejudice on one's treatment of students.

WHAT IT FEELS LIKE TO BE DIFFERENT

One can only understand the behavior of those who differ by understanding how this difference is internalized. These feelings are translated into behavior. Guidance from research can help in the understanding of how feelings of difference may result in maladaptive behavior.[2]

STUDENTS WHO DEVIATE MARKEDLY FROM THE NORM FEEL CONSPICUOUS. If the student is exceptionally bright, exceptionally slow, or is very much behind in school performance, there is an uncomfortable feeling of being conspicuous for the wrong reasons. Consequently such students often are either very aggressive, as though to say, "I'll tell you all about myself before you can find out," or very shy and retiring, as though trying to shrink into a psychological corner where nobody can see them. In either case, the aggression or the shyness is a signal to the teacher that students are uncomfortable with their differences. In no case should teachers overreact, making the "different" ones more acutely visible than ever.

STUDENTS WHO ARE DIFFERENT ARE LIKELY TO BE SUPERSENSITIVE. Whether bright or dull, students who differ do not respond well if they believe they are being singled out for extra attention. Such a heightened sensitivity is often found with minority students, particularly if the school has been recently desegregated, or if busing students is a subject of much local discussion. A white teacher, for instance, may be excessively kind to a black student just to show that no prejudice exists; the black student will resent such treatment.

The "visibility" of differences is probably more apt to produce heightened sensitivity than are differences that one can hide. A bright child can "act dumb" (as many bright girls do!), but the student with a deformed hand cannot hide this defect. The more visible the defect, and the more intense

[2] Erving Goffman, *Stigma* (Englewood Cliffs, N.J.: Prentice-Hall, 1965).

the social significance attached to it, the more sensitive the individual will be, and behavior will reflect this added sensitivity.

Persons with visible handicaps do not want their disability ignored, but they do want to be treated normally and fairly, just like everyone else. We all have a tendency to feel ill-at-ease with persons whose condition or situation is unlike our own experience; teachers must be careful not to be irritated and angry at students because their differences cause feelings of awkwardness.

ANY KIND OF EXCEPTIONAL ENDOWMENT HAS SIGNIFICANT MEANING THROUGHOUT THE LIFE OF THE STUDENT. Both very bright, very dull, and handicapped students pose special problems to their own families. Often students who are dull or handicapped have been overprotected by parents who have sought to smooth the path for them or who seek to compensate for their own vague and unspoken feelings of guilt as the probable cause for their children's deviance. Overprotection may seem acceptable at home, but when the students are at school they may be ill-equipped to deal with the everyday world of the classroom. By the time they reach the secondary school, such students may have learned many ways of coping with school which, in many instances, are counterproductive, and make their situations worse.

When parents have rejected their own children because of visible differences, the road is even thornier. Of course children who are extremely different are more difficult to rear; when parents reject and/or neglect them, there are bound to be serious personality problems.

EXPECTATIONS WHICH ARE APPROPRIATE FOR NORMAL STUDENTS MAY BE INAPPROPRIATE FOR THE EXCEPTIONAL STUDENT. In homeroom Mrs. Block spent a great deal of time early in the fall semester discussing the strategy of college applications: how to decide which colleges to apply to, how to fill out application forms, and some of the specific requirements of certain colleges, such as an autobiography. Jim sat miserably in the corner, knowing full well that he was "too dumb" to go to college. After about the tenth session on college applications he stood up, knocked over his desk, flung his books on the floor, and stomped out, yelling, "You can go————your-self, *and* college!"

The teacher who suggests life choices that presume a normal endowment will sometimes be perplexed because some students react negatively to what appear to be reasonable aspirations. Yet the rationale of the reaction is clear. Students see the aspiration as either beyond their scope or beneath their abilities. The very superior student, for example, may scorn what appears to be low-level ambitions. The motivation of these students is directly affected by goal setting. Thus, the teacher who has exceptional students should study them intensively as individuals in order to help them set goals they can accept as meaningful and reasonable.

PUBLIC LAW 94–142

An act of Congress, Education for All Handicapped Children, known familiarly as Public Law 94–142, is one of the most far reaching federal acts in recent educational history. The act requires that any school receiving federal funds (and there are hardly any schools in the country which are not recipients of some federal money) must provide an education for *every* handicapped child in the least restrictive environment, "harmonious with the child's needs and free of stigma." The popular term for this is "mainstreaming." Children who have physical or learning handicaps are no longer to be placed in special schools or special classrooms if there is any way in which those children can be integrated into the regular classroom. While this is educationally promising for many hitherto isolated or ignored students, the problems inherent in mainstreaming are tremendous. Most teachers lack the special education background required to deal with a deaf or blind child, or one who is in a wheelchair. School systems are rapidly developing in-service workshops to acquaint teachers with some of the problems which may confront them when dealing with handicapped children.

Of particular interest is the requirement, also specified by the law, that an educational plan be developed for each such student. The Individualized Education Program (IEP), which is specified by the law, requires a written statement for each student and must include: (a) a statement of current educational level; (b) annual educational goals for the student, including short-term educational objectives; (c) a statement of specific services to be provided and the degree to which the student can be expected to participate in the regular educational program; and (d) the extent of services to be provided, how long they will continue, and how they will be evaluated. Parents are given due process protection to assure that children are treated fairly when the IEP is being drawn up.

There have been numerous arguments about the scope and impact of this bill. Costs are expected to be high as many students who were previously allowed to stay out of school, or given only minimal education, are brought into regular classroom environments. Many buildings will need to be modified to allow adequate access to handicapped youngsters. It is also predicted, however, that many, if not most, of these students have adequate capacity to learn and to gain employable skills. The net social gain will be that these individuals will be able to provide for themselves as adults and not continue as social dependents. Inevitably, the years during which schools and teachers learn how to work with handicapped students will involve many adjustments.

Other differences with which the school has traditionally coped have to do with intellectual differences among students. While Public Law 94–142 also means that many intellectually limited students will no longer be segregated into special classes, the range of intellectual capacity has always been large in most comprehensive high schools.

THE EDUCATIONAL CIRCUMSTANCE OF SLOW AND FAST LEARNERS

The more complete a representation there is of any group of people, the more "normally" their achievements are distributed. If schools retain all of a given age group, achievement will range all the way from very low to very high. This range will always exist unless the people who rank very high or very low are eliminated. Whether the activity is playing a violin, throwing a football, or reading a book, all people simply cannot make the same progress in the same amount of time. Some may never reach the heights that others attain quickly.

As a beginning teacher, think of your own capacities. What is your greatest weakness: Physical dexterity? Fine arts? Now think of a fellow student teacher who is skilled in your area of weakness. Could you ever, no matter how hard you tried, reach the same degree of proficiency? What would be required?

If all children are retained in school, two choices are open: (a) to require that all children attain the same minimal degree of proficiency in the same amount of time, keeping for additional time those who cannot reach this standard or (b) to expect differences in achievement and gear instruction to these differences while keeping students of the same age together for various general activities.

When grades were first established for American schools, students progressed from one grade to another on the basis of specifically completed work: learning numbers, addition and subtraction, multiplication and division, compounds, reduction, and the rule of three.[3] The sequence for reading and writing was also specified. A student passed from one level to the next on the basis of specific competencies. Although this approach seemed reasonable, it also resulted in a tremendous rate of retardation. All students do not learn the same things at the same rate. After many attempts to resolve the problem of excessive retardation, elementary schools in mid-century adopted policies that virtually eliminated failure. Students pro-

---

[3] Ellwood P. Cubberly, *Public Education in the United States* (Boston: Houghton Mifflin, 1947).

gressed from grade to grade whether or not they had mastered the work of the previous grade. Conscientious teachers worked with those who lagged behind; less conscientious teachers ignored those who were not up to the work of the class. Students who excelled—who completed all the work in half the time—were also ignored; they just sat and waited for the rest to catch up.

The result of such policies was that when students arrived at the junior and senior high schools many were deficient in basic skills. They were adolescents in physique, but they were far from achieving adolescent competence in the skills needed to complete the secondary school. By the late 1970s public indignation came to a head over the extensive media reports of some barely literate students graduating from high school. A few school systems were sued by students who claimed they had been cheated in their education. Continued pressure was exerted by parents as well as students who felt that they were not given sufficient opportunity to exercise superior intellectual ability, although advanced placement classes were available in many schools.

A sharp shift in expectations on the part of educators and the public became evident. A call for "back to basics" resulted in sharply increased emphasis on competency as the basis for grade-to-grade promotion. It is probable that, as a result, the range of differences in achievement in the average secondary school will be reduced. More intensive emphasis on reading, for instance, will probably result in more students who will be able to read near grade level, or if grossly deficient, placed in special programs.

TO GROUP OR NOT TO GROUP

One of the issues most bitterly debated in educational circles is that of grouping secondary students by ability. The arguments on either side are persuasive, depending on one's bias. Research, although massive, does not provide a clear-cut answer; personal feelings have thus had relatively free rein in determining school policy.

Some selection occurs, of course. The academic course often intimidates the slower students, so that they choose the commercial, shop, or "general" courses of study. The bright students gravitate toward college preparatory courses. Self-selection does not always work as completely as one might wish, however. Some students are doggedly enrolled in a college preparatory curriculum when their capacities are far below those required for success. And in the smaller high schools, where there are neither sufficient students nor enough teachers to establish separate courses of study, this kind of selection cannot occur.

No matter how intensive the stress on basics may be in previous schooling, a typical class of teen-agers may contain students whose IQ ranges from dull to normal to genius, and whose reading ability is from adequate fifth grade to graduate school.

Whether the teacher is aware of it or not, attitudes toward those who will perform better, as against those from whom one does not expect special aptitude, will be conveyed to students. An ingenious research study showed that teachers, without any obvious overt signs of paying special attention to certain students, actually did encourage the progress of students (selected at random) who had been supposedly identified as "late bloomers."[4] The findings indicate that without the teachers even being aware of it, they did produce unexpected growth in the specially identified students. Since these students were actually picked at random, there was nothing in their previous record to indicate that they would show any exceptional improvement. Yet they did. One can only conclude that it was the teachers' expectations that made the difference. Despite the criticism of this research, the folk wisdom that teachers get the behavior they expect seems irrefutable. One might therefore seriously question policies which group and then label one class as "dumb" and another as "smart" since inevitably groups perform in accordance with their labels.

The basis for grouping is another source of discomfort. Are teachers reliable judges of who is "smart" or "dumb"? Might a teacher be taken in by a charming smile, a well-groomed appearance, an adroitly nuanced enthusiasm? Would a teacher's prejudices and preconceptions about particular groups influence judgment as to who "ought to" succeed and who cannot? If tests are the basis for grouping, are they any more reliable? A person who "tests" poorly may have a test phobia or lack the necessary motivation and drive to demonstrate good performance. It was found, for instance, that when promised rewards that fitted with their value system, children who previously did poorly on tests could do a great deal better.[5]

It has been found, too, that boys perform less well under stress, so that the anxiety-laden test situation tends to depress the scores of boys as a group.[6] Finally, middle-class prodding and the incidental, but important, things which middle-class children pick up from their verbally and culturally richer environment give them a major advantage in tests that measure those kinds of attributes, rather than innate ability, whatever that may be. Time and again, research has shown a close correlation between

[4] Robert Rosenthal and Lenore Jacobson, *Pygmalion in the Classroom* (New York: Holt, Rinehart and Winston, 1968); and Peter Guinpert and Carol Guinpert, "The Teachers as Pygmalion: Comments on the Psychology of Expectation," *The Urban Review*, 3 (September 1968), pp. 21–25; Robert Rosenthal, "The Pygmalion Effect Lives," *Psychology Today*, 7 (September 1973), pp. 65–63.

[5] Allison Davis, *Social-Class Influences Upon Learning* (Cambridge, Mass.: Harvard University Press, 1948.)

[6] Seymour B. Sarason, and others, *Anxiety in Elementary School Children* (New York: Wiley, 1960).

socioeconomic status and school grouping practices: The "better class" of student comes from the "better-class" home. All these factors create doubt about ability grouping based on test results or even teacher appraisal.

There are differences other than intellectual ones. Some people are talented musically; should they be in special classes in English and mathematics? What about people with superb gifts in art and design? Isn't this a good basis for separation? No one would suggest that either of these talents is an adequate basis for separate classes in all subjects. But there are special classes for the musically and artistically gifted. Thus, such differences can be expressed through choice of subject matter. In the same way, one can talk sensibly about marked differences in intellectual competence. The kinds of subject matter electives which are provided in most secondary schools do, in themselves, tend to reduce heterogeneity. Thus the typical system of electives, although far from perfect in its operation, does tend to make secondary school classrooms progressively more homogeneous. The limitations, as well as the advantages, of this kind of organization have been argued in the professional literature. Some teachers feel that the separation causes academic students to become snobs while the vocational, commercial, and general students feel socially inferior. One question prospective teachers should ask themselves is: "Have I ever been placed in a "slow" group? If not, how can I know what it feels like to be in such a group?"

In observing school grouping practices, one should note what racial or ethnic groups tend to be in the "top" or "bottom" groups. Because of an inheritance of inadequate schooling, plus disproportionate clustering in inner-city slums, black youngsters are apt to be placed in slow sections in many schools. Teachers often perceive black students as less able, when test results may be inconclusive or even nonexistent. After schools were ordered desegregated in Washington, D.C., for instance, most of the students in the basic, or lowest track, were black. School officials claimed that this was the result of various IQ tests. Under court order, however, it was found that a majority of these students had never been tested.[7] Were they so grouped because they just "looked dumb" or perhaps because they "talked poorly"? Similarly, students from bilingual backgrounds— Cuban, Mexican-American, Puerto-Rican—are often to be found in greater proportion in lower tracks.[8] The student who begins with a deficit, whether it is real or in the eye of the beholder, is then labeled as a person with less ability, given less chance to be challenged by able or more culturally

---

[7] Clifford P. Hooker, "Issues in School Desegregation Litigation," in Clifford P. Hooker (ed.), *The Courts and Education*, Seventy-seventh Yearbook of the National Society for the Study of Education (Chicago: University of Chicago Press, 1978), pp. 84–115.

[8] Christina Tree, "Grouping Pupils in New York City," *The Urban Review*, 3 (September 1968), pp. 8–15.

sophisticated students, and doomed, therefore, to a lifetime at the bottom of the heap.

If grades are the basis for grouping, then girls will be overrepresented in the top tracks, and boys in the lower tracks. Would anyone argue that boys are less intelligent than girls? Or that girls are really brighter than boys? Since boys are typically less patient and obedient than girls, their previous school records may reflect discipline problems rather than achievement. Many talented persons are probably defeated by such a system, and their talent is either distorted into illegal activities or permitted to atrophy from disuse. The injustice of such programs has made for increased intergroup tensions throughout the country.[9]

What are some alternatives? Some school systems have abandoned mass ability testing as it now exists. Through trial and error, then, students and teachers work together to try to assess each person's potential. Experiments with nongraded secondary schools, where students work on contracts geared to their own learning rate and ability, have been tried with modest success (see Chapter 14). The forces favoring ability grouping are formidable, however. Many are based on class lines: The upward-mobile and the middle-class parents resist classification (or lack of it) that would open doors to more students, which would result in more open competition with their own children. The elitist concept of the role of education—that the schools should do the best job for the very able although providing for "those others"—reinforces grouping practices.

Despite all the theory and research which suggest grouping practices are not the best solution to our teaching problems, many teachers still feel that homogeneous groups are desirable. When asked, teachers almost unanimously state that they perfer classes grouped by ability, though of course most teachers do not want to have to teach very many of the "slow" sections. Teachers feel this way when the ability range in a given class is too broad. They may lack the skills to differentiate their teaching, and thus only feel adequate when most of the class can keep together doing the same things more or less at the same time. Many teachers like accelerated classes of especially talented or able students and do not want to have to bother with the care and special preparation required to teach less able students. Teachers are undoubtedly the chief factor in retaining ability grouping.

While newer procedures and new sensitivity to individual students may produce better solutions than ability grouping, prospective teachers must be prepared to deal with groups of mostly "slow" students, or mostly able students, as well as to work with groups varying greatly in ability, interest, and motivation.

[9] Richard Leiva, "Special Education Classes, Barrier to Mexican Americans?" *Civil Rights Digest*, 1 (Fall 1968), pp. 36–39.

TEACHING THE SLOW LEARNER

Today, more young people stay in school for a longer period of time than ever before. As a result, there has been growing concern for those who are intellectually unable to meet the same standards in the same period of time, no matter how hard they try.

Elementary schools usually permit all children to move ahead with their age group, even if they are demonstrably below their peers in school achievement. It is unwise, the argument goes, to keep a big, bulky adolescent with third graders just because he has not learned to read beyond that grade level.

One can discuss the merits and failings of this point of view. But the consequences result in classrooms where some members cannot spell words more difficult than "car" or "dog" and some are unable to remember a simple set of directions, or how to file things alphabeticably or do simple arithmetic.

It must be remembered that some students are slow learners because of factors other than limited intellectual capacity.

Janice was accepted by her teachers, her classmates, and her family as being not very bright. She seemed to have trouble with her schoolwork; could not read very well; and, in general, seemed destined for routine jobs. About the middle of her high school career one teacher, after observing her rather closely, suggested that her eyes be tested. With glasses she was able to read the blackboard for the first time. Moreover, she was also able, for the first time, to read books without tiring quickly. Her problems did not disappear overnight, but by graduation she was a better-than-average student.

Persons with poor hearing or eyesight may not really be aware they have defects. One student, when given a hearing aid for the first time cried out, "Why, birds really do sing!" In the case of color-blindness, which affects many more boys than girls, an inability to select the right color may not be stupidity or insolence, but a genuine lack of perceptual discrimination.

IDENTIFYING THE SLOW LEARNER

Before jumping to conclusions about the mental capacity of an individual, the student's folder should be consulted. Test scores of students should be checked while keeping in mind the fallibility of standardized tests. Some able students may not be competent readers for a whole host of reasons, and since all group tests are based on reading ability, for some students the general achievement and ability measures will be spurious.

There is a stereotype of the very dull; the student whose face looks empty, with an expression of apathy, without spark or life. Such a student may not respond to the mood of the class since what others find amusing is beyond his or her comprehension. Such a student may not be able to find the page in the book as readily as others, may forget pencil and paper, cannot repeat the assignment, may find it extremely difficult to follow the simplest directions.

Many slow learners do *not* fit this pattern. The slower student can often be a happy, extroverted individual. The world appears simple and pleasant, particularly if there are warm and understanding parents and siblings at home. With little awareness of the consequences of any particular action, the slow learner is not worried or anxious.

What appears to be irresponsibility may actually be a more restricted view of the world. Teachers often find that when classroom tasks are appropriate to their abilities, slow learners can be the happiest, most pleasant, best adjusted students in the class. Since most teachers tend to be concerned about the larger world and aware of the many problems that life presents, such attitudes may seem out of place and unnatural to them. Some teachers may go so far as to try to make these happy youngsters worried and anxious, since they feel that it is not "normal" for students not to care about the future. Such teachers would do better to try to understand the differences between slow learners and themselves rather than to try to remake the students.

Slow learning students will be responsive to personal attention. If treated with kindness, they freely respond with greater effort in school tasks.

Mary Ann and her older sister, Alice, were in the same United States history class. The teacher discovered the reason for this when she checked the records. Although there was a three year difference between the two girls, Alice had been retained two years in elementary school. Now she was barely able to keep up with her younger sister. "It must be hard enough to be in the same grade with her younger sister," thought the teacher, "without the added torture of being in the same class."

But this was a small rural high school and there just wasn't any other class for Alice. She was far from a good student. She rarely did her homework. She giggled and teased the boys near her. The teacher scolded, frowned, berated. Nothing worked. One day the teacher, glancing up, saw Alice scowling at her as usual. Instead of returning the frown, the teacher smiled—a warm, friendly smile. Alice seemed completely taken aback, but weakly smiled in return. She went back to work, too. From that day the teacher found it easy to smile at Alice. And Alice, although not becoming a model pupil, was more amenable to requests and generally more cooperative.

Most teachers have had little, if any, close contact with people of average or below normal mental processes. By the very selection of the teaching profession, they are automatically in a "superior" group. If there was any kind of tracking or grouping in the school you went to, you were almost without doubt in the advanced or accelerated track. Few prospective teachers have experienced the humiliation of being failed or kept back a grade. Bright people usually do not select dull or slow persons as friends or associates. It is therefore difficult for a teacher to grasp the way in which even an average, not to mention below average, mind works.

Although intellectual limitations usually are the cause of slow learning, students may manifest all of the symptoms of retardation when actually other factors are at work. Sometimes emotional troubles impede learning. Conflict in the home or poor adjustment to agemates makes the world so unpleasant or so disturbing that students cannot, no matter how hard they try, take in very much of the material of the classroom. Sometimes students have had some bitter experience with failure and, rather than feel that terror again, refuse to take an active role in the classroom. Thus, they are actually afraid to learn, rather than incapable of it.

Although both physical and emotional factors may make a normally endowed child appear to be a slow learner, here the special concern is with those students who really do have limited learning capacities. How can these students be detected? What can be done to improve their opportunities to learn?

True, slow learners do put facts together differently, generalize differently and think differently. They can retain few facts, few details. They may be able to report immediate reactions, but have little insight into the whys of any response. Abstractions are most elusive; they work best from one concrete situation to another, with models available to copy or emulate. When these ways of learning are understood and accounted for, the slow learner can and does learn, and it is a joy and reward for both teacher and student when such learning occurs.

PRECAUTIONS IN TEACHING SLOW LEARNERS

Edward was practically illiterate. He came from a non-English speaking background, and although he could talk well enough, he had only the dimmest notion of spelling. He could tell you the story line when he heard a story read aloud, but had to struggle painfully to read the same story to himself. One day when the regular teacher was absent a substitute teacher whose specialty was vocal music appeared. Instead of giving the required assignment in the grammar book, Mr. Larson decided to teach the class some songs. The class responded well to the change in pace but one student seemed to shine. Clear and strong, above the rest of the group, Edward's voice just floated out. On subsequent visits, Mr. Larson took Edward aside, tested him, found he had acute musical memory and almost perfect pitch. Edward had a rare ability.

Intelligence has many facets. A student who is the star poet in one class may be all thumbs in shop or a miserable dunce in mathematics.

A student who responds with joy to the orderly sequence of a geometric proof may find sociological data incredibly confusing. A bright student in one class may be a slow student in another.

Often a student who had been identified as a slow learner is either scheduled for shop work, placed in clerical or business training classes, or in art and music courses. The teachers in these fields may rightfully resent a policy which makes their classes the dumping ground for those students who cannot function well in other areas of the school.

It is a mistake to deal with slow learners in this fashion for several reasons. First, this policy assumes that manual arts and commercial courses, or even the fine arts, require less native ability than other academic disciplines. Actually, it takes a high degree of intelligence of a rather special kind to be a good secretary, a good mechanic, or a good draftsman. The student who lacks verbal skills is not necessarily automatically interested in areas where such skills are not central. Nor is it reasonable to assume that students who do poorly in reading will do well with machines.

Furthermore, if slow learners are moved completely into nonacademic courses they are denied the opportunity to be exposed to as broad a cultural background as those with greater verbal facility. Slower students are more likely to run into conflict with society than other students simply because it is more difficult for them to understand its complexities. Slow learners as well as most others become parents; they need all the help they can get in learning how to perform that role successfully. Academic courses can possibly provide some kind of assistance toward this end. It is therefore more important that slow learners be given a full share of education in basic courses that lead to social and personal understanding.

THE BACKGROUND OF THE SLOW LEARNER

It is tragic, but true, that for many of the slower students school has become a place of terror, boredom, cruelty, or painful embarrassment, or all of these. Such students have known failure before; usually they started falling behind early in their elementary school careers. For reasons not yet understood by researchers, there are more boys than girls classified as mentally retarded.

Several sources are available for gaining insight into the background of the slow student. Consultation with previous teachers often turns up valuable information, and school records may show where the inability to progress at the expected rate first appeared. Interviews with the student, of course, should prove an important source of information. (The procedure for student interviews is described in Chapter 17.)

The teacher should indicate genuine interest in the student's problems. At no time should the teacher show disappointment, disapproval, or censure. Understanding and accepting the student's reasons for failure is a prerequisite to gaining insight into the true cause. Whenever slow learners can make a contribution to any aspect of the class work, they should be given the opportunity to do so.

TEACHING PROCEDURES WITH SLOW LEARNERS

MAKE AVAILABLE SPECIAL MATERIALS FOR THE SLOW LEARNER. Simplified texts, special reading, shorter and fewer problems, should be prepared ahead of time by the teacher for the slower student. It takes some time, of course. Once a set of such materials is available, however, the teacher can use them for a number of years. The rewards in terms of busy, motivated learners, even slow learners, makes the extra effort worthwhile.

This point needs special emphasis. Since so much of classroom work requires some reading facility, the slow learner or poor reader needs particular attention and help. Scolding the student for inability to comprehend the text is not going to help. It is necessary for the teacher to make the extra effort to find material that the student can understand. There are resources in every subject field geared to the slow learner; professional journals and special methods books review and list such material. The librarian, curriculum coordinator, special subject supervisor should be used as resources to help locate such material. It does exist, but it takes some extra initiative to find.

PROVIDE A VARIETY OF LEARNING ACTIVITIES. This is essential in any classroom, but it is particularly important in one where the range of talents and skills is great. All students cannot learn through one channel. An activity that gives one student a chance to learn may be of no help to another. The slow learner especially, needs to work at a somewhat more concrete level than the rest of the class. Community resources, role playing, and audiovisual materials will help abstract concepts become concrete.

DEVELOP GROUP WORK IN THE CLASSROOM. The teacher will want to distribute the slow students among others who can learn at the expected rate. In this way, the slower students can learn by listening to their classmates and observing the way in which they handle the material. Other students are good, and often patient, teachers when given a chance to help. Even though the slower ones may appear to be silent onlookers in a group, they often show that they, too, have grasped the material at hand.

PROVIDE AN ATMOSPHERE OF SYMPATHETIC UNDERSTANDING. Too often the busy teacher becomes impatient and overcritical of the slow learner, who never seems to get the point, who always has to ask the question that was just answered. The teacher must constantly remember the handicap that restricts such students and treat them with consistent patience and good humor.

HAVE SOME OF THE MORE ABLE STUDENTS WORK AS COACHES OR TUTORS WITH THE SLOWER STUDENTS. Used judiciously, this procedure makes the most of the talents of both fast and slow students and takes some of the burden of individual instruction off the teacher's shoulders. At the same time it provides a chance for the slow learner to keep up with the class.

DISCUSS THE STUDENTS' PROGRESS WITH THEM AS OFTEN AS POSSIBLE, POINTING OUT THEIR STRENGTHS AND BEING REALISTIC ABOUT THEIR WEAKNESSES. Slow students, like many of us, have difficulty in making objective assessments of their accomplishments. Either there is refusal to see good work, or a blissful ignoring of inadequate performance. Neither posture is helpful. It is especially necessary for the student with a history of failures to have pointed out repeatedly those things which are performed successfully. Where grading is on an absolute level of achievement, or even when grading on the curve, it is important for the teacher to cushion for the slow student the inevitable low grade. This can be accomplished by frequent individual conferences.

PLAN TO GIVE A TEST OR EXAMINATION, FROM TIME TO TIME, THAT IS DESIGNED TO GIVE THE SLOW LEARNER A CHANCE TO GET A GOOD GRADE. Despite the authors' position that current grading practices are inherently unfair and inadequate, the teacher must still give grades. It is possible to boost the morale of the slower students by including easy questions in tests, or some obvious problems on the study sheet, to avoid humiliating the slow student, who can only get a zero.

I hadn't really understood what it meant to be a person like Susan. I knew that she wasn't very bright, but she was quiet and docile and really no bother. One day I gave a test that I thought would be easy. I had really been concerned about class morale and had remembered that sometimes a class gets a lift when everyone does get a good mark on a test after a series of pretty tough quizzes. But I wasn't prepared for Susan's reaction when I returned the papers. She looked at her paper, puzzled. Then she flushed and put it away. It had, I remembered, a B on it. After class she came up to my desk, standing there rather awkwardly and shyly. "Mrs. Key," she said, "I think you made a mistake. I got a B on my paper." "Why no, Susan," I said, "That was right. That was a good paper." Her face changed utterly. She just glowed. "Why, that's the first B I ever got!" she cried with deep joy and ran out of the room. I don't know when I have seen such happiness on a student's face and felt such a pang in my own heart.

THE SLOW LEARNER IN THE HOMOGENEOUS CLASS

Some teachers find a whole class of slow learners a challenge; others dread it. Admittedly, there are many problems. Since the students usually have little intrinsic interest in classroom work, particularly in the academic subjects, the class is often characterized by a general apathy. Its slow progress makes severe demands on the teacher's patience.

Sometimes classes for slow learners include brighter students who have behavior difficulties or need remedial work. Unless these students receive extensive counseling, they may disrupt learning for everyone.

For a class composed predominantly of slow students, the following suggestions may prove useful.

THE SELECTION OF TEXT MATERIAL IS OF PRIME IMPORTANCE. It is important to find text material that is written for adolescents but which is considerably simplified. Some teachers experiment by writing their own materials. Sometimes elementary texts not used in the elementary schools can be cut up and the pages bound in folders. If the standard text is too difficult for students, current materials may be tried. Although these are written for an adult audience, the popular style, the pictures, the higher interest level may help to overcome reading reluctance as well as reading limitations. Much popular adult material actually has a vocabulary load that is about sixth-grade level.

A CAREFUL SCRUTINY OF COURSE CONTENT SHOULD BE UNDERTAKEN EARLY IN THE TERM. Normally one selects materials and projects carefully in planning for teaching; with a class of slow learners content must be drastically pruned. Whatever reading assignments are planned should be short and spaced far enough apart so that students do not become hopelessly discouraged. However, avoid belaboring two or three paragraphs of text each period. If it is obvious that the point has been missed, try to simplify the explanation and go on to the next problem or idea. Later, after reflection, one can try a new approach to the difficult concept and see if it works better.

WRITTEN ASSIGNMENTS SHOULD BE KEPT BRIEF. Students with a reading handicap usually have difficulty in written work. Even if they can read, their writing is probably considerably less than fluent. Spelling will be a problem unless concentration is given to a list of words used frequently. The procedures, so well described by Holt as well as Fader and McNeil,[10] should be utilized to develop writing skill with slow learners or those who have never felt free to write.

AS LEARNING ACTIVITIES AND CONTENT ARE SELECTED, THE TEACHER MUST DEVISE SOME WAY FOR THE STUDENTS TO GAIN A SENSE OF ACHIEVEMENT. Perhaps they can build a model stage or make a relief map or mount some common moths. School success is a rare experience in the lives of slow learners. The more they can experience success that is genuine, worthwhile, and truly their own, the more willing they will be to expend effort on schoolwork.

SINCE THE SLOW LEARNER'S CAPACITY FOR INTELLECTUALIZATION IS LIMITED, IT IS ESSENTIAL TO FIND APPLICATIONS OF ABSTRACT MATERIAL. Slow learners have

---

[10] Extensive coverage of writing activities are included in: John Holt, "How Teachers Make Children Hate Reading," *Redbook* (November 1967), pp. 50–61; and Daniel N. Fader and Elton B. McNeil, *Hooked on Books: Program and Proof* (New York: Putnam, 1966), pp. 27–44.

as varied an adolescent life as brighter students; this can be exploited to the full in relating class work to situations they know and live in. "Did you ever know a person like this?" or "Did anyone you know ever live in a place that sounded like this one?" or "What would your family do to solve a problem of this kind?" are some ways of drawing out the real-life class materials.

THE SLOW LEARNER CAN AND SHOULD WORK AS HARD AS ANY OTHER STUDENT. Such students want as much as anyone else to make something of their lives, to have fun, fulfillment, and security. They will put out much energy on a task if they know the teacher believes in them. Never make snide comments about the intellectual limitations of the group; that is destructive and unprofessional. Demonstrating awareness of the limitations of their abilities is accomplished by deeds not words. For instance, the teacher keeps as businesslike an atmosphere in the classroom with slow learners as would be expected for any group of students. Their difficulties do not provide an excuse to "goof off," tell stories, or just let things slide. Because the students are slower, they need help in working more attentively than others who can accomplish the tasks more swiftly.

> The classroom was as busy as any I have ever observed. Students and teacher were all engaged in a tremendous project. They were learning the rudiments of photography. They were going to take pictures around the school and prepare a handbook for new students. Each student had a task. I watched while they were getting their first lessons in the use of the camera, and were deciding what pictures they had to have in the handbook. I found it hard to believe that this was a class of slow learners, but the office assured me that the IQs were from 60 to 80 and all had years of school failure behind them.

Patience is perhaps the teacher's chief ally. Often the simplest instructions, the most elementary ideas, must be repeated many times. It may take every bit of self-control for the teacher to keep from lambasting the dull class if he or she has explained something for the tenth time without succeeding in getting across the essential point. For the mental health of both student and teacher, it is more useful to think of the variety of ways a single idea or concept can be presented and the many ways relearning can be guided. Using some of the more interesting "fun" ways of organizing drill and review will help immeasurably (see Chapter 12).

TEACHING THE FAST LEARNER

Consider the following students:

Johnny has all the answers. Before Miss Brown has finished explaining the contribution of Einstein to the development of the atomic bomb, his hand is waving wildly in the air—he is ready to launch into a vivid, accurate, rapid half-hour lecture of his own on $E = mc^2$.

Annabelle never has to study. Her papers come in with the regularity of a ticking clock: neat, polished, perfect. She has an aloof and bored expression during the hour's discussion of King Lear. Yet, when asked to write a theme on the major issues raised, she does so effortlessly and with remarkable insight.

Gordon is a pest. He gets every assignment done in one tenth of the time it takes the rest of the class. His work can be quite good, but it is usually sloppy, careless, tossed off in a hurry. Then he spends the rest of the time making life miserable for Mr. Jones, Mrs. Gray, Mr. Cohen—in fact, for every teacher he has. He can think of more ways to annoy teachers than a whole school of adolescents.

Rita is a menace. She wears the lowest necklines of anyone in the 11th grade. The rumor has it that she has slept with half the boys in the class, has had one abortion, and regularly gets stoned. She also gets straight Cs, though occasionally she gets an A when something catches her interest for a while.

Bill has a terrible report card. The highest mark on it was a C, and this was in physical education. His citizenship marks were equally bad. No one could get him to work in school. Laziness, perversity, cussedness? No one knew.

What do the students have in common? They are all very bright. They have intelligence quotients ranging upward from 140. Their problems, at times, seem very similar to those of the slow learner, and sometimes very different. While work for the slow learner needs to be simplified and slowed down, work for the fast student has to be accelerated and made more complex, and must provide full scope for students' inventiveness to grow.

Popular stereotypes about gifted individuals are undoubtedly held by teachers as well as anyone else. Actually, such people are apt to be overlooked because they often act like everyone else, as long as they are treated like human beings and not like "oddballs." Bright adolescents do, however, often have a somewhat harder time adjusting to daily school life. Their interests have grown faster and in different directions than many of their contemporaries. If lucky, they have had adults with whom to associate, but as a result they are then out of touch with the world of their peers. While they can grasp mature concepts, they may lag in the social graces. If accelerated in elementary school, they may be the youngest in their class, which only adds to their feelings of isolation and awkwardness.

Many bright youngsters are ashamed of their own abilities. This is particularly true of girls. Up to now, American culture has sent strong messages to girls that being too bright is a disadvantage. One result has been the unwillingness of girls to be visible competitors in intellectual activities. Girls have avoided taking advanced mathematics and science because these are considered male activities, which results in girls not having the prerequisites for later careers in science or science-related fields.[11]

---

[11] Lucy W. Sells, "High School Mathematics as a Crucial Factor in the Job Market," Unpublished study, (Berkeley: University of California, 1973).

The problem of the girl who will not work to capacity is very similar to that of the boy who uses his intelligence selectively. He may be the star on the football field because of his photographic memory for plays and his keen, quick mind in figuring out strategy. But when it comes to analyzing geometric proofs, he just will not be bothered. Or he may refuse to discuss poetry or classical music or art because he thinks of them as "sissy stuff." The problems posed by such youngsters are not easily solved. All teachers are reluctant to see bright students sit through classes without applying their intelligence to the material at hand.

> . . . to turn out students who fit the administration's idea of normal, well-adjusted individuals. This includes firm suppression of any deviation from the norm—signs of rebellion, and the like. Many of the more brainwashed students help the administration reach this goal by ostracizing members of minority groups. People who dress differently or whose opinions are different are constantly baited. In my opinion·this kind of harassing only tends to make people withdraw farther from the society that encourages it.

Such comments, collected by a high school teacher from an upper-track class, illustrates the anger and dismay of bright teen-agers who find the education provided to be hollow, if not actually hypocritical. It is a major challenge to secondary school teachers to reach and teach such adolescents.

Probably the most difficult problem in dealing with especially bright students is one's own feelings about them. Unfortunately, many teachers are not as intelligent as some of their students. Thus, having extremely bright students in class may be perceived by ordinary teachers as a threat and a menace; teachers should guard against such a reaction.

> The worst teacher I ever had was Mrs. Fucelli, who taught Italian. Italian was not introduced into my high school until my senior year so I took it as an elective. I lasted about 1½ months in her class before I finally threw my book down in disgust. I was always pretty good in languages and had previously studied French and Spanish. I knew how to approach studying a foreign language. The class I was in was composed mainly of freshmen and, for a good percent of them, this was their first attempt at a new language. The class was paced very slowly—too slowly to hold my interest. I remember feeling guilty for knowing the right answers! My hand was constantly raised and she would never call on me—that is, of course, unless she knew I was no longer paying attention. Then she'd zap me with some question and ridicule me for not knowing what she had said.

An individual teacher can be extremely influential. The Johns Hopkins project for the mathematically talented emerged in part due to the influence and interest of a junior high school mathematics teacher, Paul Binder. He had noticed the mathematical ability of individual students and encouraged them to continue and take as much mathematics as they could, wherever they could. One student, whom he identified in eighth grade, was able to complete his college work so that he would finish a Ph. D. by age 20. There are some extremely precocious young people in schools who, with proper help and nurturing, can grow up to utilize their amazing talents to the full.[12]

THE FAST LEARNER IN THE HOMOGENEOUS CLASS

The advantages and disadvantages of ability grouping for fast learners have also been debated at length. To minimize the disadvantage that may attend this kind of grouping, the teacher should plan programs based on these major principles:

LEARN TO KNOW INDIVIDUAL DIFFERENCES AMONG THE VERY BRIGHT. Although the ability of the group may be generally superior, there will be great differences in interests and motivation.

ESTABLISH A HIGH STANDARD OF PERFORMANCE, WHICH CHALLENGES THE ABILITIES OF THE GROUP. There should be a constant attempt to help students establish a standard of workmanship that makes them uncomfortable with inferior work. This is best accomplished by group discussion, by inquiry on the part of the teacher as to what more could be done, by playing down grades and emphasizing competence, by having available a rich range of resources and activities.

DEVOTE SPECIAL ATTENTION TO THE DEVELOPMENT OF ADEQUATE SOCIAL SKILLS. The teacher may use material that emphasizes social understanding and classroom techniques that promote cooperation and interchange.

ENCOURAGE INDIVIDUAL INITIATIVE AND STUDENT LEADERSHIP. Bright students may fall into leadership positions because of their ability, not because they have leadership skills. Sensitivity to the needs and feelings of followers is an important aspect of the education of the very bright. This sensitivity comes as a result of opportunities to assume leadership responsibility.

DO NOT LET THE CLASS GET A FALSE IDEA OF SUPERIORITY. Intellectual segregation may produce in bright students a spurious sense of their own competence. Showing them how much more they have to learn, and demonstrating the lessons to be learned from others regardless of IQ, will help reduce this possibility. However, the students in special advanced sections are often highly insecure and anxious, as a result of teacher prodding "to keep them from feeling too smart." Some teachers threaten to

[12] Julian C. Stanley, Daniel P. Keating, and Lynn H. Fox (eds.), *Mathematical Talent: Discovery, Description, and Development* (Baltimore: Johns Hopkins University Press, 1974).

"demote" students to regular sections if they do not continuously prove how smart they are.

SET A HIGH LEVEL OF EXPECTATION REGARDING SELF-DISCIPLINE, SELF-CONTROL, AND SELF-DIRECTION. Bright students can go a long way in educating themselves and in running their own affairs if an opportunity is provided for making mistakes under guidance. The bright student needs the mature adult as much as the slow student, but the former kind of student can learn more quickly from his or her experiences. Independent study activities should be used extensively.

THE FAST LEARNER IN THE HETEROGENEOUS CLASS

In classes where bright students are found with all other varieties of intelligence and personality, the teacher should be on the alert to give them special help. Such students profit from an enriched program. Although they must follow the curricular pattern of their classmates, they should be expected to explore many side avenues of interest as well. Some classroom techniques for meeting the needs of fast learners in mixed classes are summarized below:

MATERIALS ON AN ADULT LEVEL COVERING THE CONTENT OF THE COURSE SHOULD BE AVAILABLE IN THE CLASSROOM. Wherever possible, these should be particularly recommended to the bright student as a substitute for textbook material.

DO NOT ALLOW BRIGHT STUDENTS TO MONOPOLIZE THE TEACHER'S TIME. Sometimes the response of bright students is so rewarding that the teacher gears a whole class to these few. This does the rest of the class a disservice and is likely to interfere with the optimum adjustment of the bright students.

ALLOW BRIGHT STUDENTS TO DEVELOP ALL THEIR TALENTS. Too often the bookish interest of the bright student is exploited, as though this were the only demonstration of intelligence that really counted. The superior student may often have other talents, too. This fact should be recognized by the teacher in making assignments. For example, one very bright boy won a Merit Scholarship and a Science Talent Award, taught flute, won a prize for a short story, and organized a get-out-the-vote campaign in his neighborhood.

One bright girl was the lead in the senior play, wrote a monthly column for the school newspaper, was on the "It's Academic" team for her high school, which was the winner in the local competition, and took two college-level courses in her senior year.

IDENTIFYING VERY BRIGHT STUDENTS IS A MAJOR RESPONSIBILITY OF THE TEACHER AND THE SCHOOL. If school records are carefully used, such students may be spotted early. Sometimes bright students are not recognized because they are so bored by school that they do poorly, or show their lack of interest by being disruptive or disorderly. Often such students are made to feel guilty: "Why, a bright kid like you ought to settle down and use those brains!" Finding a challenging task in line with the students' own interests will do more to get them to use their intellect than scolding.

Teachers often vie for classes of the academically talented because of the aura of prestige that surrounds them. Presumably, rubbing classroom shoulders with bright students is "better" than being with the same number of average or dull students. This kind of thinking may result in teachers with most seniority being assigned to "bright" classes. Unfortunately, seniority is not always a sign of the kind of talent that is useful in teaching gifted students.

CREATIVITY: A PARTICULAR KIND OF DIFFERENCE

Students who deviate from "normal" expectancies are often puzzling to teachers. Among the most difficult to characterize are students who are distinctively creative. Presumably, creativity is a prized goal of education; yet observation and research indicate that schools more often discourage creativity and repress or punish creative young people.

While high intelligence and high creativity are not necessarily associated, often the highly creative student is lumped along with the highly intelligent. Such creativity is not easy for the average teacher to deal with graciously. Studies of creative individuals show that they put reality together in a new and unique way; they see shortcuts that the average mind misses; they can use fantasy to dream up unusual solutions to new questions. They often are marked by a bizarre sense of humor and are adept at ingenious ways of making mischief, particularly if bored. For teaching approaches that encourage the development of creativity, see Chapter 9.

CONFORMITY OR NONCONFORMITY?

Schools have always been criticized for rewarding conformity. Today we know that conformity can come in many disguises. We know further, that nonconformity, within limits, can be tolerated, with no terrible repercussions. However, the active encouragement of nonconformity may also be an obligation of the school. In analyzing the source of the contributions of such great people as A. N. Whitehead, J. B. S. Haldane, J. D. Bernal, and Jacob Bronowski, Carl Sagan noted that "the development of such gifted individuals required a childhood period in which there was little or no pressure for conformity." Sagan goes on to comment that there is a desperate need for the development of creative thinkers, but that instead of allowing such intellectual power to develop, "the instructional and examination systems of most . . . countries [is] an almost reptilian ritualization of the educational process."[13]

SUMMARY

While every student is different, some are more different than others. Such students, who differ markedly from the norm, present special learning problems for teachers. Students with marked physical handicaps, while often cared for in special institutions, may also be enrolled in increasing numbers in regular classrooms so that they may have a better chance at an approximation of "normal" adolescent life. Students whose intellectual capacities are at either end of the normal·distribution—either quite slow in learning or very able—pose unique challenges. Adapting instruction to meet these varying needs requires teacher imagination and ingenuity. The issue regarding the grouping of students by ability remains unresolved. So far, the "perfect" procedure for grouping students so that all may learn at their optimum level has not been devised.

The emphasis in this chapter has been primarily on the differences among adolescents. However, the universal experience of growing into and surviving the experience of adolescence provides a common denominator for all students. Events in the larger society impinge upon this adolescent period which may produce new and different points of stress and evoke new responses from young people. The teacher of adolescents needs wisdom and tolerance, as well as continued awareness of the changing climate which each generation of adolescents will experience. Having learned to live—and love—adolescents, the teacher can then begin the creative task of selecting appropriate materials for learning and the methods which will engage students in the excitement of learning.

[13] Carl Sagan, *The Dragons of Eden: Speculations of the Evolution of Human Intelligence* (New York: Random House, 1977), p. 192.

SELECTED READINGS

Ashcroft, S. C. (Ed.), "Special Education," *Theory Into Practice*, XIV (April 1975), p. 145.

Ashley, Joyce C., "Mainstreaming: One Step Forward: Two Steps Back," *American Educator*, 1 (October 1977), pp. 3–7. This position paper represents the views of the American Federation of Teachers on Public Law 94-142. Included is a summary of the main provisions of the act.

Civil Rights Digest, U.S. Commission on Civil Rights, Washington, D.C. 20425. Published quarterly by the Commission and available without cost. Invaluable resource for current information on how schools are meeting the challenge of racial and ethnic differences.

Goldberg, Miriam L., A. Harry Passow, and Joseph Justman, *The Effects of Ability Grouping*. New York: Teachers College Press, 1966. Convincing review of the research on ability grouping, demonstrating that it typically does more harm than good.

Integrated Education, published bimonthly by Integrated Education Associates, School of Education, Northwestern University, 2003 Sheridan Road, Evanston, Ill. 60201. Major resource on school activities related to all forms of discrimination and civil rights.

Rehberk, Richard A., and Evelyn R. Rosenthal, *Class and Merit in the American High School*. New York: Longman, 1978. A careful study of the extent to which socioeconomic or other factors enter into ability grouping and achievement.

Reynolds, Maynard and Jack Birch, *Teaching Exceptional Children in All America's Schools*. Reston, Va: The Council for Exceptional Children, 1977. A good introductory text which will be helpful in the implementation of mainstreaming.

The Council for Exceptional Children, 1920 Association Drive, Reston, Virginia. Publishes a journal and also other materials related to exceptionality and the schools. Good resource for topical information.

The National Center on Educational Media and Materials for the Handicapped. Columbus, Ohio: The Ohio State University. This is a newly established center for the dissemination of media materials which can be of great value in helping the teacher who is working with handicapped students.

Van Til, William, *Secondary Education: School and Community*. Boston: Houghton Mifflin, 1978. Chapter 4, "Characteristics of Young People." A wise and humane educator presents those characteristics of youth which are significantly relevant to the contemporary teacher.

part II

SHARING:
power
and
ideas

SHARING power in the classroom becomes possible when one understands the necessity for young people to learn democratic practices in all aspects of their living. Sharing ideas becomes possible when one is sensitive to the many ramifications of both verbal and nonverbal behavior.

Chapter 4 Power Sharing: Democracy and Learning
Chapter 5 Sending and Receiving: Teaching as Communication

FOCUS ON CHAPTER 4

The teacher in a democratic society is not an autocratic ruler in the classroom. Behaviors associated with democratic citizenship, if allowed to flourish in a classroom, place the teacher in a different relationship to students from that of the autocratic ruler. Proclaiming allegiance to democratic principles does not insure translation of those principles into classroom action. It is, in fact, far easier to leave democracy outside the classroom door and act as though one ruled by decree and absolute authority. In this chapter major assumptions underlying democratic teaching are presented.

Significant ideas presented in this chapter include:
- Common misconceptions about democratic education have resulted in unnecessary confusion. Rightfully understood, democratic education undergirds effective learning and creative teaching.
- The democratic classroom can be identified by six characteristics which, in turn, provide the basis for assessing the degree to which the classroom reveals a democratic mode of operation.
- Because the teacher is an authority, it is not easy to establish a genuinely democratic classroom; school procedures and student attitudes make democratic teaching difficult.

chapter 4

Power Sharing:
democracy
and learning

One of the more astonishing aspects of our society is that everyone espouses democracy, but not necessarily in education! "Let's have education *for* democracy, but let's be careful about democracy *in* education!"

The question may seem like a simple quibble over meaning, or it may be dismissed as irrelevant. Some might argue that schools are not the real (adult) world, and therefore we need not be dedicated to the democratic concept in that domain. However, a strong claim could be made for the opposite view, which holds that if there is democracy in one part of our lives, there must be democracy in every other part as well. In order to have democracy in the world of adults, the world of students must be permeated with the same values and the same interrelationships.

MYTHS ABOUT DEMOCRATIC EDUCATION

A widespread myth regarding democracy in the classroom is the notion that students in a democratic classroom are free to decide, day by day, what will take place; that confusion and disorder reign; and that students are engaged in "artsy-craftsy" projects that have little or no relevance to academic content.

Rather, this conception is one of classroom anarchy, not democracy. Arbitrary, piecemeal activity, which takes place in confusion and disorder works directly against democratic principles.

What is meant by "democratic"? It is difficult to frame a definition: World leaders use the word in different ways; and similarly, educators have difficulty describing the democratic classroom or the democratic teacher.

Part of the trouble may stem from the fact that so few people have ever experienced democracy in education.

> When I arrived at Central High School, the principal assured me that I was going to see the most experimental and democratic class in the city.
>
> I was taken to the classroom—isolated from others in the building—just before the bell rang to end class. The clamor coming from the classroom, with doors closed, was astonishing. As we approached the room, I could see students through the glass panels of the doors as they milled in the classroom. Two girls were dancing in the back of the room. The bell rang and instantly students ran into the corridor, slamming against the principal and me. None of them excused themselves; indeed, none of them seemed to notice us.
>
> I was introduced to Mrs. Eris, who gave me a hearty handshake, spoke briefly about the necessity for teaching kids "the democratic way," and promptly abandoned me as she escorted the principal from the room.
>
> Presently the bell rang for the beginning of the next class. After several seconds many students wandered into the classroom, some of them punching one another, some holding hands, some putting cigarette packages away— all of them loud and unconcerned for their subject, the classroom, the teacher, and the visitor. After most of the students were inside the classroom the teacher reappeared, yelled, "Quiet, you kids" and, in passing me, said, "Sorry, I'm late. I had to have a smoke."
>
> I don't think you could say the class ever began, anymore than you could say it ever ended. The students—who certainly appeared at least average in ability and who were from above average socioeconomic homes—did exactly what they wanted to do, which was mostly gossiping and clowning. During the period, I saw these things: a group listening(?) to a record by Yma Sumac (I was told that because she is Peruvian and they have pyramids in Peru it was important to see a relationship between her and Egypt where they also have pyramids); individual students writing in textbooks (doodling and writing personal notes); a small group planning a bulletin board (they never did decide what its theme was to be); a few boys looking at magazines and comic books; a boy and girl who played courting games in and out of a closet.
>
> Twice during the period, the teacher attempted to shout above the din, but quickly gave up and returned to whatever conversation she was involved in with individuals and groups. I was struck by how insignificant she seemed to be. Students responded to her in exactly the same way they did to one another: that is, with contempt and ridicule. Before the end of the hour, I left the room. No one noticed. I went out to my car and sat for several minutes contemplating my experience. All I could think was, "If that's democracy, we're in trouble."

Mrs. Eris is correct in her statement that students should learn the "democratic way," but her approach leads elsewhere: to alienation, contempt, ridicule, aimlessness, and irresponsibility, none of which characterizes democracy.

HOW DO YOU KNOW A DEMOCRATIC CLASSROOM WHEN YOU SEE ONE?

That democracy can, and should, be operative in education is based on the assumption that citizenship in a democracy demands practical, long-standing training in how to function in such a system. To deny students this training is to restrict their personal growth and thus to limit the resources of society.

A teacher who implements the curriculum by working with students in solving common problems and another one who implements the curriculum by allowing regimen to work its' will on individuals may both believe they are developing a curriculum that meets democratic principles. Teachers of both kinds may be able to say with complete sincerity that they are laboring to develop democratic behavior. Both may be honestly convinced that they are democratic teachers. Although teachers are people of good will, they are not necessarily democratic. Good will is not synonymous with democracy.

Democracy needs to be redefined if it is to be legitimately linked to education. Anthropologists and social psychologists shed some light on this subject. As Ruth Benedict has pointed out, there are many kinds of social systems that one can call democratic because each member of the group is able to live a good, protected, productive, individual existence. Yet these systems may look different from our own political system of democracy.[1]

Democratic education must be considered primarily as a social system devoted to developing better human relations. If the needs of students are being met, if they are progressively better able to cope with their world, if they are developing increasing self-direction in the conduct of their own affairs, if they are able to seek more learning as a result of present learning experiences, then probably the classroom is a democratic one. The teacher who permits and arranges for these experiences is, then, a democratic teacher, who, by encouraging these kinds of behaviors to occur, is also contributing to the ability of these young people to act as democratic citizens. Democracy is a learned behavior. We are not born with it. And many do not learn it at all, or learn it only partially, for themselves, or else want to find the Big Boss who can take care of everything. Citizenship is so much more than knowing how a bill becomes a law, or voting on election day. Democracy is an array of behaviors which regulate how we behave in the privacy of our homes, in our neighborhoods, on the job, and

---

[1] Ruth Benedict, "Recognition of Cultural Diversities in the Post-War World," *Annals of the American Academy of Political and Social Science*, 228 (July 1943), pp. 101–107.

in public places. It is only when young people in school experience over and over again, in thousands of individual incidents, the ways in which democracy works and feels that they are going to be able to act democratically out of school.

FREEDOM WITH RULES

A democratic classroom has an orderly procedure established; there are rules that apply to various activities, although such rules are not rigid dos and don'ts. They are rules that have evolved according to the demonstrated needs of the students and they are enforced with equality and humaneness. If someone is giving a report, others listen; if a group member has an assignment, the teacher sees to it that the assignment is completed because the group will need it. These, and similar rules, govern social living in any group and should be expected in a classroom.

But what happens if the teacher establishes a rule that the students do not like? In a science class, Miss Lynch stated that the entire class would have to finish every experiment in the unit being studied before anyone could proceed to the next unit. Three students finished much before the others and spent a week in the library while the rest of the class caught up. But even at the end of the week, two students were still several experiments short. This meant postponing the next unit of work for another two or three days. The students felt that Miss Lynch's rule had been arbitrary and should not be applied to succeeding units of work. They had a good point; the present rule benefited only the slowest students and penalized the fast ones for being ahead in their work. "Why get your work done ahead of time, or even on time?" said the students. "You'll just have to wait for the others."

The teacher, on the other hand, had a good reason for her decision: Some general class instruction would be necessary before the whole class could proceed to the experiments in the next major unit of work. It would be inefficient to give this instruction to two or three students at a time, and difficult to have supplies out simultaneously for a number of different experiments. The democratic teacher discusses with the class the reasoning behind a rule and the possible problems that might arise from it, and requests from the class a more acceptable solution. What if the rule is a school rule and such deviations and compromises are not allowed? Then the students may not be in a position to change the rule. In that case, the whole problem of rules and what to do about them should be aired.

Why do rules exist anyway? Every game has rules, and people do not change them just because they provide a temporary handicap. In a democracy rules are made to ensure good order and fair play. Students can be helped to make an objective examination of the function of rules in a democracy. They will discover that when a rule is outdated, or arbitrary, or is contrary to common sense and actually impedes the purpose it was designed to achieve, an orderly method of changing the rule should be sought. In this way, students may come to recognize that orderly change allows freedom within security.

Failure to provide ample time for students to discuss school rules, particularly if they are rules which may build resentment or anger, is potential dynamite.

One junior high school principal periodically orders boys' or girls' lavatories, or both, locked as punishment for smoking or defacing the facilities. His procedure has not reduced the number of such incidents. Lavatory behavior does not improve when there are such rules; in fact, it often gets worse. Extensive discussions with students about school problems can produce usable solutions; the pity is that so few schools trust students enough to ask them.[2]

Rules are only one element of the kind of classroom security that produces a democratic atmosphere. Another element is a clear-cut recognition, by both students and teacher, of each other's roles and areas of responsibility. The teacher who seeks to have a democratic classroom must not deceive students into thinking that they have more freedom and power than the teacher is willing to grant.

> Miss Willow was dissatisfied with the routine of the class that she had inherited in midterm from another teacher. In this class the schedule was: Monday and Tuesday, read assigned chapter, answering questions at end of chapter. Wednesday, discuss questions. Thursday, additional question recitation and short quiz. Friday, discuss current events. Miss Willow suggested a more active kind of learning situation, with projects, debates, different kinds of readings, and activities the students would suggest. After some talk in class, the students voted to keep the established routine. Miss Willow was annoyed and decided that the students would have to try things her way anyhow. The students were bitter about her previous lofty comments on democracy and freedom.

This teacher was not genuinely willing to let the class choose and yet she had provided the freedom for them to do so. The class had no security regarding the teacher's role in the class and therefore learned to distrust her. The teacher in a democratic situation must be willing to take the consequences of the freedom granted. If the students cannot reasonably be expected to make a wise choice, through lack of necessary experience or knowledge, then obviously the teacher should not offer the choice.

[2] James McPartland, et al., "Student Participation in High School Decisions: A Study of Students and Teachers in Fourteen Urban High Schools," Center for Social Organization of Schools, (Baltimore: Johns Hopkins University, 1971).

GENUINE CHOICE

It is clear that the democratic classroom allows choices, but among what kinds of things can students choose? First, the choices must be real. When people vote in totalitarian countries, they only vote "yes." That kind of "democracy" has no place in the classroom.

The concept of choice is essential to democratic teaching, just as it is essential to a democratic society. It is obvious that young people do not know all the consequences of their acts. Students do not choose whether or not to come to school—they have to come until they reach the age of choice specified by the state in which they reside. It is all the more important, then, that teachers give them many opportunities to develop the ability to make wise choices in those social and personal areas where they do know the consequences. Otherwise, one essential democratic skill will not be developed.

The teacher, by virtue of age, training, experience, legal authority, and tradition, must establish some limits in choices of subject matter and method. In many areas it is the teacher who knows best. Obviously, it would be unwise to give young people the choice between learning either the best method for freezing meats or the elements of a balanced diet; such a choice is unrealistic. The teacher may, however, discuss with the class the importance of relevant amounts of activities according to their needs and interests. Then the class may choose perhaps two days for freezing and four days on proper diet.

> Mr. Grant decided to discuss with his second period class alternatives to a final examination. He explained why a final examination would be given: "I need this information as proof of the progress individuals have made." Students pointed out that other evidence about their progress existed. "Why can't our other work show the same thing?" one student asked. Another asked, "can we vote about it, Mr. Grant?"

If student needs are ignored or suppressed and only the opinions and demands of the teacher and the institution are followed, there can be no democracy. Thus the appropriateness of the question "can we vote about it?" can be answered only when both teacher and students are informed of the needs, interests, motives, limitations, and goals they share. The democratic teacher's function is *to guide students so that they become increasingly able to choose among increasingly significant alternatives*. After all, the major decisions in life are above the level of learning 100 spelling words versus learning two lyric poems. Out of the classroom, young people are choosing whether to accede to pressures from their peers and experiment with drugs; to arrange for an abortion without informing their parents; whether to make an extra effort to make good grades for college applications or just drift along satisfied with a mediocre record.

Such choices have broad implications for the young people involved; the democratic classroom provides essential experiences in developing the ability to choose intelligently—outside as well as inside the classroom.

The concept stated above should not be confused with the requirement that every time a decision is to be made, the whole class must participate. This kind of "democracy" is just as futile as no democracy at all. One can take a lesson from society itself; many decisions are so obvious, so insignificant, that people often do not know they are making them. One does not consciously decide whether to put on one's left shoe rather than one's right shoe first. In a classroom, the class does not ponder the problem of whether books should be passed up the aisle from the left or from the right. The concept of orderly living can, and must, pervade the classroom. Where there are thirty youngsters and one adult to be considered, there are bound to be problems in management which require group decisions for order—and learning—and some which are best handled by one person, the teacher.

Besides developing an essential democratic skill, the opportunity to choose means better motivation of all learners:

> The literature book used in Mr. McKenzie's twelfth-grade English classes started with Beowulf and progressed chronologically to modern essays and stories. The teacher had found that to start at the beginning of the book was often a handicap, since the selection from Beowulf was one of the most difficult in the whole book. Therefore, at the beginning of the semester, Mr. McKenzie passed out the textbook and asked students to look through the book carefully. Then he discussed the various sections of the book, pointing out some of the more interesting and important selections. He answered questions that students raised about the book. Almost a whole class period was spent in this exploratory experience. Toward the end of the period, Mr. McKenzie asked students to gather in groups of four. Each group was asked to reach a consensus about where in the text they would like to start. The reports were given to the teacher, who began the year's study based on the students' choices. Although no two of his classes wanted to start in the same place, Mr. McKenzie found that eventually he did cover the same ground. But because he started with an area in which most of the students had some interest, each class was more amenable to following his lead into areas of lesser interest.

Choice here became a facilitating factor in learning; it meant active participation.

Even though students may have little interest in literature at the outset, the very process of choosing makes them evaluate, causes them to look at the possibilities and seek something "good" about one or the other. Then, having chosen, the students develop a stake in the subject area; they feel it is theirs, because they had an active role in selecting it. The teacher may of course find that student interest lags in spite of this. The wise teacher will not then say, "What's wrong with you? After all, you decided to study this material." It does no good to reproach the class for being unable to maintain interest in its own choice. Having once created a situation in which students make a positive choice toward some learning experience, the teacher must help in sustaining that interest. Merely allowing a class to choose, and then expecting the expressed interest to solve all further problems of motivation, is not merely foolish, it is infeasible. Nevertheless, by providing the springboard of choice, the teacher has at least obtained an initial impetus moving students toward worthwhile learning.

But, says the skeptic, "What if the students choose to do nothing? Isn't that one of the alternatives we must allow them in a democratic framework?" Of course not! A person has no choice in a democracy about whether or not to obey the law. Law is the framework that makes it possible for everyone to have maximum freedom. Without laws, we would be at the mercy of the whims and passions of everyone, and the most powerful and most selfish would destroy the others. Thus, in the classroom, students cannot have the alternative not to learn as a conscious choice, although often it is an unconscious decision that the teacher has to combat. Part of the personal obligation of living in a society is that one is educated in the ways of that society. The obligation of the teacher is to stretch every possible resource to bring this learning to every student. The teacher cannot let the student choose nothing!

In a democratic classroom, students grow into wider and wider spheres of leadership and participation, although the amount and type of participation will vary from one individual to another. Some students are better able to lead, and these students are encouraged to assume more and more leadership roles; other students excel at solving problems, and these students are expected to share this ability with the class.

DEVELOPING AND SHARING LEADERSHIP AMONG STUDENTS

The teacher can nurture leadership among students in many intimate work situations, with both small and large groups, short- and long-range projects, and by providing many kinds of leadership and quasileadership opportunities. Some of these are comparatively simple, like allowing students to collect papers, or to read notices, take roll, lead discussions, report on special research, make plans for a trip, serve on evaluation committees, right up the ladder toward full and significant leadership participation in the activities of the classroom.

But in its emphasis on leadership, the democratic classroom is concerned with all facets of participation. In a democratic classroom few students can hold back and be passive observers, having nothing to do with learning or with the teacher or with their fellow students. The teacher does not win active, full participation merely by requesting it or by punishing those who do not participate or by giving checkmarks in a roll book for those who do. Rather, many opportunities are provided for different talents to manifest themselves—choosing pictures for a bulletin board, maintaining the classroom library, becoming an expert on some special topic of personal interest related to the major content of the course. These and countless other small opportunities eventually provide an avenue for every student to become a contributing participant and perhaps even a leader! A democratic social order needs the intelligence of everyone to function; it cannot rely on the special expertise of a few leaders alone.

DEVELOPMENT OF RESPONSIBILITY

The more students can affect the world around them, the more they feel responsible for what they do. The great complaint of adults about youth today is that "they have no feeling of responsibility." And how, one asks, can they acquire a feeling of responsibility in a world that allows them to make so few important decisions, that gives them so few important jobs to do? There is a direct relationship between participation and responsibility; one cannot exist without the other. This sense of responsibility is increased when participation is significantly related to the adult world. Too often students feel that there are two distinct worlds—the in-school world and the out-of-school world—and that the out-of-school world is more important. The teacher should therefore constantly seek those bridges between school and community which relate classroom learning to daily living.

Students can:

- Keep records of supplies used and arrange for reordering.
- Organize and supervise in-class library.
- Check safety of all machines and compliance with safety rules.
- Act as liaison with central office for discussion of rules.
- Arrange for visitors, parent conferences, trips.
- Check traffic hazards in and around school.
- Plan furniture arrangement in class.
- Take responsibility for maintenance of typewriters, business machines, other equipment, and report and monitor repairs as needed.
- Organize and run in-class meetings to resolve specific problems.

Responsibility is as much learned behavior as is democratic behavior. Each teacher can inventory those areas where students can be helped to take responsibility, and then let them do so. Just as parents have to learn to let their children go as they grow up, so do teachers have to learn to trust their students, and to let them have responsibility for decisions as well as their consequences.

SENSE OF BEING VALUED

The phrase "all men are created equal" points to a fundamental assumption underlying democratic society, which is that all individuals equally deserve the respect and protection of the social group. People are far from being equal in talents, in their contributions to society, in an infinite number of other characteristics. But in a democratic social order each human being has value simply by being a human being. Similarly, in the democratic classroom every student feels that, as a person, he or she is given due consideration. Students recognize that their personal, subjective, and unique needs, interests, motivations, and goals are considered in the total learning process.

A democratic classroom does not distribute its rewards on a narrow basis. Each person is given the maximum opportunity to achieve learning in his or her own way. True, these individual differences make democratic teaching difficult. In some classrooms, for example, reading may range from fourth- to twelfth-grade level. The teacher who genuinely values each student as a person has an obligation to find reading materials suited to each level, whether in mathematics, science, home economics, or history. Only in this way can every student be helped to his or her own best performance.

What we feel about ourselves is the key to our happiness; we feel good when others like us and our unique characteristics, and we are thus able to deal more successfully with the problems of home and job. Delinquents among young people are often those students who feel that no one likes them and who, in turn, do not like themselves. School failure is a public way in which people are told that they are "no good." Such a message becomes a self-fulfilling prophecy; the person then in truth does become less "good."[3]

When this principle is fully applied, the implications for the teacher are revolutionary. As discussed in Chapter 14, on grading practices, our current grading system which is based on the so-called "normal curve" *requires* failure of a set percent of students. Obviously, students who fail despite their best efforts can hardly believe that the school or the teacher cares about them, and they in turn reciprocate by not caring about school or education. According to Bloom, this state of affairs is unnecessary. If we are

---

[3] Robert Rosenthal and Lenore Jacobson, *Pygmalion in the Classroom* (New York: Holt, Rinehart and Winston, 1968).

diligent as teachers, creative in our approach to differences, and do not require all students to learn at the same pace, then almost all students could eventually learn the basic curriculum of the school.[4] A teacher who wishes to practice democracy in education in a consistent fashion should heed the data which Bloom presents.

THE EXPERIENTIAL APPROACH TO LEARNING

Democratic classroom procedure depends to a great extent on the experiential approach to learning, where nothing is known until it is tried out.

The realm of athletics highlights this thesis. A student is not expected to learn tennis by reading a book about it; he or she must come in contact with tennis rackets, balls, courts, rules, and opponents. Democratic education utilizes this inquiring approach in dealing with all subject matter. In United States history the experiential—and, therefore, democratic—teacher will develop the student's understanding of government through intensive interviews in the field with government officers of all kinds, rather than depending merely on the textbook. In a music class, records, radio, television, magazines dealing with popular culture, and music criticism in daily newspapers become the basis for developing judgments about "good" music rather than students' merely absorbing selections provided by the teacher.

Democratic education, it is clear, is not merely a matter of method and relationship, nor merely a matter of content; democratic education utilizes both content and method to achieve democratic ends. Some observers have attempted to see a difference here and to put either method or content in a prior position. But a careful analysis of what actually happens to the student in the classroom shows clearly that the best method will fall far short of its fullest promise if the content is irrelevant to life, and the best content will be rendered ineffective if the method of instruction is inhumane.

EVALUATING THE DEMOCRATIC CLASSROOM

Democracy in education is a developmental concept. Students, like all people, are not naturally democratic. *Democratic behavior is learned.*

Learning democratic behavior is most difficult, since it demands so much of every individual in the way of selflessness, responsibility, objectivity, restraint, and passion. Many teachers must start with groups of students who are unskilled in democratic procedures and relationships.

---

[4] Benjamin Bloom, *Human Characteristics and School Learning* (New York: McGraw-Hill, 1976).

Such classrooms will, of course, look different from those where democratic skills are well developed. Democracy in the classroom will also look different depending on the age of the students and the subject. Seniors in high school can usually be given much more freedom of choice than freshmen. With these warnings in mind, observers may ask questions such as these:

1. *Are students able to make genuine choices?*
   Are increasingly significant areas of choice provided to develop more adult discrimination among alternatives?
   Does the teacher seem genuinely open-minded about choices the students may make?
   Does the teacher follow through on the choices students make?
   Do students, in talking about their class work, often use such phrases as, "We decided to do this," or "When we chose that . . ."?
2. *Do students have freedom?*
   Are students free to express opinions without fear of "retaliation"?
   Do students have freedom in making rules?
   Do students have freedom of movement? Are they free to move around the room if they are engaged in purposeful activities?
   Is there a relaxed give-and-take among students, not only about the material being studied, but about other school and personal affairs?
3. *Are students participating in all classroom activities?*
   Is participation well distributed among the class members.
   Do students participate in planning important phases of the program?
   Do students participate in the evaluation of class and individual learning?
4. *Are students developing responsibility commensurate with their age?*
   When students agree on a project, do they follow through on their decision and complete the work according to standards of good workmanship, and without prodding or threats?
   Do students increasingly take responsibility for one another by volunteering to help those needing special assistance?
   Do students and teacher share responsibility if something goes wrong with their class plans?
5. *Do the students feel valued as individuals?*
   Are students of low ability taking an active part in class activities?
   Are superior students making unusual contributions to the class?
   Are opportunities available for developing special interests and talents?
   Are praise and criticism easily shared by both teachers and classmates?
6. *Does the subject matter relate to significant democratic goals?*
   Is subject matter at every possible point related to real-life situations faced by youth or adults in our culture?
   Are the ethical bases of democratic processes made explicit throughout the course?
   Is subject matter periodically revised in the light of changing social needs?

The democratic teacher strives toward these goals knowing that some may be achieved sooner than others. One teacher may be better able to relate content to daily living; another may give students a genuine sense of being valued. Each teacher has strengths worth conserving; the democratic teacher recognizes these strengths and seeks to minimize areas of lesser competence.

DEMOCRATIC VERSUS OTHER KINDS OF LEADERSHIP

At this point, it may be useful to see what happens to students under democratic leadership in contrast with autocratic or laissez-faire leadership. It should become apparent why all teachers must work toward democratic leadership, even though no one teacher can hope to perfect it.

Under the authoritarian leader, members seek approval from the leader rather than from one another; there is marked rivalry for the leader's attention. When all rewards and punishments come from one omnipotent source, only the relationships with that person become important. Other members in the group are looked upon as being in the way, as competitors, or as persons to whom one hopes punishment will be diverted. Under such leadership, member–member relationships are not likely to be constructive.

An autocratic leader makes many, though not all, members fearful or angry. Since he or she may seem too powerful to rebel against, members of the group get relief for their pent-up feelings by going after another member of the group. The autocratic leader fosters attacks on scapegoats and thus keeps tensions in the group directed away from personal attacks on the leader.[5]

"Madame Defarge" runs her classroom like the army. All the desks and chairs must be in line with the masking tape on the floor, every item must be "letter perfect" and arranged in "neat piles." No one moves or speaks without permission. The kids hate her, but there is such a need to escape her wrath that they betray one another and pretend to seek her approval. Slower students suffer miserably from the ridicule she encourages other students to heap on them. She is an amazingly cold and aloof individual who is, ironically enough, always talking about her church involvement. When "Madame's" class precedes mine, it takes me ten minutes to get the class together.

A leader may also be too permissive. In such a group the student feels that anything goes; nothing is definite. The leader seems indifferent to members and what they do. Members feel a strong need for leadership, and they may seek an autocrat. There may be rivalry among them to organize the situation in some fashion or other. Members show their dissatisfaction

[5] Ralph White and Ronald O. Lippitt, *Autocracy and Democracy* (New York: Harper & Row, 1960).

with the anarchic situation in many ways. Students express hostility and dislike for the teacher who shows no evidence of planning, is disorganized, and acts on the impulse or mood of the moment.

One is more likely to find autocratic than laissez-faire type teachers in the schools. The system, for a number of reasons, supports the teacher who dominates and rules the class with the ardor of a dictator. The appearance of order and compliance seems, in many schools, to be more important than the other outcomes of such a teaching style. Laissez-faire teachers, however, do not last very long. The chaos in their classes is too obvious to be overlooked, and either they learn different ways of organizing their classes, or they leave. In the name of permissiveness, or the antiauthority ideology of the 1960s, some beginning teachers wanted to lead their classes without being domineering. The approach they tried did not work. Many left teaching, disillusioned with reality, and convinced that public schools were basically authoritarian institutions. As we have seen, the school or the class is only as authoritarian as the adults in the system wish it to be. An individual teacher *can* be a model of democracy in practice, but it takes dedication, sensitivity, and intelligent assessment of what is going on in the complexity of the classroom.

THE TEACHER HAS MANY AUTHORITIES

Basic to the inability of schools to be run as permissive communes is the fact that the role of teacher is endowed with many implicit and some specified authorities which surround and limit all teachers:

1. The teacher has legal authority; the students are compelled to attend school.
2. The teacher is in the classroom because of special knowledge and skill; the students expect to learn.
3. The teacher must grade the students.
4. The teacher is older.
5. The teacher is a quasiparent.

These characteristics of the teacher inhibit the kind of group leadership that may emerge, by contrast, in voluntary groups such as 4-H Clubs, Y-Teens, or Boy Scouts. The school as a cultural institution is by tradition authoritarian; students develop an expectation of "being run." This expectation of authoritarian procedures is a major problem for the democratically oriented teacher. In a voluntary group, of course, the expectation is different; the members, for the most part, expect to run the group themselves.

Accepting the authorities which are inherent in the role of the teacher is the first step toward developing into a democratic teacher.

KEY CHARACTERISTICS OF THE DEMOCRATIC TEACHER

It may be helpful to sum up the key characteristics of a democratic teacher-leader as follows:

1. Gets genuine satisfaction out of seeing the group do for itself something that the teacher may previously have done (for example, lead a class discussion; set up rules for a field trip).
2. Considers all learning as a means of meeting individual and social needs.
3. Is willing to take a back seat as often as possible in order that students may learn how to exercise self-direction.
4. Is patient with the seeming slowness of the discussion and joint-planning approach.
5. Is sensitive to student needs for security and guidance, and therefore is not afraid of providing a firm touch as often as it is required.
6. Recognizes the variety of human personalities to be found in any classroom; does not penalize students for their economic, racial, or ethnic background, or for their level of ability.
7. Encourages creative thinking on the part of students; recognizes that any given unit of learning may be approached in an infinite number of ways.
8. Is able to respond objectively to student aggression; recognizes that the leader should not overreact to personal attacks by young people.

DEMOCRATIC TEACHING IS NOT EASY

Why is democratic teaching so difficult to achieve in the average high school? There are a number of significant reasons.

Institutional Traditions

As has already been mentioned, the school today has evolved from past eras when authoritarian relations were the rule in families, government systems, religious institutions, and at all school levels. Teachers who seek more democratic ways sometimes find that a number of their colleagues strenuously oppose their different approach. Classrooms have always been teacher-dominated; it is the familiar pattern. Students know exactly how to respond to such a situation; each person knows his or her place.

Difficulties in Finding Significant Areas of Choice

The traditional curriculum in many fields presents a course of study, from which is derived a seemingly logical sequence of subject matter. Students may make some decisions and choices regarding rules of conduct, but such decisions and choices are limited.

Students Have Difficulty Accepting Freedom

Frequently teachers with the best will in the world begin a class with democratic procedures without finding out first how much capacity the group has for self-direction and self-discipline. If order has always been imposed, students will not be able to discipline themselves without being very gradually inducted into this style of teaching.

> In a class where very strict routines had always been followed—the read-recite-quiz sequence—Mr. Murrone, a student teacher, decided to introduce a small element of self-direction. He suggested that a bulletin board committee might take over the bulletin board, with contributions from class members, particularly those who had done poorly in the usual work. The idea, relatively simple though it was, took about half an hour of class time to convey. After he had appointed the committee, including two top students, Mr. Murrone was amazed to be bombarded constantly with numerous petty questions. What color shall we use? Can we use pins or thumb tacks? Who will put up the materials? These students were so unskilled in self-direction that any teacher would have to move very slowly with them.

Too often, when a teacher does have such an experience, the conclusion reached is that the class just cannot have "democracy" in education. This is an unfortunate and unjustified conclusion.

Inability of Teachers To Share Control

Teachers are often fearful about allowing their students too much freedom because "one never knows what the demons will do next." This uncertainty is a genuine hazard; the adolescent is unpredictable: moody and stubborn one day, cheerful and cooperative the next. The teacher who is sensitive to these forces, as well as the one who suspects that the ill-repressed primitive urges in adolescents may at any moment get the upper hand, often feels compelled to exercise rigid control over the classroom.

Student Frustration and Aggression

Teachers who use democratic approaches to teaching are often surprised at the violent reaction of some one or two students who, for no obvious reason, become genuinely upset. It must be remembered that democratic procedures put a great burden on individuals to be self-disciplined, to adhere to group-made standards, to share their talents with the group. Many individuals find these disciplines severe, especially if a harsh and rigid parent or—surprisingly enough—an overindulgent one has hindered the development of an individual's self-control.

In a democratic situation, latent hostilities toward authority may come bursting forth; again, the teacher is likely to think that the fault lies in democratic teaching procedures rather than in the student's own social adjustment. It is true that democratic teaching may permit more direct expression of aggression than repressive teaching, where aggression is usually displaced upon scapegoats such as minority group members, other classmates, brothers, sisters, or parents. In a democratic situation the more permissive atmosphere allows the aggression to be directly focused on the teacher, who appears to be the source of frustration.

A teacher who wants to be democratic must be alert to signs of frustration. If too many props are taken away from students too soon and no adequate substitutes are provided, aggression may become widespread. For example, a teacher may suggest to students who have been used to working for grades that grades are not of paramount importance, but that what is learned is very important. Eventually, the group can be brought around to accepting somewhat more realistic methods of evaluation; yet for a short time, the class may be agitated and rebellious, complaining that they do not know how they are doing in their work. The new methods sounded good to them intellectually, but they were not emotionally meaningful. If a group is not used to self-direction, a careful and slow approach is essential.

THE FREEDOM OF THE TEACHER

Teachers who are themselves subjected to authoritarian treatment may come to believe that students should be treated in the same manner.

Observers had noted a very tense atmosphere in all the classrooms of a suburban high school. Students were reprimanded for merely slouching in their chairs. Whispering to anyone was a cardinal offense. Later, a faculty meeting was visited. There, the principal treated the faculty as the students were being treated. He shouted at them, shook his finger at them, and in general conveyed the impression that the faculty were to be ordered around. Interestingly enough, most of the faculty seemed to feel that their school was much superior to all neighboring schools; that rigid discipline, limited textbook study, few extracurricular activities, and a "tough" marking system meant better education.

Teachers themselves may reject a principal who does not want to be the kind of tyrant described in the preceding anecdote and who tries to be democratic. Whether the attitudes originate with the teaching staff or with the administration, it is difficult to maintain democratic relations on one level without the active support of the other.

However, it is also apparent in observations of many secondary schools that teachers have a great deal of individual freedom in establishing the kind of climate they prefer in their own classrooms. A teacher who genuinely practices classroom democracy probably will not find the administration ordering a change. Other teachers may be critical, and there may be a sense of being identified as an oddball, but most schools do allow for flexibility in teaching styles. Sometimes teachers who claim they cannot utilize more democratic methods because "they" won't let them, are very possibly using excuses for their own inability or lack of inclination to drop authoritarian procedures. There is, in most schools, far more freedom for teachers to teach as they want to than most teachers ever use.

Competition or Cooperation?

Because the spice of competition is present in most social and work situations, individuals sometimes forget that the leaven of cooperation must also be present wherever people live and work together. In the democratic classroom, cooperation is regarded as a skill as important as competition. Furthermore, competition is encouraged between groups rather than exclusively among individuals. And the goals are of a different kind; competition is not for prizes or grades or special dispensations, but for higher achievement or for the more adequate solution to a group problem.[6]

Teachers sometimes feel that it is unwise if competitive situations are played down. They fear that students really work hard only to get ahead of someone else, not because of any real interest in learning. Such teachers view the democratic classroom with alarm, because in it cooperative enterprise accompanies individual competitive work; and the teachers do not see how it can result in the same learning. What motivation will there be to get the grade? It is possible that democratic education will not produce the same motivation to get the grade; but it will produce learning that is highly significant, based on different motivations. A democratic teacher may use competition when different groups have bulletin board displays, and the class is asked to judge which group made the best display. Will the group that made the best one get an "A"? Where a pervasive grading system is in operation, this may be necessary. A democratic teacher would strive to produce a situation where the recognition of what had been learned was all the reward desired; adult life rewards not with grades, but only with recognition for performance and the self-satisfaction of earned achievement.

SUMMARY

There is a great deal of pious talk about democracy, yet few people seem comfortable with the idea of the democratic classroom. It is impossible to be *against* democracy—like being against God, country, and Thanks-

[6] James S. Coleman, *Adolescents and the Schools* (New York: Basic Books, 1956).

giving—yet there are some critics of education who feel that democracy has no place in the school. However, it is difficult to see how democratic citizens can emerge from twelve years of schooling unless they have experienced democratic classroom practices. Political democracy and classroom democracy are not the same thing, yet democratic classroom practices do share many characteristics with democratic behavior in the world outside the classroom. The principles of democratic classroom practices can be applied by any teacher. The results will be a sense of shared purpose, with students and teachers in productive partnership.

SELECTED READINGS

Benne, Kenneth, *A Conception of Authority.* New York: Teachers College, Columbia University, 1943 (Contributions to Education No. 895). This tightly argued dissertation analyzes the role of authority in democracy.

Borton, Terry, *Reach, Touch, and Teach: Student Concerns and Process Education.* New York: McGraw-Hill, 1970. A personalized report on how some skilled educators tried to utilize democratic processes in reaching students. Many exciting examples of creative teaching.

Dewey, John, *Democracy and Education.* New York: Macmillan, 1924.

——. *Experience and Education.* New York: Macmillan, 1938.

——. *Individualism, Old and New.* New York: Minton Blach and Company, 1930. These three titles represent many democratic teaching procedures that stem from Dewey's formulations. The second work cited here has been particularly influential.

Jackson, Philip W., *Life in Classrooms.* New York: Holt, Rinehart and Winston, 1968. How students develop strategies for dealing with institutional membership. Discussion of the evaluation climate of the classroom and the castelike status structure governing the flow of power between teachers and students.

Kurfman, Dana G. (Ed.), *Developing Decision-Making Skills.* Forty-Seventh Yearbook of The National Council for the Social Studies, 1977. Provides a rationale for democratic decision making in classrooms, and gives specific detailed suggestions for classroom applications.

Kelley, Earl C., *Education for What Is Real.* New York: Harper & Row, 1947. A classic attack on some of the common myths of education by which we delude ourselves.

Rogers, Carl R., *Freedom To Learn.* Columbus, Ohio: Merrill, 1969. This eminent author describes his belief that students can be trusted to learn and enjoy learning when directed by someone who provides a solid environment and encourages "responsible participation" in selecting goals and means of reaching them.

Schimmel, David, and Louis Fischer, *The Civil Rights of Students.* New York: Harper & Row, 1975. Students as citizens have distinctive rights. When these are understood and observed by teachers and administrators many causes of conflict may disappear.

Seaberg, Dorothy I., *The Four Faces of Teaching: The Role of the Teacher in Humanizing Education.* Pacific Palisades, Calif.: Goodyear, 1974, ch. 3, "The Political Environment of the Classroom," pp. 17–25. Well-developed presentation of the power/authority system of the classroom.

Van Til, William (Ed.), *Issues in Secondary Education,* Seventy-Fifth Yearbook of the National Society for the Study of Education, Part II. Chicago: University of Chicago Press, 1976. The twelve chapters in this yearbook, written by well-known educators, make clear the recurrent problems facing secondary education.

Wittes, Simon, *People and Power; A Study of Crisis in Secondary Schools.* Ann Arbor, Mich.: Center for Research on Utilization of Scientific Knowledge, University of Michigan, 1970. Insightful analysis of the power system in schools dealing well or poorly with student disruptions.

FOCUS ON CHAPTER 5

While one does not have to be a scholar to be a good teacher, one does have to be a good communicator. Language, verbal and nonverbal, is the medium through which we send and receive ideas. The more skillful one is in communicating, the better able students are to learn from the environment the teacher arranges. Four language components have strong implications for students: reading, writing, speaking, and listening. All subjects require expertise in all four. Nonverbal behavior plays a significant role in supporting or negating verbal messages and also in the rapport between students and teachers.

Significant ideas presented in this chapter include:
- The process of communication enables us to send and receive messages better.
- Listening and reading are probably the most significant ways through which people learn in schools.
- Every teacher is a teacher of reading. Knowing how to encourage and foster reading within subject areas is recognized as a major need in American schools.
- Listening skills are generally ignored as part of classroom work. Specific techniques exist to aid people in improving their listening skills.
- "Actions speak louder than words"—and the implications of that fact are far-ranging for classroom interactions.

chapter 5

Sending and Receiving: teaching as communication

Nearly everybody talks, many can read and write, and some listen.[1]
Action speaks louder than words.[2]

B ecause talking, reading, writing, and listening are concerned with words, they make up the components of
verbal communication; they contribute 70 percent of all human exchange.[3]

Facial expressions, body posture and movement, tone of voice, vocal
emphasis, rate, and pacing are the principal aspects of nonverbal communication; they account for 65 percent of all social meaning in interpersonal communication.[4]

All teaching and learning involves both verbal and nonverbal expression.
Frequently, but not exclusively, the nonverbal serves to underscore the
verbal. Obviously, good teachers are proficient in both forms of communication. Individuals need not be scholars to be good teachers, but they
must be good communicators.

All parts of the school curriculum depend on the communication process
—on the sending and receiving of messages. For that reason all teachers
are teachers of communication skills. Each discipline has its own language,
structure, and organization, and each student must understand them in
order to send and receive messages within the discipline. All people have

---

[1] Joshua Whatmough, *Language: A Modern Synthesis* (New York: New American
Library, 1956), p. 16.
[2] Traditional wisdom.
[3] David K. Berlo, *The Process of Communication* (New York: Holt, Rinehart and
Winston, 1960), p. 1.
[4] Stewart L. Tubbs, and Sylvia Moss, *Human Communication: An Interpersonal Perspective* (New York: Random House, 1974), p. 163.

unique, as well as shared, nonverbal means of expression; each student and teacher must be able to decode those expressions if teaching and learning are to occur.

THE COMMUNICATION PROCESS

Understanding the way in which communication occurs should help in understanding some of the problems of teaching–learning.

One explanation of the process depicts three basic elements: source, message, and destination.[5] A message (idea or feeling) is sent from a source to a destination by way of a signal (in this case language). Each source contains an encoder, which translates the message into a signal; each destination contains a decoder, which retranslates the signal into the message. An idea, then, exists in an individual who translates the idea into language so that a second person may understand. When the words reach the ear of the second person, they are retranslated into idea form. Or course, it is necessary that both the source and destination have similar experiences if the idea is to be shared. The process is depicted this way:

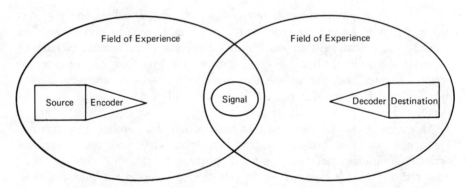

Think of the circles as the accumulated experience of the two individuals trying to communicate. The source can encode, and the destination decode, only in terms of the experience each has had. If the circles have only a small area in common—that is, if the experience of source and destination have been strikingly unlike—then it is going to be difficult to get an intended meaning across from one to the other. This is the difficulty we face when a person who does not have a science background tries to read Einstein or when we try to communicate with another culture much different from ours.[6]

[5] Wilbur Schramm (Ed.), "How Communication Works," *The Process and Effects of Mass Communication* (Urbana: University of Illinois Press, 1945), pp. 3–26.
[6] Schramm, p. 4.

In oral language, the speaker usually receives feedback that indicates to what extent the message is "getting through." An experienced communicator then alters the message according to the behavior seen or heard, in order to make it more understandable to the audience.

In its passage from source to destination, the message may encounter "communication noise" or static (inattention or fatigue on the part of the receiver, ineffective signal, sounds or sights that vie for attention), which either prevents the message from being delivered or distorts it when it does arrive.

Since teachers and students are constantly in the act of sending and receiving messages, it is obvious why they should understand the process of communication. To what extent do teachers send messages to students out of a frame of experience which students do not share? To what extent do the distractions of the classroom create communication noise that prevents the message from getting through? To what extent do students attempt to send messages for which there is no teacher experience or for which the teacher provides the static? Communication should be a two-way experience; a sender and a receiver are required. Both must participate actively for real communication to occur. This is a give-and-take situation, which involves language experience and concepts.

> Language carries with it a two-part concept. Language is . . . a body of words, a vocabulary . . . but it is also a scheme for the use of the words. Language also includes the way authors . . . join words together to suit their purposes for communicating, whether that purpose is to give instructions or to inform, compare, persuade, or entertain.[7]

MASTERING FOUR VOCABULARIES

Actually, we have four verbal language vocabularies: listening, speaking, reading, and writing. (In which of the four is your greatest strength? Weakness? To what extent are your strengths and weaknesses those of an average eleventh grader?) Within any one of the four vocabularies problems of communication may arise because of the fact that all people do not share exactly the same meanings for words. (Poll your colleagues for the meaning of "attractive.")

Experience is significant in the communication process because it provides commonalities that allow us to share ideas with one another (see the diagram on page 94). Ideally, the best communication occurs when there is a similar background of experience for the sender and the receiver.

Concepts develop out of experience. While two people may agree in

---

[7] Dorothy Piercey, *Reading Activities in Content Areas: An Idea Book for Middle and Secondary Schools* (Boston: Allyn and Bacon, 1976).

general about the idea of "snow," people who live in Florida will hold vastly different concepts about it from those who live in Alaska. Many abstract concepts (truth, honesty, integrity, respect) are more difficult to understand where common experience is absent.[8]

The remainder of this chapter is concerned with ideas and procedures for fostering two-way communication and has as its focus the give and take which permits language, experience, and concepts to allow good teaching and learning to occur.

READING AS COMMUNICATION[9]

For most students, the key to success in school is their ability to read. Most of the work they do either individually or in groups, and most of the ways in which they are evaluated, depend primarily on how well they read. Despite the fact that this reliance on reading increases as students move farther up the educational ladder, the formal teaching of reading skills is usually abandoned by the beginning of junior high school; reading development, while obviously fundamental to achievement, is left to chance. And yet, evidence shows that reading efficiency develops only when it is directly taught.

There are good reasons that all teachers should teach reading in their content areas:

1. As indicated above, each subject has its own language, relies upon its own experiences, and presents its own concepts. ("The sum of the areas of the squares constructed on the adjacent sides of a right triangle is equal to the area of the square constructed on the hypotenuse." "Comparisons: Avoid including within the class or group the object or term being compared, if it is part of the class or group. Use *other* or *else* to exclude the object being compared." "History is the record of the whole of human experiences within a chronological framework. It includes generalizations relating to: (a) chronology, sequence, and change; (b) main tendencies in the growth of civilizations; and (c) historical interpretations. Because the role of history is interpretative, the generalizations often involve some of those from other social sciences.")

2. It is the nature of schools that students of diverse reading abilities are usually grouped together for learning. In order to work effectively with what may often be a reading ability range of five grade levels in the average classroom, all teachers must be prepared to teach the "reading" of their subjects.

3. The modern curriculum makes it necessary for students to have multiple reinforcement in all areas for developing reading skills. Marshall McLuhan

[8] Allen Berger, "So You Want to Know," *Wilson Library Bulletin*, 45:3 (November 1970), p. 254.
[9] Some states now require course work in the teaching of reading for teachers; this section is intended as a general overview for those without such background.

predicts that written language will diminish in educational importance as students—nourished on electronic media—grow in sophistication. Increasingly, he says, students will learn through "immersion" of all the senses. While McLuhan[10] may be accurate in his prognostications, today's classroom teacher must deal with students now and most classroom activity still depends on reading materials for teaching and learning.

4. Educationally disadvantaged students usually need special assistance in reading material whose subtlety, vocabulary, or complexity possibly lie outside their fields of experience. How often do such students, whose interest and ability may be high, meet failure or discouragement because they cannot "read" their way through semantic or technical jargon?

Anticipating what students need to know in order to know more is one of the distinguishing marks of the good teacher; anticipating ways of aiding young people to break the reading code that may stand between them and success is therefore imperative. The widespread concern for teaching basics, and the particular stress for developing reading skills, creates an atmosphere within which all teachers must now function. While much in-service education is being provided regarding the teaching of reading, it is also important for individuals to develop competence in this area on their own.

GUIDES TO BETTER READING

What specific things can teachers do to help all students read better? Here are some suggestions:

DIAGNOSE THE READING LEVEL OF MATERIAL PROVIDED FOR THE STUDENT. Examine all texts and collateral reading carefully to see what special reading difficulties may be encountered. Clues will, of course, be found in introductory material. For what grade level was the material written? On what basis was this reading level set? The teacher must, of course, read the material to discover special problems which may hinder the understanding of concepts employed. In addition, familiarity with reading levels makes it possible for teachers to recommend appropriate materials across a period of time.

One effective way to determine the grade level at which materials are aimed is the *Cloze Procedure* (see page 98).

ARRANGE AN ENVIRONMENT CONDUCIVE TO THE ENJOYMENT OF READING. The room should be a pleasant place in which to read silently. Color, light, pictures, comfortable tables and chairs, growing plants, and other decorative features with all aid in creating a place in which reading can thrive. Do not underestimate the power of an effective bulletin board in developing

---

[10] Marshall McLuhan, *Understanding Media* (New York: Signet Books, 1964).

CLOZE PROCEDURE

I. PURPOSE

To obtain an informal estimate of student's ability to read specific materials that is, science, social studies texts)

II. VALUE

A. Can be used with many types of materials
B. Can indicate frustration and instructional reading levels
C. Easy to construct and score

III. PROCEDURE

A. Use material not previously read by the students.
B. From the material, take a well-organized sample of about 100–250 words.
C. Leave a complete sentence at the beginning.
D. Delete every fifth word thereafter (not proper nouns or numbers), leaving equal sized blanks. Delete every tenth word for expository material.
E. Score the sample, allowing only responses which are exact approximations of the author's responses (spelling does not count).

IV. INTERPRETATION

70% +   = Independent Reading Level
40% +   = Independent Reading Level
Below 40% = Frustration Reading Level (students probably SHOULD NOT use this book!)[11]

---

[11] Adapted by Dr. Beth Davey, University of Maryland, College Park.

interests that may be satisfied by some pertinent reading material. A special bulletin board (or part of one) that encourages reading relationships between a particular subject area and newspapers, magazines, and books can often mean the difference between an uninterested, or bored, student, and one who reads for study and enjoyment.

PROVIDE A VARIETY OF READING MATERIALS. After diagnosing the reading level of the text, have on hand books and other reading materials that are both much more difficult and much easier than the text. In this way, students can be guided to individual levels of difficulty.

Each classroom should have its own library of supplementary reading material. Here the teacher can have at hand appropriate items for the students without having to go through the procedures required in a school or public library. A browsing shelf, with new items displayed prominently and invitingly, and a lending system for checking books out will be of inestimable help in encouraging reading in any subject field.

The classroom library should also include magazines and booklets, not only those that deal directly with subject matter but those of general interest to teenagers.[12] Assist students in special problems of reading peculiar to the subject area. Make lists of the specialized vocabulary that will be encountered in the week ahead and go over it with the class. It is useful to have large, lettered charts on which difficult or special words are presented and defined, with both a dictionary definition and an illustration of usage. Use the chalkboard liberally in writing out new words and phrases and give students an opportunity to raise questions about words. Remember that abbreviations, acronyms, symbols, formulas, and signs (e.g., #, $, &) are included in the term vocabulary.

GEAR CLASS DISCUSSION TO THE KIND OF READING SKILL DESIRED. If reading is to be for enjoyment, do not hinder this goal by seeking detail, fact, and intricate analysis as an outcome of the reading. Instead, raise problems of attitude, feeling, emotion, and bias and try to stimulate new ideas.

DIVIDE THE CLASS INTO READING LEVELS FOR SOME ASPECTS OF INSTRUCTION. Often a teacher can obtain copies of different texts at different reading levels. Since most texts in a given field cover approximately the same material, although with varying emphases, this procedure can make for rich learning as each reading group contributes to the total class discussion those aspects of the problem particularly emphasized in its book.

CONSULT SCHOOL FILES FOR THE READING SCORES OF STUDENTS. Many schools conduct routine reading tests of all entering students, but teachers do not make adequate use of this information. Teachers can save themselves much worry and confusion by having reading scores beforehand. Moreover, the job of planning reading material for individual abilities is then made easier.

CONDUCT A STUDY OF CLASS READING INTERESTS AND HABITS. A simple inventory will often provide a teacher with important information about the general interest range and reading level of the class.

READ ALOUD TO YOUR CLASSES. Teachers often forget that reading aloud can be an exciting teaching technique. If there is some highly dramatic, interesting, or complicated portion of the subject matter, take time out to read a few paragraphs aloud. If this is followed by discussion, reading can be a less mysterious process for many students. Do not read aloud if you

---

[12] Scholastic Magazines (904 Sylvan Avenue, Englewood Cliffs, N.J. 07632) offers a variety of magazines such as *Voice, Action, Junior Scholastic, Scope, Art and Man,* and *Co-Ed.* Other publishers who issue magazines aimed at secondary school students (of wide reading range) are Xerox Publications (245 Long Hill Road, Middletown, Conn. 06457) and King Features Syndicate (235 East 45th Street, New York, N.Y. 10017).

cannot do it well; you will produce an opposite reaction from the one desired.

DO A CASE STUDY OF A READING PROBLEM. Each beginning teacher should focus attention on a reading problem during an early period of teaching. A valuable project is a case study of a student with a reading handicap. Using your own knowledge about reading, and seeking the expertise of a reading teacher or of other experienced teachers, analyze this individual problem, considering the remedial and instructional techniques which can be used to correct it. An analysis of this kind will prove beneficial in working with other students with reading difficulties.

EXERT INFLUENCE TO HAVE PAPERBACK BOOKS AVAILABLE FOR SALE IN THE SCHOOL. Most students who own books, read books. Even in the most poverty-stricken areas it has been found that students will purchase inexpensive books, if they are available.

DEVELOP A READING COLLECTION IN YOUR SUBJECT. See if the school library has an adequate collection of material in your field. If not, try to develop one. Publicize the need for books and journals and give specific titles. Parents and school patrons often like to give books or will help in purchasing them. "Book fairs" are another resource; so is the roving Combined Paperback Exhibit in Schools, which whets the appetite of adults and students alike. (Information can be obtained from the Combined Book Exhibit, Inc., Scarborough Park, Albany Post Road, Briarcliff Manor, N. Y. 10510).

DO NOT ASSUME THAT LOW READING ABILITY MEANS LOW INTELLIGENCE.

THROUGH FACULTY COMMITTEE ASSIGNMENTS, WORK TO ESTABLISH SPECIAL ALL-SCHOOL READING SESSIONS. Arranged in alternating time slots, the reading sessions are times when all students and all school personnel put other activities aside and read. The purpose of the sessions is for students and adults to read for pleasure, either bringing their own magazines, newspapers, or books, or obtaining them from sources made available in the classroom or which are circulated by carts placed in the corridors. In schools where this procedure has been followed, teachers testify to increased reading proficiency.[13]

CLUES TO READING RETARDATION

Retardation in reading usually results from a complexity of causes. Mental, physical, and emotional factors may all be involved. None of these can be treated in isolation, but only in association with the others.

[13] Richard M. Petre, "Reading Breaks Make It in Maryland," *The Journal of Reading*, 15:3 (December 1971), pp. 191–194.

Retarded readers may often be identified by the following characteristics:

1. They are dissatisfied with reading, revealing dissatisfaction either through specific complaint or through objections to any reading assignment.
2. Their reading test scores are in the lowest fourth for their grade level.
3. They can use words in speaking which they seem unable to comprehend when seen.
4. They are average or above average in achievement if they are required to do school work that does not call for any reading.
5. They show special personal problems, such as poor attitude toward school, unusual nervousness, extreme hostility toward teachers, extreme apathy toward classroom occurrences, sluggish physical performance.

THE DIAGNOSIS OF READING DIFFICULTY

Many excellent reading tests can aid in discovering group and individual reading problems. Some of the most widely used are the following: Iowa Silent Reading Tests (New York: Harcourt Brace Jovanovich); Nelson-Denny Reading Test (Boston: Houghton Mifflin); Diagnostic Reading Test Survey (Chicago: Science Research).[14] (See Chapter 13 for additional comment about testing for content rather than reading ability.)

In addition to the Cloze Procedure, discussed on page 98, teachers may want to devise simple reading tests of their own. This is easily done: Choose a selection of reading matter that seems to be typical of the kind of reading expected of students. Count the words in the selection carefully. Then make duplicate copies of the passage and give them to the class under optimal conditions of relaxation and motivation, setting a time limit and asking students to mark where they finished when time is called. The group is given a set of questions to test their comprehension of the selection, the questions being similar to those that will be asked on reading material in class. One teacher may seek overall understanding of mood or point of view, while another may want students to grasp the sequence of thought or retain particular details. A careful checking of several such simple tests will quickly reveal individual reading patterns. Some students may read slowly, but grasp all they read; others may read rapidly, but be confused and vague about content. With this knowledge the teacher will be able to guide individuals toward more adequate reading habits.

GENERAL REMEDIAL PROCEDURES

Increasingly, schools are developing special reading classes for poor readers, and thus specially trained reading teachers are coming to the assistance of classroom teachers. However, there are still not enough special

[14] For detailed descriptions and reviews of these and other reading tests, see latest edition of O. K. Buros, *Mental Measurements Yearbook* (Highland Park, N.J.: The Gryphon Press, periodically updated).

classes or specialists to provide the help needed. At the secondary level, particularly, the provision of special reading skills and the remediation of poor ones are apt to be neglected. For this reason, the classroom teacher should know what can be done to aid students with reading problems.

Classroom teachers who wish to help poor readers must acknowledge that they are not experts and that they must proceed with caution lest they compound students' problems. However, numerous guides are available which provide teachers with sound basic principles in reading. University programs in the teaching of reading are growing in number, and participation in such a program is a valuable asset to all teachers. For individuals untrained in reading instruction remedial techniques are suggested in the following paragraphs.

DEVELOP SPECIAL RAPPORT WITH STUDENTS WHO NEED REMEDIAL ASSISTANCE. Such students are often delighted to have someone take an interest in their problem, although they are sometimes extremely discouraged about the possibilities of doing anything about it. The teacher will have to set aside some time several days a week for individual work if a remedial approach is taken.

HELP STUDENTS GAIN INSIGHT INTO THE BASIS OF THEIR OWN DIFFICULTY. After giving students some reading tests, review the results and discuss their study habits with them; perhaps they have prevented themselves from overcoming their handicaps by poor study conditions, failure to wear glasses, or other reasons.

PROVIDE FOR RECREATIONAL READING. Often, a start will have to be made at a very low level of reading; perhaps poor readers should be allowed to work from comic books, paperbound books, and magazines, if that is all they are interested in. Because most poor readers are negatively conditioned to any kind of reading, teachers should permit students to read material of their own choosing even if this deviates considerably from the course content.

FIND A PROBLEM IMPORTANT TO STUDENTS. Require them to use some reading skill in order to obtain a solution.

DISCUSS READING MATERIAL WITH STUDENTS BOTH BEFORE AND AFTER READING. Through a friendly and informal chat, teachers can aid students to look for meaning by reducing the initial anxiety that occurs when the poor reader confronts the printed page. Some discussion about the content can aid students to transfer their concern about "the words" to attention for the ideas in the passage.

CONCENTRATE ON ASSISTANCE. After rapport has been achieved, concentrate assistance on the work of the class. Do not make the remedial procedures so different that students feel left out and isolated and cannot understand the essence of daily work.

DISCUSS POOR READERS WITH OTHER TEACHERS. It often helps if the cooperation of all the teachers of students needing remedial aid can be enlisted so that students get support in all classes. The confidence gained in one area will not then be undermined through repeated failure in another. It is also important to see that duplication of effort is avoided. If one teacher has better rapport with a student, then that teacher should be the one to undertake the greater portion of the remedial aid.

READING SKILLS FOR SURVIVAL

Most reluctant readers will acknowledge their need, and probably desire, to read materials that will help them function in a verbal world. Even students who read well discover that there are areas in which they have to read with particular skill. Everyone is eventually confronted with directions, terminology, and "gobbledegook" that demands translation for survival. Adolescents who do not acquire these survival skills will find their adult life needlessly burdened, and perhaps even marred, by the consequences.

Following directions on income tax, applications or membership forms may prove troublesome to the point of serious error. Failure to read fine print in a legal contract may result in the too-late reminder, "Buyer, beware!" Inability to read quickly may be a great hindrance in traveling on rapid-speed highways, just as failure to understand telegraphic road signs such as "Yield" and "SLOW Children at Play" may cause tragedy. Regional road terms such as "Rotary," "Median," "Ped Xing," and "Soft Shoulders" may cause confusion. Obtaining subject-related materials for poor readers can be difficult. It is important to be on the alert for materials as one reads magazines and newspapers, browses in museums and bookstores, and visits teacher conference book exhibits. General interest magazines (discussed on page 99) are particularly helpful for slow readers and provide high interest, low-level reading material for bilingual students, as well.

Low-level reading materials are also available from consumer agencies and from local, state, and federal governmental agencies. A phone call or visit to nearby union offices or community training programs may produce additional materials that will help convey to students that reading is a survival skill.

Certain states now require that students pass a basic competency test for high school graduation. These tests deal with basic reading and mathematic skills. Many of them contain actual examples from loan statements, recipes, guarantees, government notices, advertisements, application forms, catalogs, bills, transportation schedules, and other everyday reading materials. Obtain samples of these materials and integrate them into your instruction. If possible, obtain a copy of an old basic competency test and share it with students; examining the test is a good way to help them understand the "real world" and its demands.

> My ninth-grade social studies class has been working throughout the semester on an extended unit called "The World of Work." The students are not good readers nor have they been highly motivated to success in school. I soon recognized that they knew little about the requirements for survival in the world of work they are studying. After several failed attempts to establish relevance through the textbook, I decided that the textbook could be only one minor reference. What they need are encounters with people in the work world who can convince them of the hazards of survival. Many resource persons have been solicited to work with the class and many formal and informal field trips have been arranged. In the classroom, students spent much of their time reading job descriptions, promotion requirements, work manuals, applications, and an assortment of other job-related materials. The difference in student attitude—and competence—was obvious by the end of the second week.

Teachers can help students develop survival reading skills through effective bulletin board displays, by continual correlation of course work with the world of work, and, as with all other reading development, by patience and encouragement which develop self-confidence, and, thus, positive self-concept.

READING CAN BE FUN

Helping students to read better should help them to enjoy reading more. Whatever the subject, enjoyment of the reading experience is essential to full understanding and appreciation of content. Too often students find reading painful rather than enjoyable. "From the very beginning of school we make books and reading a constant source of possible failure and public humiliation. . . . Before long many children associate books and reading with mistakes, real or feared, and penalties and humiliation."[15]

To assume that the cultivation of reading enjoyment is the province of English teachers is to suggest that no other discipline can provide reading pleasure. Biographies, historical fiction, and historical accounts like those of Barbara Tuchman and Garrett Mattingly permit students to discover for themselves the excitement and enjoyment often obscured by textbooks. The abundance of paperback books is particularly advantageous to the social studies. The accessibility and attractiveness of most of these publications make it easy for students to know history directly, through biog-

---

[15] John Holt, "How Teachers Make Children Hate Reading," *Redbook* (November 1967), p. 50ff.

raphies, memoirs, and reportorial accounts. Readings in fiction, such as a comparative study of Margaret Mitchell's *Gone with the Wind* and Margaret Walker's *Jubilee*, enable students to see contrasting viewpoints in dramatic terms. Exposure to magazines such as *American Heritage* and *Horizon* does much to reveal to students that history is "alive." Authors such as Paul de Kruif, Margaret Mead, Loren Eisely, Rachel Carson, Donald Peattie, Eric Temple Bell, and Annie Dillard have made scientific writing as thrilling as a mystery story. There is abundant current material in the popular magazines on most of the topics taught in secondary school science classes, and the articles are written so that science becomes an exciting and satisfying experience. For the study of languages, the personal anecdotes of travels abroad, the lives of immigrants of the various nationality groups in America, and the translated fiction of the foreign culture are all excellent materials, as are newspapers and periodicals from other countries.

My first genuine interest in French—as a language that had something to say about people—came in Mr. McArthur's French·II class. His room was a magnificent jumble of French language novels, biographies, nonfiction, magazines, and newspapers. You couldn't miss the point that he loved the language, that he devoured it daily, and that what he read helped to make him the exciting person he was. I started slowly with the magazines and newspapers and eventually got hooked on the books, as well. I'm studying to be a translator now; it was that heap of materials in Mr. McArthur's class that got me started.

TEACHING READING IN ALL SUBJECTS

All teachers teach reading when they assist students in understanding the specific purposes of reading assignments. Aspects of understanding are:

- factual comprehension: order; incident; cause and effect
- assimilation: connecting the written experience to the reader's experiences; connecting reading experiences to other areas of living (knowledge of other people, subject areas); making judgments based on reading; giving illustrations of specific, related references
- comparing and contrasting: finding similarities and differences among things read as well as among nonreading experiences
- summaries: reducing material to a few sentences; synthesizing principal points established; briefly paraphrasing; identifying an author's point of view (prejudice or bias); outlining principal points

In addition, teachers teach reading when they assist students to develop vocabulary in relation to the subject matter. This can be done by:

- presenting in advance words students will encounter in reading assignments
- taking the time to help students study words in context, and identifying syllables; identifying prefixes, roots, and suffixes
- requiring students to use new words in sentences of their own invention

Finally all teachers teach reading when they:

- display enthusiasm for reading and written subject matter
- provide clear goals for reading assignments
- demand a variety of skills and reading rates
- show patience with slow and reluctant readers
- reward all students for their accomplishments

LISTENING AS COMMUNICATION

More than any other communication skill, listening is taken for granted. It is assumed, somehow, that competence in recording and reacting to spoken language develops on its own. The fact that students engage in listening more than in any other school activity may give rise to the idea that listening skills perfect themselves. Nothing could be farther from reality. Listening, like all other language arts, develops more reliably when it is taught directly.

All teachers will want to consider three areas of importance that affect the development of listening skills: classroom atmosphere, techniques of listening, and hearing handicaps.

CLASSROOM ATMOSPHERE

Some situations encourage listening while others discourage it. Physical environment and psychological atmosphere contribute greatly to whether or not a student "hears" or "listens"—and how well. The actual classroom and its surroundings contribute many distractions to effective listening. Furniture squeaks, scrapes, and bumps; doors slam in the corridor; chords and discords filter in from the music room. In some rooms heating fixtures hum, or poor acoustics create echoes. And in every classroom there is always the possibility of interruptions from the public address system.

Out-of-class noises affect what happens in the classroom. Sometimes schools are near train tracks or airports, on streets with heavy traffic, or classrooms are adjacent to playing fields. Such conditions impose a handicap on teaching and learning. One of the difficulties of many city schools is that they are ancient structures which stand amidst factories and other dingy, unattractive buildings, attempting to function on hyperactive thoroughfares where air pollution competes with ear pollution. One solution to noise distraction—although unfortunately only in new, experimental schools—is the carpeting of all floor space. This provides a successful effort to muffle sound, and also manages to remove some of the "coldness" of the typical classroom.

A direct control of noise in the school building can be effected by teachers self-monitoring noise they themselves create or allow. Often disturbances can be controlled by closing doors or windows, moving to a more restricted area of the building, or, not infrequently, by teachers lowering their voices.

> I was called to the north wing of the school this afternoon by several teachers' protests. "Miss Tebaldi," the voice teacher who was afraid she would strain her voice, was teaching with the help of a hand microphone. It certainly saved her voice, but it completely disrupted classes in nine other rooms.

Play or music rehearsals, group projects, or sports practice all have the right, and the need, to make more than usual sound; however, none of these activities has the right to produce noise that disturbs other classes.

"YOU'RE NOT PAYING ATTENTION!"

During a working day, average individuals spend 11 percent of their time writing; 15 percent reading; 32 percent speaking; and 42 percent listening.[17] Only about one-fourth of all listening is done efficiently.

TECHNIQUES OF LISTENING

Improvement of listening skills, like all other communication skills, can be learned. But first we must understand the distinction between "hearing" (awareness that sounds are being made) and "listening" (the active process of paying attention). An activity which draws attention to this distinction calls for students to sit silently for one minute without warning. At the end of the minute, students are asked to list those things they heard during the silence. After some lists are read, the teacher asks how many people heard more subtle sounds, such as air from the heating unit, the buzz in an overhead light, the sound of rustling clothing, and so on. Once more students are asked to be silent, this time *listening* for all possible sounds. The lists which are then read lead easily to distinctions between hearing and listening as well as to the necessity of developing the aural sense.

Another hearing–listening exercise may involve the use of high-fidelity test recordings that employ a wide array of sounds to be identified by the listener. This technique may be equally effective in an introduction to the study of sound in a science class or in the introduction or development of skills in other areas of the curriculum.

A major deterrent in perfecting listening habits is the notion that whenever students sit still to listen, they must be entertained. Students unfortunately develop a pattern of listening that says, in effect, "We are

[17] John W. Keltner, *Interpersonal Speech-Communication: Elements and Structures* (Belmont, Calif.: Wadsworth Publishing Company, 1970), p. 11.

either entertained when we listen, or we are bored; there is no middle ground." This attitude interferes with adequate listening in class and certainly militates against listening to recordings, radio, television, and films that require critical reaction.

In many situations, some teachers require students either to take notes, write a summary of material presented, or to fill in details in a teacher-prepared outline, copies of which are given to everyone. In discussions, it is effective occasionally to require that any speaker must repeat the statement made immediately prior to theirs. Both techniques—writing and restating—require time and patience, but both produce results.

Practice in each area of listening described below can provide specific development of listening skills.

- Casual listening—the kind we do in everyday conversations
- Recreational listening—for light music, stories, entertainments
- Discriminative listening—used to detect changes which reflect the speaker's changing moods
- Informational listening—the kind that goes on when we listen to directions about how to perform an activity or how to get from one place to another
- Listening for organization—what we do when we take notes and try to find the pattern of the speaker's ideas
- Critical listening—used to detect purpose and bias, to edit out propaganda, to analyze the reasons behind words
- Creative listening—used to change and develop the speaker's material into our own forms, ideas, patterns.

To ensure application of what is discussed the teacher must provide activities which require students to use (and distinguish among) the kinds of listening.

Good listeners are individuals who:

1. are prepared to listen, physically as well as mentally; they recognize and accept the fact they have a task to do and they focus on doing it
2. think of the topic beforehand, raising a few questions in their minds about it
3. distinguish among the main parts as they listen, holding in their minds a few significant words or phrases that deal with those parts
4. concentrate; they use self-discipline to keep themselves attentive to the speaker
5. are flexible enough to move with the speaker over a range of ideas, attitudes and style
6. compensate for emotion-arousing words; they are not misled or distracted because a speaker uses words which trigger strong feelings in them
7. are always building their vocabularies so that they are better prepared to listen about many things

Obviously students will learn these principles best if classroom activities provide the opportunities to practice them. Because good listening is not easy and requires continued practice, teachers must be willing to provide time for the development of this skill as it relates to individual disciplines, and they must also provide creative activities which cause students to actually engage in the seven characteristics mentioned above.

It is important to bear in mind that good listening is not dependent on intelligence nor is it necessarily related to reading skill.

SEMANTIC OBSTACLES

A special concern for all speakers and listeners is the kind of communication noise (static) which can be identified as semantic obstacles.

Semantics is the study of the meaning of words. The study is divided into two parts: denotations and connotations. Denotations are those meanings which reside within the dictionary; connotations are those meanings which reside within our own experience. For example, the word "blood" is denoted as "the fluid that circulates in the principal vascular system of man and other vertebrates . . ." but it frequently connotes fear, nausea, or revulsion. Both definitions can exist side by side in our minds.

Semantic obstacles, those words and phrases which either distort a message that is transmitted or actually prevent the message from getting through, are of particular concern to the teaching/learning process. Basically three kinds of semantic obstacles exist:

- misunderstanding one word for another
- emotional arousal that distorts the message transmitted
- lack of understanding because definitions are not known

Misunderstanding one word for another can occur in any context. Essentially the misunderstanding occurs because the receiver believes another word has been used. Teachers report such confusions as "saddle lights" for "satellites," "Blue Bonnet Plague" for "bubonic plague," "Round John Virgin" for "round yon virgin, mother and child," and "The Grapes of Raft" for "The Grapes of Wrath."

Emotional arousal that distorts the message transmitted occurs when individuals feel embarrassment, hostility, confusion, fear, or some other strong emotional reaction that springs out of an association they make with the word or phrase. Words such as "intercourse," "mother," "bitch," (referring to a female dog), "gay," "mankind" (and many other "man" words), and "Negro" have created communication noise sufficient to prevent learning. Typically, students who experience this kind of semantic obstacle are either too embarrassed to ask for clarification or are sufficiently upset by the obstacle to say so, regardless of the circumstances.

Frequently, lack of understanding because definitions are not known is the case in the typical secondary school classroom. Most often students do not acknowledge that they do not know a word's meaning. Sometimes they will misunderstand it for another word, but most often they will experience a blank in the message transmitted, much like the "blip" that sometimes occurs when a word is censored on television. Occasionally, students may supply a correct meaning by the context of the sentence, but if the teacher speaks rapidly, the message is usually lost.

Extremely valuable in discovering the extent to which semantic obstacles exist in the classroom—and extremely valuable in understanding the range of their kind—is the maintenance of a communication journal over a four- to six-week period. List the date and one or two of the semantic obstacles you have observed during the day. Weekly review of the journal and a final full overview of the gathered obstacles can provide rich information which will assist in monitoring one's own speech as well as that of students.

> Looking back over the last few weeks, I see clearly how much of my class-room language is based on faulty assumptions. I have a strong tendency to think that my students know the language of mathematics as well as I do. (And how embarrassing that three times last week I said "triangle" when I meant "rectangle.") I also see that one faction within my fourth period class uses language that offends some of the others. I'm not sure how I'm going to deal with that, but it is clear something has to be done.

HEARING HANDICAPS

A student who has a hearing handicap presents a special problem in developing communication skills. Some school systems provide a hearing test for all entering students, and the information obtained from it is entered on students' permanent records. Teachers are informed of the results at the time the test is taken; but, like all such information, it will not be useful in succeeding semesters unless all teachers consult the records of all their students.

The student who constantly says, "But I didn't hear you make that announcement," or "I didn't catch the page number when it was given," may have a genuine hearing difficulty. Before judging such a student as lazy or provocative, it might be more humane to determine whether the student has a hearing problem.

> Nancy consistently failed to get her homework in on time, offering the excuse "But I didn't hear you." After audiometer tests were given, her teacher discovered that she had no hearing at all in one ear. When her seat was changed to the other side of the room, so that her good ear was in the best position to catch what was said from the front of the room, Nancy's work improved considerably. Nancy herself had not realized that she had a hearing disability until the test was administered.

There is some disagreement about the meaning of "deafness" and "hearing loss." However, most studies of school children indicate that between 5 and 10 percent have some definite hearing defect.[18] The available studies on hearing loss make it clear that this physical limitation makes personal and social adjustment difficult. Since so much of school activity depends upon what can be "heard," teachers must be especially sensitive to this problem.

What can teachers do about a student whose hearing is impaired? They can employ several methods of making directions clear and they can provide additional materials for learning. In addition to giving assignments orally, it is also wise to write them on the chalkboard. In that way, both sight and hearing can be used to obtain important information. Teachers can also see that hard-of-hearing students are seated advantageously in the classroom, that other students assist them (if they will accept such assistance), and that assignments allow those students to capitalize on their other senses.

All students may face some hearing loss as they move from one part of the room to another. Some rooms have "dead" spots in which only the loudest of sounds can be heard. In large rooms, seats in the back may be sufficiently remote from speakers in the front; seats on the window side may be close to outside noise. Sometimes noise spills over consistently to certain parts of the room from adjoining rooms. The problem of other-group noise is a recurring problem in many open space schools.

WRITING AS COMMUNICATION

> I hate to write. Teachers don't pay any attention to what you say, anyway. All they look for are mistakes—like grammar, spelling, and punctuation— and whether you're giving them back what they want. It's like a game, and it's almost impossible to win.

While this student's comment may be something of an exaggeration, it is worth considering. Do teachers consciously or unconsciously preoccupy themselves with the form of what students say to the point of impairing what they say? Certainly, form is important, but it is easy in the daily routine of multiple evaluations to seize on the "how" and ignore the "what." When this happens, the students assume, as the one above suggests, that minutia is what is important to teachers, and not substance. If concentration on form does emerge, then teachers have an obligation to reevaluate their goals. To fail to capitalize on adolescent concern for values

[18] R. G. Barker, B. A. Wright, and M. R. Gonic, *Adjustment to Physical Handicap and Illness* (New York: Social Science Research Council, 1946), p. 163. See also C. D. O'Connor, and Alice Streng, "Teaching the Acoustically Handicapped," *The Education of Exceptional Children* (Chicago: University of Chicago Press, 1950), p. 156.

and for involvement in the adult world and to fail to encourage students' ideas about these concerns is to deprive them of an important aspect of their education. It is true that what we say is either enhanced or minimized by the form in which it is said, but to emphasize form to the exclusion or detriment of content is to discourage students from wanting to think through and say anything.

There are several ways in which the classroom teacher of any subject can assist students in gaining fluency in conveying important ideas and emotions and cause them to discover, at the same time, that acquiring this skill is a pleasant process: Students should be encouraged to write when they have something important to say. Too often students try to express ideas that do not interest them, the sole motivation being punishment or fear. The pressure on students to write "because it is required" is an extremely inhibiting factor. The class itself might try to get a letter on a local issue published in the local paper; the subject might be reverse discrimination, maintenance of life support systems for the terminally ill, minimum wage legislation, human rights, or drug violations, to suggest just a few. Or students might want to communicate with the principal or superintendent or a local politician about a matter of importance to the school. Some incentive that places the stress upon the outcome, rather than on the process of writing, may serve to release many students from the dread of writing for a teacher's correction.

If students fail to write complete sentences in answering an examination question in history, in physics, in German, or in commercial law, then those teachers should provide class time to discuss elements of good writing. Too often teachers expect that students will make automatic transfer of knowledge from one subject to the next. Through reward and praise, by posting on bulletin boards examples of good written work, by reading aloud to the class some of the better materials turned in by students the teacher can do much to develop an affirmative attitude toward writing.

The best practice for the teacher attempting to foster a positive attitude is to make comments on the student's written work, pointed most of the time toward the recognition of good material. Even if the work is not of the best quality, it is important that the teacher find positive observations to make. Such comments as "good try," "fine start," "shows considerable improvement," or "good choice of words" do a great deal to prepare students for absorbing more critical comments and will help them feel that it is worthwhile to continue.

The teacher should avoid overemphasis on errors. When reading examinations or reports, the teacher is tempted to circle all spelling errors, to make large red checks where incorrect punctuation has been used, to point out all incomplete sentences. Students who spell poorly probably have had many years of failure in that area. To continue to point out all failures is probably the least profitable thing the teacher can do to help them improve. It is worth the effort to assist students with words common in writing; but class time spent in learning to spell infrequently used words might better be employed in developing ideas, concepts, and attitudes. Large charts with correct spellings, definitions, and appropriate illustrations help make important words useful tools for students whose fear of misspelling may keep them from demonstrating knowledge.

There is little evidence to support the notion that students who consistently make errors in spelling, punctuation, and grammar look at the corrections made by the teacher. It has been suggested that students take them for granted and that their eyes pass over them in search of the grade and overall comment.

> I'll never forget the first batch of essay examinations I corrected and returned to my tenth graders. I had spent hours meticulously correcting each error of content and language. I confess the papers were bright with my red pencil markings. At the end of class I returned the tests; most of the students immediately looked at the grade, then crumpled them up—and dropped them in the wastebasket as they left class.

At this point a basic concept of good teaching should be stressed. Grades should never be wholly dependent on written examinations; that is, they should never exclude all other modes of evaluation. Some people express themselves well orally, some in writing, some in the graphic arts. Good teachers provide many ways for students to demonstrate learning. Overemphasis on writing, to the exclusion of other ways of showing competence, has caused many students to drop out of school and has retarded the growth of many others who have remained.

SPEAKING AS COMMUNICATION

In general, students will speak better if the situation is relaxed, if they have something important to impart, and if the nature of the occasion is less significant than the sharing of a vital experience. The use of group work (see Chapter 10) will help to provide opportunities for this kind of speaking. The low level of oral communication skills in most secondary school students implies that all teachers should focus their efforts on aiding students to speak better, to speak more freely, and to speak with greater enjoyment.

Oral work in a classroom should be preceded by a class discussion of what makes a good oral presentation. No matter what the subject matter, when a student is asked to impart knowledge to the rest of the class, to make an explanation, to give directions, or to report progress, it is important that these activities aid in the development of speaking skill. This can be assured if teachers and students discuss what goes into a good oral report, then list together criteria that may be used in evaluating these efforts. Then, when agreement has been reached by the class, the list should be posted in a conspicuous place. When a report has been given, the teacher and the class may refer to the list with the question, "How can we improve?" As in correcting student writing the teacher should focus on good points and direct students toward establishing goals for improvement.

In setting up a list of factors that contribute to good speaking, the teacher should see that these criteria are included: clarity, interest, ease of audience understanding, directness of contact with audience, poise and relaxation, and absence of distracting mannerisms. A class can quickly and easily build with the teacher a list of such factors. Using an evaluation sheet for oral work or allowing a committee to assess progress also helps students focus on skill development. But this should not be overemphasized. It is important to keep adolescents, already self-conscious, from being so disastrously self-conscious that they are completely tongue-tied and emotionally upset by stage fright.

Teachers should be careful that certain behaviors of their own do not destroy an atmosphere conducive to speaking freely and well.

> Mr. Church said on several occasions that he believed it was absolutely necessary for students to practice good speech in class. He couldn't understand why his students consistently refused to practice what he told them was good for them. After all, he explained to other faculty members, he insisted on an answer—right or wrong—whenever a student was called on; he insisted also that students stand when they spoke so they could have practice in posture; he interrupted when they made errors and saw to it that they repeated themselves correctly. When he was approached about his behavior, he remarked, "I'm just trying to help."

It is amazing that Mr. Church's students spoke at all. Every tactic he employed is all but guaranteed to ensure speech resistance in students. Why must students answer every time they are called on? What purpose is served when students stand to answer? Do they really develop good posture by standing to answer a question? When students are criticized and corrected publicly, do they attend to their errors, or to their peers' reactions? Does repetition of a "correct" speech pattern become a part of a student's behavior when it is repeated only once, and then under scrutiny?

Many students have problems that require special help. One particularly important problem exists for students who come from homes where a foreign language is spoken most of the time. For these students, learning good habits of expression in English is especially difficult. They require more sensitive help than other adolescents, particularly because of the embarrassment they may feel when speaking in front of a group.

Considerable discussion has occurred regarding appropriate ways of dealing with the special dialect of educationally deprived students. Such students may come from isolated rural America, or inner-city slums. Their speech patterns vary from "standard" English. Observers and linguistic scholars point out that many times this speech utilizes nuances missing from standard English. Yet most teachers are strong advocates of removing all traces of speech that differ from the middle-class norm. The pros and cons of this discussion may be pursued by the interested student. The point emphasized here is that teachers must be sensitive to the personal meanings of a student's language and speech habits. Deviations from what the teacher considers correct should be carefully considered before any kind of public judgment or pointed effort toward change is made. However, the hazards, of speaking a "different" kind of English in terms of job placement must be made clear to students.

Students who are shy or withdrawn in class probably utilize few opportunities to talk with other classmates and therefore have little chance to develop skill or confidence in presenting ideas in a school setting. It is particularly important that they have experiences in circumstances that will develop skill and confidence which allow them to verbalize their attitudes and beliefs as well as their grasp of subject matter. Using small group procedures is particularly helpful with such students.

Students with speech defects should of course receive the specialized training of therapists. If speech tests are not administered to students, it becomes the teacher's responsibility to refer these students to the proper agency of the school. As with introverts and students for whom English is a second language, the speech-defected adolescent must be accorded special consideration in the oral activities of the classroom.

NONVERBAL BEHAVIOR AS COMMUNICATION

In the broadest sense, nonverbal communication concerns not only people but the environment in which they function. Most people are influenced by their surroundings just as they are influenced by the interactions they have with others. For optimal learning to occur, teachers should consider both people and the space in which they behave.

While the messages conveyed by a working environment are sometimes subtle, they are, nonetheless, real and affect the self-concept, and thus the working attitude, of individuals. Size, openness, and decoration of space have marked effects on the degree to which people are comfortable. In learning situations, those things influence discussion, discipline, attentiveness, and what might be called "the ability to work." While they may seem mundane matters, part of the teacher's task in creating an atmosphere that encourages learning is to monitor lighting, ventilation, heat, furniture, and cleanliness.

I hated Sociology 100 because I was always uneasy in the classroom where it met. I didn't realize why until about the third class meeting and when I did things only got worse. I was constantly distracted by the filth of the room. It was just across from a room with food vending machines and was a popular place for eating when classes weren't in session. The floor was strewn with bits of food, wrappers, and spilled coffee. Cigarette butts were mashed out on the floor, also. In addition, the room itself was painted an ugly green, a venetian blind was broken and hung askew. The pipes overhead rumbled and I felt miserable.

An overstated reaction? Perhaps. Perhaps not. To what degree have you been influenced by your working space? What are the things which interfere with your productivity? What are the things that help you to work quickly and well?

CONGRUENCE VERSUS INCONGRUENCE

I never trusted Ms. Segal. I don't think many people did. She seemed to be a nice enough person, but somehow you were never sure whether she meant what she said or not. It wasn't until I read a book on nonverbal communication that I understood why. She had a tone of voice, mostly inflection, that seemed to say the opposite of her words; her "I'll be glad to help" somehow came out sounding like, "Whatever you do, don't ask for help." She struck a recurring pose with her arms crossed, she always slightly backed off when you approached her, and she avoided looking you in the eye. She could have used a few lessons in body language.

Whether nonverbal behavior is concerned with learning space or with people engaged in the learning act, a basic concern is the extent to which the message being sent is congruent with how (or in what circumstance) it is being sent. When incongruence exists, people are confused. From their confusion may spring suspicion, anger, distrust and other negative reactions. Actions *do* speak louder than words and at an unconscious level we are always testing out the sincerity of those who send us messages. When we are in doubt, we accept the nonverbal message over the verbal one—and that is when much of the difficulty of classroom communication occurs.

Because of the way in which most secondary school classrooms are arranged, the nonverbal behavior of the teacher is unusually significant in hindering or helping communication. Gestures, facial expressions, posture, movement, vocal intonation, pitch, pauses—each conveys feelings—whether they be excitement, boredom, involvement, detachment, self-confidence, uneasiness. More than any other aspect of nonverbal communication, the use of the eyes suggests to students an array of reactions about teachers and their capabilities. Recall teachers you have known and enumerate with others both positive and negative memories you have about the way in which they used their eyes to express themselves.

Sister Catherine could use her eyes like few people I've ever known. Her eyes seemed to glow and she was able, with amazing swiftness, to make them change from approval to delight to annoyance to scorn. She had a particular "look" that could squelch an offender; it was her "double whammy special." It said volumes. Behind her back we sometimes called her "Sister Whammy."

Of course, nonverbal behavior exists on both sides of the teacher's desk. Students use their bodies and voices, just as teachers do, and they can confuse or manipulate teachers by the way they use them. (See the discussion of "Bright Eyes, Scaredy-Cats, and Dummies" on pages 366 and 367.)

A significant aspect of nonverbal behavior in the classroom deals with how teachers use the space of the classroom. Behaviors such as always remaining at a distance from students, never walking into certain areas of the room, clinging to a podium, or remaining behind the "security blanket" of the desk all convey specific messages which can translate as "I'm afraid of you," "I don't trust you," "I'm unsure of myself." Working with students at eye level and moving about in all parts of the room are important practices. It is of prime importance in classrooms where informality and a strong feeling of working together is desired, that the teacher does not establish one piece of furniture or one part of the room as his or her sacrosanct province.

Mrs. Shimoda seldom moved from a four-foot high podium her husband had made for her. She leaned on it, walked around it, stood behind it—but she almost never left it. People vied for seats in the back; you could get away with murder there. Whenever she came near you, you were so surprised you spent the whole time looking at her bushy eyebrows or noticing the wrinkles or smelling a terrific perfume she wore.

ATTENDING BEHAVIOR

Attending behavior is a term given to describe those aspects of nonverbal behavior which suggest that students are attentive to the work of the classroom. All teachers need proficiency in "reading" the signs that indicate that students are bored, confused, or distracted. That kind of feedback is a signal that the teacher's approach needs some adjustment, that students need to be called to attention, that additional clarification is required. To ignore or be unaware of student feedback is to take the risk of wasting time, energy, and opportunity for learning.

As you observe secondary school classrooms, or on-campus ones, note the behaviors of students that suggest that they are attending to the teacher's comments or to the questions and comments which other students raise. What are the clues to attending that you are able to identify. Discuss with your classmates what you observe.

SUMMARY

The communication skills of teachers determine, to a considerable degree, their success or failure. An understanding of the communication process can help in facilitating the sending and receiving of messages. In addition to perfecting skills in reading, writing, speaking, and listening, it is important to be alert to the ways in which nonverbal communication underscores or contradicts our intentions.

SELECTED READINGS

Brunner, Joseph F., and John J. Campbell, *Participating in Secondary Reading: A Practical Approach.* Englewood Cliffs, N.J.: Prentice-Hall, 1977. A how-to volume that concentrates on basic reading and study skills students need regardless of subject matter.

Daniels, Steven, *How 2 Gerbils, 20 Goldfish, 200 Games, 2,000 Books and I Taught Them How To Read.* Philadelphia: The Westminster Press, 1971. A creative teacher's account of working in an urban school. Illustrated with anecdotes and presenting a variety of practical suggestions for teaching.

Exploring Nonverbal Communication. Columbus, Ohio: Center for Advanced Study of Human Communication, 1977. Two filmstrips concerned with proxemics (the use of space) and kinesics (body language). Well-illustrated information important to teachers.

Fast, Julius, *Body Language.* New York: M. Evans and Company (distributed in association with J. B. Lippincott Company), 1970. Easy-to-read, practical primer in kinesics. Eleven chapters deal with space, masks, touch, body positions, eyes.

Ginott, Haim G., *Between Parent and Teenager.* New York: Avon, 1969. While obviously directed at the communication process, teachers as well as parents can profit from this practical example-filled guide for improving communication between adolescents and adults.

Hall, Edward T., *The Silent Language.* Greenwich, Conn.: Fawcett, 1961. A leading anthropologist reveals how people communicate without words and how behavior reflects a nation's influence on world affairs.

Hennings, Dorothy Grant, *Mastering Classroom Communication: What Interaction Analysis Tells the Teacher.* Pacific Palisades, Calif.: Goodyear Publishing Company, 1975. Three areas of focus (The Communication Process, The Teacher as Receiver/Decoder, and The Teacher as Source Encoder) provide close examinations of the interactive processes involved in teaching.

Improving English Skills of Culturally Different Youth. Washington, D.C.: U.S. Department of Health, Education, and Welfare, 1964. Includes many practical suggestions as well as a summary of research.

Lorayne, Harry, and Jerry Lucas, *The Memory Book.* New York: Stein and Day, 1974. Techniques for developing the memory.

Nilsen, Alleen Pace, et al., *Sexism and Language.* Urbana, Ill.: National Council of Teachers of English, 1977. Eight essays exploring long-standing sexist attitudes in language and literature. Also includes "NCTE Guidelines for Non-sexist Use of Language."

Piercey, Dorothy, *Reading Activities in Content Areas.* Boston: Allyn and Bacon, 1976. A thorough "ideabook" for middle and secondary school teachers in all subject areas. Practical activities clearly presented.

Postman, Neil, *Crazy Talk, Stupid Talk.* New York: Delta (Dell Publishing Company), 1976. "How we defeat ourselves by the way we talk—and what to do about it." An excellent aid for all who want to perfect their communication skills.

The Reading Teacher. Journal of the International Reading Association, 800 Barksdale Road, Newark, Del. 19711.

Report of the National Council of Teachers of English Task Force on Teaching English to the Disadvantaged, *Language Programs for the Disadvantaged.* Champaign, Ill.: NCTE, 1965. Excellent summary of what is known to date about promising programs and practices, with recommendations and selected annotated bibliography.

Robinson, H. Alan, *Teaching Reading and Study Strategies: The Content Areas.* Boston: Allyn and Bacon, 1975. A detailed and helpful guide for teaching reading and study skills in science, social studies, mathematics, English, and, more briefly, other subjects.

Seymour, Dorothy Z., "Black Children, Black Speech," *Commonweal*, 95: (November 1971), pp. 175–178. Helpful explanation that shows clearly that ghetto speech is a dialect with a form and structure of its own.

Walter, Tim, and Al Siebert, *Student Success: How To Be a Better Student and Still Have Time for Your Friends.* New York: Holt, Rinehart and Winston, 1976. Just what the title says.

part III

LOGISTICS: management, planning and resources

LOGISTICS require careful thought, thorough organization, and a knowledge of materials. Managing the typical secondary school classroom calls for concern with order, detail, and timing. Unit and lesson planning that facilitates the act of learning requires teachers to demonstrate a thorough knowledge of both content and methodology, along with a keen understanding of young people. Resources for teaching and learning are increasing in their variety; effective teachers know and use those which do the job well.

Chapter 6 "Minding the Store": Management of the Classroom
Chapter 7 "Here's My Plan . . .": Organizing and Planning for Teaching
Chapter 8 Getting It All Together: Teaching and Learning Resources

121

FOCUS ON CHAPTER 6

Teaching is like juggling: One has to keep all the balls up in the air at the same time, smiling while doing so. Or so it seems. The routines of the classroom are sometimes overwhelming and annoying, but because they determine how well time, space, and resources are used, they are important to master. Classroom housekeeping, careful record management, and getting, using, and returning such things as audiovisual equipment require careful planning and good timing.

Significant ideas presented in this chapter include:
- Classroom management is closely related to discipline and to the establishment and maintenance of a democratic atmosphere.
- Administrators place a high premium on careful, on-time recordkeeping.
- The physical appearance of the classroom—in all aspects— either facilitates or hinders learning.
- Knowing "the rules" of the school is important with regard to the way in which a teacher functions both with students and administrators.
- There are numerous ways in which students can be seated in a room other than in rows. For true interaction, people must be able to see—and read one another's faces and being seated in rows works against that end.

chapter 6

"Minding the Store":
management of
the classroom

Nobody told me. I had no idea how important
housekeeping details are in a classroom. I also had
no idea of where to begin.

Organization, whether readily apparent or not, is one
of the keys to day-to-day survival in the secondary
school classroom. Beginning teachers, like the one quoted above, are
typically astonished, overwhelmed, frustrated, and even angered by the
amount and kind of organizational tasks demanded in so complex an institution as the contemporary secondary school. By mastering organization and
management the teacher is placed in the happy position of being able to
concentrate on the act of teaching itself; by allowing management details
to become master, one's potential for teaching is thwarted.

Classroom management is closely related to success in discipline and to
democratic atmosphere. The condition of the classroom and how things are
organized determines much of how students will perform there. (You may
wish to read this chapter in relation to Chapters 4, 15, and 16.)

FACING REALITY

Teaching may be compared to juggling: The trick is to keep all the
balls up in the air while looking graceful and offering a big smile. The new
teacher (juggler) is frequently concerned with getting just one ball (activity)
into the air. Unfortunately, one activity automatically casts other activities
(balls) into the air at the same time. Consider the organizational management implications of the following:

- "Pass up your papers."
- "Will each of you get a book from the side shelf?"
- "Break into groups of four for the next fifteen minutes . . ."
- "Answer 'here' when I call your name."
- "Will somebody take this to the office?"
- "I know the print is small, but I hope everyone in the back can see . . ."
- "No, don't turn the lights on, I think I can fix the projector without them."
- "I know the bell has rung for the end of class, but I have just one more thing . . ."

Have your considerations included confusion, wiseacre remarks, blank stares, scuffling, gossiping, flirting, catcalls, variations of "whaddyouwant-ustdo?", and an assortment of noises and chaos? All are possible reactions to the previous instructions and comments. To prevent the array of disheartening reactions possible, a teacher must know ahead of time the best possible strategies for achieving desired results.

Probably the best way to learn organization for management is to start vicariously, to observe (in the practice of others and through reading and discussion) the things that do work and those that do not. An immediate application of this premise is to return to the eight teacher statements above and seriously to consider with fellow students specific instances in which those statements caused good and poor results. Offer alternative management ideas for each. If you have not already begun to student teach give particular attention to classroom organization and management with which you cope as a student and which you can observe in a secondary school setting. Careful attention to those procedures will be instructive even if the procedures are disastrous. We can learn from vicarious as well as real experiences; sometimes what we learn is what *not* to do.

After considering with classmates the reactions to the eight statements above, it will be helpful to consider the ideas which appear in this chapter. Finally, of course, you must have organizational and management experiences of your own which will tell you quickly whether you are causing any of the variety of reactions suggested earlier in your classroom.

As you begin to juggle the activities of the classroom, there is this reassurance: One need not take on all management burdens at once. Before beginning teachers try classroom methods that involve extensive management problems, they must develop a feeling of some mastery of the ordinary routines. Mastery can be attained by moving gradually from simpler toward more complex ways of working.

If teachers can manage to get the roll taken efficiently and effectively at the beginning of the hour, if they can return test papers with little confusion, if they can distribute and collect equipment and supplies in a speedy and orderly way, if they can stop whatever they are doing for an interruption from the principal's office and not have the class dissolve into complete chaos, then they are ready to employ greater variety in class routine. At this stage they may introduce a motion picture, have a resource visitor, plan a short-run group experience, send part of the class to the library, plan a field trip, and even discuss problems of discipline and control with the class.

It is important to underline this thesis: Ability to manage grows gradually. Beginning teachers may be somewhat skeptical. If it is so easy to move from traditional to modern methods, they may ask, "Why don't we see more modern methods used in the classrooms we visit?" There are many answers to this question. Some teachers adhere to the more conventional methods because they have not achieved a basic sense of security in classroom management; they are still afraid that there will be complete loss of control if they once shift the focus from the teacher to the learning problem. Some teachers remain unconvinced that the newer methods achieve true learning goals; some are familiar only with older methods of instruction. Often school administrators discourage departures from familiar patterns, and sometimes teachers are intimidated by custodians who complain when desks are rearranged. Some teachers have had unfortunate experiences with innovative practices and have shied away from new attempts to use them. And, unfortunately, some teachers are unimaginative, tired, or lazy.

SETTING THE STAGE

For the most part, students respond to teachers, to one another, and to their studies according to how comfortable they feel in their surroundings. The classroom that says "Welcome" throughout the school year is the classroom to which students come with high expectations and in which they perform at their highest level.

As young people enter a classroom, they sense almost immediately the kind of spirit that prevails. The following student comment is typical of how youth react to the classroom environment a teacher sets up:

I like to go to Miss Lynch's class. Partly because she's a good teacher, but also because her classroom is a nice place to be. In fact, it's the best classroom I've ever been in. The bulletin boards are terrific. They're really interesting and they look good too. Miss Lynch always has magazines and newspapers in the back of the room and she has some plants along the side of the room. She always puts out projects and other assignments where we can see what others have done. There are so many interesting books and other stuff that she's always bringing to school that you'll always find kids poking around in her room before and after school. Maybe the best thing, though, is that the desks and chairs aren't like they are in all my other classes—you know, all in rows, facing the teacher's desk in front. Miss

Lynch's desk is in the back corner and our desks are arranged in groups, or sometimes in a horseshoe or a circle. It's really a funny thing, but I'm positive everybody feels more comfortable.

It is a great help, of course, if the teacher is assigned to the same room for all classes. In schools which are crowded, however, it is not always possible for each teacher to have a specific room. Sometimes a teacher may have a few classes in one room, then "float" for several periods.

This certainly narrows interest in and opportunity for room arrangement. Students may also feel displaced, which only intensifies the problem. In addition, interpersonal problems among faculty members may be aggravated because of having to share rooms: One teacher is compulsive about neatness and order, whereas another has a mighty disregard of such "mundane matters." A compromise must be reached, and it should be one that puts the welfare of the students first. An understanding about procedures for making the room attractive, storage and display facilities for each class, and shelf space for reference material should be sought among teachers who share rooms.

Whether it is the individual's fault or not, a disorderly environment breeds disorderly conduct. Even if it means doing more than one's share, the concerned teacher will help deter antisocial and destructive behavior by personal example that encourages order and respect in others.

A consultant to a junior high school was walking down the hall with one of the central office staff. Suddenly the visitor stooped and pushed back a piece of metal that protruded below a locker. As they went down the stairs he poked with his shoe at a big hole in the lineoleum. A broken window with tape ineffectually keeping the sagging ends together next caught his eye. The door to the classrooms swung on broken hinges.

After a pregnant silence he finally voiced his feelings: "I seem to remember that Redl,[1] in his research with delinquent youngsters, made a point about disturbance contagion. He said that not only did the excitement generated by a child serve as a point of infection for other susceptible children, but chaotic environments were also sources of infection and produced chaotic behavior in youngsters. How can we expect young adolescents to be disciplined and self-respecting when we put them in environments which are disturbing and dislocating?"

An administrator of long experience has observed:

Across the years, I have been interested to observe that the classrooms in this building that are least damaged by student abuse—desk carvings, graffiti, damaged equipment, mutilated text and reference books—are those belonging to teachers who see to it that their rooms are friendly and interesting places to work. When students are interested in where they are and

[1] Fritz Redl, *Children Who Hate* (New York: Free Press, 1951).

in what they're doing, they don't have time to build up frustrations that release themselves in destruction. ·

It is dangerous to be complacent about "mere classrooms"; they are an integral part of the total learning environment.

ORDER IN THE CLASSROOM

It may seem obvious to say that the prime rule guiding the teacher in the organization of a classroom is "a place for everything and everything in its place." It is disastrous when the chemistry teacher plans a certain experiment but cannot find the necessary chemicals, or when the distributive education teacher plans a lesson around an advertising mock-up, which is nowhere to be seen. These frustrations are the result of poor management and poor housekeeping, and can add up to poor teaching.

However, there are many classrooms in which the needed items are simply not available. Are they lost, strayed, or stolen? No one knows. It is a useful habit to make a daily check before school opens to be sure that the room and its materials are neat and orderly, ready for another day's work.

There are several places in the classroom that seem to attract clutter, such as the teacher's desk, the top of a file cabinet, or the book case. Particular care should be taken to keep the teacher's desk neat—not a model of rigid order, but a place where one can quickly find the class roll-book, the text or model needed in a lesson, an extra sharpened pencil, a piece of scrap paper. A teacher's desk is a reflection of the person who uses it; disorder among the tools of one's profession usually indicates disorder within the organization and management of the professional. Students frequently become uneasy when they encounter a desk that is always piled high with carelessly strewn papers. It is easy to think, "Why hand in careful work here? It is not going to be treated with care."

INSTRUCTIONAL ROUTINES:
SEATING, ATTENDANCE, RECORDS

Even for experienced teachers, the first days with a new class can be hectic. Students and teachers both have a host of adjustments to make. In a sense, a new social organization is being born, and it is inevitably attended by some pain. For these days, well-planned routine is imperative, since impressions are being formed and exchanged by students which may help or hinder the teaching process indefinitely. It helps to be at or near the door of the classroom when students enter and to make a deliberate effort to speak to them by name. This recognition of individuality helps establish a rapport that has many subtle effects on teacher–student relationships.

Discovering activities in which students are engaged may suggest impromptu remarks to be made to them. Of course, these casual conversations need not be limited to the classrooms; in any setting, the teacher should always recognize students and say something to assure them that the teacher knows each one personally.

In almost every secondary school classroom in the country, there is one prime order of business at the opening of each hour—taking roll. But how can one plan to organize students for efficient management?

There are several possibilities, and each has its consequences:

Seating Plan	Consequences
Seat all students alphabetically.	This plan helps in learning students' names. It is fair, and likely to separate cliques and best friends. Of course, students whose names are at the end of the alphabet always sit in the rear (or front). (This plan might be utilized only long enough for the teacher to recognize students.)
Let students sit where they wish.	With this procedure one can quickly see the social organization of the classroom. Cliques and groups emerge; isolates can be spotted. Friends like to be close together. Most students will not sit in front seats. Troublemakers often sit near each other and in the rear. In addition, students do not extend their friendship range.
Seat students according to size or special problem, such as vision or hearing defects.	Smaller students sit in front so that they can see, as do students with glasses or a hearing deficiency. Seating all the big boys in the rear may spell trouble.

Unless there is good reason to the contrary a teacher might begin with the free-choice system. True, one should take into account the particular physical needs of youngsters as soon as they become apparent. But for the first few days, it may be advantageous to allow students to sit where they please. What about the noisy cliques? The teacher should know about them as soon as possible. Once they are identified, the teacher will have learned something valuable about the social structure of the class. The teacher is apprised at once of the hazards of developing self-discipline within the group.

The other great advantage of the free-choice system is, of course, that students, like other human beings, prefer to be next to people they know and like. Even if students do not talk to their neighbors, it is simply easier to get work done if they feel comfortable with the people around them. For this very human, very understandable reason, then, adolescents may react more positively to free choice than to an imposed seating arrangement.

During the first days of the school year the teacher's major task is learning students' names. If students are allowed to sit where they please, then the teacher should request that these seats be retained during the early weeks of the class. A seating chart is a must at this time, which can be obtained quickly by making a plan of the room showing the desks, and having students write their names in the appropriate squares.

The importance of knowing and pronouncing correctly students' names cannot be overstated. Human beings make such identification with their names that in a sense the names are the persons. In certain nonliterate cultures, "real" names are so important that they are often kept secret lest evil spirits cast a spell upon the person. In some societies an individual does not get a "real" name until puberty, when he or she is recognized as a "real" person. While Americans do not apply this same kind of mysticism to their names, they do regard the sight and sound of them as unique. Many teachers find it hard to learn the names of 165 students in one day, or even one week or one month. But this is one task to which they should immediately devote their full energy. The sooner they know all the names of all their students, the sooner routines and teaching tasks will become a matter of working with individuals rather than with bodies. The effect on student morale is positive; the feeling of belonging to a group can now occur.

Activities such as taking the roll and seating students, then, have ramifications beyond mere management. After a seating chart is made it should be used! Students do not mind if teachers refer to the seating chart when calling upon them. Whether to call students "Miss Jones" or "Mr. Smith," or use their first names is largely determined by local custom and school level. Sometimes the practice differs from class to class; whatever the practice, teachers should avoid calling students by last names only. Many adolescents find it either clinical or rude. If you have freedom to do as you wish, be careful about first names. Do not use them until you find the form preferred. Horace may prefer Butch, and Antionette may wish to be called "Tony."

RECORDKEEPING SKILLS

Armed with the knowledge of the power of names, who is to keep track of the names listed on the roll, and how? During the first days of school, teachers will want to take the roll themselves. This is an invaluable aid in learning the names of students quickly. The importance of taking roll is clearly appreciated by all experienced teachers; beginning teachers, however, may not know how crucial this procedures can be. In most states, the daily attendance roster is used as the basis on which funds are allocated to school districts. It is vital to know who is in school, and for how long. Unless a careful and complete roll is taken, school authorities cannot know who is truant or put the proper machinery in motion to find out why the student is not in school. There are few things more disturbing to an administrator than a teacher who does not complete attendance accurately and promptly.

What kind of attendance procedures work best? The seating chart, as indicated, is a great help during the early days of the semester. An empty seat indicates an absent member. The question arises, however, "How long do students have to stay in seats originally assigned or selected?"

As soon as the teacher learns to manage any degree of flexibility in class arrangements, students may be permitted, even encouraged, to shift seats. This renders the initial seating chart obsolete, of course. Reading a roll aloud is time consuming, and unless each voice that says "Present" is checked, some wise adolescent may answer for his or her friend. It has been suggested that students sign a roster. The same problem exists, however: Someone may sign for someone else. Thus these methods may not work very well.

The use of student assistants is an effective way of taking roll. To assure accuracy, two students may be assigned this task. By rotating the job arbitrarily through the class, the issue of favoritism is eliminated. Students may also enter into the teacher's rollbook a check to indicate who is absent on a given day.

In many schools the teacher is issued an "official" rollbook, where one enters the names of all students, usually alphabetically, with a page for each class. If student assistants take the roll and enter attendance reports, the teacher will want to have two rollbooks—one for attendance and one for grades and other data. It is not wise to give students ready access to personal material about other students.

The rollbook in which students' grades are recorded is an important document, for it provides a record of returned assignments, test grades, final examination grades, many of the items on which a final grade is to be based. A neat rollbook not only is a great help to a teacher, but has other functions as well. A parent may come to school to protest an assigned grade, and the rollbook may have to be produced as evidence for what was used to determine the grade. A messy, smudged rollbook, with hit-or-miss entries, will not help a teacher defend the validity of the grade assigned. This record has some attributes of a public record. The grade given cannot —and will not—be changed by anyone unless it can be proved that evidence was deliberately distorted. Part of a teacher's management routine, then, is learning to keep a rollbook and entering in it the data needed to make an evaluation of students. It is wise to keep old rollbooks for several years if the administration does not automatically file them at the end of the school year. Requests for recommendations are sometimes more quickly and efficiently handled by referring to them.

It is always possible that some curious adolescent will find a grade book when the teacher is not present. If standardized test scores are entered, they should be placed in the record in code. Devise a letter code, for example, whereby high scores are designated by an X and low scores by an M.

One great need in secondary education is to know more about the numerous students encountered daily. Some personal data can be gathered about each student through a questionnaire (see Chapter 17). In addition, cumulative records in the main office or the counselor's office, report the results of standardized tests taken by students. These provide information that may be helpful. Learning their value is the problem. It is suggested that after the students in a class have become individuals in their own right in the view of their "new" teacher, the teacher can obtain their test scores and transfer them to the rollbook. Obtaining such scores too early may cause prejudging, and as the chapter on grading points out (Chapter 14), such records are full of human error and bias. So give each of your classes a "blank slate." It is often surprising that an innocent teacher, who is unaware of Bill's reputation for stupidity, and treats him as though he were intelligent, actually produces a metamorphosis of "stupid Bill" into "smart Bill." The "self-fulfilling prophecy" or Pygmalion effect must never be underrated.[2] Not everyone agrees with this point of view; some practitioners believe it is important to use student records, as well as other information about students, as soon as possible. Regardless of philosophical viewpoint, it is unanimously agreed that there must be strong effort to avoid prejudging and that those who employ records from the beginning must strive to maintain an ethical use of the records as well as an ethical silence about information which those records may contain.

The class is seated, the teacher knows the students' names and has taken the roll. What other management problems will occur?

CLASSROOM LOGISTICS

Having the right supplies at the right time and in the right place requires that teachers—in addition to other things—must be logistics experts.

Each subject area has its own supply problems, and each school has established procedures by which supplies are obtained. In some schools there may be a supply clerk who issues material when requisitioned. Sometimes the amount of a given item is limited by a departmental budget,

[2] Robert Rosenthal and Lenore Jacobson, *Pygmalion in the Classroom* (New York: Holt, Rinehart and Winston, 1968).

with requisitions approved by the department head, area supervisor, or building principal. In smaller schools, the supplies may be open to any teacher. Certain supplies—for subjects such as science, art, home economics, and industrial arts—may be expensive and take a long time to replenish once they are depleted.

At the opening of the school year the teacher will want to check on the supplies available. An inventory may or may not be on hand. A personal check is essential. Are the materials in the chemistry supply room adequate for the experiments anticipated? What about the typewriters, the sewing machines, the welding equipment? Not only will teachers want to check supplies on hand and the source and possibilities for new ones, but they also will want to investigate all items which require maintenance, repair, or replacement. Who repairs a broken sewing machine? What procedure is followed to obtain the repair in the shortest amount of time? Who makes the decision to replace it with a new one? Enumerate some of the supplies which are required for a week's activities in your subject area. In your student teaching assignment, as well as in your first permanent assignment as a teacher, identify school procedures for ordering supplies.

Among audiovisual materials, motion pictures most often present requisition problems. Usually the films must be ordered long in advance of the date on which they will be used. Teachers who plan instruction with their students will have difficulty predicting just when a motion picture may be needed, and compromises will be inevitable. But better compromises can be effected if it is known at the beginning of the school year just how, and when, films may be requested. Larger secondary schools may have an audiovisual coordinator to assist with the scheduling. Even if they do, however, the coordinator will appreciate the teacher's familiarity with the catalog of the principal supply sources for the school, the necessary requisition forms, and the other required administrative procedures.

Many audiovisual materials require equipment: projectors, recorders, screens. Most, if not all, equipment will also require advance scheduling. A quick way for new teachers to become unpopular is to remember just before class time that they must have a piece of equipment. Although many schools have student service clubs that distribute and operate the equipment, it is advantageous for teachers to know how to operate equipment.

THE CLASSROOM IN ACTION

Let us assume that it is 8:15 on a Monday morning. Mrs. Collier has planned to give a test during second period, to review the text material during the third period, and to work on group projects during the fourth period. Mrs. Collier considers the supplies that will be needed for those three classes. Looking at her lesson plans she is able to identify quickly the need for an extra supply of notepaper for the test, pencils and pens for the inevitable few who forget to bring their own; for the review a few extra textbooks may be needed, again for those who "forgot"; construction paper, crayons, tracing paper, rulers, magazines, and glue will be required for the group projects. She also decides that it is not a bad idea to empty the shavings from the pencil sharpener and to open a new box of Kleenex since a rash of colds has been making its way through the building.

As the morning passes and students arrive for each of the classes it becomes obvious that student assistance can facilitate the logistics required.

With a modicum of direction, a few students can pass out the paper, pencils, books, and other supplies while the teacher discusses the lesson that is to come. Too often a good half of the time of such laboratory classes as chemistry, biology, physics, art, and mechanical drawing is consumed in simply getting the material to the students at the beginning of the period and collecting it again at the end. Such a waste of time is difficult to defend: It cheats the students of vital instruction and it is an indication of poor management.

Teachers can help themselves in these matters. A storage cabinet, properly used, is a great aid. Here papers of various kinds can be kept, along with related materials. Students, assisted by labels on shelves and drawers, can keep the supplies in order. The bookcase should shelve currently used references. A simple check-out system can be organized so that books are circulated as needed. No file cabinets? No bookcases? Bricks and boards can serve as a temporary bookcase. A sturdy wooden box may be found that is the right size for storage. Crude as these materials may be, they will hold supplies and are better than either a disorganized mess stacked in a corner or no supplies at all.

A useful activity for one of the first days of class is to distribute duplicated statements describing basic routines of the class (distributing and collecting materials, forms for reports, checking out reference books, and so on). The statements should be regarded as a basis for discussion. It should be understood that the routines may be modified as the class devises more efficient procedures. Sometimes a group can be immediately appointed to codify management patterns to be presented later to the class. When students devise routines for the class, their peers are more likely to observe those routines.

Wisely used, student assistants can relieve teachers of the supervision of much necessary routine. This use of students need not be exploitative. Many will gain status and develop maturity from the experience. Because it is a learning experience, student assistants should be rotated. It should not be the exclusive property of the academically gifted, nor used as a way of "keeping busy" those students who "can't do anything else." Students themselves should have a voice in who does the jobs, what the responsibilities are, and how long they should be enjoyed.

Before the class hour ends, a few minutes spent in general housekeeping are well justified. The next class should come into a neat and orderly room. This is especially important when the room is shared by several teachers. The incoming teacher's morale will be helped by clean chalkboards, bookshelves in good order, chairs or desks in place, and a floor clear of papers. At the end of the day, the custodian will be appreciative. Furthermore, the beginning teacher will earn a reputation for being a good manager.

ARRANGING THE CLASSROOM ENVIRONMENT

For different activities during the class hour, some changes in seating arrangements will be necessary. Even if the seats cannot be moved (and it may come as a surprise to some that there are still schools—many in the "inner city"—where desks are nailed to the floor), the students need not be immovable for the hour. They can and should move, to facilitate discussion, group work, project and study activities. Of course, it is even more important that the teacher not be fastened to the front of the room, for this encourages the old recite-for-the-teacher pattern. If there is space, the teacher's desk, should be moved to the rear of the room: Supervision is more efficient from this vantage point, private conversations with students are facilitated, and teacher domination of the classroom is less likely. If the furniture is movable and the class is working as one group, seats may be arranged in quarter or half circles facing away from the windows from front to rear, so that no one has a direct light glare. In small-group activity, work around tables or at desks arranged in squares or circles is, of course, most efficient, because face-to-face working fosters group unity. Students arranged in small groups enable a class to improve overall academic performance and assist teachers "to stay on top of disruptions."[3] The diagrams on page 135 illustrate some possible room arrangements for whole class and group work.

MANAGING TIME

The management of classroom routines is a task best learned early and mastered early. At the same time, teachers must carefully consider use of time. Regardless of good qualities, teachers can be successful only when they are reasonably fresh in mind and body. The teaching day rarely ends with the bell signaling the end of the last period. Students come for extra help, for advice, for disciplinary adjudication, or just for chit-chat. Similarly, colleagues may come by to confer, gossip, or mutually commiserate. There are books to be replaced, supplies to be checked, and the

[3] Terry Kirkpatrick, "Watch It Kids! This Teacher's Got Your Number," *The Washington Post* (January 1978).

SUGGESTED ROOM ARRANGEMENTS

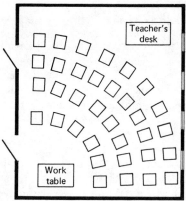

Front of Room

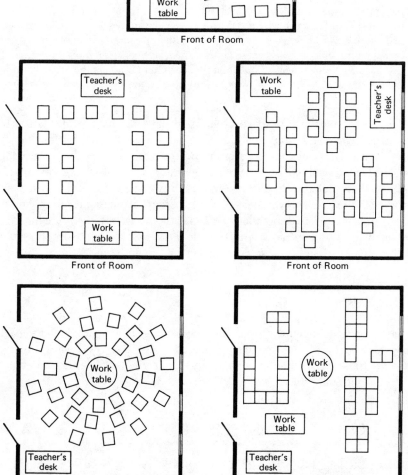

Front of Room

Front of Room

Front of Room

Front of Room

next day's plans to be reviewed for last minute changes. Finally, the teacher packs for home.

One student teacher learned about time-management the hard way:

> I had worked arduously over the unit test. I had prepared two multiple-choice items, 10 matching, and 3 essay questions. My supervisor felt it was a good first try. I was elated! Fortunately I bribed a girl friend into typing the test on ditto masters and I ran them off and stapled them so that they could be administered on Tuesday, the day announced, to four classes. Well, it worked; in fact, it worked so well, that I worked until 2 AM three nights in a row correcting the tests.
>
> I had promised the test back on Friday. I had forgotten—and no one had warned me—that four times 35 is 140, which meant I had 140 test papers to grade and 140 grades to record. I also found, to my horror, that the seventh-period class, which I had never considered a very alert group, had done remarkably well even on the essay questions. It dawned on my feeble mind that maybe the seventh-period students were brighter than I thought: They had checked out the test questions with pals in earlier periods during the day. So now I'm wondering, how much of that correcting time did I waste?

The above anecdote has two obvious morals: (1) having all classes take a test on the same day has consequences for the teacher's time and energy and (2) students do communicate with each other. The latter problem can be solved by varying the timing, as well as the coverage, of the test. The first problem, that of too many papers to grade at one time, involves the teacher's awareness of the problems of managing time. Looking ahead, one is able to schedule major class experiences, tests included. As you identify holidays and special school events, do not forget personal involvements as well. It's no fun correcting papers on your birthday.

SUMMARY

Management—in and out of the classroom—is a major key to teacher survival. Creating order, mastering classroom logistics, and using time well are essentials for those who wish to give their greatest talents and energies to the teaching act itself.

SELECTED READINGS

Callahan, Sterling, G., *Successful Teaching in Secondary Schools*. Glenview, Ill.: Scott, Foresman, 1966. See Chapter 17, "Directing Cocurricular Activities."

Davis, Janet, "Teachers, Kids and Conflict: Ethnography of a Junior High School," in James P. Spradley and David W. McCurdy (Eds.), *The Cultural Experience:*

Ethnography in Complex Society. Chicago: Science Research, 1972, pp. 103–120. This ethnographic vignette shows the ways in which the structure of the school introduces elements which create potential conflict.

Dawson, Helaine S., *On the Outskirts of Hope.* New York: McGraw-Hill, 1968. See especially pages 18–26 for a description of a sensitive teacher's awareness of the impact on disadvantaged older adolescents of seating arrangement and classroom atmosphere.

Gores, Harold B., "The Habitats of Education," *American Education*, 10 (October 1974), pp. 16–23, 26. The old, fortress-like building has given way to the factory-style building; what are the consequences for student and community perception of school purposes?

Green, Alan C., "The Schoolhouse Revisited: Problems and Opportunities Missed," *Phi Delta Kappan*, 56 (January 1975), pp. 36–62. Points out some of the missed problems of the new school design which does not always reflect the realities of teaching approaches.

Ohles, John F., *Introduction to Teaching.* New York: Random House, 1970. See "The School Society," pp. 97–120. This selection describes the intricate network of social relationships institutionalized by the school.

Smith, Louis M., and William Geoffrey, *The Complexities of an Urban Classroom: An Analysis toward a General Theory of Teaching.* New York: Holt, Rinehart and Winston, 1968. An educational anthropologist looks at a junior high classroom, dissecting the interactions in an unusually stimulating and enlightening manner.

Sommer, Robert, "Classroom Ecology," *Journal of Applied Behavioral Science*, 3 (October–November–December 1967), pp. 489–503. A research study showing that classroom arrangements play a key role in how students interact and also on the amount of participation evoked.

FOCUS ON CHAPTER 7

The responsibility and complexity of teaching is so great that successful teaching cannot occur without organization and planning that allows teachers and students to know clearly what they are doing and why. The more clearly students understand what is expected of them the more likely they are to produce results that are appropriate and satisfying. Many factors contribute to the kind of organization and planning which allow teaching and learning to have genuine meaning.

Significant ideas presented in this chapter include:
- While it is not always possible, or desirable, to do so, it is important to involve students in planning the work of the classroom.
- Objectives for teaching may be classified as hunting (behavioral) objectives or fishing (affective) objectives. Knowing the difference between them is significant for the kinds of activities selected for the classroom.
- In most schools, the year's study is broken into units; units are composed of daily lessons. Knowing how to organize and plan both is fundamental to the smooth operation of the classroom.
- Variety in activities and materials is important in establishing and maintaining student interest.

chapter 7

"Here's My Plan...": organizing and planning for teaching

It wasn't until the end of the second week of student teaching that I began to see the real value of planning. A kid asked me how what we were doing had to do with the objectives I had handed out previously (and which I had taken unquestioningly from my cooperating teacher). I didn't know. It suddenly dawned on me that I had only a vague notion of what we were doing and why.

Another way to conclude the anecdote above is: If you do not know where you are going, you may not get there. Similarly, while you may know where you are going, it is prudent to have a map.

It is hard to believe that Mrs. Bradford's kind of teaching can go on in the second half of the twentieth century, but this is exactly the situation in which I spent some miserable hours. Mrs. Bradford was compulsive. The seats in her room were all placed in perfect rows, with the places for each desk and chair marked on the floor. On her desk was a green blotter, a small flag, and her record book. On the window sills were neat, exactly spaced flower pots of artificial geraniums. Her rigidity extended to her "planning." She had figured out the days of the school year, the pages of text material in the assigned book, and divided one by the other. And we read that much— no more and no less—every day of the year. Presidents could come and go (in fact one was killed during my unpleasant stay in her classroom), and we did not deviate from the assignment. She also had decided that our spelling was inadequate, so, although this was not the subject she was supposed to teach us, she systematically gave us two words a day sampled from the dictionary, starting with the letter "A." We got to "Z" the day before school ended.

One of the teachers we all hated was Mr. Hughes. It was a small high school, and in order to get to college we had to take our required science from him. The problem was that he never taught us the subject. He scoffed at the text, regaled us with tales of his years in the service, and sometimes startled us by announcing an exam on five chapters we had never discussed in class. Plan? He probably couldn't even spell the word. We felt cheated and angry because we knew our lack of science instruction would show up when we took the college entrance exams. I found out by accident that he actually had a very good background in science, but just never got around to organizing his material, and to this day I do not understand why.

Our favorite teacher in tenth grade was Mr. Griggs, who not only cared about us as people, but who let us know exactly where we were going and who gave us the directions for getting there. He patiently explained objectives to us in all the work we did; he was well organized, and he respected our abilities—whatever they were. A thing he did I'll always remember and be thankful for: He posted one or two objectives on the chalkboard for each class. We felt secure in what was expected and at the end of each class we had a sense of accomplishment.

After completing a college methods course in which planning is stressed, student teachers observing their resident teachers at work may conclude that little planning occurs. This is an unfortunate conclusion because good teaching cannot occur without careful planning.

PLANNING IS ESSENTIAL

While there is great variation in the amount and kind of planning by experienced teachers, good teachers invariably are those who have carefully planned their work. It is true that the plans of experienced teachers are not always as detailed as those required of student teachers. What the observer needs to bear in mind is that what may appear to be a skimpy list of reminders is actually a condensation of many years of teaching. The "skimpy list" may be, in fact, a shorthand compilation of materials and notes, mental as well as written, a refinement of an individual personality and style, and a list only because the resident teacher has years of experience with a particular subject, probably at a particular grade level. Until beginning teachers have reached a comparable level of knowledge and skill, they will be wise to plan carefully for every minute. Teachers must remember that during any given class period they are responsible for the meaningful use of approximately thirty hours of human time.

A recurring criticism of student teachers by public school personnel is that they do not know how to organize and plan effectively. Careful organization of classroom activity based on clearly stated objectives is essential if learning is to occur. Only through thoughtful planning can students and teachers work together toward clearly understood purposes. As one begins to teach, it becomes obvious how well-planned lessons provide the teacher and students with confidence and assurance. As teaching expertise develops, one finds that detailed written plans, as such, are not as important as the thought and preparation which they represent.

PLANNING WITHIN A FRAMEWORK

Of course, the plans which teachers make are not created without a context. Indeed, the plans are needed partly because they deal with components of a larger nature, and also because they follow up on as well as precede other learnings.

Almost all school systems have designed a total curriculum spanning beginning grades through high school. That total curriculum contains educational aims (also called rationale or goals) which the school system strives to achieve with all its students. The educational aims of one school system include the following:[1]

> In order to aid in inducting youth into responsible and effective citizenship in this dynamic society, nine major functions of living have been identified as goals of the Chicago public schools. These are:
>
>> practicing American citizenship
>> using the tools of communication effectively
>> developing economic competence
>> improving family living
>> protecting life and health
>> building human relationships
>> enjoying wholesome leisure
>> satisfying spiritual and esthetic needs
>> meeting vocational responsibilities.

These aims are achieved by students moving systematically from one grade to the next engaging in experiences which carefully break down the many components of a particular aim. To achieve many aims it is necessary for students to be enrolled, at secondary level, in numerous courses which deal specifically with one aspect of a component, such as social studies. Some aims are achieved by students being enrolled in courses that range over several subject areas.

In the case of subject areas, work is divided by grade level, and, in some instances, even into semester courses. In the subject area for a grade level, specific year or semester-wide learning objectives are determined. Content for the year is scrutinized and objectives are achieved by breaking the overall content into pieces called units.

[1] Board of Education of the City of Chicago, Illinois, 1964.

THE UNIT

A unit is a series of related learning experiences built around one central topic or problem area (e.g., the Expansionist Movement, Family Interpersonal Communication, Oral Interpretation, Mathematical Sets, Harlem Renaissance Painting, Writing Effective Business Letters, Techniques of Badminton). Whatever it is concerned with and however it is explored, the unit is a pattern of organization that allows teachers and students to examine closely some aspect of a larger subject.

All units should include consideration of six major components:

1. Scope—how much content is to be covered? (and consequently, how much time is required?).
2. Sequence—in what order are the elements of the content to be studied?
3. Objectives—what learnings are to be achieved?
4. Learning activities—in what day-to-day experiences will students engage that will allow them to achieve the objectives?
5. Materials—what things will teachers and students need to examine to complete the learning activities?
6. Evaluation—(a) how successfully did the teacher perform? and (b) how successfully did the students perform?

Some teachers prefer to think of the unit process itself as having three major parts: objectives, developmental activities, and culminating activities.

In order to accomplish the work of the unit, which may last from a few days to several weeks, it is necessary to divide the work into daily segments, called lessons. Finally, daily lessons are themselves divided into specific learning activities. In the pressure and rush of daily work in the classroom the job at hand (terminology, dates, dexterity) may seem remote from the aims described by a school system. But seen in the context of students' learning over a twelve-year period, learning components, however small, can be perceived as essential to intellectual, social, technical, and aesthetic development.

WHO PLANS THE UNIT?

The most significant learning is that which people *wish* to achieve. It is, therefore, learning that answers questions which individuals have asked themselves; it is learning that is based on self-motivation and frequently it is that kind of learning which responds to certain basic concerns—survival, success, status, and self-concept. Also, it is learning that is rooted in individual curiosity. Therefore those who plan for maximum learning should be all those who are involved in the process, students as well as teacher.

Although beginning teachers have many other things to learn on the job, none is probably more important than that of obtaining and using student involvement in the planning process. If students ask fundamental questions, they work more readily to obtain answers, and in so doing automatically present more willing attitudes, accept more responsibility, and engage in detail; in the process they minimize their own boredom (and misbehavior).

A good unit is planned to take into account differences among students. To do this a variety of learning activities is required. In addition, while a unit often begins and is carried out in one area of concern, it frequently cuts across subject lines and makes use of related learning areas.

For instance, in a study of water pollution, a science class may delve into the politics of water legislation (or lack of it), may make a survey of the attitudes toward federal versus local control over industrial pollution, and may be led into the historical-legal anachronisms that impede water-control legislation, such as having selected rivers for state boundaries. The international implications of water use is a fascinating bypath for study. Analysis of water pollution would lead to both chemical and biological inquiry, and certainly mathematics could be employed, as data are gathered regarding the incidence of pollution in its various manifestations.

The same area of study might be used as an aspect of a social studies unit, concerned with federal–state relations or international problems. Again, to determine the dimensions of the topic, students might well go far afield into the sciences involved and also utilize mathematics to organize data obtained.

A unit can develop as described above and yet be based on two distinctly different premises. On the one hand, the assumption may be that the goals of the secondary school can be reached through the presentation of logically arranged knowledge. In that case, the unit may center on a subject-matter topic: the halogens; the short story; the Civil War. This is sometimes called a subject-matter unit. On the other hand, the assumption may be that the goals of the secondary school can be reached through experiences enabling students to meet their individual and social needs. In that case, the unit will center on social and personal problems: "How can we prepare for happy family living?" "How can we make democracy work better?" This is sometimes called an experience unit.

The experience unit is the more difficult to conduct. It requires broad knowledge on the part of the teacher, careful planning, plus the involvement of a wider range of activities and materials. Moreover, it requires greater elasticity in time allotment. The results may not satisfy the school administration, which may be primarily concerned with uniform outcomes. The expectation may be reinforced both by schoolwide testing programs and by the desires of other teachers. It is sometimes difficult to obtain the same outcomes from experience units as from subject-matter units. Furthermore, as a beginning teacher, it is often difficult to get an experience unit started in the typical fifty-minute school period, and also difficult to maintain continuity from day to day. Fellow teachers may complain because students get involved in the unit at the expense of other assignments.

On the other hand, there are distinctive and positive rewards in teaching problem-centered or experience units if they can be managed. Through them, resources of vitality, interest, and creative motivation are opened up because students feel that they are working with the "real stuff" of life. The difference in classroom implementation between subject-matter and experience units may not have to be so sharply drawn. Subject-matter units can be planned to take account of student and social needs, can have subject-matter goals oriented to these needs, can utilize materials and activities to meet both the short-term subject-matter expectations and the long-term goals of the high school, and can include a broad evaluation program.

As stated earlier in this chapter, all units require attention to scope, sequence, objectives, learning activities, materials, and evaluation. Scope and sequence are subjects peculiarly rooted in the various subject areas and will not be discussed further here. The remainder of this chapter, however, will examine specifics related to objectives, learning activities, materials, and evaluation for both units and daily lessons.

OBJECTIVES: KNOWING WHAT IS EXPECTED

While objectives are the first things thought about, they are the last things achieved. In order to be achieved, they must be carefully stated and clearly communicated to students. One of the reasons teacher–student planning is important is that it provides students with the opportunity to participate in the decision about objectives to be pursued. In this situation both teacher and students know where they are going and how they are going to get there. Together they have decided that the topic under consideration can contribute something of value to their education and jointly they will pursue that end.

WHAT KINDS OF OBJECTIVES?

Because the aims of a school system are designed to produce well-rounded, competent individuals, school subjects with their varying objectives have been identified, in order to produce those kinds of people. Some subjects stress factual understanding; others stress the development of skills and abilities; and still others concern themselves primarily with attitudes, appreciation, or values. Of course, all significant learning should produce a mixture of these qualities. No subject, after all, is an end unto itself, but a means to an end.

One recurrent criticism of education is that most teachers do not really know why they are teaching what they teach. For instance, when pressed, a teacher may defend spending several days on the War of 1812 because "It is part of American history." When asked why students should study American history, the same teacher would typically fall back upon the cliché, "Why all citizens ought to know their national heritage." Others might claim that the study of history, like any other subject, is an end in itself.

While many teachers are able to offer more concrete reasons for the study of the subject they teach, they have rather unformed ideas about what their students should (and do) learn. They speak in generalities not easily translated into action.

For the most part, objectives can be divided into two categories: hunting objectives and fishing objectives.[2] A hunting objective exists when teachers and students know precisely what "game" they are after. (More formally, hunting objectives are concerned with cognitive and psychomotor [skill] learnings which can be described in measurable behaviors. The term "behavioral objective" is most often used in this regard.)

- "Given a simple slide rule, the learner will construct the product of two three-digit numbers correctly in three out of four examples."
- "The learner will sand and prepare wood surface according to procedure demonstrated in class."
- "In three out of four instances, the learner will state two facts, two opinions, and two inferences about photographs which the teacher displays."
- "In a 250-word essay, the learner will correctly use ten words from the vocabulary list."
- "The learner will perform a batting swing as demonstrated."
- "The learner will operate a 16mm film projector correctly."

A fishing objective exists when teachers and students are not sure what kind of "game" they may catch. (More formally, fishing objectives are concerned with feeling and emotion, such as interests, attitudes, appreciation, and methods of adjustment. The term "affective objective" is most often used in this regard.)

- "The learner will respond sympathetically to the plight of the Joad family in *The Grapes of Wrath*."
- "The learner will appreciate his or her freedom of speech in the American democracy."
- "The learner will understand Picasso's emotional frame of reference in 'Guernica.'"
- "The learner will enhance self-concept through successful completion of a career inventory analysis."

Hunting, or behavioral, objectives mainly deal with specific intellectual learning, such as acquiring information or skills. Fishing, or affective,

[2] The terms "hunting" and "fishing" are adapted from Robert F. Hogan, "On Hunting and Fishing and Behaviorism," *Media and Methods*, 6 (March 1970), pp. 42–44. Hogan's article is a strong plea for recognition of the fact that both behavioral and affective objectives are required in education.

objectives deal more with esthetics and emotions. Subjects such as mathematics, science, industrial education, business education, or physical education lend themselves easily to description through hunting objectives. English, social studies, art, drama, speech, music, home economics lend themselves less easily to the task. However, it must be stressed that all subjects of the curriculum, if they can be justified as contributing to the formation of the whole person, the functioning citizen, the happy and productive private person, require the achievement of both hunting and fishing objectives.

Whether a particular part of a subject is suited best to one or the other kind of objective, it is true that the surest way to produce genuine learning is through the clearest possible statement of objectives. Whether hunting or fishing, terminology and structure should be clear and outcomes should be as specific as possible.

An objective may be defined as "an intent communicated by a statement which describes a proposed behavioral change in a learner."[3] It is the description of a behavior or performance desired in a learner. In the statement of an objective, the verb is of key importance. Some verbs (fishing ones) are open to a wide range of interpretations, while others (hunting ones) are specific in the behavior they require.

The following are examples of verbs which allow many interpretations:[4]

to know
to understand
to grasp
to enjoy
to believe
to be involved

Some verbs which permit more specific interpretation are:

to identify
to define
to write
to recite
to construct
to list
to compare
to contrast

You may wish to examine more closely the objectives that have been stated throughout this discussion in order to be familiar with their format and with the specificity they attempt—whether they be hunting or fishing objectives.

Regardless of the kind of objectives used, experienced teachers find that

[3] Robert F. Mager, *Preparing Instructional Objectives* (Palo Alto, Calif.: Fearon, 1962), p. 3.
[4] Adapted from Mager.

learning occurs when separate statements exist for each objective desired; indeed, "the more statements you have, the better chance you have of making clear your intent."[5]

Further discussion of objectives is best restricted to your particular subject area. Certainly, the objectives a teacher establishes are directly related to his or her philosophy of education, and for that reason it is wise for beginning teachers to examine basic works in the philosophy of education as well as in the writing of objectives.[6]

ACTIVITIES: KNOW HOW

In the following discussion of how one goes about building a unit, the assumption is made that teachers want to, and will, develop their own units. There is some reason to question both assumptions, however. In many school systems a resource guide, or a series of resource units, has already been prepared by teachers and consultants in the system. An individual is expected to use the prepared material as a guide for teaching; the decisions about the unit have already been made, and the materials and activities have already been defined. Some beginning teachers may feel that there is little left for them to do. This may be true, depending on the rigor with which the school district expects conformity to its own pattern of instruction. In most school systems, however, the guide is a suggested one. Teachers are expected to keep more or less within the subject-matter limits defined by the guide for obvious reasons: Students might be confronted with two or three units in two or three different grade levels all devoted to the same topic.

There are other limitations on teacher-developed units; one is the textbook. It takes an imaginative and hard-working teacher to find extra materials and devise varied activities that make a textbook a minor partner in the educational task. The construction of most texts inhibits the

---

[5] Mager, p. 53.

[6] For an examination of objectives compiled from a national assessment of the purposes of education, see National Assessment Objectives, Educational Policies of Education, National Education Association, Washington, D.C. For an examination of making objectives specific, in addition to Mager's work, see Benjamin Bloom (Ed.), *Taxonomy of Education Objectives: Handbook I, Cognitive Domain* (New York: McKay, 1954). (Originally published in New York by Longmans, Green). Also see references listed on page 169. For philosophical issues, see Charles J. Brauner, and Hobert W. Burns, *Problems in Education and Philosophy* (Englewood Cliffs, N.J.: Prentice-Hall, 1965); Robert S. Lynd, *Knowledge for What?* (Princeton, N.J.: Princeton University Press, 1939) (Paperback edition published in New York by Grove Press, 1964); George F. Kneller, *Existentialism and Education* (New York: Wiley, 1956; paperback edition, 1964); Robert L. Brackenbury, *Getting Down to Cases: A Problems Approach to Educational Philosophizing* (New York: Putnam, 1956); Alfred North Whitehead, *The Aims of Education* (New York: New American Library of World Literature, Mentor Books, 1949); and Earl C. Kelley, *Education for What Is Real* (New York: Harper & Row, 1947).

teacher from devising another approach or rearranging the sequence of learning activities (see Chapter 6). However, with the development of more teaching aids and the extensive publishing of paperback materials, the predetermined unit set by the chapters in the text will disappear as quickly as teachers demonstrate initiative and devise their own units.

Finally, there are prepackaged units being developed by many new curriculum-revision projects. Some, like the Physical Science Study Commission and the Biological Sciences Curriculum Study programs come with text, laboratory manuals, films, and filmstrips all ready for instant utilization. The task of the teacher is to press the right button or open the right pamphlet at the right place. Some of the teacher's manuals that accompany these new materials are so detailed that even the questions the teacher should ask are provided. Several commercial instructional modules (also known as LAPS, HELPS, IPIS, and UNIPACA) are also available to provide students with material for independent and semi-independent study.[7]

Although these materials are often imaginative in their departure from the read-recite-quiz sequence of the standard academic class, they do, in their own way, inhibit teacher creativity.

However, given the vastness of the subject matter to be considered, as well as the changing nature of the subject, the creative teacher has much opportunity to roam; the new prepackaged units, when they are well done, are better training models than a wall-to-wall curriculum. Once an underlying philosophy behind the particular approach to a subject is understood, and after adjustments are made to styles in thinking and teaching, an individual can then restructure packages to fit immediate circumstances.

STAGES IN BUILDING A UNIT

Stage One: Preparing and Initiating the Unit

When a unit 'of instruction is undertaken for the first time, a complete, if tentative, plan should be roughed out. It has already been said that a good unit is planned cooperatively by teachers and students. So it is. But in order to maintain orderly direction for instruction, one must have in mind some distinct aims and objectives, some definite activities, some specific sources of materials, and some well-defined evaluation measures that can be used. Tentative choices of content will be based on data collected about student differences and estimates of what experiences will meet their

---

[7] For an overview of instructional modules, see Charles R. Duke, "Learning Activity Packages: Construction and Implementation," *High School Journal*, 58 (April 1975), pp. 312–321. See also Kenneth Chastain, "An Examination of the Basic Assumptions of 'Individualized' Instruction," *Modern Language Journal*, 59 (November 1975), pp. 334–344; Errol M. Magidson, "Is Your Module Good? How Do You Know?," *Audiovisual Instruction*, 21 (October 1976), pp. 43–44.

developmental needs. Moreover, rough plans will be modified in accordance with students' suggestions. But it is unwise to venture far without pre-planning.

The initiating stage of a unit includes certain key steps on which the unit's ultimate effectiveness and success depend:

1. Preliminary realistic diagnosis by the teacher of: (a) curriculum require-ments; (b) student interests, capacities, and needs; and (c) relevant learning to date.
2. Tentative selection by the teacher of possible significant problems or areas of learning geared to the preliminary diagnosis.
3. Tentative preplanning by the teacher to clarify the ways in which possible problems and areas may be approached most effectively.
4. Open, direct, and stimulating discussion with the class, designed to involve them in further diagnosis and choice of a problem or area for further study.
5. Sufficient preliminary exploration with the class to ensure that all students understand the why and what of the unit enterprise finally chosen.
6. The use of special materials, films, and activities (such as field trips) that will both clarify understanding of the unit problem and focus interest upon it.
7. Development of teacher–student plans adequate for the effective comple-tion of the unit.

The last point is worth special attention. Once the unit topic has been chosen, careful joint planning of the scope and sequence of study is essential. The scope is usually indicated by dividing the problem into principal subquestions. Beginning teachers often have trouble at this stage because the limits of the problem are not clearly defined. Usually both teacher and students are eager to get into the problem if the initial steps of the unit have been stimulating. They see no point in mulling over the statement of key questions. However, unless the energies of the group are mobilized by a clear plan, they will be expended in 100 directions and will never be utilized to bring the unit to a satisfactory culmination. The sequence of study is equally important. For example, it must be clear how the data necessary to answer subquestions or solve subproblems will be collected and who will do the job.

Stage Two: Developing the Unit

It is somewhat artificial to separate initiation from development of the unit. Actually, the second stage evolves naturally from the first. Although class participation is greatest during the second stage, the teacher continues to play a vital leadership role.

For example, the teacher performs an important function in helping the class define the objectives of its action and study. "Just what are we really after? What will we have when the unit is completed?"

Of course, this goal setting really begins during the initiation of the unit, when plans are being agreed upon. But the closer the students come to action in the unit, the more important it is that their goals be concrete and clear. By asking the right questions, by guiding the discussions, by helping the class verbalize and criticize its goals, the teacher plays a significant role. The teacher plays an equally important role in helping students decide which activities will best help them attain their objectives.

Development of the unit gives the teacher unusual and complex opportunities to provide student assignments that will maximize individual development. Because the unit is almost inevitably a complex undertaking that requires a variety of activities to carry it forward, student capacities may be challenged at many levels and in many areas. It is part of the teacher's function to guide the assignment of students to various activities according to both their ability to contribute and their ability to grow. Here the teacher makes decisions not so much on the basis of who will do a specific job best, or most quickly, but on the basis of who will learn and grow the most.

As the work of the class on the unit progresses, the teacher continues to act as a guide, both for individual students and for their working groups. A class working on a unit is comparable to a busy laboratory or a workshop. Students work either in small groups or as individuals; they move about to use room facilities or to confer with others or consult files or the classroom library. The teacher's voice is not the only one to be heard in the room. Conversation and discussion are necessary parts of work going forward. The teacher moves among the students, visiting individuals and groups, offering assistance, listening, observing, and guiding. The teacher, too, is a learner in the unit and may be frank to say so.

The unit moves forward in time to its agreed date of completion. Individuals and groups in the classroom eventually feel their deadlines close at hand. These are times agreed to in planning, and progress toward them has been checked in the class plan book or unit log.

The second stage reaches completion when the students present their findings to the class. A panel format may be used, or other members of the class may select one individual to explain their findings to the whole group. Dramatizations, displays, prerecorded interviews, and a variety of other techniques may be used. Bit by bit, as the unit comes to its conclusion, students find themselves rounding up data and insights they did not have previously. If the unit has gone well, all participants, including the teacher, will feel that they have shared in an important, meaningful venture.

Stage Three: Culminating and Evaluating the Unit

Whether a feeling of accomplishment is really warranted, what strengths and weaknesses the unit had, how it might have been improved and made more effective—all these are concerns of the teacher and the class in the culminating stage of the unit. The main business of the third stage in a unit of learning is evaluation.

Certainly the emphasis in the unit should be on the quality of the process as well as on the end product. A unit is not evaluated solely on the basis of a beautifully illustrated or dramatic report. The processes of learning leadership and "followership," developing good group attitudes and skills, fostering problem-solving abilities, and increasing student self-direction also deserve major consideration. If most of the gathered facts slip away in the ensuing years while these essential processes remain, the efforts of the unit will have been justified. A good culmination includes an evaluation of these processes by both teacher and students. The success or failure of a unit is not measured solely by a pencil-and-paper test of facts.

Evaluation, in the sense in which the word is used here, is where all concerned assess the findings of the study, the procedures that were used by the class, and the future implications of what has been learned. Evaluation should always refer to the goals established at the beginning of the study and should always help individuals raise new goals for academic and social performance.

FORMULATING THE UNIT

At this point, it should be helpful to examine the plan of a unit designed to be used with an average to above average group of eleventh graders. While the unit has a decided English emphasis, it could be adapted easily to a social studies or humanities course. In any case, its inclusion here is intended to illustrate broad concepts regarding organization and planning. The nature of the topic removes it from the more restricted concepts of certain subject matter.

Title: Facing Death: Preparing for the Inevitable
Time: Five weeks (five days per week; 50 minutes per class)

I.   Unit Aims

    A.   "Fishing" Aims—The learner will:

        1.   Recognize that confronting the death of a loved one is a difficult, universal experience.

        2.   Assess personal awareness about death as well as individual strengths and weaknesses for encountering the death of loved ones.

        3.   Make a comparative judgment about the intellectual and esthetic quality of the three books read.

        4.   Share with others reactions to the varied experiences of the unit.

B. "Hunting" Aims—The learner will:

1. Orally recount sequential details from *Brian's Song* by William Blinn, *A Death in the Family* by James Agee, and *On Death and Dying* by Elizabeth Kubler-Ross.
2. List three ways in which the film treatment of *Brian's Song* is similar to the film treatment of *A Death in the Family*.
3. List three ways in which the film treatment of *Brian's Song* is different from the film treatment of *A Death in the Family*.
4. Complete information and discussion review forms at the end of discussions concerning the readings and viewing.
5. Complete an evaluation form concerning the group processes observed during one session in which he or she serves as a discussion leader.
6. Score at least 70 percent accuracy on an objective examination based on *On Death and Dying*.
7. Obtain at least five commercial sympathy cards and complete an analysis based on classroom established criteria.
8. Present evidence of research about death in another culture; share that information with the whole group orally.
9. Complete interview forms developed by the class following interviews conducted in the community concerning death-related subjects.
10. Score at least 80 percent on a take-home essay based on major concepts encountered in the unit.
11. Score at least 70 percent on an in-class essay examination based on readings, viewings, and discussions.

II. Learning Activities

A. Initiatory Activities

1. View videotape "Dying and Death."[8] Discuss central issues in relation to statistics on death and young people, death and terminal illness, death and cultural attitudes toward it.
2. Teacher reading of brief excerpts from the three books students will read.
3. In-class beginning of *Brian's Song*.

B. Developmental Activities

1. Read and discuss: *Brian's Song, A Death in the Family, On Death and Dying* (whole and small groups).
2. View and discuss: *Brian's Song, A Death in the Family* (whole and small groups).
3. Engage in interviews.
4. Perform research.
5. Collect and analyze sympathy cards.
6. Listen to and interview a resource person.

[8] Available from the Center on Aging, University of Maryland, College Park 20742. This fifteen-minute tape is intended to provoke classroom discussion. Users of the tape are urged to duplicate it for further use.

C. Culminating Activities

1. Complete objective examination.
2. Write brief essays.
3. Share results of interviewing.
4. Share results of sympathy card analysis and relate to the unit topic.
5. Share results of research.
6. Synthesize learnings from the unit and set goals for future learning.

The following calendar, to be shared with students, is essential both so that the teacher can establish reasonable daily objectives and so that students can obtain an overview of the unit and recognize assignment responsibilities over many weeks' time.

UNIT CALENDAR FOR FACING DEATH
(Shared with students in mimeographed form)

WEEK ONE

Monday: Videotape, introductory discussion; begin reading *Brian's Song*.

Tuesday/Wednesday: Examine Unit Calendar/read and discuss *Brian's Song*.

Thursday: View *Brian's Song* (Special arrangements have been made for you to remain in class until the completion of the film; because your other teachers have agreed to your late arrival at next period class, discussion of *Brian's Song* will be delayed until Friday.)

Friday: Small group discussion/begin (and complete for homework) essay reaction to it.

WEEK TWO

Monday: Share and discuss essays in small groups; begin *A Death in the Family*.

Tuesday/Wednesday/Thursday: Complete *A Death in the Family*. Discuss (whole and small groups.)

Friday: Complete chart for comparing and contrasting reactions to the reading of *Brian's Song* and *A Death in the Family* (individual and large group).

WEEK THREE

Monday/Tuesday: View *A Death in the Family*. (Because of the film's length, two periods will be required to see it in its entirety. It is important that you be in your seat and prepared to view the film promptly at the ringing of the bell.)

Wednesday: Discuss viewing of *A Death in the Family* and compare/contrast film treatment of *Brian's Song* to book.

Thursday: Teacher explains: (a) collection and analysis of sympathy cards; (b) interviewing process; (c) other culture research project (all with examples); students begin one of these activities.

Friday: Continue activities from Thursday; teacher and student reading from first few pages of *On Death and Dying*.

WEEK FOUR

Monday/Tuesday: Read and discuss *On Death and Dying* (in small groups).

Wednesday: Resource person.

Thursday: Total group summary of *On Death and Dying* and reactions; summary to resource person.

Friday: Objective examination on *On Death and Dying*.

WEEK FIVE

Monday: Return and discuss examinations; work on continuing activities (individual and small group).

Tuesday: Report of interviews, conclusions about sympathy cards (small groups).

Wednesday/Thursday: Presentations about other culture research projects.

Friday: Essay examination synthesizing the unit topic; tie-in to next unit, goal setting for further growth.

In examining both the overall unit plan and the unit calendar, specify the topics, concepts, themes, generalizations, problems, and questions which are stated or implied. In what ways would you make adjustments in either the unit plan or the unit calendar? Justify the changes you would make.

THE DAILY LESSON PLAN

The unit of learning at its best requires of the teacher long-range planning for resources and materials; but, as indicated earlier, day-to-day planning is also necessary. Typically, beginning teachers function best working with lesson plans that provide a somewhat uniform scheme for an entire class. While this approach has value for those adjusting to the complexities of teaching, it is an approach which eventually stifles individual needs and interests because it automatically enforces a lock-step approach on people with diverse intellects, interests, and talents. Obviously, the one-lesson-for-all approach implies that the teacher does most of the preliminary screening in order to insure that the subject matter will be covered.

Because the unit plan protects against disconnected lessons, each class session examines one or more small aspects of the unit topic. As with the unit itself, the daily lesson is concerned with:

1. Objectives
2. Learning activities
3. Materials
4. Assignments
5. Evaluation

LESSON OBJECTIVES

The lesson plan should take cognizance of the long-term aims of the secondary school in order to place the immediate objective in perspective. Daily objectives must be realistically modest. Both teachers and students tend to overestimate what can be accomplished in a fifty-minute period. If the unit has been broken down by a weekly calendar, it is easier to estimate what may occur in a fifty-minute period. No formula exists for such a calculation; only experience can indicate how long your teaching style and the personality of the group will need to complete the work. Even with experience, one is sometimes surprised that planned time and actual time do not jibe.

For the unit "Facing Death," notice that the first "fishing" aim is "The learner will recognize that confronting the death of a loved one is a difficult, universal experience" and that the first "hunting" aim is "The learner will orally recount details from *Brian's Song* by William Blinn, *A Death in the Family* by James Agee, and *On Death and Dying* by Elizabeth Kubler-Ross."

In daily lesson plans parts of both of these objectives can be attained. A daily lesson objective for one day might read:

"The learner will reflect on and discuss reactions to Brian's death. Discussion will focus on evidence from the text which shows the reactions of Gale and Joy (Brian's wife) to Brian's dying moments. What specific things do the characters say and what things does the script indicate they do nonverbally? What real or other vicarious experiences do students have which support the difficulty of this experience for Gale and Joy?

"The learner will read the final pages (118–119) of *Brian's Song* in class, following the discussion above."

Transferring unit goals into daily objectives is a matter of breaking down the subject of study into smaller, manageable portions.

ACTIVITIES

There can of course be no hard-and-fast rules about how many activities are required for a secondary school class period. But it is certain that there should be some variety within the period. The class should rarely discuss, listen, or even meet in groups for the entire period.

Some kind of time budget will be necessary. Nothing is as awkward or conducive to chaos as a slice of idle time—time when nothing has been planned. Beginning teachers should always have a number of alternatives and extras in their plans, which they will regularly need. Moreover, beginning teachers invite disaster if they trust to their ability to improvise on the spot.

Continuing to think about a daily lesson for the "Facing Death" unit, and using the two objectives listed above, it is easy to consider activities which will lead to achieving the objectives. In order to reflect on and discuss Gale Sayer's reaction to Brian's illness and impending death, students will need time to reexamine passages in which this is explained and they will need a circumstance in which to express their views. One way in which this might be expressed in a lesson plan is:

1. Individual review of pages 88–119; students formulate responses to Gale Sayer's reactions to Brian's illness and impending death (10 minutes).
2. Class breaks into groups of five, using same group arrangement as yesterday, with same chairperson. Discussion time: 20 minutes.
3. Chairpersons share group reactions with total group (10 minutes).

MATERIALS

Variety is the key word again. Many sources which can provide direction, information, and illustrations are necessary in all classrooms. Materials of many reading levels and a good supply of nonprint resources will also be helpful. Materials must fit the precise need of the lesson and must be available at the right moment. (See Chapter 6 concerning classroom organization.)

A teacher's comments about materials for the lesson from the "Facing Death" unit might state:

1. All students share or use their own copies of *Brian's Song* for reference to pages 88–119. (Extra books on shelf.)
2. Notepaper and pens necessary for individual notes and for group sharing. (Extra paper and pencils in supply closet.)

In a class session in which other activities are planned, the organization of materials can be far more complicated.

EVALUATION

Evaluation of the day's work does not imply merely a five-minute quiz, grading an assignment, or conducting an oral question-and-answer period. Each of these may have its place, but the effective teacher will take equal note of how well students worked in their groups, what resources they found to supplement their investigation or presentation, and the quality of the questions asked. There are useful ways of observing behavior in the classroom, and they belong in a sound scheme of evaluation. (Evaluation techniques are presented in detail in Chapter 14.) Most important is that the evaluation be consistent with the lesson itself. Did it achieve what was intended? If not, what reasons should be considered? How does one go about achieving the same objectives another day?

In addition, teachers need to evaluate themselves on a daily basis. A self-evaluation, using the daily lesson plan as a reference, might include these questions:

1. Did I state objectives clearly?
2. Did I build on preceding lessons?
3. Did I allot time correctly?
4. Did I arouse and capture the interest of students?
5. Did I emphasize important points?
6. Did I use teaching aids effectively?
7. Did I succeed in getting maximum class participation?
8. Did I relate the lesson to practical problems?
9. Did I allow time to evaluate class performance?
10. Did I plan to expect the unexpected?
11. If I were to teach the lesson again, in what way(s) would I change it?

DEVELOPING THE DAILY LESSON PLAN

Here is a daily lesson plan which might be used for the first day of the unit, "Facing Death." Other formats for lesson plans appear on pages 159 to 163.

Teacher: *Carrie Collier*   **Unit: Facing Death**
Period: 4   **Date:** February 17   **Lesson:** Introductory (First day)
Time Period: 50 minutes

A. "Fishing" Objectives—The learner will:
    1. Begin to consider "fishing" aims of the unit (Nos. 1 and 2).
    2. Demonstrate some interest in pursuing the unit.

B. "Hunting" Objectives—The learner will:
    1. View videotape "Dying and Death" and record reactions to it.
    2. Examine and question (in total group) central ideas presented in the videotape.
    3. Participate in the initial reading of *Brian's Song*.
    4. Continue reading *Brian's Song* for homework.

C. Learning Activities
    1. View "Dying and Death" (15 minutes).
    2. Teacher-led discussion of reactions to videotape; teacher presentation (using overhead projector) of statistics regarding:

  a. death and young people
  b. death and terminal illness
  c. death and cultural attitudes toward death (15 minutes)
 3. Small group brainstorming to generate questions students have about facing death of a loved one. No discussion (10 minutes).
 4. Teacher reading of three brief excerpts from *Brian's Song* (pages 105–107), *A Death in the Family* (pages 146–147), *On Death and Dying* (pages 144–145) (5 minutes).
 5. Students begin *Brian's Song* (remaining time).

D. Assignment
Read at own rate in *Brian's Song.* Book to be completed by beginning of class on Thursday. Write notes and questions as needed.

E. Materials
 1. Videotape and videotape machine (extension cord).
 2. Overhead projector and prepared overlay.
 3. Marked copies of *A Death in the Family*, *On Death and Dying*, and *Brian's Song* for teacher reading.
 4. Copies of *Brian's Song* for each student.

F. Evaluation
While examining this daily lesson plan, discuss ways in which the learning activities fulfill the "fishing" and "hunting" objectives established. Based on the information so far provided about the unit "Facing Death," and this lesson in it, in what ways might a teacher comment in the evaluation segment?

Teacher _____   **Subject** _____

Unit _____   **Date** _____

Period _____

    I. Topic:

    II. Aims (Long-range Goals):

    III. Objectives (Short-range Goals):

    IV. Materials:

    V. Procedures:

    VI. Evaluation

    VII. Outcomes:

    VIII. Sources and Resources:

Unit _____   Student Teacher's Name _____

Topic _____   Class _____

Objectives: Date _____

Time Allotments	Activities and Procedures

Assignment:

Materials and Equipment	Advance Preparation and References

Subject _____ Teacher _____ Presentation Date _____ Per 1 _____ 2 _____

Purpose: 3 _____ 4 _____

5 _____ 6 _____

Time (Minutes)	Content	Method	Materials	Evaluation

Assignment:

Subject _____   **Teacher** _____

Presentation Date _____   **Period 1** ___ **2** ___ **3** ___ **4** ___ **5** ___ **6** ___

I. Purpose (what you want the student to learn):

II. Assignment:

III. Procedures and Time Indicated (Lesson or Demonstration Outline)

IV. Resources (Tools and Equipment Needed)

V. Evaluation and Suggested Presentation Improvement.

VI. Reminders and Special Notes

A TEACHING UNIT
(Science)

Unit Title:

Approximate Teaching Time:

Major Concepts to Be Developed:

1.

2.

3.

Student Teacher:

Cooperating Teacher:

School:

Behavioral Objectives:

1.

2.

3.

General Content Outline	Instructional Methods	Instructional Materials and Equipment	Evaluation Methods and Procedures	Advance Preparation; Reference Materials	Comments

163

CRUCIAL FACTORS IN PLANNING

STUDENTS AND TEACHERS PLAN TOGETHER

The teacher's plan should be tentative only; the final plan for action should be conceived jointly by students and teacher. The planning will revolve around such questions as "What are the divisions of this problem?" How shall we go about finding out how people feel on this subject?" What rules do we need in order to go on that trip we proposed?" These are questions of classroom procedure and student conduct, as well as of choice of subject matter. Such planning is fundamental to democratic teaching.

One word of caution concerning the use of student–teacher planning: Avoid overdoing it. Constant insistence on student choice can be just as frustrating as its opposite. Time should be set aside for student–teacher planning shortly after the initiation of a new unit. There should be short planning sessions for the day as the work progresses. Evaluative sessions are important in keeping standards of work and conduct at an acceptable level, but the balance of class time should be devoted to problem discussion, study and research, and individual and small-group work.

Planning sessions should be stimulating and well paced. Students should feel that the opportunity to choose and evaluate is real. Teachers must bring a genuine enthusiasm to the planning sessions, showing their own eagerness to learn and evaluate progress along with their students. They should seek exciting opportunities for learning even in their students' most mundane and naive suggestions.

Can planning be applied in such logically organized classes as algebra, geometry, chemistry, and physics? Yes! Although some teachers do not develop large, problem-centered units in these subjects, there is still ample room for student–teacher planning. Such questions as, "How much time do we need for study in class?" "Should we do lab work in pairs, in groups, or individually?" "How much credit should be discounted on homework if papers are messy and untidy?" are pertinent in all classrooms and best answered by students and teacher working together. Although valuable class time must, of course, be spent on this planning, the teacher will find that much less time will be spent later in pushing reluctant students and in checking up on neglected assignments.

RECOGNIZING STUDENT NEEDS

When teachers draw upon all they know about adolescents in general and those in class in particular they are attempting to recognize students' needs. They identify those needs relevant to the course, content, and experience. For example, the biology teacher knows that adolescents must understand and accept bodily changes. Therefore, if biology content gives students a chance to understand their own physical equipment better, they will be motivated to learn. A physical education teacher who encountered a similar problem handled it this way:

> During the year Mr. George became aware of the variety of hygiene problems of his physical education class and concluded that the upcoming health unit should evolve from the interest of the students. Since he wanted to ensure that they realized their interests and concerns, he arranged for his students to spend two class periods browsing in a variety of reference works, magazines, hygiene and health texts, and through a file of hygiene-related materials he had collected across the years. The school nurse gave a short talk to the class, outlining some hygiene problems she had encountered among teenagers. Mr. George saw to it that students met in small groups to voice their concerns; finally, a committee collated the interests indicated by the various groups. Committee reports were given in class. Mr. George helped the class divide their concerns into two basic lists. Students were given their choice of the two categories for study and pursued their work on both an individual and small-group basis. At the end of the unit each group, working under the direction of student leaders, made some form of presentation to the class, sharing the learning each had gained.

Employing materials not immediately related to classroom study can enlist the interest of students who may not otherwise "be hooked." The use of such books as History of the Lathe to 1850 or A History of Civil Engineering[9] may well lead boys who are interested in mechanical or hand skills to a study of history. A pamphlet such as El Primero Paso Importante[10] which describes, in easy-to-read Spanish, "the first big step" of entering school, may also be an interest tool. Not only can foreign-language students profit from reading about content already familiar to them from experience, or from which they may profit because of interest in children, but if they are suffering from difficulties of the English language, they may find it helpful background to one phase of American life. Such a student would also be able to share the material with parents and thus aid them to smooth the school entry of younger children still at home. Another blending of interest may occur through the use of resources like The Letters from the Captain's Wife, a portfolio of New England materials containing historical

[9] Robert S. Woodbury, History of the Lathe to 1850 (Boston: Massachusetts Institute of Technology Press, 1968). Hans Straub, A History of Civil Engineering (Boston: Massachusetts Institute of Technology Press, 1968). See also Eric Sloane, A Museum of Early American Tools (New York: Funk and Wagnalls, 1964).
[10] National School Public Relations Association, El Primero Paso Importante (Washington, D.C.: The Association, 1966).

information and adapted recipes of the nineteenth century—presented in letter form.[11] An inexhaustible array of possibilities exists for using "unusual" materials to stimulate or develop areas of interest.[12]

HELPING STUDENTS BECOME AWARE OF THEIR NEEDS

Often people do not know what they need! Thus, adolescents believe they have no need to learn about lenses and the refraction of light in physics class. But a skilled teacher, who shows them all kinds of lenses— in eyeglasses, microscopes, car headlights, binoculars—can excite their curiosity and create "a need to find out" why and how light can be bent. Creating such an awareness in a psychologically sound manner means that the teacher has a medium for widening the experience field of the student.

CONVEYING ENTHUSIASM FOR LEARNING

Enthusiasm is contagious. The wise teacher does much to convey and capture enthusiasm by utilizing units focused on genuine concerns of the students. The problem-centered unit is, in a sense, its own motivation. It is the teacher's task to see to it that the problem is of deep concern. Adolescents readily respond to, and just as readily reject, a work that only pretends to be a "problem." One reliable test of what is a good problem for study is the speed with which students comprehend it. If a teacher has to do all the work of building enthusiasm over the "exciting" material, then it can be assumed that the problem is not really important to adolescents.

SETTING GOALS IMPORTANT TO STUDENTS

Too often the real thing a student works for is a grade. Actually, of course, this is motivation too: Some students can and will work hard to get a good grade. But the result is low-level learning. The student actually is

[11] *The Letters from the Captain's Wife* (Washington, D.C.: US Department of the Interior, 1966).

[12] "Unusual" resources for motivational or developmental purposes include such possibilities as: *London: A Pilgrimage* (a book containing illustrations by Gustave Doré of Dickens' time); *Foxfire* (nos. 1, 2, and 3—all of which contain material gathered by students from the inhabitants of southern Appalachian mountain folk); *How the Other Half Lives* (Jacob Riis' collection of photographs of ghetto life at the time of the Great Migration); *Technology in the Ancient World* (mechanical ingenuity as seen through the tools and implements of agriculture, of transportation, of the home, of commerce, and of war); *How Did Sports Begin?* (the origin of athletic sports and games); *The Renaissance Cookbook* (authentic recipes with principles of Renaissance cookery); *George Washington's Expense Account* (good history but funny because of the book's treatment); *The Good Old Days—They Were Terrible!* (just that); *Montgomery Ward & Co: Spring and Summer Catalogue for 1895*. What other "unusual" resources can you add to this list of real (and available) books? Brainstorm with your classmates ways in which these resources might be used for secondary school teaching.

not concerned with what or even how he or she is learning, but only with a status label. Good motivation establishes goals that are in themselves important: to be able to read recipes, to be able to fix simple electrical circuits, to appreciate the culture of a foreign people, or to have greater skill in taking dictation. To endure, learning must be based on more than earning a grade.

RELATING THE GOAL TO THE STUDENT'S RANGE OF ABILITIES

Tasks remain challenging so long as students are fairly certain that they can perform them and perform them with some pride in accomplishment. Success must taste good, must not be too cheaply won, and must leave important resources for further learning.

Good motivation is positive and is based on learning that makes sense to the learner. It is not negative. Too often, the motivation used by a teacher takes one of the following forms:

- "If you don't do this well, you will have ten additional problems!"
- "We'll have a test tomorrow if you waste this study period!"
- "We can't stay on this topic all semester! You'd better start studying harder or you'll flunk the exam."
- "Since you did do badly on that last test, we'll have to spend more time on this material."

Such phrases, and their underlying negative attitudes, do not motivate— at least in the positive sense. Whenever teachers express this attitude they build student antipathy to learning. From then on, it is a dull and dreary struggle for both teacher and student to plough through the drab desert of psychology, chemistry, German, or bookkeeping.

THE ASSIGNMENT IS CRUCIAL IN PLANNING, TOO

If assignments are used to carry the day's work forward, they should make clear what things to do, how they are to be done, and why they are to be done. Assignments must be specific: Who is to do what? What difficulties are involved? What is the deadline? In order for assignments to lead to further learning, it is important that they be made at the right time—on the basis of inadequacies in discussion, perhaps as the result of or to complete a problem-solving experience.

It was near the end of the period in a junior class. Bored students were slowly closing their books, calculating exactly how many more minutes were left to the period. The minute hand jerked on with a slow, dull click. Ms. Mac-Pherson always waited until the last possible moment to make the assignment for the next day. Often the crucial words were spoken as the bell shrilled out, effectively drowning her voice. Then students anxiously and irritably demanded, "What pages are we supposed to read?"

Today she seemed particularly labored in giving the assignment. "Now I want you all to read Chapter 3 in your text. That is about forty pages. You should be able to do that at home in about an hour. Be ready to answer questions on the chapter, and perhaps we'll have a short quiz if you aren't prepared well enough. I'm going to check in my record book and call on those of you who haven't been doing much in class lately."

Does this description seem exaggerated? Or is it a typical episode in hundreds of secondary school classrooms? A look at a teacher performing the assignment function at a higher level should be informative:

It was near the end of the period in a junior class; Ted was in front of the room, answering questions about a report he had made on a visit to the telephone company. He had brought back some advice from the personnel manager on what high-school students should do to prepare for telephone company work. Questions were being fired at him right and left. Ted was having difficulty remembering all of them. Just then Miss Murphy interrupted: "Ted, I think our time is about up. That was a splendid report, and there are many more questions to be asked. Since we haven't time now to answer all the questions, let's all jot down three or four really important questions tonight. We'll ask Ted to answer them the day after tomorrow."

Miss Murphy then turned to the board and wrote: "Assignment for Period 2, Wednesday: three or four questions on the telephone company visit."

"Also," she said, "There are some books here in the classroom and in the library on how to prepare for a job. After we hear from Fred and Mary tomorrow on their visit to the cannery, it would be helpful to have some summaries of these books for those who could not make trips. Each of you take one article or book and prepare it for Thursday. Anyone else interested can see me." These directions were put on the board, with the names and topics. There still remained a few moments of class. Students gathered their books; Tony, Bob, and Tyrone came to the shelf and discussed books in which they were interested. The teacher briefly chatted with them and made an appointment to talk with them before class the next day.

In this example of a different approach to giving assignments, the teacher capitalized on what was occurring in the class at the moment and within the framework of a continuing activity. Specific students were given special work to do. No threats were made; instead, the assignment was stated so that it followed naturally out of the discussion. (It may be wise at this time to read "Out of Class Study," Chapter 12.)

SUMMARY

A teaching unit brings together various related areas of knowledge, ideals, values, and attitudes into a cohesive whole. The unit attempts to show students the whole and the parts of the whole as well as the relationships which exist among the parts of the whole. Daily lessons are the manageable components which allow the work of the unit to be accomplished. Not only can the daily lesson stand, in some part, on its own, but it also provides a link with what has gone before, develops new insights and skills, and establishes a link with what is to come.

The organization and planning that make good teaching (and effective learning) possible are basic skills in a teacher's repertoire.

SELECTED READINGS

Cohen, Edward, "If You're Not Sure Where You're Going, You're Liable to End up Someplace Else," *Media and Methods,* 6 (March 1970), pp. 39–41. Lucid and persuasive arguments for the use of behavioral objectives.

Gardner, Leonard, "Humanistic Education and Behavioral Objectives: Opposing Theories of Educational Science," *School Review,* 85:3 (May 1977), pp. 376–394. "The cult of efficiency . . . unabashedly admits that it has no idea of the purposes of education."

Gronlund, Normal E., *Stating Objectives for Classroom Instruction.* New York: Macmillan, 1978. A lucid pamphlet dealing with all aspects of instructional objectives. Two appendices provide a checklist for evaluating a final list of objectives and lists illustrative verbs for the statement of objectives.

Instructional Objectives Exchange, Box 24095, Los Angeles, Calif. 09924. Wide array of resources in testing and planning aids. Extensive "Measurable Objectives Collections" are also available. Ask to be placed on mailing list.

Mager, Robert F., *Preparing Instructional Objectives.* Palo Alto, Calif.: Fearon, 1975 (paperback).

Popham, W. James, and Eva L. Baker, *Establishing Instructional Goals.* Englewood Cliffs, N.J.: Prentice-Hall, 1970. A programmed text for writing instructional objectives. The chapter "Selecting Appropriate Educational Objectives" is probably the most helpful.

Vargas, Julie S., *Writing Worthwhile Behavioral Objectives.* New York: Harper & Row, 1972. A self-instructional book concerned with identifying and writing objectives in the cognitive domain. Helpful is the section entitled "Developing a Unit."

FOCUS ON CHAPTER 8

Good teachers arrange environments that allow students to learn through all their senses and by using a variety of challenging resources. Knowing what resources to use within a subject area and for young people is a task that continues as long as one teaches; new materials appear daily in such number that keeping abreast of them is taxing, although informative and stimulating.

Significant ideas presented in this chapter include:
- A frequently overlooked resource for teaching is other people, both those in school and in the community at large.
- Experiences away from school, usually in the form of field trips, can have direct, productive relations to classroom study. Field trips must have careful planning and follow-up.
- Close scrutiny must be given to all print and nonprint media. Appropriateness, bias, quality, accessibility are all important in the making of decisions about choice.
- Many resources are free.
- Many teachers make some of their own resources, which are frequently among the most effective ones.

chapter 8

"Getting It All Together": teaching and learning resources

An overhead projector, two sets of books to be
distributed, a visiting speaker, one set of
mimeographed guidelines, a model of the heart,
one set of answer sheets, colored chalk. . . . Just for
my own curiosity I counted up all the helping
things I used in teaching today. The total? 27.
I feel like a control manager.

Examining the activities of good teaching plans over
several weeks one is struck by the number of resources
which are employed to make teaching and learning significant and enjoyable.

In a classroom where maximum effort is made to reach all the students—
each with different interests, abilities, and goals, as well as different ways of
learning—it is essential to utilize a wide variety of materials, people, and
tools to provide motivation, offer examples, develop concepts and skills,
inspire creativity, suggest relationships, and summarize and synthesize
knowledge.

VARIETY IS THE SPICE OF RESOURCES

When teachers make use of direct and vicarious experiences they automatically employ variety in learning resources. But how can teachers plan
the details of that variety in addition to everything else they are supposed
to do? Actually, variety in learning experiences follows naturally when
planning starts with student interest and experience, since those interests
and experiences are themselves different at different times.

For example, a teacher of social problems might plan a discussion on developing worthwhile leisure interests (in order to lead into a study of the problem of leisure and recreation in an industrial civilization). The discussion might focus on students' activities during their free time. Several important points would probably arise. First, recreation costs money; second, there are not enough recreational facilities in town; third, "our parents won't let us do the things we want to do in our leisure time," and fourth, "facilities are not open at times when working students want to use them." On the basis of these points, a teacher could foresee such variety of activities as these:

- General assistance from, and an informational presentation by, a health and recreation teacher or supervisor.
- Interview of local politicians concerning support of recreation facilities.
- Class interview of community recreation department personnel.
- Examination of public records to understand bureaucratic red tape and to examine costs and tax support.
- School survey of student interests and use of community recreational facilities.
- Letters to state agencies and personnel responsible for supporting and subsidizing local facilities.
- Examination of federal government reports and statistics to understand the relationship of local to nationwide programs.
- Use of reference works on recreation and related topics.
- Library research to see what has been written on this subject.
- Interviews with a local recreation commission member to see what is available in the community.
- Panel discussion of the findings from the activities above.
- Quiz on how much is known about recreation in town.
- Individual oral reports on findings.
- Essay examination on problem topics in the area of recreation.
- Poster and bulletin board displays on desired and desirable recreational activities.
- Photographing and videotaping facilities and their uses.
- Individual scrapbooks of advertisements, newspaper clippings, and so on, on recreation and health.
- Evaluation of commercial recreation offerings, including television and radio.
- Diaries by students of their own recreation habits.
- Written proposals for improvement of recreational facilities within the community.
- Drawings and models for improved facilities.
- Tape recording, or transcription, of interviews with older citizens on the topic "What We Did for Recreation in 1920."

These are some of the many experiences that can evolve into a single unit of work when instruction starts with immediate student interests and activities.

Variety is not only important in any single class, but year after year different approaches to the same subject matter are needed. The first reason is that each class is different. For example, no two eleventh-grade groups in chemistry can be quite the same. Each has a different assortment of young people, with different home and school situations, needs, and interests.

The second reason for a change in approach is its effect on the personality of the teacher. To do the same things five periods a day for ten months, year after year, is bound to have a deadening effect on the teacher's spark and interest. For the sake of sheer self-preservation, the teacher must seek new approaches to subject matter.

Third, subject matter changes. New ideas and new discoveries mean that some concepts taught in today's chemistry, for instance, may be archaic by next year. Outmoded subject matter is as much a fraud as uninformed instruction.

IN-SCHOOL PEOPLE AS RESOURCES

Personal contact is one of the most important, and most effective, sources for enlarging experience. The opportunities for such contacts in the school community are many.

Immediate to the classroom are other school personnel and students. Whenever the ability and interest of administrators, supervisors, helping teachers, and other faculty members are found, they should be used. Such people frequently are not utilized. Yet often these resource people are simply awaiting the opportunity and invitation to meet students on new ground and with new areas of contact.

Working in a school near Washington, D.C., I was happy to discover within my own school system a variety of interesting people who were delighted to spend time relating their experiences and enthusiasms to my students. Our principal had once been a handwriting expert for the FBI; our band instructor, a soloist for a major symphony orchestra; our shop teacher, a Peace Corps volunteer whose hobby was karate; our cafeteria manager, a ten-year resident of Thailand. One supervisor was a professional writer; our pupil personnel worker had been a computer programmer. Another teacher was an amateur expert in space exploration, and another supervisor was a student of Zen Buddhism. For all the possibilities of my core curriculum classroom, I'd hit the jackpot; but then, I'd also looked for it!

Students, themselves, can be invaluable resources. The wise teacher capitalizes upon students' experiences and interests as much as on those of "outsiders." Many times students have traveled to, and sometimes lived in, parts of the nation or world which are relevant to classroom study. Their impressions, experiences, and mementos are first-hand opportunities for stimulation and investigation, as are those of their parents and other relatives. Students' job experiences are also important as resources—not only the substance of work itself, but the procedure for getting and keeping a job, the responsibilities of the "world of work," and the experience of meeting and dealing with new and different people: All are fodder for the formulation, expression, and discussion of ideas and extending experiences of others. Many students have had dealings with police, courts, or with welfare and other social agencies. They can give an "insider's view" if they wish. In every school, there are students who have pursued personal interests to such an extent that they qualify as amateur experts. A teacher will find it useful to make an inventory card for each student to get an idea of these resources. Such a card might look like this:

Name _____ Class _____ Period _____

Your Hobbies:

Travel Experiences (yours):

Travel Experiences (parents, other relatives):

Other things that are of special interest to you: (for example: church group)

Parents' Occupations:

Parents' Hobbies:

Whether the interest lies in a special phase of science, music, art, sports, or in some other area related to school, it can usually be woven into the pattern of the classroom. And students also participate in community activities—attending conferences, 4-H meetings, entering in rodeos or meeting public figures.

VISITORS AS RESOURCES

The use of visitors in the high school classroom is probably more common than any other method of utilizing community resources. Some community workers make numerous trips to schools as a regular part of their work. Police chiefs, probation officers, traffic court judges, fire chiefs, health officers, directors of recreation, all recognize the importance of informing young people about the kind of community service they perform. There is a certain glamour about seeing and hearing a police chief in person. The presence of the chief, who is both more formidable and more human than the students anticipate, helps the law become more than just "Thou shalt not . . ." An effective way of helping to dispel prejudice or misunderstanding, as well as opening students' eyes to a broader understanding of community makeup, is to invite individuals such as a Chinese dentist, a female judge, or a black legislator to speak.

In areas where relations between the community and the authorities are strained or misunderstood, the school has an obligation to bring students and authorities together so that they may understand and educate one another. As frequently as possible, school visitations by community figures should correspond with student visits to the physical environments in which these figures work. Seeing a police station, a jail, a courtroom, a hospital, a fire house, a library, or an employment office, contributes to a sense of the reality of institutions which are mysterious, threatening, or actually unknown to many students.

Often when resource persons from outside the school appear in the history, science, mathematics, or foreign language classroom, they are believed when the teacher may be doubted; they are able to inspire young people when the taken-for-granted teacher goes unheeded.

> Talking to my social studies class, I discovered that students generally refused to accept as fact much of the information they had uncovered about living conditions in areas of the Middle East. When their incredulity persisted, one student suggested that her mother, a former Iranian princess, might be willing to talk to the class. In two ensuing visits—she was that popular and successful—the students came to accept that not only what they had read was true, but indeed was frequently understated. In addition, however, the students discovered a whole new appreciation for the culture of the Middle East, from eating customs to the beauty of the Koran. So interested and delighted was the visitor by her contact with the students that she volunteered to return each year. Until she moved to another part of the country four years later, she was a stimulating and exciting guest for each succeeding group of students.

Individuals of the community often have special knowledge or special expertise, that the average teacher cannot hope to have. A veteran of Vietnam can make that part of history far more vivid than any text. Knowledge that such people live in their area may inspire young people to take more interest and pride in the community, give them goals for which to strive, show them in flesh and blood the complexity and fascination of the twentieth century.

However, resource visitors can sometimes be utter failures. Teachers may then become cynical about using resource visitors at all. Yet the fault as often as not lies with the teacher and students. Few visitors are in touch with groups of adolescents; they do not know much about them, their interests, ideas, or level of understanding. Teachers invite into their classrooms those people who are successful in their spheres, but this very success may place a barrier between them and high school students. Many experts cannot share their knowledge without using language that may be gibberish to secondary school students. Sometimes the teacher may have to interview such persons and transmit the special knowledge to students. Prior to inviting an expert, teachers and individuals or groups of students should make their acquaintance; if this is not feasible, at least the ability to interest students should be checked with other members of the faculty and with students.

When deciding whether to invite visitors, teachers and students might consider some of the following questions:

1. Are the potential visitors interested in adolescents or do they have negative attitudes toward young people? If they do not respect young people their attitudes will show and the information or skill they share will be tainted by them.
2. Do the potential visitors ordinarily speak in an overly academic fashion? A person who speaks in a complicated or abstruse way about specialized information will probably confuse or annoy the typical secondary school student.
3. Do the potential visitors ramble and stray from the subject? A raconteur may be suitable for a social event, but if specific content is to be covered, this kind of person is hopeless in the classroom.
4. Are the potential visitors basically entertainers—always ready with a joke? While they may amuse the class for an entire period, student knowledge will not be increased. Of course, it is not necessary to be serious all the time, but if the content is serious, it is out of place to have people who are merely entertainers.
5. Do the potential visitors express strong prejudices? It is fine for people to be convinced that their jobs or hobbies are the best, but sometimes visitors use an audience to express pet hates. If these are directed against any group represented in the class, it can be most unfortunate. Moreover, the classroom must not be used for propaganda unless both sides can be heard.
6. Will students confuse the potential visitors or offend them? It takes an abundance of poise sometimes to answer the naive, testing, or innocent questions of young people. Community members should not be exposed to such questions unless they can stand up to them with ease and humor. If they get incensed because students ask "dumb" questions, then they probably will not be good resource persons.

With these and other questions in mind, teachers and students can interview prospective resource visitors and be fairly sure of the degree of success they would have with a class.

GETTING READY

There are ways the teacher, and the class, can make sure that the visit of a guest speaker is pleasant and profitable for all concerned. Here are some suggestions:

Brief the visitor ahead of time. A list of student questions can be composed by a student committee and presented to the visitor. Probably the questions should be personally presented, since the visitor at that time can review the questions with the students and make sure that student interests are understood.

Prepare the introduction. When the student or teacher introduces the visitor to the class, it should be made clear that the visitor will speak for ten minutes, or whatever the time allotted, and then will answer questions. Stating the time period to the visitor with the class as audience is a kind of gentle blackmail. It takes a rugged individualist to overlook this kind of time limit. Often a visitor is more aware of a student chairperson than of another adult and is more likely to comply with requests.

Request permission to interrupt. Either the teacher or the student chairperson can ask the visitor, with the class as audience, if it is permissible to interrupt if something does not seem clear. This provides a needed wedge if the speaker rambles far off the topic, gets boring, or becomes too academic.

List questions on the board. The questions that have been given previously to the speaker may be written on the board and the speaker placed so that the list is observed by all. This keeps the speaker from spending too much time on one question.

Use a group interview. A group of students may be especially interested in the field the visitor is to discuss. Perhaps these students have some knowledge about it and are ready with intelligent, and significant, questions. Then the visitor and the interviewing group are placed in front of the room and encouraged to proceed as though no audience were present. This prevents the visitor from making speeches and ensures that student questions will be answered.

Prepare the class. In discussing the area on which the visitor is to speak to the class, the teacher or student committee may make a point of raising important issues. The class may then be divided into groups. (See Chapter 10 for directions in setting up groups.) Each group will write out questions and assign responsibility to students for asking the questions.

Contrary to common opinion, most adolescents are attentive and polite to visitors. Students will usually greet the break in classroom routine with interest, appreciation, and commendable behavior.

THE FIELD TRIP

Almost all teachers acknowledge the value of field trips, yet many students go through secondary school with no experience of this kind. The most significant deterrent is the organization of the typical secondary school day. When the student has only one fifty-minute period with a teacher, it will obviously cause a major disruption if the teacher wishes to undertake a field trip lasting for more than a single class period. It is also clear that few worthwhile field trips can be conducted in fifty minutes. Moreover, the teacher must face a different class each hour, and in good conscience cannot slough this responsibility off on another faculty member or assign students to the library.

Can these barriers be overcome? Approval of the school administration and cooperation by other faculty members are essential. If a field trip means encroaching on the class time of another teacher, then clearly no teacher is justified in asking for such a dispensation very often. If, however, a good reciprocal arrangement can be worked out ("If you will excuse my students for an industrial arts field trip, I'll be happy to excuse yours for the PTA concert rehearsals"), the field trip can be used more frequently.

Modular schedules, in which subjects and classes are not scheduled every day at the same hour, lend themselves particularly well to these arrangements. Such schedules are established to build in flexibility, to provide, for example, a whole day for one subject area; the class would not necessarily meet again during that week—or if it did reconvene it would be scheduled in order to accommodate the field trip.

Warning: be alert to the obstacles to field trips within your school. Frequently, there are a number of permission forms to be completed and filed in the proper offices. Understand from the beginning what is required —and fulfill those requirements. The field trip experience will make it worthwhile.

PLANNING THE TRIP

Although many schools have established rules for field trips, actual planning is sufficiently time-consuming that a teacher can rarely expect to make many during a semester. If, for example, a teacher has five classes, a mass of detail must be confronted for five different field trips or the logistics of a field trip involving two or more classes. The very thought of this kind of planning is enough to discourage most teachers. The planning problems may, however, be solved in a number of different ways. First, the preplanning may be done almost wholly by students.

A simple outline, planned by teacher and students, will suffice for a framework:

1. What is the purpose of the field trip?
2. Where can we go? What places will allow our class to visit?
3. How do we get there? What transportation is needed? Where can we get it? How much will it cost? Who will pay?
4. How long will it take?
5. Whose permission must we have? How do we obtain it? (Principal, parent, other authority).
6. Is there an admission charge (museum, concert, play, exhibit)?

7. Can students be excused from other classes?
8. What are we to look for?
9. How will students report on the trip?
10. What study is needed for the trip to make it more meaningful?
11. What follow-up activities will be appropriate?

"WHOSE JOB IS IT?"

The preceding list will set a framework within which to assign specific individual or committee responsibilities. After a few days of exploration, the committees may report back to the class. Then, after some consultation with the teacher, the trip is practically arranged. If the teacher has previously collected a few suggested community resources for possible field trips, students will be able to plan with a minimum of fumbling. Much of the student planning can be done after school, or perhaps during a judicious amount of released time from class. In arranging the field trip for the whole group, students save time from the teacher and, just as important, are given practice in assuming genuine responsibility.

Soliciting the assistance of parents, of retired citizens, or other interested community members in the supervising of field trips can produce highly favorable results. Not only are students frequently on their good behavior because of "outside" chaperones, but many times there is an unusual opportunity for cross-generational understanding and sharing.

Often overlooked are the possibilities for exciting "field trips" that may be no farther than the nearest empty lot, shopping center, traffic interchange, or wholesale truck depot. For instance, an empty lot can be used by both biology and geography teachers in the study of ecology. What plants grow there? What insects or other life appear in the morning hours? What appear in the afternoon hours? Students may even have an all night camp-out in a vacant lot (with prior permission, adequate chaperonage, and a discreet notification to the police, to observe the night life of the empty lot). How human activities affect other living things in this small sample of a city or any area would be interesting. Similarly, a shopping center studied at different times of the day, and different days of the year, can reveal many things about shopping habits, advertising methods (and their effectiveness), job opportunities, consumer attitudes, international trade, business finance, and business law.

An article in the newspaper about a reporter who sifted through the Kissingers' trash caused one of my classes to engage in one of the most profitable projects of the year. Following up on a student's joke about finding out about her neighbors, I focused the class' attention on how we could, indeed, find out a great deal about our neighbors and our own reliance on services and products, about consumption of luxuries versus essentials, about us of energy and about waste. They were fascinated but disbelieving. By the time we finished the project three weeks later everyone, me included, was amazed at the variety of information that had been learned. Isn't it funny how a kid's wisecrack sometimes pays off in a big way?

AFTER THE FIELD TRIP

Visiting the location of the field trip is not the end of the experience. It is important, later in class, to ask students to summarize their experiences, to indicate the highlights of what they have learned, and to consider follow-up experiences that will capitalize on the visit.

It will be beneficial to brainstorm (see Chapter 9) with others—either within or outside your subject area—unusual field studies that are possible in your community. After you do so, itemize the various content areas which are required to complete the field study.

THE TEXTBOOK AS RESOURCE

The extent to which teachers acknowledge what good teaching is and what they actually do in daily teaching can generally be gauged by the way in which a textbook is employed as a learning resource. Regardless of what they say about creative teaching, those who anchor students and themselves to a single textbook, and its slavish mastery, are not engaging in innovative teaching. Textbooks have special structures—framework, chapter organizations, questions, and suggested activities—which can seriously hinder a creative approach to the specific needs of a group. In addition, most textbooks also have annotated teachers' editions which explain exactly how to employ the textbook as a blueprint for the course. If they do not wish to, teachers need not think about what they are going to teach or how they will go about it.

Textbooks, because they are neat packages of information, also contain their own generalizations and conclusions. What is left, then, for students to do? In the process of digesting the content of the textbook and accepting and remembering the generalizations and conclusions, what happens to the process of critical thinking? Of discovery? Of creativity? Of values clarification?

A student newspaper poll reported that among the top five complaints against teachers in general is that of relying on textbooks as the basis of class work. Should textbooks be outlawed then? No, but the textbook should be used as only one aide to learning. It is only one resource in what should be an ever-growing storehouse of learning materials.

In an age of information explosion, textbooks have a way of becoming quickly outdated. To rely on one text is to diminish the scope and depth of the material offered to students. The best of textbooks—and there are many excellent ones—can provide only a broad, general approach to a subject area. Such broadness and generality lead almost always to a superficial presentation. This superficiality is frequently demonstrated in the bland approach that attempts to be objective and to satisfy a wide range of potential buyers. The result is that much material that would generate discussion and further investigation is eliminated. A preponderance of factual material also does little to encourage the clarification of values. Another problem is that students are also in danger of believing that once a textbook is mastered, the subject matter it deals with is also mastered. Finally, textbooks cannot accommodate the range of intellectual or experiential needs in any group.

Textbooks are helpful and meaningful when they are used as one of a variety of resources. Having several copies of many textbooks on hand will enable students to discover that there are many approaches to subject matter; that different organization and illustrative materials offer varying points of view not available when a single text is used.

KNOWING WHICH TEXTBOOKS ARE WORTHWHILE

Beginning teachers may not have a say in choosing textbooks for their classes. Nevertheless, they should know how to judge the strengths and weaknesses of the books selected for them. First of all, teachers should see how well the authors of the textbook seem to know the adolescent. Does the book relate the interests, needs, abilities, backgrounds, and experiences of adolescents to the content presented? Is the style brisk and alive rather than overdignified or stilted? Is the format attractive? Are the illustrations relevant? The teacher should also ask if there is adequate coverage of material and whether there are open-ended sections or suggested activities and questions that encourage discussion and problem solving. The teacher must always check for accuracy or distortion of information. A textbook designed for use in a state history course contains this observation:

> The slave's condition had its advantages. He usually worked the accepted work week of the colony—from sunrise to sundown daily except Sunday. But he enjoyed long holidays especially at Christmas. He did not work as hard as the average free laborer, since he did not have to worry about losing his job. In fact the slave enjoyed what might be called comprehensive social security. Generally speaking, his food was plentiful, his clothing adequate, his cabin warm, his health protected, his leisure carefree. He did not have to worry about hard times, unemployment, or old age.[1]

In another instance a biology textbook contains a chart of the development of man in an evolutionary progression which depicts an Anglo-Saxon

---

[1] Virginia Council of Human Relations, "What Pictures of America Does Your Child Receive from His High School Books?" Leaflet, no date.

male as the culmination of the process.[2] While other sources available to students may also contain incorrect or slanted material, the opportunity for students to accept faulty information as correct is greater when the only reference available is a single text out of which the class operates and which the teacher does not challenge.

Some evidence should be offered by the publishers that the development of concepts, attitudes, and skills in the text has been tested in the classroom. This evidence, presented to schools by publishers, should include analysis of the vocabulary burden; systematic provision for repetition of key data, summary, and review; and suggestions for a wide range of supplemental materials and activities.

Almost any departure from the deadly read-recite-quiz format for textbook study should be utilized. If certain pages are assigned for reading, groups of students can make up questions about the content on the basis of "What concepts or facts or information ought anyone to remember ten years from now?" These can form the basis for a classroom game, an oral quiz, or a short test. Different texts can be assigned to the class, all covering the same general content; and again in groups, students reading the different texts can compare how the same data is treated, try to figure out why the textbooks differ, and come up with a "new version" by rewriting the material assigned. This could lead students to nontext sources, too, to amplify or verify data. Students can be asked to look over the questions at the end of the chapter or assigned section and to select that question which seems to get the most significant item or idea conveyed. They need not necessarily answer the question, but each must defend question choice. In so doing, the student will have to do some evaluation of the other material and probably end up answering the question! If the text is outmoded, the teacher can put one sentence on the board and ask the students to consider it. For example, one textbook stated that "many large cities have streetcars."[3] The city the students lived in did not; what was wrong with the text? They proceeded to check the copyright date. From there they went to the problem of defining "many large cities." Then they went back to study the public transportation in their own city: Would the statement have applied to their city at the time the text was written, and if so, to what extent? Thus, even an inaccurate, misleading or wrong statement can be used. Textbook pictures are another source for elaboration. Questions raised could concur authenticity, relevance, and data provided by the picture not related to the text: All of these are possibilities. Students can evaluate whether the picture is worth the room it takes up in the text or whether another kind of illustration, or none, would be better.

[2] J. H. Otto, and A. Towle, *Modern Biology* (New York: Holt, Rinehart and Winston, 1965), p. 548.

[3] H. Millard Clements, William R. Fiedler, and B. Robert Tabachnick, *Social Studies: Inquiry in Elementary Classrooms* (Indianapolis: Bobbs-Merrill, 1966), p. 155.

Working with slower students in geography, Mr. Daniel asked them to study the pictures that illustrated a chapter on India. The students were asked to list those things about India which they had learned from the pictures. A sizable and interesting list was compiled. Next, the students were asked to list those things they thought they knew about India from all previous experiences. Again the list was lengthy, if somewhat farfetched. With a variety of materials—using many resources other than the textbook—the teacher led these slow readers into research that proved and disproved what students knew. The end result was a collectively written and illustrated "textbook" that was presented to the school library.

Paperback books are being increasingly employed in classrooms from elementary school onward. The list of subjects available in softcover edition is extensive; the books are attractive, inexpensive, and easy to handle. More important, they allow easy access to materials that can satisfy interest and supply resources in a host of areas.[4]

WHOSE MEDIA CENTER IS IT?

I didn't go to a library for four years after graduation from high school. I hated the sight of them. My worst experiences were in the high school library, but a few unpleasant ones happened at my local public library, too. In both places, the librarians acted as though every book in the place belonged to them personally and each librarian reigned over the premises as though they were tombs. Students were afraid to ask for help for fear of ridicule by the librarians who always seemed to be filing cards in a box or loudly shushing people who made little or no noise. It was an awful experience. Last year, at last, I got up my courage to use the public library again. I finally asked myself, "Whose library is it, anyway?"

Just as bubonic plague is a thing of the past, it is to be hoped that the kind of stereotyped media specialist who hordes books and maintains martial order is also obsolete. For if media centers are not clearly inviting and pleasant places, they are surely going to provoke apathy and rejection in school as well as out. It is not sufficient that materials exist; they must be easily accessible—indeed enticing. Increasingly, media centers are comfortable, attractive workshops and fortunately the services available to students are increasing as the idea grows that books, magazines, and non-print resources provide pleasure as well as impart information.

But it is part of a teacher's task—in every subject area—to see that students discover how to make the most of media center resources.

Mr. Soure, the physical education teacher, refused to participate in reading week, a schoolwide project in which thirty minutes in the morning and

[4] John Egerton, "Paperbacks Are Better Than Pool," *Southern Education Report*, 3:9 (May 1968), pp. 21–26.

thirty minutes in the afternoon were set aside so that everyone—school workers as well—could read anything they wanted. He laughed at the suggestion that his students might want to spend an hour in the media center browsing among sports-related books and periodicals. "Reading doesn't have anything to do with physical education," he said. So everybody else in the school read—and overwhelmingly most of them enjoyed themselves—while Mr. Soure's students went about their regular exercises.

Subject area teachers share the responsibility of seeing that students also become familiar with public library facilities. A field trip may be in order if only a few students have been there previously. A conducted tour, meeting a librarian, and perhaps obtaining library cards can do much to help students become pleasantly familiar with one of their most valuable lifetime community resources.

THE CHALKBOARD HASN'T DISAPPEARED YET

Whether it's black, brown, or green the chalkboard is a vital resource for both teacher and student. A kind of public scratch pad, it allows clarifications and illustrations to be more immediate and relevant than other resources permit. The chalkboard is probably still the most effective device for aiding students to focus attention and to understand quickly.

The chalkboard also allows for economic use of class time. Assignments, announcements, reminders, spellings for new and difficult terms, and drill exercises can all be placed on the chalkboard before class, and can be utilized immediately or covered by a map or taped construction paper until needed. Colored chalk is effective for indicating structure and order, as well as for indicating emphasis. Graphs, diagrams, and other pictorial designs are also enhanced by the use of colored chalk.

In classrooms with limited chalkboard space, many teachers employ construction or wrapping paper and crayon or felt-tip pen to list assignments, announcements, or reminders. If prospective teachers have not had wide experience in writing on chalkboards, they should seize the opportunity to do so before assuming a teaching assignment. Legible chalkboard penmanship that is large enough to be read easily from the back of the room is essential.

BULLETIN BOARDS: WHEN, WHY, FOR WHOM?

Just as all other resources available to teachers and students are educational in purpose, so are bulletin boards. While they should be decorative to the classroom setting, their function is to aid teaching and to reveal learning.

How often changes are made in bulletin board displays must be determined by the activities of the classroom since, in all but a few cases, they will reflect the study of the class. After several weeks a display becomes boring and the paper materials become faded and dog-eared. A long outdated bulletin board also may suggest to the casual visitor (or confirm to the frequent one) that the teacher's attitude is either static in content or approach or that the teacher is limited in awareness of how to use resource materials and lacking in sensitivity to other people.

In addition to their function of presenting information or revealing learning, bulletin boards are important because they allow students the opportunity to exercise a variety of creative skills in a meaningful, direct way. Selecting the purpose and theme of a bulletin board, identifying the means of presentation, and executing the presentation—both in personnel and materials—all allow young people opportunities in responsibility and group dynamics, as well as in critical and creative thinking, that are both honest and real.

If bulletin boards are educational, are they intended to educate anyone besides students? Yes and no. Their basic operating goal is always directed toward the students of a class. If they achieve this goal, they will be by their nature instructive or informative to others who may see them. Classroom bulletin boards do not exist to convince parents or other school personnel that "something is going on in here."

With rare exceptions, bulletin boards should be the work of students. The first display of the year will probably have to be the teacher's, although as time passes, student materials from former years can be used.

Many students throw away their work when it is returned ("What am I gonna do with it?" or "My mother will just throw it away anyhow"). Instead of losing quality work, it can be used as part of a "Students' Gallery of Accomplishments," a bulletin board device that rewards effort and, at the same time, indicates to students the importance of pride in one's work.

Some guidelines in the creation of bulletin boards should be discussed with students. Principles of presentation and arrangement that might be agreed upon include:

1. Use color wisely. It is effective in attracting attention, showing boundaries, indicating classification, providing contrast for lettering and other displayed items. Be sure to use harmonizing colors. Red, orange, and yellow attract attention; blue, green, and purple attract less attention. Generally, background colors should be less brilliant than the subject displayed.
2. Consider the eye level of the reader. If there is material to be read, be sure that those who are expected to read it can see the print without difficulty.
3. State the theme through the title. The message of the display should be evident through the title as well as through what is displayed.
4. Use legible lettering that is consistent with the theme. Ornamental or gim-

micky lettering should be avoided. Use a single color for titles and lettering. Remember that horizontal lettering is more effective than vertical lettering.

Popular advertising techniques that are frequently intended to shock or puzzle viewers are generally not useful for classroom bulletin boards. In order to serve their purpose, bulletin boards must be clear and direct. Class time should be provided for students to examine and read bulletin boards. Imaginative teachers find ways to incorporate bulletin boards in lessons (motivation, drill, review, discussion), thereby making them everyday teaching tools.

TELEVISION, MOTION PICTURES, AND VIDEOTAPES

Motion pictures, television programs, and videotapes are similar in the kinds of learning experiences they can provide. All have the unique ability of showing the world in action through sight, sound, and color. It is possible to watch the drama of human relationships, real and imaginary, or to transport the viewer to places and events distant in time or space. Microscopic life can be made to fill the screen. The explosion of a bomb, which in reality takes a fraction of a second to occur, can be studied for minutes through slow-motion photography. Conversely, the unfolding of a flower, which in reality takes hours, can be seen in a few moments through time-lapse photography. The complicated workings of a giant machine can be simplified as the camera focuses on one relevant operation at a time. Through animation, the operation can even be viewed from within, as in the case of the cylinders of an internal-combustion engine.

The first criterion for selecting motion pictures, television programs, and videotapes is that they should exploit these unique advantages. An instructional motion picture or television program should not be merely a photographed lecture or a series of still pictures or an entertaining travelogue. Keep in mind that impact will be weakened if the experience is burdened with commentary about action that is never seen on the screen. Some of the most exciting recent educational (and commercial) films are documentaries, with an explanatory narration, or completely without words.

Just as motion pictures, television programs, and videotapes have unique advantages, they also have special disadvantages. Both present the material for learning at a fixed pace. The student is therefore forced to move along at the speed determined by the producer of the material. This disadvantage can be overcome to some extent with motion pictures and videotapes since scenes within them can be reshown. But to promote the most efficient learning, both motion pictures and television programs should take account of the psychological principle of pacing. In simplest terms, this means that material of intellectual complexity or emotional intensity must be presented in deliberately planned intervals that permit the viewer to mull over what has been seen, heard, and felt. If enough time is allowed, the learner is then ready to accept another difficult or tense sequence. But if the learner is hit hard again and again without time to recover, preoccupation with the first blow may shut off further receptivity, and learning is interrupted. In a film demonstrating the graphing of algebraic functions, for example, students would soon "tune out" if they were to be shown all the processes of computing a table of values, placing points on a graph, sketching the curve, and identifying geometric shapes, without time to reflect, question, and practice each of the steps involved. Here is an instance where eight-millimeter film (discussed later in this chapter) could be put to excellent use. In a series of "single-concept" installments of four or five minutes, shown on an inexpensive projector with instant installation cartridges and continual replay as needed, students can see and perfect the steps separately, repeating those with which they have difficulty.[5]

The problem of paced selection is particularly acute in the motion picture and the television program because these are expensive media. Producers have a tendency to overload the typical twenty-minute motion picture or the half-hour television program with learning material just because it costs so much to provide those few minutes. The idea seems to be to appeal to the greatest number of teachers. If enough concepts or skills, attitudes, or appreciations are packed in, the argument runs, many people will find something they teach. With regard to learning, this is, of course, an utterly false kind of economy. Films and programs in which so much material is concentrated are meaningless to most students.[6]

Also important in the selection of motion pictures and television programs is the existence of a good teaching pattern. For example, the film or program should employ sound means of motivating the student. This may mean that unfamiliar material has been set in familiar surroundings to facilitate engaging students in the problem. Or it may mean that actors the same age as the students have been used. To sustain interest, the film or program should challenge the students to work along, at least mentally, as the action unfolds. Corollary problems not covered in the film or program may be directly suggested by the actors or commentator. In the closing sequences, the film or program may have the actors or commentator speak directly to the students about their responsibility for further exploration of the problem, or leave the issue unresolved and open, thereby inviting class discussion and further study.

[5] Louis Forsdale (Ed.), *8MM Sound Film and Education* (New York: Teachers College, 1962), p. 16.
[6] Mark A. May, "Word-Picture Relationships in Audiovisual Presentations: The Acquisition of Skills, Concepts, and Understandings in *Instruction Process and Media Innovation*, Robert A. Wiesgerber (Ed.) (Skokie, Ill.: Rand McNally, 1968).

TELEVISION: SOME SPECIAL CONSIDERATIONS

Increasing developments in national and local educational television should make better use of television possible both in and out of the classroom. Where television is available in the school, there are many opportunities for class viewing which allow immediate follow up. Programs scheduled on commercial television are sometimes useful during school time, too. At present, most such programs are probably of greatest assistance in science, social studies, English, dance, drama, and music classes. The innovative teacher, though, may find relevant material in programs that do not immediately suggest relationship to the subject.

Assignment of any outside experience with nonprint media must be handled thoughtfully. Not all students have access to these resources. Since it would be unfair to embarrass or penalize them for this inaccessibility, an alternate choice should be open to them. No outside assignment in any nonprint media should be accorded any less preparation or follow up than is given to printed materials. Indeed, since time will intervene between preparation, viewing, and follow up, the teacher must provide safeguards of simplicity and restatement which will enable students to make the most of their exposure. Providing students with take-home guide questions or an imaginative "reporting sheet" that requires them to list major points or observations will help them to focus more clearly on the program at home. An opportunity to "recap" the experience, questioning for clarity, will enable students to comment more intelligently and to discuss in depth the larger issues of the presentation. An opportunity for critical insight can be developed by asking students to pretend they are critics for a particular magazine. For instance, students could be "reviewers" of a television program or a film for *Parents Magazine, Teen Scene, TV Guide, Better Homes and Gardens, The New Yorker,* or *Rolling Stone.*

In viewing nonprint media, students need training in skills that allow them to understand both the special nature of a medium and what it permits and restricts.[7] The eye of the camera and the ear of the microphone are not all-encompassing any more than are the eyes of human beings. Indeed, because they may be especially restrictive in order to convey their particular thesis, they may observe less than a person would in a real situation. This may be demonstrated to students by showing them a large photograph on which all but one section (or detail) is covered. Attention and discussion around the question, "What is this picture about?" should follow. Then a larger area of the picture, incorporating other details, should be revealed and discussed, and so on. This experience can be related to what happens

---

[7] Edgar Dale, *Audiovisual Methods in Teaching,* 3d ed. (New York: Holt, Rinehart and Winston, 1969).

when people are exposed to an experience containing so many elements that they are unable to concentrate on the details of only one.[8] Students need to know the special focusing attributes that the camera and the microphone possess. Their ability to magnify, to explore from extraordinary angles, and to distort can all be dynamic and exciting ways of experiencing that stretch far beyond individual human possibilities. Students can be helped to see the agility of the camera's eye through a bulletin board display that utilizes photographs whose effects are created through the techniques mentioned above. In what ways can such a display be prepared to correlate with science, music, art, English, history, industrial arts, distributive education, home economics, and physical education? Videotaping, which allows recording and instant replay, suggests possibilities that are limited only by the imagination of teachers and students. A large number of learning experiences can be enhanced through the videotaping of student performance, followed by a developmental critique and reapplication of student effort. On-the-spot filming out of the classroom, whether in the school building or away from it, can allow students to collect information in a unique manner that permits analysis, in some instances, of incidents and comments that would otherwise be elusive. As with the use of all resources, teachers should know the restrictions of the latest copyright laws.

MOTION PICTURES: SOME SPECIAL CONSIDERATIONS

What has been said about the use of television for educational purposes is generally true about the use of motion pictures. Films that have been created for use on a theater screen, however, raise special considerations. The picture quality of theatre films is inevitably larger and clearer than that of television. Color is truer, as are the contrasts possible in blacks and whites. Subtle as these effects may be, they contribute to one's reaction to the two media. The fact that images are larger than life, and that they are clearer than television images, gives them greater dramatic force. The fact that most students take television for granted may also add to the impact of seeing a film projected on a screen rather than emanating from the familiar "box."

In addition to educational films mentioned earlier, teachers should familiarize themselves with the numerous commercial films available. All

[8] The relatively new term "visual literacy" has been coined to describe, among other things, the ability to decode pictures. The exercise described here is one among thousands that help to develop visual literacy in students. For further information, write to the Conference on Visual Literacy, Gallaudet College, Washington, D.C. 20002. Also contact Educational Markets Services, Eastman Kodak Company, Rochester, New York 14650. Have yourself placed on the mailing list of Documentary Photo Aids, P.O. Box 956, Mount Dora, Florida 32757. Also write to National Instructional Television Center Headquarters, Box A, Bloomington, Indiana 47401. See Bernard C. Hollister, "Using Picture Books in the Classroom," *Media and Methods*, 13:5 (January 1977), pp. 22–25.

teachers will find films that deal with subject-matter concepts and illustrations as well as with discipline-related values. Some films worth consideration are "The Bridge," "Abandon Ship," "The Lion in Winter," "Little Big Man," "The Grapes of Wrath," and "Sounder" in social studies classes; "Fear Strikes Out," "Bang the Drum Slowly," and "Brian's Song" in physical education classes; "Oedipus the King," "Romeo and Juliet," and "Lord of the Flies" in English classes. Other choices might include "Citizen Kane" (psychology), "Metropolis" (sociology), "The Turning Point" (dance), "The Friendly Persuasion" (home economics), "2001: A Space Odyssey" (science), and a wide array of classic as well as popular genre films (film study or popular culture).

An interesting use of film might be made in a humanities class by utilizing the full-length film of Cyrano de Bergerac and then the 20-minute film of the ballet Cyrano de Bergerac. If the viewing of the films were to come after the reading of Rostand's play, which could include a study of the historical setting and an investigation into the life of the real Cyrano, along with the study of the role of dance, music, drama, art and French culture and history, then tremendous insights could be gained. Not only would students have the opportunity to examine the films for their own merits, but they also would be able to make comparisons and contrasts and be able to synthesize isolated learnings. An advanced French class could go further and compare the French and English translations.

Catalogues of commercial films which may be rented for classroom use are available in public libraries or from film distribution companies and also from film depositories at universities.

Perfection of eight-millimeter sound-track film and equipment, and experiments, still in progress, suggest a variety of ways in which this inexpensive resource may be used. In classroom situations where students can learn skills through simple example or explanation, the use of eight-millimeter film allows individualized instruction in the same way that equipment in an electronic language laboratory allows students to progress at their own speeds and in many areas. The fact that film and equipment of this kind are compact and less expensive makes their use feasible at two important levels.

Homemade movies, usually eight-millimeter film, are also of practical advantage as a classroom resource. With a sound track, eight-millimeter film can perform in the same way as videotape except that the film must be processed and an eight-millimeter projector must be used. The time delay for film processing may be an important factor in deciding whether or not to use this resource. On the other hand, the relative costs and accessibility (when compared with videotaping) may outweigh the inconvenience of the time lapse.[9]

[9] For a broad view of eight-millimeter films for your school, use Forsdale (footnote 5).

One creative teacher arranged for his students to make their own three-minute films developing an aspect of English study. Each student wrote his or her own script, oragnized its production, and filmed the color–sound movies himself. In addition to knowledge gained about film and movies, his students ". . . had enlisted the help of parents and friends, had creatively used and learned about their community."[10]

Related indirectly to television and motion pictures is the use of still pictures: photographs, drawings and one-dimension illustrations of all kinds. Next to the chalkboard, pictures are probably the teacher's most immediate way of supplying needed images. A comprehensive file of pictures (as well as other "realia") is a must in the classroom. The availability of such material in magazines and newspapers, as well as through educational supply companies, is inexhaustible. Student- or teacher-made photographs are superb documentation of a field trip.

AUDIO AND VIDEOTAPES AND RADIO

Realizing that emphasis is only on sound, the same application to the classroom can be made of radio, tape recordings, and records as with films, television, and videotapes. The purpose in all cases is to enrich classroom activity with the sight and sound of reality. Because they deal only with sound, radio tape recordings, and records are generally more limited in their application. They demand greater skill on the part of young people who have grown up in a world of noise. To use these one-sense resources effectively, students must be able to distinguish between "hearing" and "listening," and must perfect the latter (see Chapter 5).

As with television programs viewed during the school day, radio broadcasts may be used in the classroom or tape recorded (as with out-of-school programs) for later use. Records are invaluable in many areas because they are permanent, of high quality, and inexpensive. While all of these audio resources are valuable in the learning process, the same care and consideration must be given to their selection and use as with any other classroom resource.

Tape recorders and tapes are now widely accessible to classroom teachers. The potential of the tape recorder is great since it can be easily and unobtrusively employed. It can serve as a substitute for the teacher in drill, review, or quiz situations, and act as a verbatim secretary for presentations, meetings, or oral testing.

When the tape recorder is used as a substitute for the teacher, it allows individual and structured attention to those who need it, while

---

[10] Frank McLaughlin, "Teacher of the Year," *Educators Guide to Media and Methods* (January 1969), p. 47.

freeing the teacher to work with other students in less mechanical activities. Of course, it also saves the teacher the time and monotony of repetition. In situations where individuals have been absent during important presentations, discussions, or lectures, the tape recorder allows opportunity for experiencing the activity and the resultant questions and comments that were elicited. The significance of classroom give-and-take—frequently of tremendous importance—has been preserved.

Recorded presentations that are especially effective can be filed for reuse later in the year or in other classes.

Desired change in students' speaking habits, as well as in organization of thinking, can best be effected by students listening to themselves. "Is that me?" is the usual response, followed by a grimace and smile. "Boy, do I stink!" is frequently the next statement, which allows discussion and goal setting based on self-motivation.

English, speech, drama, or music teachers who are working in a concentrated way on speech or vocal quality will find tape recordings invaluable for accumulating evidence of improvement throughout the year.

In all classes, teachers may find ways of having students demonstrate learning by recording their responses or by showing mastery of pronunciation, reading, or musical skills, or in answering individualized questions intended to allow them to show their ability to think and respond on their feet.

In the use of audio resources, attention is engaged longer and the effect strengthened if the listening material has an easily recognizable structure. Outlines for understanding and appreciation should be joined in a coherent organization. Students should be told early and explicitly what the point of the program is and should be reminded of it as the program develops. They should be assisted in making a summation when the program ends. In dramatization, for example, the number of scenes and characters in each program should be sharply limited unless the group has had a great deal of training in listening. Each scene and each character should be carefully introduced because, if the student fails to make the essential identifications, the interest plummets. Sudden shifts in time and place should be held to a minimum for similar reasons. At the end, brief comments or suggestive questions by the announcer concerning what happened in the drama make learning more efficient.

When the class is expected to retain much detail, a program or recording should be chosen which provides repetition of detail in a variety of ways. For example, if the radio program hopes to establish several qualities in the character of President Kennedy, each of these qualities may have to be given in two or three revealing episodes.

The last criterion is obvious, yet crucial to the success of these media: The narrators, speakers, or participants in drama must employ good diction and clear enunciation. The presentation is to the ear alone, and if the ear cannot clearly distinguish the words, no learning can take place.

CHOOSING FILMSTRIPS, SLIDES, AND TRANSPARENCIES

Filmstrips, slides, and transparencies for overhead projectors are similar to radio programs and audio recordings in that they appeal to one sense only, but they are different in that they permit study and discussion at any point and for as long as the class or an individual wishes. Therefore, filmstrips, slides, and transparencies should be chosen for their adequacy in stimulating study and discussion.

To accomplish this kind of stimulation, the amount of detail and the number of captions or labels in any one of these illustrations should be limited. For example, so many parts of a flower may be labeled that the student either becomes confused or never focuses attention at all. The appeal of a series of slides or pictures in a film strip can be strengthened by close-up, medium, and long photographic shots. The possibilities of diagrams, cut-a-ways, exploded views, graphs, and cartoons should not be overlooked.

Whenever possible, the use of mechanical equipment for all classroom resources should be entrusted to students. Responsibility, pride, and greater interest in the learning activities themselves will result.

SELECTING NEWSPAPERS AND PERIODICALS

Two kinds of newspapers and periodicals are available for classroom use—those especially prepared for instructional purposes and those published for the general adult market.

Probably the most important consideration with respect to the newspaper or periodical designed for classroom use is the quality of its interpretation and its selection of news stories, articles, and library materials. These newspapers and periodicals do not pretend to be abreast of each day's events. When they reach the classroom, the news is somewhat dated. Students will be familiar with a good many of the facts from reading adult newspapers, listening to the radio, viewing television, and hearing their parents', and others' conversations. A simple record of the news, then, is not enough. Students need interpretive comment to stimulate thinking about the significance of the facts; the quality of this comment should be the first criterion of selection. Naturally, it is important that the interpretive comment be nonpartisan and that opposing points of view be fairly stated.

Next in importance is the vocabulary of the material. A number of guides to readability, prepared by reading experts, are available (see Chapter 5). A teacher will do well to make use of these in order to avoid an unrealistic vocabulary burden.

Some attention should be given also to the makeup of a newspaper or periodical designed for classroom use. It ought to invite attention through good design, avoiding the arrangement of articles like tombstones in a solemn row. Pictures, cartoons, maps, and graphs should be liberally used.

Finally, newspapers and periodicals can be chosen for the quality of the teaching guide offered. This supplemental sheet, published for the teacher, should emphasize how students can be guided to read with increasing discrimination in the particular subject area.

Selection of adult newspapers and periodicals for the classroom is a more difficult problem. The number of publications available is overwhelming and they manage to violate most of the precepts listed above. Adult newspapers and periodicals are rarely nonpartisan, their vocabulary is not geared to the classroom, and their makeup ranges from the sensational to the ultraconservative.

Still, these are the materials on which students will depend to an important extent when they are adults. It would be foolish to exclude these resources from the classroom since they offer an excellent opportunity for critical examination and for development of more mature tastes. What is important is to offer a comprehensive sampling from these materials. In many communities, only one newspaper is published. Students should become acquainted with other newspapers, differing in quality and approach, in order to be able to view their own community newspaper in proper perspective. In many homes, the only periodicals read are chosen from the five or six national leaders in circulation; in still other homes, no periodicals of any kind are read. Students therefore must be given the opportunity to examine and compare, in the objective atmosphere of the classroom, not only the popular favorites but also some of the lesser known magazines.

It is probable that racial tension will not decrease for some years to come unless educators are sensitive and adroit in helping students understand the complex issues involved. Most students, both black and white, are unaware of the black press. Most large cities have a weekly or bi-weekly newspaper particularly aimed at the black population. These should be available in the city schools for classroom study, and in suburban and rural communities also. In areas not served by such metropolitan papers, deliberate efforts should be made to select several of the best and include them as routinely as one uses the local newspaper, or the *New York Times,* the *Washington Post,* or the *Christian Science Monitor.*

In the magazine field, *Ebony* is a good source for pictures and articles; *Time* and *Newsweek* are good once-a-week summaries of news reporting.

Many metropolitan centers also have other papers addressed to particular ethnic or special interest groups: *Variety,* for the stage-struck, *Women's Wear Daily* for the fashion-minded; the *Wall Street Journal* for the economics student and future businessperson. Labor unions have both local and national newspapers and journals. There are Spanish-language newspapers and magazines in many areas with large numbers of Spanish-speaking people.

"IT'S FREE!"

Millions of dollars are spent by commercial firms and public and private agencies on materials to influence public opinion. A large portion of these materials is aimed at the classroom. But whether or not especially tailored for the schools, the materials may constitute a valuable resource. Certainly they should not be used without carefully educating students to discern bias and slanting of information. Directed experience in the classroom can help adolescents to develop discrimination that will continue to be valuable. As in the case of adult newspapers and periodicals, students will be assailed by special interest materials all their lives. In choosing free materials for classroom use, teachers should consider such questions as these:

- Is the material genuinely related to curricular objectives?
- Is it in good taste?
- If it is an advertising piece does it keep advertising to an absolute minimum?

MAKING RESOURCES

As sophisticated machinery allows the making of transparencies for overhead projectors, film-making, photocopying, and the reproduction of pictorial, as well as printed, copy to become cheaper and thus more accessible to classroom teachers, it will become necessary for teachers to understand the potential of such material for the classroom and also to know how to develop these materials.

Increasing numbers of media centers are securing such equipment. Almost all school systems have a center where various kinds of machinery are available for classroom use. Even if the media specialist or some other staff member is not trained in how to develop these materials, manufacturers' representatives are often available and eager to visit schools to conduct training sessions for staff members.

Once more, teachers must be cautioned about the possibility of infringing on copyright laws. Frequently material that teachers wish to duplicate is readily available in some form from publishers or permission to reproduce can be easily obtained. Some manufacturers of copying machines publish weekly periodicals containing materials in many subject areas. These periodicals are especially prepared to ensure clear printing and are designed to enhance classroom use.

SUMMARY

To work effectively with contemporary secondary school students, it is imperative that teachers use a wide variety of resources so that the greatest number of students can learn in ways that are appropriate to their abilities, interests, and goals. The range of resources begins with people and extends to a wide assortment of audiovisual devices. Whatever resources are employed in the classroom, they work best when they stem out of students' interests and needs and when they add dimension to the learning process.

SELECTED READINGS

Audiovisual Instruction. Published by Association for Educational Communications and Technology, 1126 Sixteenth Street, N.W., Washington, D.C. 20036.

Beach, Don M., *Reaching Teenagers: Learning Centers for the Secondary Classroom.* Santa Monica, Calif.: Goodyear Publishing Company, 1977. Useful "cookbook" for designing learning centers. Ideas offered in five subject areas of junior and senior high schools.

"Bulletin Boards and Display," two filmstrips subtitled "Planning the Bulletin Board" and "Bulletin Board in Action." Bailey Films, Inc., 1966. Reino Randall, producer. Address: Bailey Films, Inc., 6509 DeLongpre Avenue, Hollywood, California 90028. Excellent principles of design for maximum effectiveness of bulletin boards. Helpful sections include illustrations of related color and shape concepts.

Dover Publications, Inc., 180 Varick Street, New York, New York 10014. Have yourself placed on the mailing list for announcement of inexpensive reprints of fascinating books which can be used to enhance study in numerous areas.

Gordon, Arthur, "Throw Out the Textbooks," *American Education,* 8 (September 1967), pp. 5–7.

Grambs, Jean Dresden, *Intergroup Education: Methods and Materials.* Englewood Cliffs, N.J.: Prentice-Hall, 1968, Part II "Films." Provides a discussion of the use of open-ended films and a recommended list.

Grambs, Jean, and John C. Carr (Eds.), *Black Image: Education Copes with Color.* Dubuque, Iowa: W. C. Brown, 1972. Nine articles which explore racial distortions in social studies and English textbooks. The first chapter "Storytellers and Gatekeepers" serves as an excellent introduction to the problem of hidden censorship in all textbooks.

Horkheimer, Mary Foley (Ed.), *Educators' Guide to Free Films.* Randolph, Wisc.: Educators' Progress Service, annual editions. *Educators' Guide to Free Filmstrips.* Randolph, Wisc.: Educator's Progress Service, annual editions.

Marcus, Lloyd, *The Treatment of Minorities in Secondary School Textbooks.* New York: Anti-Defamation League of B'nai Brith, 1961.

Media and Methods Magazine, P.O. Box 13894, Philadelphia, Pa. 19101. Published nine times a year (subscription: $9.00), this attractive and readable resource focuses on nonprint and alternative print materials for secondary school use.

Yellow Pages of Learning Resources. Cambridge, Mass.: The MIT Press, 1972. From "Accountant" to "Zoo," a collection of community resources and activities for students with the opportunity to study outside the school building.

part IV

METHODOLOGY:
teaching
and
learning

METHODOLOGY is what the professional teacher utilizes to maximize student learning. Gaining skill in a variety of teaching methods is a fundamental part of the education of teachers. Research into the conditions of learning has provided clues about what kinds of classroom experiences will most likely engage most students in active learning. Such activities as brainstorming, discussion, role playing simulations and gaming, and drill and review are techniques of teaching which observation as well as research have shown to be effective in improving student achievement along the whole range of student abilities and talents. In addition, skill in the processes of creativity, inquiry-discovery, and values clarification permit students to work at the higher levels of intellectual functioning.

FOCUS ON CHAPTER 9

Intellectual functioning ranges from the simple to the complex. Unfortunately, many students are not challenged to the more complex aspects of thinking as often as they should be. Using the work of psychologist J. P. Guilford, a hierarchy of intellectual functioning may be examined. In order to work at the higher levels of thought, students need skill in the ability to think divergently. Processes which utilize that skill and which encourage —and challenge—students to greater intellectual mastery are creativity, inquiry-discovery, and values clarification.

Significant ideas presented in this chapter include:
- While both convergent and divergent thinking are necessary for intellectual development, skill in divergent thinking is prerequisite to complex problem solving.
- An effective technique for helping students to think divergently is brainstorming. It is easily learned and can be used in every subject area.
- In order to function at higher levels of thought students must encounter on a regular basis questions which range across seven areas of difficulty.
- Specific activities can be used in all subject areas to assist students develop their creative abilities.
- The process of inquiry-discovery requires students to be active participants in the act of learning.
- Values clarification is a process which allows people to determine the significance of their knowledge, feelings, and behaviors.

chapter 9

Three Processes for Learning: creativity, inquiry-discovery, values clarification

It is better to ask some of the questions than to know all the answers.—*James Thurber*.

The psychological fact that every learner is unique has been expounded so many times that the significance of the statement is lost in the repetition. Periodically, it is wise to ponder the fact and to consider its implications for the day-to-day work of the classroom. If a class is composed of thirty students then thirty different ways of responding to the environment and knowledge are present. While many of these ways will overlap, ultimately, each of them is different. Intelligence, emotion, experience, talent, goals, all present in each student, have been individually patterned to create truly individual ways of learning.

Teachers faced with the uniqueness of all learners are confronted with the problem of how to help each one develop his or her abilities at the highest possible intellectual level. In order to do that, a teacher must be proficient in directing learning in many ways. Individualized work permits many opportunities for students to learn in ways best suited to them, but most work in most classrooms is conducted in groups or with the whole class. In these instances, how does the teacher promote high level thought and activity which allows everyone to stretch and grow? In general, this is accomplished when teachers find methods and techniques that require attention to all levels of intellectual functioning. The greater the accommodation to the varied learning styles present in the class and the more inclusive of intellectual challenge, the greater the possibility of helping each student to learn.

Psychologist J. P. Guilford's work in describing the "structure of the intellect" classifies the primary mental abilities as cognition, memory, divergent production, convergent production, and evaluation.[1] An aware-ness of these classifications can be helpful in making decisions which pro-vide for the uniqueness of students and at the same time cause them to work at all levels of intellectual endeavor.

1. *Cognitive* abilities are those that allow discovery, recognition, and compre-hension of information.
2. *Memory* abilities are those that permit the storage and retention of infor-mation.
3. *Convergent Production* is the generation of specific (right answer) informa-tion from other information.
4. *Divergent Production* is the generation of varied ideas based on given (or known) information.
5. *Evaluation* abilities are those employed when a decision must be made about accuracy, appropriateness, or suitability of information.

Experience shows that all these categories are important in learning. Unfortunately experience also shows that the prevailing mode of operation in too many classrooms is that which directs students to the lower levels of thinking—cognition, memory, and convergent production. While it is relatively easy to create circumstances in which students are required to work at those levels (for example, "read the chapter and answer the questions"), it is not so easy to create circumstances in which students are required to explore the higher levels—divergent production and evaluation. This chapter is concerned with three processes for learning that can stimulate the learner's intellectual functioning at those higher levels. The three processes are creativity, inquiry–discovery, and values clarification.

The format of the chapter includes five principal parts: brainstorming, questioning, creativity, inquiry–discovery, and values clarification. The discussion of the three processes for learning is preceded by sections on brainstorming and questioning, since skills in those areas provide students with essential tools for working within the processes.

An ideal strategy for helping students understand the importance of divergent thinking and for helping them to generate divergent thought is brainstorming. In its most complete form, brainstorming also includes evaluation; through this simple strategy, then, students can experience both forms of the higher categories of thinking.

Brainstorming in some form is fundamental to the development of skills in creativity, inquiry-discovery, and values clarification, since each of those processes rests upon the generation of alternative thought and behavior.

---

[1] A good summary of Guilford's ideas can be found in Robert Wilson, "The Struc-ture of the Intellect," reprinted in Mary Janes Aschner and Charles E. Bish, *Pro-ductive Thinking in Education* (Washington, D.C.: National Education Association, 1965), pp. 21–32. See also J. P. Guilford, "The Structure of the Intellect," *Psycho-logical Bulletin*, 53 (July 1956), pp. 267–293.

BRAINSTORMING

One of the advantages of brainstorming is that it is an enjoyable exercise in which there are no right or wrong answers.[2] All students can have the opportunity to participate without fear of error; the easy-going nature of the exercise allows for spontaneity and sense of humor, as well as the sharing of intellectual endeavor.

In a brainstorming session, the members of the class: (a) are confronted with a question or problem; (b) generate possible answers to the question or solutions to the problem (hypothesis-making); and (c) evaluate the possible answers or solutions.

When brainstorming is used as an introductory activity for helping students develop skill in divergent thinking, it is not necessary to go beyond the first two steps. As they express interest and develop competence in the process, they can progress to the third one.

Mr. Krikstan had put the desks aside before students arrived for fifth period. The chairs were arranged in a circle so that each person could see the other's face; Mr. Krikstan's chair, which was also in the circle, had a cassette tape recorder under it, ready to record the session that followed. As students came into the room they sensed that something special was going to happen; the noise level was higher than usual and it took Mr. Krikstan a few minutes to settle the class (Donna and Joanne were giggling, Roland was "on stage," Tammy looked lost without her desk). When he had everyone's attention he said, "Yesterday when we were trying to understand why people who live in recurring flood areas return to their homes year after year, I realized that we haven't given enough attention to thinking about all the possible answers that might exist for a question. Oh yes, Twanna is always thinking of lots of reasons why we shouldn't do something (everybody, including Twanna smiled—it was one of the class's private, friendly jokes), but we haven't taken the time to help ourselves consider alternative answers to questions and alternative solutions to problems. Well, I have an activity that I think will help us to do these things. I'm going to put a question on the board and we're going to see how many possible answers we can think of to the question. Yes, I'm going to participate, too. There are a couple of rules, though. Number one: Once the question is up, the only talking permitted is to offer a possible answer—a hypothesis. Number two: No questions can be asked about the possible answers which are offered and no comments can be made about them either, which means, Hugh, that you can't roll your eyes back in your head and that you, Sharon, can't say "Now wait a minute." (More friendly smiles in the group about behavior every-

[2] For an extensive overview of brainstorming, see Alex Osborn, *Applied Imagination* (New York: Scribner, 1957). See also Sidney J. Parnes, "Do You Really Understand Brainstorming?" in Sidney J. Parnes and Harold F. Harding, *A Source Book for Creative Thinking* (New York: Scribner, 1962), pp. 283–290.

body recognized.) Number three: Try not to talk when someone else is and be loud enough to be picked up by my cassette. I'm using the cassette so that we can have a record of ideas which we'll use later."

After several students asked clarifying questions about the procedure and a few laughs were shared about those people whose self-control would be tested, Mr. Krikstan wrote on the board, "What are all the uses we can think of for one red brick?" Several expressions showed confusion, some amusement, a few annoyance at what appeared to be an irrelevant question. Mr. Krikstan quickly pointed to the outline of the brainstorming procedure he had previously put on the board, ran his finger underneath the "red brick" question he had also written there and turned to the class with a large quizzical gesture. Slowly responses began: to put under a car tire, to throw through a window, to hold a door open, to use as a bookend, to use as a paperweight, to displace water in a toilet, to act as an anchor, to heat and use as a footwarmer, to use as a table for mice, to bore a hole through and use as an earring, to keep as a pet brick. . . . The ideas continued. Finally Mr. Krikstan said, "All right, let's stop there."

As the session moved to the next stage, Mr. Krikstan led students in estimating the number of ideas they had generated together, allowed them to say that they had enjoyed themselves, and listened to their expressions of surprise that so many ideas could be generated so quickly for just one brick—although some people thought some of the ideas were "weird." Next, Mr. Krikstan helped the class to understand things about the brainstorming process, such as that:

1. "Far out" ideas are more likely to produce "new" possibilities and to encourage others to do likewise.
2. The way in which brainstorming is done allows 'hitchhiking or the formulation of an idea based on one that precedes it. (He pointed out the hitchhiking between "To displace water in a toilet" and "to use as an anchor").
3. Brainstorming is best when there is both fluency (many ideas) and fluidity (a steady flow). (He pointed out that the flow of ideas came to an apparent stop twice and that he waited patiently for them to start again, after which time there was a spurt of new ideas.)

Because it was a first effort, and he wanted the students to experience it simply as a rewarding introduction, Mr. Krikstan did not lead the class to the level of evaluation. He continued to use brainstorming as a "warm up" activity, requiring five minutes at the beginning of class for the next three days. On Friday he returned to the original question that had made him realize that his students were lacking in the ability to think diversely and hypothetically. Several smiles of recognition greeted the question on the board, "Why do people in recurring flood areas, return to their homes year after year?" This time the responses were gratifyingly different. Mixed with hypotheses indicating an understanding of day-to-day realities were an array of responses that showed subtleties of psychological and sociological understanding. When the responses were listed—this time on the chalkboard—the class went on to an evaluation session from which twelve "usable" ideas were retained. (For example: "people don't have other alternatives"; "tradition"; "they take the floods for granted"; "people think it won't happen again.") Dividing into twelve pairs, the class next proceeded to do research using books, interviews, and nonprint media. They spent a week accumulating facts and opinions to test their hypotheses.

At the end of two weeks in which original plans were necessarily rearranged, students had "answers" to a significant human question, had engaged in carefully focused research, and had learned a technique that can be profitable for life-long learning.

As students work with the brainstorming process, it is important to stress five rules:

- Do not evaluate or discuss ideas as they are being expressed; defer comments and questions until later so that all participants can feel free to contribute.
- Present ideas briefly, without explanation or justification.
- Listen to the ideas of others and add to them.
- Do not engage in any negative behavior since that deters others from expressing their ideas.
- The teacher will not participate except to encourage, preferably nonverbally, additional comments.

Obviously, brainstorming is not a magic device that will cause divergent thinking in all students and in all situations. Once it is understood and some competence has been developed in the technique, it is an unusually effective tool for learning.

Brainstorming is particularly useful for:

- motivating at the beginning of units and lessons (a short brainstorming session can quickly raise issues about which students are interested)
- suggesting possible plans of action
- obtaining group solutions to organizational or social problems
- using information already mastered
- generating thought about complex subjects

While teachers, counselors, and other group leaders report immediate results from the introduction of brainstorming, it must be remembered that the greatest results will be produced when students are given regular opportunities to use it in relation to subject matter. (For example: "What resources can be used to get information about . . . ?" "What experiences might cause a person to behave as . . . (a fictional character, a case study subject, an historical figure, a family member)?" "What explanations can be given for the fact that an ice cube sinks to the bottom of a glass of clear liquid?") Brainstorming is a skill, and as such, must be practiced regularly.

At the same time students are developing skill in brainstorming and using that skill to develop their divergent production and evaluation abilities, it is important that they be exposed to questions—from teachers and in learning materials—that also cause them to move beyond the lower levels of intellectual functioning. Questioning, which is sometimes referred to as an art, is one of the most important tools of teaching, and also one of the most difficult to master.

QUESTIONING

Questions, which are probably the principal stimuli for causing thought, are essentially problem-solving devices. While it is frequently important to be able to answer them, it is equally important—for teachers and students —to be able to ask them.

Obviously, all questions do not have equal value. J. P. Guilford's work in describing the "structure of the intellect", referred to earlier in this chapter, provides a framework from which questions of varying degrees of intellectual complexity may be formulated. In a related way, the work of Benjamin Bloom[3] has facilitated the classification of questions according to intellectual complexity. Using Bloom's research, a hierarchy of questions, ranging from recall to evaluation has been formulated.[4] Learning to move from the lower level questions ("Who is the main character?" "What is the meaning of 'zygote'?" "What is an F chord?") to higher level ones ("On what basis is it fair to conclude that Dreyfus was innocent?" "What are some implications for our economy of an embargo of Arabian oil?" "If you had teenage children, what rules would you establish about their behavior?") is not a simple task. Asking good questions—and being able to ask them spontaneously—is not quickly learned. Much classroom experience, as well as professional "homework" is necessary to develop questioning proficiency. Without that proficiency it will not be possible to direct students to the significant outcomes of the processes of creativity, inquiry-discovery, and values clarification.

The questioning levels derived from Bloom's work are based on his taxonomy of cognitive objectives. All seven categories can be used in some way at every grade level in every subject. These seven levels of questioning are:

MEMORY

Recognition or recall of information.
Memory questions deal with

    (a) definitions
    (b) facts

[3] Benjamin Bloom et al. (Eds.), *Taxonomy of Educational Objectives: Handbook I, The Cognitive Domain* (New York: McKay, 1958).
[4] The hierarchy of questions presented on the following pages has been adapted from Norris M. Sanders, *Classroom Questions: What Kinds?* (New York: Harper & Row, 1966).

(c) generalizations—recognition of common characteristics of a group
(d) criteria (bases for judgment)

TRANSLATION

Expression of ideas in different form or language (written, oral, pictorial).

INTERPRETATION

Explication of relationships among facts, generalizations, values, etc.
Several kinds of interpretations exist:

(a) comparison/contrast (ideas which are same, different, related, or con-
     tradictory)
(b) implication (ideas based upon evidence)
(c) induction (application of a generalization to a group of observed facts)
(d) quantitation (use of a number of facts to reach a conclusion)
(e) cause and effect (recognition of events leading to a conclusion)

APPLICATION

Solving lifelike problems that require identification of an issue and the selection and the use of generalizations, facts, and skills

ANALYSIS

Recognition and application of rules of logic to the solutions of problems

SYNTHESIS

Using original (creative) thinking to solve problems

EVALUATION

Making judgments based on clearly defined standards

A look at some specific examples within the seven categories may be
helpful. The following questions could be raised during and after a unit
concerned with smoking.

MEMORY

Definition: What do the following words mean: carcinogen, tar, emphy-
                  sema?
                  Define "hazardous."
Facts: What is the Surgeon General's Office?
                  What percentage of physicians smoke?
                  Who is affected more by cigarette smoking—men or women?
                  Where in this community can you obtain information about
                  the effects of cigarette smoking on health?
Generalization: Why is tobacco advertising not permitted on television?
                  What is the effect of peer pressure on teenage smoking?

Criteria: Explain on what basis you do (or do not) believe the government should require the Surgeon General's "Warning" on all packages of cigarettes.

TRANSLATION

Restate in your own words the "Warning" which appears on all packages of cigarettes. (Be careful to consider the phrases "has determined" and "may affect.")

In what way could the Surgeon General's warning be expressed pictorially rather than verbally?

INTERPRETATION

Comparison: How are the effects of cigarette smoking like those of cigar smoking? In what ways are the effects of cigarette smoking and cigar smoking different?

Implication: According to information we have studied, what effect may cigarette smoking have on an unborn child? What overall effects may result from smoking two packages of cigarettes daily over a ten year span of time?

Induction: What conclusion do you draw from the fact that tobacco is a cash crop in sixteen states, dominating the agriculture of some—notably North Carolina and Kentucky?

Quantitation: Name five diseases related to cigarette smoking. Name five ways in which cigarette smoking effects human behavior. What conclusions do you draw from the table below?

TABLE 9.1   Estimated Years of Life Expectancy at Various Ages for Males in the United States, by Daily Cigarette Consumption.

Age	Never Smoked Regularly	Number of Cigarettes Smoked per Day			
		1–9	10–19	20–39	40 and over
25 years	48.6	44.0	43.1	42.4	40.3
30 years	43.9	39.3	38.4	37.8	35.8
35 years	39.2	34.7	33.8	33.2	31.3
40 years	34.5	30.2	29.3	28.7	26.9
45 years	30.0	25.9	25.0	24.4	23.0
50 years	25.6	21.8	21.0	20.5	19.3
55 years	21.4	17.9	17.4	17.0	16.0
60 years	17.6	14.5	14.1	13.7	13.2
65 years	14.1	11.3	11.2	11.0	10.7

Source: E. C. Hammond, Life Expectancy of American Men in Relation to Their Smoking Habits. Presented at the World Conference on Smoking and Health, New York City, September 11–13, 1967, 23 pp. Reprinted by permission of the American Cancer Society.

Cause and Effect: What physiological changes are produced in the body by the inhalation of cigarette smoke?

APPLICATION

What research design would you use to conduct a science fair project concerned with the effects of cigarette smoke on the breathing habits of white mice?

How might the government mount a nationwide program to discourage smoking?

ANALYSIS

The American Cancer Society reports that, "Thirty million Americans have quit smoking cigarettes for a very good reason. Evidence accumulated in recent years has now proved beyond doubt that what was once considered merely a bad habit is the No. 1 threat to the health of this country, according to the US Surgeon General." Using a variety of sources, determine the validity of these sentences.

SYNTHESIS

Pretend that you have been awarded a grant of $2,000,000 to aid schools to (1) discourage students from beginning to smoke and (2) help those who smoke to stop doing so. Present your ideas under the two listings.

EVALUATION

Based on what you have read and heard about this subject, is it fact or opinion that smoking causes physiological harm to human beings? What is the evidence that supports your response?

Based on what you have studied, would you discourage your own children from smoking? Why?

It would be profitable to select an area of study within your discipline and construct questions at each of the levels illustrated above. Share your questions with people outside your subject area in order to check the degree to which you have made assumptions about what students may or may not understand. Pool your best questions with others in the class and share the examples so that you can begin a file of question models which may be helpful in your teaching.

You might wish to examine the seven Bloom-based categories against Guilford's five levels of intellectual difficulty. Explain what relationships you discern. What differences exist? Which of the categories formulated from Bloom's work come under Guilford's classification of convergent production? Which under divergent production? Which under evaluation?

It will be informative to examine the questions above about smoking and classify them according to whether they are convergent or divergent. How many fall at the lower level of the questioning hierarchy? How many at the upper level?

It is important to bear in mind that all students are capable of some kind of thinking throughout the hierarchy. As teachers come to know their students' abilities and to recognize the areas in which greater intellectual development is required, they can determine where to place emphasis within the hierarchy. The recurring problem for teachers is devising questions which stimulate each student to intellectual growth. Knowing where to best put time and energy can only be determined through awareness of students' needs and readiness.

The formulation of questions of all kinds is itself an important skill. The correct choice of words, directness, and clarity of expression, as well as focusing on genuinely significant content, are all important in stimulating appropriate thought. Poor questions may produce results that show only that the teacher is a poor communicator, not that students have not learned. (It may be valuable at this time to read Chapter 13, "Testing, Testing . . .")

In order to provide students with fair test questions which range over the seven levels of the questioning hierarchy, it is imperative that the full range of questions be employed as learning occurs. If students are expected to respond well to certain types of questions in a testing situation, they must have experience with those questions on a day-to-day basis. One does not suddenly develop the resources to respond to various kinds of questions without dealing with those kinds of questions in classroom study. As teachers are learning to ask the full range of questions, it is wise to incorporate those questions, with their categories marked, in lesson plans.

ENCOURAGING QUESTIONS AND ANSWERS

How many classroom questions have you answered in your educational career? How many times were you unsure of your responses? How many times did you have to answer when you were sure your answer was wrong or weak? How many times were you praised for your responses? How many times have you been able to ask questions that were concerned with content rather than form? How many times were your questions considered seriously by teachers? How many times have you received satisfactory answers to difficult or unusual questions you have asked?

Remembering your own experiences in asking and answering questions as a student, it should be helpful to remember these do's and don'ts as a teacher. The teacher should:

1. Ask a question first, then call upon a student to answer.
2. Allow time for a response. Many good questions require time to consider as well as time to formulate answers.
3. Call on many students, not just the same few. Be careful about embarrassing students who seldom volunteer responses.
4. Avoid "yes" and "no" questions. If a partial reply is given, ask a follow-up

question which will cause the student to provide more information. (See below.)

5. Reward good answers with either verbal or nonverbal behavior.

The teacher should not:

1. Ask "double-barrelled" questions (for example, "Why was Mary, Queen of Scots despised and when did she ascend the throne?")
2. Ask questions which contain or suggest the correct answer.
3. Embarrass or otherwise penalize students who give wrong answers.

Determine why students give wrong answers and help them to correct them.

HELPING STUDENTS ANSWER THROUGH PROBING

Many times students require assistance in providing complete responses. Sometimes they need additional questioning which helps to reaffirm answers about which they are unsure. Occasionally, it is necessary to ascertain that an answer is not just guess work. For these and other reasons, it is frequently appropriate to pose follow-up questions and comments such as:

- How do you know that is so?
- Where did you find that answer?
- What evidence exists in the material to prove that point?
- Isn't that a contradiction of . . . ?
- How does your answer jibe with . . . ?
- Why do you like that one better? (Yes, but *why?*)

The value of questions and the ability to ask good questions well cannot be overestimated. For both teachers and students the following observation might serve as a daily reminder: "Once you have learned to ask questions—relevant and appropriate and substantial questions—you have learned how to learn and no one can keep you from learning whatever you want or need to know."[5]

BRAINSTORMING, QUESTIONING, AND THREE PROCESSES FOR LEARNING

True teaching and true learning are more than simply the imparting and regurgitating of information. They are also more than isolated mastery of what has been described earlier as intellectual functioning. Teaching and learning which have life-long implications are activities that develop process as well as product.

[5] Neil Postman and Charles Weingartner, *Teaching as a Subversive Activity* (New York: Delacorte, 1969), p. 23.

The three teaching–learning processes explored in the remainder of this chapter depend to a considerable degree upon the expertise of teachers in accepting, promoting, and developing divergent thinking and evaluation. The strategy of brainstorming is ideally suited to many aspects of creativity, inquiry–discovery, and values clarification. Fundamental to these processes is the ability to pose questions that touch all levels of intellectual functioning.

Each of the three processes is experiential, requiring continuous reference to the learner's activities, interests, and motivations. Each of the processes, causes learners to challenge assumptions which spring from activities, interests, and motivations. As assumptions are challenged, assessment and realignment are automatic, and thus intellectual and behavioral change, with which education is concerned, occur.

The processes of creativity, inquiry–discovery, and values clarification all depend on the ability to respond to and to ask provocative questions. Each process leads students to generate their own questions and thereby their own motivation. When people are able to say to themselves "What might be the answer to this problem?" "How can I find out?" "How might things be different?" "What does this (information, encounter, feeling) mean to me?" they are ready and eager to learn. No degree of teacher motivation can equal the self-stimulation of curiosity.

CREATIVITY

Frank is the school's leading nonconformist. In a school of middle- and upper-middle-class students, from a conservative community, he "hears a different drummer." His appearance—hair, clothing, shoes, demeanor—are all distinctive. While he is never anything but courteous, he has the tenacity of a determined clam when he fastens on to a question for which he seeks an answer. This is frequently embarrassing to most of Frank's teachers, staid authoritarians whose notion of learning is certainly not Frank's. Because he is not at all interested in grades, he is encountering difficulty in gaining college admission. Only two of his teachers have gone to bat for him. The others, who show a decided stiffening of muscles when his name is mentioned, regard him as a troublemaker who "will wind up on drugs or something else just as bad."

All of this would be laughable if it were not so patently absurd. Frank is clearly the most gifted student I have found in my seven years of teaching. His approach to problems is genuinely innovative; his thinking is profound for a person his age; and his ability to see and relate issues, problems, and possible answers is sometimes unnerving. And yet he is already being shelved by society—or at least that part of it he has met—because society isn't able to see or adjust to the creative potentials he possesses.

Despite the treatment given to countless Franks, teachers say they want their students to be creative. "The trouble is" (as one teacher put it), "that we want it only in manageable amounts, because its offspring, innovation, rocks the boat. So the only 'creativity' we tolerate in school is the kind which follows the rules, pleases teachers and parents, and isn't noisy."

Frank is one of those creative students who also has strong academic ability, although he does not always choose to use it. Further, he is one of those creative students who is not restricted by delayed skill development. While some students are blessed with the array of natural abilities Frank has, not all creative students have high academic ability, just as not all of them have abilities which match their physical maturation. Unfortunately, many highly creative individuals go unidentified, and thus unencouraged.

Until recently it was common belief that only certain people were born with creative ability and that one either "had" it or did not. No thought was given to providing experiences which could develop or enhance creative thinking in all students. Art, drama, and music were provided for most students in order to increase their appreciation of the work of others— not to foster their own creative expression. Research now indicates that all people have some degree of creative ability and that there are many learning activities which can help develop that ability.

All learning is affected by the environment in which it occurs, just as all learning is affected by the personality and effectiveness of the teacher. The development of creativity is especially contingent upon all three factors. Because creative thinking is, by its nature, divergent thinking, it requires intellectual as well as emotional risk. Being different in thought and behavior can be dangerous—especially for adolescents who are constantly pressured to conform by teachers, by parents, and particularly by peers. Providing a stimulating atmosphere in which individuals can think and experiment is of paramount importance; providing encouragement and also protection for divergent thinking and experimentation are equally significant.

A classroom which is attractive and contains a variety of stimulating resources—projects, books, magazines, newspapers, plants, animals, games, equipment—is a constant reminder that there are many views of life and learning and that a multiplicity of views is valued in that space. The environment is a stimulus to investigation as well as a comfortable place in which to inquire. A teacher who reveals an acceptance of people and ideas in all their variety is, by example, also a stimulus to creativity. Numerous other factors are involved in fostering creativity. Among the more important things all teachers can do are:

- **Encourage individual thinking.**
  Help students to challenge assumptions.
  Provide recurring opportunities for development of observational skills.
  Encourage the belief that "nothing is ridiculous if you think it will work."
- **Provide growing experiences.**
  Use creativity exercises (such as those on the following pages) on a regular basis.
  Help students to see the relationship between the arts and sciences.

Help students accept, understand, and "deal with" their emotions.

Ask divergent questions daily; ask at least one "open-ended" question daily; provide alternative assignment possibilities; include divergent and open-ended questions in tests.

Require hypothesis-making as part of the learning process.

Provide nonreading and nonwriting learning opportunities.

Dispel the idea of "genius" and "masterpieces."

- **Stimulate a sense of satisfaction.**

See that students share the results of their work.

Reward the unusual, the "far out"; share "far out" ideas with students.[6]

Do not grade assignments that are designed to promote creativity.

Protect the creative person from peer sanctions.

Consistently demonstrate that you value creative ideas and behavior.

Explore with students the personal rewards that result from original thinking.

Participate in creative activities with your students.

Avoid being predictable.

Use your sense of humor.

Share your creative thinking and work with your students.

The suggestions above apply to all teachers in all classrooms. They should not be viewed as behaviors reserved for those who teach English and the arts. All aspects of life, which are reflected presumably in the curriculum, are enriched by creative thinking and behavior.

In order to think divergently about one's environment, it is necessary to be aware of it as it is. That requires sensitive observation. Observation is possible only through the five senses; the training of those senses is fundamental to the fostering of creativity. Within the context of each subject it is important for students to have experiences which require them to sharpen their observational skills. In what ways can students gather information in your subject area by using each of their senses? In what ways might they begin to think divergently about those things they take for granted within your subject area? Perhaps students need basic training in how to look, listen, touch, smell, and taste. (See page 107 which suggests some basic observation skill exercises.) One technique for assisting students to record and use their observations is to have them maintain an observational log (a notebook in which they occasionally note unusual sensory findings) related to subject matter. The log can provide extra credit as well as serve as the source for many related topics, projects, and interests that students uncover and share with their classmates. It may contain not only written observations but clippings of articles, pictures, cartoons, student sketches, as well as other forms of expression (e.g., mathematical problems, music, maps, science experiments, puzzles, etc.). If the observational log

---

[6] Examples of ideas to share are found in A. E. Brown and H. A. Jeffcott, Jr., *Beware of Imitations!*, a reprint of a 1932 publication of records from the United States Patent Office. Available from Dover Publications, 180 Varick Street, New York, New York 10014.

is maintained, it is important for the teacher to see it occasionally—in order to demonstrate that it is valued—but it is also important that the book not be graded. Extra credit can be given for its maintenance but to grade it is to judge materials not intended for that purpose. Indeed, judging creative material in a classroom all but guarantees that students will not be creative, but will second guess the teacher's taste.

When teachers maintain their own observational logs and occasionally share the contents with students, students are dramatically reinforced in the realization that teachers value the exploration of the senses and, thus, diversity. The teacher is also modeling a willingness to risk by sharing as well as modeling in the presentation of unusual ideas.

Another way in which teachers can facilitate creative thought is to provide specific, short creative exercises. Used as "warm-ups" these exercises are excellent techniques for fostering many kinds of divergent, or lateral, thinking, and can frequently be used as lead-ins to current study. Some of the basic techniques include these activities:[7]

1. What are all the uses for . . . ? (See the red brick exercise described on page (204.) A different object is substituted each time the question is used (e.g., a rubber tire, a coat hanger, a phonograph record, a man's shoe). The exercise is limited to a few minutes in which students make individual lists which they later share in a group. The exercise produces both fluency and fluidity of thinking. Research shows that the more people are encouraged to produce "far out" ideas, the more unusual the ideas will be and the greater the number of ideas produced. At base, this exercise calls for a challenging of the assumption with which we regard common objects. It is an excellent beginning exercise in divergent thinking. Teachers who use this and the other exercises described here find that students quickly vie for presenting the class with problems to be thought about laterally.

2. This reminds me of this, which reminds me. . . . Individuals are asked to write their word associations in a series that will eventually contain five words. The problem might be: red ———— ———— ———— beer. Students are asked to fill the first blank with a word they associate with "red." The second blank receives the word they associate with the word before it; the third blank receives the word they associate with the one before it and, which, in turn, they associate with "beer." In order to avoid producing sentences the finished product should not contain verbs. One seventh grader solved the problem this way: red *forest trees birch* beer. In another circumstance using the series fuzzy ———— ———— ———— money, seventh graders responded with: fuzzy *bear tree green* money; fuzzy *bear honey sweet* money; fuzzy *wuzzy bear fur* money; and fuzzy *beard Santa Claus present* money. The thinking required in this instance is the same as that required by people who know where they are and where they want to get but who must find a strategy for moving from one place to the other. By making free associations the problem of attaining the goal is made possible.

---

[7] Eugene Raudsopp, "Four Tests for Creativity," *Science Digest*, 52 (October 1962), pp. 42–47.

3. Why is it true that . . . ? This exercise, best done by letting students call out their ideas as they occur, calls for the participants to accept the content of the problem as true and to work from that assumption. "Why is it true that most people who commit suicide do so during the month of April?" As students express their ideas, it is extremely important to enforce the brainstorming rules discussed on pages 203–205. No discussion; present ideas briefly; listen to the ideas of others and add to them; no negative behavior; no participation of the teacher except to encourage additional statements (preferably by nonverbal means). One of the most significant experiences which students can learn from this exercise is the value of hitchhiking on others' ideas. In the discussion which follows it is important to ask students to indicate those ideas which they developed based on hitchhiking. The kind of thinking employed in this exercise is that of generating hypotheses, within specific limitations, which is itself a high level of thinking and one which is employed repeatedly under many names in all subjects.

4. What would happen if . . . ? In this exercise people working in a group, expressing themselves aloud, consider such problems as "What would happen if, when we all awoke tomorrow, we found that we had grown two additional eyes in the backs of our heads?" Again hitchhiking will encourage a wide range of diverse ideas. This exercise loosens the tendency to be rigid in problem solving, by encouraging thought beyond the commonplace and the ingrained. It is an exercise which can eventually lead students to the practice of confronting problems with the thought, "What if we did it this way . . . ?"

Other exercises which generate alternative thinking include those with nonverbal symbols, symbolic and metaphoric thinking, art materials, musical instruments, junk materials, creative drama and dance, and scientific instruments.

In addition to providing environment, encouragement, and direction, it is important for teachers to make clear that they have high expectations that everyone will think creatively. After that, patience and the provision of time for creative thinking and behaving is a necessity. Two other factors are important: (a) reward for both thought and product and (b) systematic and continuous opportunities for exploration and growth. Creative results will not occur because five minutes is reserved every now and then for a creative exercise. A continuous effort at encouraging creative insights and expressions is fundamental.

Equally important, as indicated earlier, is the readiness and ability to ask questions. Every activity of the classroom should lead students to say "How?" "Why?" "Could there be another way of doing this?" When students ask teachers, fellow students, and themselves questions and seek answers they are—in one sense—already involved in the creative-thinking process.

An atmosphere that encourages creative thinking is one in which daydreaming is not the worst possible thing a student can do. One of the great shortcomings of secondary schools is that many do not allow needed time for thinking. It is through the daydream that out-of-the-ordinary thinking has a chance to catch hold. What opportunities for creative thinking are strangled when daydreaming is ruled out as a "waste of time"?

Teachers with highly creative students need extra doses of insight and tolerance. To be too bright or too creative is apt to strain relationships in living: at home, at school, with peers. Teachers who are alert to the particular needs of students can help channel their unique attributes in ways rewarding to the individual and in ways that also deflect them from interfering with the slower and more pedestrian ways of their fellows. For instance, if Jack, who has a real flair for music, wants to spend the period experimenting with an original composition on a twelve-tone scale, while the others are barely managing to recognize the difference between B and B-flat, then it seems reasonable to permit Jack to try his luck and test his talent. If Linda has finished all the chemistry experiments that the rest of the class will struggle with for the whole semester, in two months, she can be encouraged to see if she can invent better experiments to demonstrate the same principles or to carry out her own research and investigation. Why not?

Some school systems have established special programs to provide intellectual and artistic enrichment for the highly creative. In some situations, it has been possible to work out arrangements with local colleges or universities to let students attend college classes or work in college laboratories or studios—a far better solution than just handing them library passes and saying, "Go do what you want till the rest of us catch up." Both teachers and administrators need fortitude, good judgment, and belief in the essential reasonableness of young people to be flexible; but it is damaging and socially wasteful to maintain things as they are, just because it is the easiest way.

Whether one agrees with Albert Einstein that imagination is more important than knowledge, it is certain that students of today cannot become the happy, productive citizens of tomorrow without finding and perfecting their creative powers.

Many of the same teaching and learning attitudes concerning creativity also apply to the process of inquiry–discovery. Divergent thinking, evaluation, and the ability to pose significant questions are all day-to-day components of inquiring and discovering. Additional ingredients of the process are discussed in the next section.

INQUIRY–DISCOVERY

Inquiry–discovery is an approach to teaching and learning in which the responsibility for learning is placed clearly on the student. It is a system which requires that the student ask questions and then examine possible solutions. The system is based on the scientific method of investigation which requires posing a problem, generating hypotheses about the problem, testing the hypotheses, and applying solutions. While it is a system that deals more with concepts, it cannot ignore facts. The process cannot be implemented without an exploration of facts and the use of basic skills.

The idea of inquiry–discovery, according to Jerome Bruner, is for students to put things together for themselves, to be their own discoverers.[8] In the inquiry–discovery process teachers act as catalysts, rather than as dispensers of information. They offer students problems, issues, and questions, and then provide encouragement for inquiring into the nature of the problems and guidance for seeking solutions. In the inquiry–discovery process, teachers help students find or pose problems, investigate, and clarify positions and conclusions. To function, students form and test hypotheses they develop, ultimately arriving at statements of conclusion, generalizations, or solutions.

Although some learning theorists, such as Ausubel[9] claim that the term "discovery" should be applied only to original insights and solutions, it is generally agreed that people "discover" when they find something previously unknown to them—usually the operation of a principle or generalization. Most educators hold that it is irrelevant whether students discover something original: What is important is that they have the fulfilling experience of saying, "Aha! I have found a solution!"

Inquiry and discovery can be employed quickly, as in determining grammatical generalizations, examining principles of density in chemistry, or observing properties of numbers in mathematics. It may also be study that requires either a laboratory or a project approach, demanding involved investigations over an extended period of time: for instance, the causes of slum deterioration; the causes of health and safety hazards in the home and on the job; or the philosophical relationships existing among selected works of literature, art, drama, and music.

The concerns of inquiry—and the possibilities of discovery—are limitless within each subject area. Since every group is unique, teachers have the responsibility of helping students find the most appropriate method of inquiring into, and making discoveries about, the problems they face. Teachers are generally helped in this choice since new curriculum materials in almost all fields currently utilize variations of the inquiry–discovery approach. You might wish to review professional journals and curriculum materials, with others in your subject area, to determine the inquiry–

[8] Jerome S. Bruner, *The Process of Education* (Cambridge, Mass.: Harvard University Press, 1960).

[9] David P. Ausubel, "Learning by Discovery: Rationale and Mystique," *Bulletin of the National Association of Secondary-School Principals*, 45 (December 1961), pp. 18–58.

discovery approaches and resources that are available. Share your findings with your classmates so that the entire class can see a wide range of inquiry–discovery possibilities.

As with the fostering of creativity, successful teaching for discovery demands that teachers possess and demonstrate patience. Discovery through questioning, investigation, and experimention requires a longer period of time than lecture or textbook approaches allow. Teachers therefore must discard the notion that they will "cover" a specified amount of material. Instead, they must accept quality versus quantity and realize that students will be exploring the material in depth and the experience, because of its process and self-involvement, will prove to be of lasting significance in students' lives.

Teachers must be prepared, as well, to remain comparatively silent, lending guidance and clarification only when needed, so that students can indeed fulfill their responsibility of teaching themselves.

Even though his tenth-grade students were all residents of the suburbs of a large cosmopolitan city, Mr. Ily discovered that only a few of them had ever been to a professional theatre and not many more had ever seen a full-length play. When a much-respected regional theatre announced a production of Arthur Miller's *The Crucible,* he determined to do something about the gap in his students' experience. The play was listed as one of the recommended plays for students to read during that school year. In addition to the reading, Mr. Ily decided to incorporate the reading of the play into a larger framework in which students could inquire and discover many things about themselves as well as about the theatrical experience. "I believe all art exists in order to help us explore our existence; therefore, it makes sense to approach a work of art with our own experience as a major reference," is the way Mr. Ily explained himself to his class. From that frame of reference, the class was able to engage in a series of discussions, role plays, readings, and projects which led them eventually to read *The Crucible* and to attend a performance of it.

Mr. Ily developed an inquiry–discovery unit concerned with theatrical experience which called for three components: (a) recognizing the child, the storyteller, and the actor in all people; (b) reading Arthur Miller's *The Crucible*; and (c) seeing a production of *The Crucible*.

Basic considerations that were used in creating the first component of the unit are presented below.

While this framework is only the "bare bones" of the inquiry–discovery process with which Mr. Ily's students worked, it clearly indicates the extent to which three significant components were present: questions (ranging along the hierarchal scale), experiential exploration, and student activity.

The framework presented here lists questions after-the-fact; that is, it includes questions which both Mr. Ily and the students raised.

A THEATRICAL EXPERIENCE UNIT
COMPONENT ONE[10]

Major Concept for Investigation: All people possess the qualities of child, storyteller, and actor.

Additional Concepts for Investigation: (1) it is healthy and helpful to possess the qualities of child, storyteller, and actor; (2) participating in and understanding theatrical experience can be revealing, pleasurable, and satisfying.

Inquiries	Activities
• What is the earliest story you can remember hearing? How old were you? How did you respond to the story? What is the earliest story you remember seeing (on television, in a film, in a play)? How old were you? How did you respond? What comparisons or contrasts can you make for the two experiences of hearing and seeing? Can you say to which you responded more? Why?	Large group discussion. Several students retell stories they remember.
• As far as we can tell, people have always told stories; what human needs are satisfied by storytelling?	
• We first hear and enjoy stories as children but we continue to respond to them throughout our lives. What childlike quality remains in us that allows us to story-listen and storytell?	Small group discussion. Students list stories they heard and read as children and young adolescents. In parallel columns, they list emotions aroused.
• List some emotions aroused by stories.	
• What are some meanings for the word "play," "role," and "mask"?	
• Recall some ways you played as a child. How do teenagers play? What are ways adults play?	Repeat the procedure above, making three columns to show kinds of play.
• What is meant by "playing a role"? How many roles have you played today? What are those roles? Why did you change roles in different situations? Why isn't it "safe" to be the same with everyone? In what situations do you "act" the most?	Large group discussion. Role play.

[10] Adapted from John C. Carr, *Cuesheet: An Inquiry–Discovery Guide to Dramatic Literature and Theatrical Experience* (Washington, D.C.: National Players, 1977).

Inquiries	Activities
• How is role playing like wearing a mask? • If you were to design two masks—one for your most private self and one for your most public self—how would they be different?	Demonstration of and discussion about "masks" from pictures, false faces, and costume masks. Small groups and individual work to create two masks. (Not necessarily "most private," but two masks which students are willing to acknowledge they wear.) Masks to be shared. Bulletin board display using masks entitled "The Actor in All of Us."
• What stories have you seen recently with characters whose behavior was like any of the "acting" you have done today? What happened to the characters because of the way they behaved? Has the same thing ever happened to you?	Whole group discussion.
• When you watch stories on television, in films, in a play, which interests you most: plot or character? Why? What are some of your favorite television or movie stories? What are some of your favorite television or movie characters? Why?	Whole group discussion followed by individual work in which students make brief written statements and notes. Small group discussion. Large group discussion.
• Not everyone in the group shares your opinion. What are some differences that have been expressed? What are some similarities? How can you account for the differences in opinion? What is taste? How do we get it? Is one person's taste better than another's? Why?	Large group synthesis.
• What is the difference between reading a story and seeing a story performed? What differences are there in watching a story on a television screen and the larger screen of a movie theatre? Which experience do you prefer? Why?	Large group discussion.
• Have you ever seen a play? How is watching a play different from watching a story on television or in a movie theatre? What plays have you seen? Where did you see them? Explain what you did or did not like about them.	

Inquiries	Activities
• If you have seen a play, can you recall what your reaction was to the fact that there were live people playing the roles in your presence? Have you ever acted in a play? How did you feel performing in front of others? How did the audience affect what you felt and what you did?	
• When you watched a play or acted in one, how did the audience and actors affect one another? What happened at serious, comic, or thrilling parts? What happened at the end of the play? How did the audience react at the curtain call? Why?	Large group summary, generalizations, synthesis.

Some outcomes of this component of the unit were recognition that:

- Storytelling is probably as old as language.
- A desire to "share" is important in storytelling.
- Curiosity, amazement, delight, horror, mystery, playfulness, and amusement are some feelings aroused by storytelling.
- All people respond to both plot and character.
- We "recognize" characters and frequently "identify" with them or "reject" them.
- Our emotions are aroused when we see a story; it is helpful to know what those emotions are and why they affect us.
- The unique quality of seeing a play is the existence of live performers and a live audience.
- Not only does the audience respond to the actors, but the actors respond to the audience.
- The actors and the audience share a common experience on which they collaborate.
- All humans, all their lives, maintain as part of their necessary makeup the qualities of child, storyteller, and actor.

In addition, students had the opportunity to practice small- and large-group process skills; speaking, listening, writing, and reading skills; non-verbal skills; interpersonal communication skills; as well as explore the major and additional concepts on which this part of the unit was based. Overwhelmingly, the learnings which were sought in this component are affective—or fishing—ones (see page 145) and therefore traditional testing was inappropriate. Much of this part of the unit was preparatory to what followed. As experienced teachers recognize, it is success in this part of the unit that is essential if satisfactory development of the entirety is to occur.

The other components of Mr. Ily's unit on theatrical experience included exploration of the concepts of "willing suspension of disbelief" (or what Mr. Ily called "saying I believe to make-believe"; and understanding of the role of the audience in the collaborative experience of a play. Students read Arthur Miller's *The Crucible*, frequently acting out the roles in the classroom. Occasionally students showed previously recorded videotapes or played cassette tapes they had made. During and following the reading, students were able to refer to the "discoveries" they made during the first component. When students attended the production of the play, which was followed by a discussion period with the actors and director, they were well prepared for the experience. At the end of the unit, a comprehensive examination was given which included many "hard" facts as well as many opportunities for students to show an integration of their knowledge through responses in all seven parts of the questioning range. Because Mr. Ily was ultimately more concerned with the larger goals of helping students to see the relationship of a new experience to their lives and to lead them to an experiential understanding of how literature can illuminate human existence, he was happiest with a comment made by one of the actors following the post-performance discussion: "We've simply never had an audience like these kids. They were up here with us: living it, feeling it, making it work with us. I think they understand the play better than some of us do."

Examples in other subject areas where the inquiry–discovery approach has been effective include the following:

Subject Area	Topic	Content
Science	Are Rules Natural?	Study of natural phenomena that exhibit regularity and of rules that govern human and social interaction.[11]
Home Economics	"And Baby Makes Three"	Study of what constitutes the modern family: its strengths and problems.
Music	Why does "foreign" music sound so strange.	An examination of scales, rhythm, and instruments used in various cultures.
Art	"Who Built This Picture?"	Study of the influences of architecture on medieval painting.

[11] Adapted from the Biological Sciences Curriculum Study, Boulder, Colorado, 1974.

Subject Area	Topic	Content
Social Studies	"Understanding the System"	An investigation of a local political structure and how and why constituents do and do not receive benefits.
Mathematics	Natural Geometry: Beauty and Purpose	A study of geometric shapes in nature.
Business	"Career, Career, Who's Got the Career?"	An investigation of career possibilities and requirements with particular reference to local community needs and local preparation agencies.
Physical Education/ Health	"Is Sex Necessary?"	Sex hygiene study with an emphasis on psychological and social implications.
Foreign Languages	"Saying It in French but Saying It Silently."	Nonverbal aspects of a foreign culture.
Speech	Whose Maneuvering Whom?	Investigation of the seven propaganda techniques and how they are used in the media.

With other students in your subject area, list at least five topics for which inquiry–discovery units can be developed in your discipline. Provide a title for the units and present a one- or two-sentence statement about their content. As a way of educating classmates outside your discipline to current content in your field, present your ideas to the entire class.[12]

INDUCTION: A KIND OF INQUIRY–DISCOVERY

The traditional approach to teaching/learning requires students to be exposed to rules, principles, and generalizations and then to practice application of them on a series of problems or samples. This kind of learning is called deduction. A typical example in mathematics is: Students read and clarify the rule, "Two triangles are congruent if all three sides are equal." Students then solve a series of problems in which they employ the stated rule. A typical example in English is: Students read the rule "Use commas to separate parenthetical words, phrases, or clauses from the rest of the sentences" and then place commas in a series of sentences provided by the teacher. In the deductive mode of learning, one memorizes a rule

[12] You may wish, also, to investigate the content of *Jackdaws*, publications of Grossman Publishers, 44 West 56th Street, New York, New York 10019. These packets contain primary source materials, a guide for use, and descriptive materials about the topic presented. Topics cover a wide range.

and then applies it. Many educators question the long-range value of this kind of learning. They argue, for example, that an inquiry into the way in which mathematical and language symbols are used will yield a natural understanding of rules governing them. The inquiry and discovery which occurs requires internalization, and therefore application of what is learned will have greater meaning and remain operative within the learner for a longer period of time.

The kind of inquiry that calls for students to investigate rules, principles, and generalizations is called induction. As stated earlier, it is the opposite of the deductive approach. Induction requires that the students examine an array of models, finally concluding what law is operating within them. The learners state the law in their own words and then create examples. In addition, they identify further examples provided by the teacher or other students.

As with longer range inquiry–discovery investigations, inductive lessons are appropriate in all subject areas.

The math teacher, Miss Danaan, wanted her students to discover the principle of determining the square of numbers ending in 5. She presented students with statements showing the squares of 15, 25, 35, 45 and 55 ($15^2 = 15 \times 15 = 225, \ldots$). Next Miss Danaan asked them to tell her the square of 95 without figuring on paper. When students admitted they were stymied, Miss Danaan led them through a series of questions about the given arithmetical statements which showed that all such squares ended in 25. Next, students discovered that the first digit(s) of the answer turn out to be the first digit(s) of the initial number multiplied by one more than the number represented by the first digit(s). Once the principle was uncovered, students quickly gave the square of 95.

In seventh-grade home economics class, Mrs. Herbert presented students with numerous pieces of different fabrics, asking them to suggest ways in which the materials were similar and dissimilar. Through examination of the fabrics and a series of observations and questions ("In what ways are they alike?" In what ways are they different?" "Describe the way they feel." "What causes the difference in appearance and touch?") the students concluded that fabric differences occur because of fiber content, weave, and finishing procedures.

In physical education class, Mr. Jarboe had his students stand, lean forward and backward, and return to position, considering as they did so, what was happening to their bodies in the process. Ideas such as "weight shift" and "balanced state" were clarified in a discussion centering around "how one maintains balance." Students ultimately generalized that in order for balance to be maintained the weight mass (or center of gravity) must fall over the base of support. Following student-given examples of bases of support other than feet, the principle was applied to the squat balance tumbling skill as the first of a series of tumbling activities.

English students were confronted by Mr. Ball with a series of sentences, all of which contained appositive words or phrases. Through analysis of the sentences, and a generalization reached about them, his students not only determined a definition of appositives but also made conclusions about case, number, and punctuation. Mr. Ball then asked the students to write a series of paragraphs in which appositives were freely employed.

Obviously, not everything within a subject area should be pursued either from the long-range inquiry–discovery approach or from the short-range inductive approach. Basic skills probably are best learned by rote through frequent (but pleasant, even humorous) drill, review, and application.

Some things beyond the basics are more efficiently and effectively learned that way, too. But for those significant concepts in all subject areas, inquiry–discovery will produce learners who not only think but feel. Commenting on the importance of individual "meaning-making" and the ways in which inquiry–discovery can promote it, Postman and Weingartner observe:

> If teachers *acted* as if their students were meaning makers, almost everything about the schooling process would change. For example, most school practices are based on the assumption that the student is fundamentally a *receiver*, that the object ("subject matter") from which the stimulus originates is all-important, and that the student has no choice but to see and understand the stimulus as "it" is. We now know that this assumption is false.[13]

In the day-to-day activities of the classroom, numerous things occur simultaneously as well as parallel to one another. In one lesson it is possible for students to be exposed to several topics, to a variety of teaching-learning techniques, to many resources, to questions in every category of intellectual functioning, and also to experiences which are creative, which require individuals to inquire and discover, and which, at the same time, clarify their values. The final section of this chapter attempts to show the relationship of brainstorming, questioning, creativity, and inquiry–discovery to the process of values clarification.

VALUES CLARIFICATION

When students become actively involved in learning, when they learn the skill of asking good questions, when they learn to use their creative abilities, and when they inquire and discover, they are automatically confronted with the issue of values. "Why have people sacrificed their lives for others?" "Why do some politicians flout the public trust?" "What is

---

[13] Postman and Weingartner, p. 92.

it about vivisection which is repugnant to some?" "Is abortion a matter solely of the mother's rights?" "If others cheat in order to win the game why shouldn't I?" "Who am I?" "When I have finished my education what kind of person do I want to be?"

Active learning, learning which values questioning, must of necessity be one that raises issues of vital concern to people as they are and as they may become. In order to facilitate the value concerns which students face, a systematic and rational process called values clarification has been derived.[14]

The term "values clarification" is a general label for an array of approaches which use reflection and thoughtful activity for the purpose of identifying and understanding motivations and behavior. Values clarification is not values instruction. "Clarification" is a neutral position that relies heavily on continued posing of questions which probe beyond surface responses. Value instruction attempts to tell students what they are to believe and then tests them on the degree to which they behave according to those instructions.

Values clarification is:

> . . . a form of questioning, a set of activities or "strategies," and an approach toward subject content, all of which are designed to help individuals learn a particular *valuing process* and to apply that process to value-laden areas and moral dilemmas in their lives. Use of the valuing process helps individuals (and groups) to develop and clarify their values in such a way that they are more likely to experience positive value in their own lives and to act more constructively in the social context.[15]

Developed by Louis Raths, values clarification has been found to be particularly helpful with students who are apathetic, flighty, over-conforming, or overly rebellious. Its premise is that society, and individuals within it, are confused either by a lack of value orientation or by conflicts within that orientation. Values clarification can help individuals to focus on or deal with the problem of life purpose and can also affect relationships with others.

As described by Raths, the values clarification process is concerned with three major dimensions: choosing, prizing, and doing. By reacting to questions in each of these areas, individuals can focus on those things which have greatest significance in their lives and raise questions about whether those things should be retained or changed.

Raths has seven criteria for determining values, grouped in three areas.

[14] Louis E. Raths, Merrill Harmin, and Sidney B. Simon, *Values and Teaching: Working with Values in the Classroom* (Columbus, Ohio: Merrill, 1967). We are indebted to the work of Raths for many of the ideas presented in this section.

[15] Howard Kirschenbaum, et al., "In Defense of Values Clarification," *Phi Delta Kappan*, 58:10 (June 1977), pp. 743–746.

To be considered a value, a behavior must be the result of each of the following:

Choosing: (1) freely
            (2) from alternatives
            (3) after thoughtful consideration of the consequences of each al-
                ternative
Prizing: (4) cherishing, being happy with the choice
            (5) willing to affirm the choice publicly
Acting: (6) doing something with the choice
            (7) repeatedly, in some pattern of life

While it may be inappropriate to confront all students with this system, per se, the various parts of it are easily adopted to subject-related discussions and activities as well as to teacher-student counseling sessions.

From the standpoint of most daily interractions between students and teachers, the issues of alternatives and consequences may have the most far-ranging possibilities. Time after time adolescents will state that they have no reason for their behavior ("I don't know. I just did it.") When asked what else they could do, they most often remark, "Nothing," or again, "I don't know." When asked to consider the consequences (short-range as well as long-range) of their actions, frequently they are unable to respond. Through the subject matter of every discipline, as well as in the informal situations in which students and teachers came together, it is possible to raise issues of alternatives and consequences with great frequency, and thus to assist dramatically in aspects of values clarification. Certainly, other areas of Raths' schema can be implemented in daily lessons and in other school contacts. (At this point, it may be well to peruse Chapter 17, "I Have This Problem.") Some of the most effective counseling sessions are those value clarifying moments which come in brief encounters outside the classroom. Familiarity with Raths' seven categories of value affirmation can allow teachers to ask the right thing at the right time.

Examples of clarifying questions include:

Is this something that you prize?
Are you glad about that?
How did you feel when that happened?
Did you consider any alternatives?
Have you felt this way for a long time?
Was that something that you yourself selected or chose?
Did you have to choose that; was it a free choice?
Do you do anything about that idea?
Can you give me some examples of that idea?
What do you mean _____; can you define that word?
Where would that idea lead; what would be its consequences?
Would you really do that or are you just talking?

Observe that the questions reflect the seven criteria discussed earlier. Add five clarifying questions to this list. Test them on your classmates.

In addition, many activities and projects have been designed which allow students opportunities to consider their actions against the seven criteria of the Rath's framework. Sometimes these activities are used as nonsubject restricted counseling devices and sometimes as subject-centered activities.[16] Some value clarifying activities that can be used with individuals and groups are:

- Make a Decision: Tomorrow you will lose one of your senses. Decide which of them you will give up and write a brief explanation of your decision.
- Make a List: Write down ten things you most like to do (when students have finished they code the items using such symbols as P for items they prefer doing with others, R for items that involve some kind of physical or emotional risk, $ for items which require expenditure of more than $5 at any one time), and a date for the last time the activity was performed. A discussion follows.
- Send a Telegram: On real or simulated telegram forms, students send one-sentence statements to real people which begin, "You must . . ."
- Make a Collage: Using bits of magazines, newspapers, and other materials, students create statements about themselves or their environment.
- Design Your Tombstone: Draw the kind of tombstone you would like to have. What designs will appear on it? What things will it say?
- What Do You Say? Students complete value sheets which raise several questions about a motivating topic, either verbal or nonverbal. Three examples of values sheets follow on pages 230 to 232.

[16] Adapted in part from Louis E. Raths, Merrill Harmin, and Sidney B. Simon, *Values and Teaching*, 2d ed. (Columbus, Ohio: Merrill, 1978).

VALUE SHEET 1   **The Visible Self***

1. Draw the way you
would like others
to see you.

2. Draw your
favorite dream.

3. Draw the object
whose smell pleases
you the most.

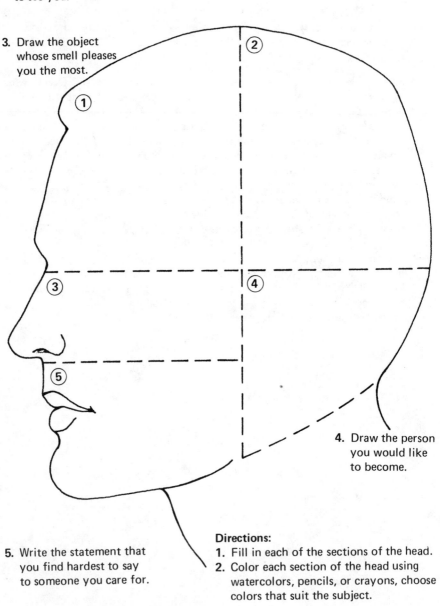

4. Draw the person
you would like
to become.

5. Write the statement that
you find hardest to say
to someone you care for.

Directions:
1. Fill in each of the sections of the head.
2. Color each section of the head using
watercolors, pencils, or crayons, choose
colors that suit the subject.

* Printed by permission of Robert Goldman.

VALUE SHEET 2

ANNAPOLIS, Feb. 7—State Sen. Peter A. Boznick (D-Prince George's) today apologized on the floor of the state Senate for publicly calling Pope Paul VI that little spaghetti-bender in Rome.

Boznick said he made the remark in a "moment of stress and heated exchange" and wanted to apologize "for so labeling a great spiritual leader."

Article in *The Washington Post*, February 8, 1973

1. My reaction to the remark "that little spaghetti-bender in Rome" is

2. The last time I called someone a name was:

   The name I used was _____. The reason I called the person the name I did was

3. Do you agree with the saying "Sticks and stones may break my bones, but words can never hurt me?" Explain.

4. If you did not like Mr. Boznick's remark—or if you thought he should not have made it where he did—does it make any difference to you that he publicly apologized?

   The last time I apologized to someone was:

5. Did you find the article amusing? Explain.

VALUE SHEET 3*

```
OOOOOOOOOOOOOOOOOOOOOOOOOOOOOOOOOOOOOO
OOOOOOOOOOOOOOOOOOOOOOOOOOOOOOOOOOOOOO
OOOOOOOOOOOOOOOOOOOOOOOOOOOOOOOOOOOOOO
OOOOOOOOOOOOOOOOOOOOOOOOOOOOOOOOOOOOOO
OOOOOOOOOOOOOOOOOOOOOOOOOOOOOOOOOOOOOO
OOOOOOOOOOOOOOOOOOOOOOOOOOOOOOOOOOOOOO
OOOOOOOOOOOOOOOOOOOOOOOOOOOOOOOOOOOOOO
OOOOOOOOOOOOOOOOOOOOOOOOOOXOOOOOOOOOO
OOOOOOOOOOOOOOOOOOOOOOOOOOOOOOOOOOOOOO
OOOOOOOOOOOOOOOOOOOOOOOOOOOOOOOOOOOOOO
```

1. To me, this picture suggests . . .

2. When I'm at a party with a group of people I don't know, I . . .

   Why?

3. The last time I did what the gang wanted to do, but I really didn't want to do myself, I felt . . .

   Because . . .

4. The last time I did something by myself, that the gang didn't want to do, I felt . . .

   Because . . .

6. What books, short stories, or poems have you read that have dealt with the question of the individual in society?

* Reprinted by permission of Ronald Stup.

From among the following motivators, select two and construct value sheets. Bear in mind that value sheets should not contain more than five or six questions; and should not be of the yes/no variety.

Cheating is socially accepted . . . everyone does it.

> High School Student quoted in
> *The Washington Post,* December 9, 1977

It would be a mistake to think that high schoolers are the pliable little morons we are made out to be. We are not.

> High School Student quoted in
> the Letters-to-the-Editor column,
> *The Washington Post,* February 10, 1978

The average American preschooler spends 64 percent of his time watching television. By the age of 14, this child will have seen 18,000 murders on TV, by the age of 17, some 350,000 commercials. In the course of his life the TV will have consumed 10 years of his life.

> *Parade,* January 16, 1972

Don't let your schooling get in the way of your education.

> Mark Twain

I only know that what is moral is what you feel good after and what is immoral is what you feel bad after.

> Ernest Hemingway

The surest way to corrupt a youth is to instruct him to hold in higher esteem those who think alike than those who think differently.

> Friedrich Nietzsche

What are some pictures, cartoons, or other graphic devices on which you could construct value sheets?

Some teachers prefer to talk about the responses to the value sheet with students individually; some have been able to establish a class rapport which permits discussion about issues to which students have responded. It should be noted that one of the basic rules of values clarification is that individuals always have the right to say "I pass" indicating that they choose not to discuss an issue or some part of it. *The rule must always apply.* When a student says "I pass," no discussion ensues. *It is imperative that, as in fostering creativity, the teacher must be ready to protect students who receive negative feedback from others. The issue of "I pass" is fundamental in assisting students to deal with issues of strong concern.*

While every decade seems to have its popular subjects of concern and discussion, Raths' has determined that basic topics are enduring in the way they relate to individual and societal values. Value-rich topics he lists are:

1. Money
2. Friendship
3. Love and sex
4. Religion and morals
5. Leisure

6. Politics and social organization
7. Work
8. Family
9. Maturity
10. Character traits

When students demonstrate an interest in further pursuit of values clarification and that pursuit extends beyond the opportunities of the classroom or the teacher's ability to clarify, students must be helped to locate those who can assist them: school counselors, local hotlines or problem switchboards, members of the clergy, or others with counseling experience. (See Chapter 17, "I Have This Problem.")

In all values clarifying activities, it is important to remember that students are being asked to apply their growing intellectual abilities to the answering of questions personally significant and, perhaps, life-lasting in nature. Just as they are aided to move from lower to higher levels of thinking about cognitive concerns, they can be helped to deal at a complex level with affective issues. In the three processes of creativity, inquiry–discovery, and values clarification, students are led to challenge the assumptions of thinking and behavior and to consider and explore alternative solutions.

In some communities of the nation, negative reaction to values clarification exists. The controversy over this process is based on the simplistic notion that teachers are able to change students' value systems through the kind of strategies described earlier. In a carefully controlled study it was concluded that, in fact, values clarification does clarify but does not change, students value systems.[17]

The processes discussed in this chapter require special behaviors from teachers, predominantly patience and a willingness to allow students to find out things for and about themselves. Patience is required not only on a daily basis (allowing students to make errors in order to discover correct or more appropriate answers and solutions; restraining a personal desire to "get to the heart of the matter"), but in the year-long operations which promote the notion that the responsibility for learning rests with the learner and that each individual must integrate personal experience and development with outside experience and knowledge. Persistence is a key word for teachers concerned with the processes of creativity, inquiry–discovery, and values clarification. Many times the effects of these approaches are not visible until the year is almost over (and sometimes not until after it is), but when they occur they manifest their worth in ways that tests cannot measure.

[17] Richard Solomon, *The Effect of Values Clarification Instruction on the Values of Selected Junior High School Students*. Unpublished doctoral dissertation, The University of Maryland, College Park, 1977.

SUMMARY

Research shows that intellectual functioning exists at various levels. Most classroom activity, unfortunately, deals with the lower levels of that functioning. Three processes for learning which can help students to function at the higher levels—requiring divergent production and evaluation abilities—are creativity, inquiry–discovery, and values clarification. Skills in brainstorming and in formulating questions are basic to the development of the three processes, all of which have significant implications for continued learning as well as for students' lives outside of school.

SELECTED READINGS

QUESTIONING

Duke, Charles R., "Questions Teachers Ask: By-Passes or Thru-Ways?" *Clearing House,* 45:8 (April 1971), pp. 468–472. A discussion of the various levels of questioning with sample questions included.

Hunkins, Francis P., *Questioning Strategies and Techniques.* Boston: Allyn and Bacon, 1972. Written with an emphasis on process, this helpful, brief volume deals with question types, the formulation of effective questions, questioning strategies, and evaluation.

Sanders, Norris M., "A Second Look at Classroom Questions," *High School Journal,* 55:6 (March 1972), pp. 265–277. An "effort to review experiences and problems of educators who have been working with patterns of questions in an effort to improve the curriculum." Helpful information is provided in response to a series of questions about questioning.

———, *Classroom Questions. What Kinds?* New York: Harper & Row, 1966. Clear presentation of the levels of questions derived from the work of Benjamin Bloom. Well illustrated with examples.

CREATIVITY

Parnes, Sidney J., and Harold F. Harding (Eds.), *A Source Book for Creative Thinking.* New York: Scribner, 1962. An extensive collection of articles ranging over the entire subject of creativity. The last two sections are particularly useful for teachers.

———, *Creative Behavior Workbook.* New York: Scribner, 1967. The contents of a "course" for developing creative thinking. Numerous strategies provided.

Raudsepp, Eugene, and George P. Hough, Jr., *Creative Growth Games.* New York: Harcourt Brace Jovanovich (Jove Publications), 1977. A "comprehensive training program" for the development of creative powers, this brief volume covers the full range of verbal and nonverbal techniques referred to in this chapter.

Safan-Gerard, Desy, "How To Unblock," *Psychology Today*, 11:8 (January 1978), pp. 78–86. An informative article which explains that "creativity occurs between a person and his work."

Smallyan, Raymond M., *What Is the Name of This Book?* Englewood Cliffs, N.J.: Prentice-Hall, 1978. Subtitled "The Riddle of Dracula and Other Logical Puzzles," this collection of brainteasers is both instructive and amusing.

Torrance, E. Paul, *What Research Says to the Teacher: Creativity.* Washington, D.C.: National Education Association, 1963. This pamphlet provides an excellent, brief guide to the meaning of creativity, ways it is manifested at different levels of school, how it is measured, what teachers can do to foster it, and how they can develop their own creativity.

—— **and J. Pansy Torrance,** *Is Creativity Teachable?* Bloomington, Ind.: Phi Delta Kappa Educational Foundation, 1973. A pamphlet that presents clear, strong arguments that teaching can increase the probability that creativity will occur.

Upton, Albert, and Richard W. Samson, *Creative Analysis.* New York: Dutton, 1961. Intended for use in high schools and colleges, this workbook, which utilizes a language approach to solving problems, is also suitable for general use.

INQUIRY-DISCOVERY

Arlo, Richard, "Inductive Teaching: A Philosophical Rationale," *Dialog* (Spring 1966), pp. 15–19. Brief, interesting article which focuses on induction and a rationale for its implementation in the classroom.

Massialas, Byron G., "Inquiry," *Today's Education*, 58:5 (May 1969), pp. 40–42; see also Zevin, Jack, "Mystery Island: A Lesson in Inquiry," pp. 42–43; Sugrue, Mary, and Jo A. Sweeney, "Check Your Inquiry–Teaching Technique." Three excellent articles which provide clear insight into inquiry–discovery teaching and learning.

Postman, Neil, and Charles Weingartner, *Teaching as a Subversive Activity.* New York: Delacorte, 1969. Exciting, provocative approach to the "inqury classroom."

VALUES CLARIFICATION

Casteel, J. Doyle, and Robert J. Stahl, *Value Clarification in the Classroom: A Primer.* Pacific Palisades: Goodyear Publishing Company, 1975. An extensive compilation of value sheets touching almost every category of interest to young people.

"Conflict in American Values: Life Style versus Standard of Living," "Deciding Right from Wrong: The Dilemma of Morality Today," "The Mass Mind: Conformity and Individualism." Three "sound-slide programs" produced by Society and Mankind, Inc. (The Center for the Humanities), Two Holland Avenue, White Plains, New York 10606. Thematic programs which provide dramatic insights and raise important questions about the topics.

"Conflict and Awareness: A Film Series on Human Values." Produced by CRM McGraw-Hill Films, Del Mar, Calif. 92014. Thirteen short films which begin with believable vignettes "portraying young adults in the midst of pressing judgmental dilemmas." At the peak of each story, the story stops and a commentator poses questions which are to be discussed by groups who have watched the films.

Howe, Leland W., and Mary Martha Howe, *Personalizing Education: Values Clarification and Beyond.* New York: Hart Publishing Company, 1975. An extensive array of strategies and work sheets intended to make values clarification an integral part of subject matter study.

Raths, Louis, Merrill Harmin, and Sidney J. Simon, *Values and Teaching,* 2d ed. Columbus, Ohio: Merrill, 1978. Lucid, well-organized revision of the seminal work in the field. A must for those interested in values clarification.

Simon, Sidney, Leland Howe, and Howard Kirschenbaum, *Values Clarification.* New York: Hart Publishing Company, 1972. Following a good summary statement of what values clarification "is," the authors present a collection of clarification activities, easily used in or adapted to classroom use.

Shannon, William V., "What Code of Values Can We Teach Our Children Now?" The *New York Times Magazine* (January 16, 1972). Poses significant questions and raises important concerns about the shift in contemporary values.

Shaver, James P., and William Strong, *Facing Value Decisions: Rationale-building for Teachers.* Belmont, Calif.: Wadsworth Publishing Company, 1976. Straightforward presentation for educators about the need for (as well as implications of) values education.

Volkmor, Cara B., Anne Langstaff Pasanella, and Louis E. Raths, "Values in the Classroom," Columbus, Ohio: Merrill, 1978. A multimedia kit containing six cassettes, and filmstrips and a teacher's guide, plus a handbook of values activities. Also includes Raths *Values and Teaching* (see above).

FOCUS ON CHAPTER 10

A common characteristic of social life is that it occurs in groups—in the family, on the job, in the school—everywhere human beings interact with others to get a task done, to solve a problem, to have fun, to give and receive affection and support. Learning how to be productive and at ease in these group settings is part of being socialized. Ideally, the school assists individuals in learning how to be part of a group and at the same time retain separate identities.

Significant ideas presented in this chapter are:
- A class of 35 students is not a group; a group is a small unit in which each person can interact with every other person in solving a common problem.
- Small group work is one of the most effective procedures for enlisting the talents of all students in a learning activity.
- There are many ways of organizing small group activities, from groups lasting for a few minutes or class period to groups which may work together for weeks or months.
- While group work is easy to inaugurate, there are specific guidelines to insure productivity and efficient use of time.
- Evaluating group work is essential; it is a task which can be profitably shared with students.
- The subgroups which emerge in any social unit can be analyzed using a sociometric test.
- Variations in group process illustrate some of the creative adaptations available to teachers.

chapter 10

Face to Face:
groups and
group processes

It has been a very lively discussion. Many hands had been raised. Ideas pro and con were listed on the board. Mrs. Jackson felt quite pleased with the quality of the thinking that had been displayed. She had only one small nagging doubt: Although the discussion had been lively, she remembered that Alice had made quite a few of the suggestions. Virginia had made some. But Sue and Tony and Jack had not said anything. And George, while nodding earnestly from time to time, also had been silent. How many others had been unresponsive?

As the discussion closed, finally, Mrs. Jackson's doubts could no longer be silenced.

"We have had a very good discussion," she said, "and many people have contributed. Or I think many people have. I wonder if you will be quite frank with me. Will all of you who participated put up your hands? I just want to know how many really took part in the discussion."

A scattering of hands went up. Mrs. Jackson quickly counted them: 13. There were 36 in the class. Two were absent. That meant that 13 out of 34 students had carried the "lively discussion." What happened to the other 21? Were they interested? Did they agree or disagree? What did they think? Were they thinking at all?

Mrs. Jackson thanked the class and went on with the business at hand. But she could not help feeling somewhat let down, just a bit cheated, and concerned as well. Her questions remained unanswered and disturbing.

Comparable situations could be reported in many secondary school classes. Good discussion procedures encourage some spread in participation but they cannot typically involve all students; time is too short and classes are too large. Often, involvement of the whole class is desirable. Is it possible? In recent years considerable progress has been made in knowledge about the personal–social climate in which learning is encouraged or discouraged. The small group setting is the best procedure to involve every individual. In this chapter, the group within the larger class will be discussed. How does one identify subgroups in a class? How can group techniques be utilized for short- or long-term purposes? The small group activity, with its many variations, may help solve the problem posed by Mrs. Jackson and echoed by many of her colleagues.

A CLASS IS NOT A GROUP

The literature of education abounds with phrases such as these: "The class then decided . . . ," "The class then began the next phase . . ." What do these phrases mean? The usual class in the junior or senior high school contains about thirty-three students. Most classes are together for fifty-minute periods; then the students are reshuffled as they proceed to the next class period. Another thirty-three students, including some new faces from another class, then convene for quite different instruction. Are these classes genuine "groups"? Can a class of thirty-three actually "decide" anything, particularly when the "meeting time" is so short?

Emphasis in the standard classroom is put upon individuals competing with other individuals. Some students, who know they will succeed, have a head start and are active participants; others, who think they will fail, may already have "dropped-out" symbolically by not participating or learning.

When there are a few articulate and aggressive students who participate readily in any and all class discussions, it is very easy for others to sit back and let them take over. Many adolescents find it difficult to speak up before their classmates; they may fear the possible humiliation of saying the wrong thing, or making an obvious remark which will be greeted with scorn, or making a grammatical error which will be publicly corrected by an insensitive teacher. Some students who are slower in formulating their thoughts than others may arrive at a response but find that by the time they are ready to voice their ideas the discussion has already moved along to another point. And, of course, they are many students who are not motivated or interested in such class activities. No kind of prodding or challenge will rouse them to take part. Such students are among the very bright as well as the intellectually limited.

When a genuine group is working on a common task, every member has a significant place; the presence and participation of all are needed and used. An athletic team is the best example of the kind of group in which each player works toward team goals and team achievement. The same feeling pervades a band or orchestra, and motivates members of a school drama production or the staff of the newspaper: These are group efforts in which each individual is involved in working with others toward the group goal. To refuse to participate means elimination from the group effort; therefore everyone tries to contribute in order to be included.

Although it is difficult indeed to create such a group feeling among thirty-five diverse individuals, the teacher can develop similar group involvement through the use of *small groups*. When the larger group is subdivided into manageable groups of five or fewer, each person can be reached.

THE POWER OF THE GROUP

Psychologist Kurt Lewin has said that the group is the ground we stand on. People are social beings. We need others at every point in our lives. To be alone is one of the harshest of punishments. There is probably no more powerful influence on our behavior, thoughts, or feelings than that of the group with which we have identified ourselves—family, religious, racial or ethnic group, professional or work group—and, in the case of students, the group of peers in the classroom and school.

Indeed, during adolescence the power of the peer group is especially potent. It is from the peer group that one gets an assessment of self; the acceptance or rejection meted out by peers is crucial for individual growth. Every biography, autobiography, and novel which touches on adolescence repeats this message: The peer group can make or break the individual.

I really never thought I cared much about the opinions of the other kids in my class. I had a few friends, but mostly I didn't pay much attention to what the others were doing or saying. Then there was an election for student body representative. Someone put my name up. I heard a few whispers, "Yeah, Janie would be a good candidate." I was absolutely astounded: they like me! They thought I was good! I won the election and from then on I found out how important it was to me to have others approve of me.

It was quite clear that Mike was the most miserable person in the class. I would watch him when the class came in and when it left at the end of the period. He spoke to no one; no one spoke to him. How, I wondered, could anyone be so isolated? He was, for one thing, fat. He had pimples. He always seemed confused about where we were in the math text. He sometimes seemed "spacey" and I wondered if he were on drugs. The counselor told me when I checked that Mike was in trouble because he never seemed able to make one single friend.

Typically, in today's culture, boy meets girl for serious discussion only under the most exceptional circumstances. The contact is usually restricted to a few undercover words in class, a brief conversation in the hall, or the bantering chitchat at McDonald's. School may have made it very difficult indeed for boys and girls to talk normally together about important things.

What is life like in many classrooms? Each student is a separate island. Little real interchange is permitted, although much goes on surreptitiously. Students are expected to learn the same material, some lagging far behind, others impatiently surging ahead of the rest. This uniformity of procedure has earned many secondary schools the condemnation of teaching for mediocrity.

In the large classroom group, it is easy for a few individuals to do all the work and the rest to wander or check in and out as the case may be. The advantage of small group work is that the attention and participation of everyone is *required*. When there are only five people solving a tough problem, the ideas of each one are needed. Research on small groups has shown that in fact they are more efficacious than individual effort in arriving at the "right" answer.[1] The power of the group to involve others and support members is attested to by the success of such groups in helping people. There are groups for alcoholics, for dieters, for consciousness raising, for parents of twins, for single parents, for people with very high IQs.

The classroom small group is essentially a learning group. Only incidentally is it utilized for the psychological support it provides. Classroom groups are *not* therapy groups. The literature of psychology and mental health is full of small group procedures which are designed for improving individual adjustment. Some teachers may use such procedures in their classrooms, but only if they are trained and understand what they are doing. The typical classroom is not the place for such ventures into healing. However, our experience with small groups suggests that, in fact, they do work indirectly to provide a great deal of psychological support, although their prime objective is the enhancement of learning.[2]

While there are many techniques described in this book, it is important to emphasize that *if there is one method which the teacher should master, it is that of utilizing small groups in the classroom.*

Using small groups is one of the easiest procedures available. Small groups require:

no special expenditure of funds
no special equipment
no permission (usually)
no special teacher talent

Why then do so few teachers use group work? It has been advocated and espoused for over twenty years, and yet one can walk down the

[1] Donald Cartwright and Alvin Zander (Eds.), *Group Dynamics: Research and Theory*, 2d ed. New York: Harper & Row, 1960).
[2] Helley R. Krantz, "The Impact of Experiential Education," *Media and Methods*, 1r (September 1977), pp. 34-35, 112-123.

corridors of the typical high school and see all the seats in rows, the teacher at the front, and the old, weary, boring read-recite-quiz format in use. Frequent teacher explanations for not using group work are:

"Students misbehave when in groups; they gossip instead of working."
"The other teachers complain of the noise."
"The principal won't let me because he says it is too noisy" (or chaotic looking).
"I tried it once and it didn't work at all."
"The students don't like it; they prefer lectures because they know they are 'covering' the material."
"The teacher who has the room the period after mine wants the chairs all in rows, so I can't place them in small circles for groups."
"I've never done it."
"It's inappropriate to my subject."
"It sounds too much like progressive education."

Some of the comments have some validity; noise that bothers other teachers has to be considered. A principal who objects needs to be educated. But the other objections are merely rationalizations. The students can put the seats back in rows at the end of the period if the next teacher requires it! Because group work failed once is not evidence that it does not work at all.

GROUP WORK: GETTING STARTED

Group work should not be an odd and rare activity any more. Some students report group work in their secondary school experience. There are courses on group discussion in speech departments, and small group research is carried on in many psychology and sociology departments. It is helpful if the methods courses taken by prospective teachers involve them in many group activities so that they can learn by doing.

As a demonstration, in one teacher-education class, a student decided to use small groups to gather student opinion about an issue facing the University student government association at the time. The issue concerned the right of a student publication to publish without faculty censorship. The student leading the class said, "All right, we all know there is a lot of talk on campus about whether there should be censorship or not. Get into groups of no more than five—and don't be in a group with your best friends or people you know—and get a summary of the feelings of the group. I will give you 10 minutes for this." The class shuffled around. How does one find such a group? There was great confusion, and most of the allotted ten minutes went by with many students not attached to any groups, and with only a few groups tackling the problem with real enthusiasm. What went wrong? When the ten minutes were up, instead of reporting their feelings about censorship, the class, with the assistance of the instructor, went step by step over the procedures the student had used to organize the group activity. Although almost every mistake in the book had been made, both the student-leader and the other potential teachers in the group learned a great deal from the exercise. The "guts" of small group work were visible; they had actually been inside the situation, and could see some of the problems and possibilities.

There are two commonly used ways of starting group work in a classroom. One method is to develop several small committees to assist in administering the classroom. Such committees, for example, can supervise the supply room for a chemistry class. Committees can regulate the distribution of paper in a typing class. Bulletin board committees can keep current-events corners up-to-date in social studies classes. A second method is to start a class with a number of short-term groups, sometimes called "buzz" groups, whose purpose is to canvass opinion or make suggestions for class plans in a minimum of time with a maximum of participation.

Which approach to use depends in large measure on the level of self-confidence of the teacher. A teacher who has little familiarity with group activity might start with the committee system, since it is most nearly a logical outgrowth of other kinds of club and youth-group activities.

The physical arrangement of some classrooms and the content of some subject-matter areas, lend themselves more easily to one type of group activity than to another. But, with experience, most teachers, can successfully employ many kinds of groups.

One warning: Beginning teachers sometimes consider it appropriate to ask the students themselves whether they would like to use group procedures for doing their work. It is certainly part of good student-teacher planning to permit choices among approaches to learning. However, to ask a group of students, "Do you want to try buzz groups now?" when the class has no idea of the nature of a buzz group, is to ask them to render judgment from ignorance.

A better way to begin is to follow the natural sequence of unit development. When the class is at the point where decisions are needed about what problems should be studied in the unit, buzz groups can be initiated. Instead of having thirty-five youngsters try to reach agreement, the teacher can say, "We want to get everyone's opinion on what problems we ought to cover in this unit. I will put you in small groups of five, for about five minutes. If we all put our heads together, we ought to be able to make better choices." Meeting places in the classroom are then designated. Leaders, for this first time, are appointed. And group work begins.

SHORT-TERM GROUPS

Short-term, or buzz groups, which are typically used to attack specific jobs, are limited in scope. The tasks can usually be completed in a short period of time—from five to twenty minutes. Good preplanning enhances the probability of success of buzz groups, with all the accompanying bonus of improved morale.

DECIDING ON THE PROBLEM FOR THE GROUPS TO DISCUSS. The task of the buzz group must be clearly defined in the mind of the teacher and fully recognized by the groups. Typically, buzz groups are useful for getting a quick reaction to a controversial issue, for planning the next steps in a unit, for assessing the relative importance of proposed topics of study, and for setting up rules or regulations for class activities or materials.

CHOOSING THE STRATEGIC MOMENT TO INITIATE THE BUZZ GROUP. A buzz group may serve to organize a discussion and extend the involvement of the class. For example, a group might be engaged in a heated discussion about athletic policies. Since sex discrimination has been ruled illegal, schools have had to rethink athletic programs. What makes for "equal treatment" of boys and girls in athletics? It is soon obvious that everyone in the class has an opinion, but not everyone can be heard no matter how long a discussion is continued. This is the ideal point at which to set up buzz groups. In fact, the moment everyone in the class is excitedly arguing and bedlam seems to have descended, is precisely when the teacher can exclaim, "Aha! You are all talking at once. Everyone wants to say something on this issue! Great! Let's get into buzz groups so you can all talk at once!" Group members are then quickly announced, group size established, a time limit given, and the groups are told to get to work.

A buzz group could then occur in the middle of a discussion; buzz groups could also precede a general discussion, to warm the class up and clarify the issues. Buzz groups could also be used to summarize a discussion coming at the end of a period of study.

DETERMINING HOW THE BUZZ GROUPS WILL BE CHOSEN. The several ways of choosing buzz groups are important enough to require a separate discussion. For the moment, let us say that the method of choosing will be based on which kind of group composition will "jell" fastest and still suit the purpose. The buzz group will usually number about five persons, though any number from three to six can "buzz" effectively. A group that is too small has too few resources to call upon; a group that is too large lets some members take a silent role or become disruptive when not involved.

SETTING THE TIME LIMITS. Time is the most effective discipline for keeping lively adolescents focused on the problem to be solved. The time allowed should be as short as possible while still allowing members to explore the topic. It is always better to allow too little time than too much.

It does take experience to determine how long adolescents can talk about something productively before the discussion degenerates into horseplay. If the teacher underestimates the time, the students can then be told that, since the task has not yet been accomplished, they can have another three or four minutes to finish. Or, if some groups finish sooner than expected, time can be called. The students will not be watching the clock if the problem is real.

ESTABLISHING GROUP ORGANIZATION. Only a chairman and a recorder or reporter are needed for organizing each group. But how will they be chosen? Sometimes the teacher can select them ahead of time on the basis of known qualities of leadership or knowledge of the field. Sometimes the tasks can be used to bring in students who do not usually participate. It is often good policy to use very arbitrary means: "The person whose name is nearest the top of the alphabet will be chairman; the person whose name is nearest the bottom of the alphabet will be recorder." If the group members are strangers to one another, such a procedure means that they have to introduce themselves by name. And it makes retreat from the assigned role difficult.

The teacher may also use the alphabetical selection as a way of insuring that a particularly shy or inarticulate student is given an important function.

After five weeks of school Nancy Anderson had not said a word in class. She never raised her hand to volunteer an answer, and when called on blushed furiously and mumbled that she didn't know the answer. Yet her homework papers were as good as anyone's, and showed that she knew what was going on. So when the class first went into buzz groups, I determined that she would talk! I watched the group she was in and noted that no other student whose names began with "A" were in her group. So I confidently announced that the group reporters would be the persons whose names began with A. Of course, Nancy had to report for her group. It was a pleasant surprise to hear her give a well-stated report. Her shyness did not disappear over night, but she did show more interest in general class participation after this. I also, of course, made sure to compliment her on her poise in reporting.

Giving the class clown a responsibility in the group will have a salubrious effect on him or her. Each group wants to show it can do as well as the next group and group members soon quiet someone who wants to show off or act up. Another important outcome can be giving leadership to students who typically are not chosen by their classmates. It has been observed in racially mixed settings that the white students assume that they are naturally the intellectual leaders, and ignore or put down black students.[3] Small groups with arbitrarily assigned leadership roles provide an opportunity for all students to be perceived as competent, sooner or later, and to feel in themselves that they too have a positive role to play.

Giving the group its leadership rather than allowing the group to choose its own is useful particularly if the class is unfamiliar with group work. Later, the roles will be assumed rather naturally. But at the beginning, structuring the group helps get work under way quickly. In long-term

[3] E. Earl Baughman, *Black Americans*. (New York: Academic Press, 1971).

groups the selection of leadership is vital; in short-term groups it is less important.

ARRANGING FOR GROUP REPORTS. Usually the appointed reporter will tell the rest of the class what was decided in the group. These decisions may be listed on the board; they may be the basis for further discussion by the whole class; or the reporters may be asked to form a group to summarize all the findings. If the reports are brief and to the point, it is ordinarily useful for each group to hear and see its own report presented to the total class. Then a certain pride of ownership encourages the youngsters to want to engage in this kind of activity again. The involvement of each person in "our" group's report is assured as each reporter tells what the group accomplished.

WAYS OF CHOOSING MEMBERS OF BUZZ GROUPS

The method of choosing members for buzz groups must be simple and easily executed. The groups are too temporary to justify elaborate selection procedures. Several illustrations of feasible methods are given below.

Groupings may be based on the established seating pattern. Instead of moving students around, the teacher can designate the five students sitting nearest to one another as constituting a group. However, to avoid confusion, the teacher will want to go around the room, pointing out specifically the groups to be formed. If the seats are in rows, students may be grouped either horizontally across the room or vertically from front to back.

Prearranged groupings may be developed. Any one of these factors can be used to divide the class: (a) an alphabetical listing of the students; (b) a sociometric test (see p. 265); or (c) talents, backgrounds, or interests. These may be used to set up homogeneous or heterogeneous groups.

When prearranged groupings are used, duplicated lists, with a copy for each student, facilitate rapid organization. At the time the groups are designated, a number should be given to each for purposes of easy identification. A rough sketch on the chalkboard may be used to show where in the classroom each group will meet. Then it is easy for students to move into their buzz groups without confusion. The lists of group members should not be distributed until the moment arrives for the groups to convene, because the listing provides a very tempting occasion for comment (either aloud or undercover) about who is in what group, and with whom!

Instead of duplicating the list, the teacher may put it on the chalkboard before class and pull a map or chart over it until the list is needed. Reading the list aloud is generally unsatisfactory. Students forget their group assignments; reactions to the names of those grouped together may be loud and prolonged; and, invariably, at least one student just does not hear his or her name.

A counting-off device is sometimes useful. Some classes are seated according to their own wishes. Friends sit near friends. When the teacher seeks to widen the circle of acquaintance, counting-off will produce a thorough reshuffling. And it's fun besides. Starting in one corner of the room, the first student is number 1, the next is 2, and so on. The final number is determined by the size of the class. If there are thirty-five students, and groups of five are wanted, the numbering continues through to seven and then starts over again. This gives seven groups of five members each. All the "ones" are in the first group; the "twos" in the second group, and so on.

Numbered cards can be made ahead of time. These cards contain the buzz group numbers. If there are to be seven groups of five members each, there will be five cards with the number 1 on them, five with 2, and so on to number 7. These can be shuffled and passed out at random by student monitors. The number received designates the student's buzz group. There is some danger that students will trade cards clandestinely with each other in order to get into a particular group. This may be halted by an admonition from the teacher to keep the card one is given; or the teacher may choose to ignore it if it is not widespread enough to defeat the purpose of the procedure. When the groups have been organized, the numbered cards may be collected and used again another time.

Whatever device is used for setting up buzz groups, the important thing is to do it speedily.

To facilitate speed in setting up groups, particularly if students are to move from their regular seats, the teachers should warn them: "Gather all your movable belongings because you are soon going to be sitting someplace else." Without such a warning, there is apt to be a mad scramble to collect belongings that are on the desk, in the desk, on the floor, in the shelf under the seat; even these few moments of chaos are wasteful, and preventable.

Observation of adolescents quickly reveals that disorder and disturbance in classrooms occur when there is nothing to do. Whenever seats are to be moved or rearranged, there is an opportunity for someone to wander off on private pursuits. Quick and efficient transitions from general discussion into buzz groups lessen the likelihood of disturbance. Of course, if the students are genuinely interested in what the groups are going to do, that motivation alone will get them into their groups quickly.

WAYS OF USING BUZZ GROUPS

A substitute teacher was faced with a class of seniors who had been studying some of the problems of vocational selection. Although the substitute was entirely new to the class, he felt that anything would be better than the usual teacher–student battle that goes on when a substitute comes in. So he took the class by surprise. He asked them to shift chairs into groups of five, and to list as a group some of the problems they felt they would face when they entered the world of work after June. The class took to the discussion with vigor; and, when the time was up, a provocative list of problems had been put on the board. The class was led into a discussion of "Which problem is most important now?" and then, "Which problems can we do something about ourselves," and "Which can we get help on from the school?" Next day, when the substitute returned, the class demanded another buzz session.

The buzz-group technique, as we have outlined it, has a host of uses. Early in the term buzz groups may discuss questions they would like to have answered in the course. Sometimes, when students have few questions regarding the course, the teacher may outline the variety of possible topics to be covered. The list should include more topics than can be taught. The problem for the groups then is to select those they would like to study. This device gives the students a chance to think critically about the course work ahead, gives them a feeling of proprietorship in the course work to be covered, and also provides an opportunity for them to meet others in the class early in the semester.

Another use for the short-term group is in working out routine problems or exercises together. For example, students may spend part of a period selecting from a list the sentences they consider most "vivid." Or they may grade the quality of a set of anonymous compositions, a procedure that gives them significant practice in critical judgment. The same sort of group situation is useful for judging various musical compositions, artistic productions, translations, lettering charts, floor plans, breakfast menus, recreation habits, propaganda slogans, and the like. One teacher allowed students in groups to correct their examinations together. Where morale is high and competition for grades has been deemphasized, this procedure minimizes the chance and the need to cheat or fabricate. It also provides all the students with an opportunity to learn the right answer, not just to find out theirs was wrong.

Short-term group activity may be devoted to the group game. This is particularly useful in those classes where a certain amount of drill is needed. The imaginative teacher can devise simple games that small groups can play while the rest of the class is engaged in other activities. Or, the whole class may play them together in small groups. This latter method ensures a maximum of practice for all, not merely for the most able or the most backward. It also makes routine drills somewhat more palatable. Classroom learning games (see p. 302) often depend on some kind of small group or team for decision making.

One of my most successful small group activities has been with the use of flat pictures. I cut pictures out of magazines which are vivid or interesting, showing people, places, events. These are pasted on ordinary paper. I arrange them in groups of seven or eight, being sure that each set has a good variety. After the students are placed in buzz groups, I give them a set of pictures. I ask the groups to select the picture they would most like to write a story about; they are not to write the story, just indicate their preference. After about five minutes, depending on the augumentativeness of the groups, I ask each reporter to hold up the group selection, and tell the class why each picture was chosen. I then turn to the class to make any comments they wish about the pictures or the process.

The use of flat pictures lends itself to many continuations of the buzz-group process. The groups may in fact be asked to write a group story about their chosen picture. Or the whole class can then select one picture, and each group set to the task to see what kind of story each group can devise. Before they know it, a class is engaged in creative writing—painlessly!

Or if the pictures show social conflict, the students can develop generalizations about what values make social conflict inevitable, or alleviate social conflict. Pictures that show men and women in stereotyped or unusual role situations could be used, and students asked to select those which are most or least liked, out of which could come a valuable discussion on sex-role expectations.

Discussion and analysis of films through buzz groups is another classroom application. Too often, as pointed out in Chapter 8, films waste class time because there is inadequate audience preparation and participation. If buzz groups are set up before the film and instructed regarding a task of analysis to be completed after the film, then students' attention is more likely to focus on the film, because there is a purpose in watching. Open-ended films, designed specifically for class discussion, are particularly good for buzz groups; all students will have a chance to react and be heard.

THE LONG-TERM GROUP

The buzz group is useful for small group activities which take up only a portion of a class period, and whose membership dissolves as soon as the group task is over. The long-term group is a more permanent working party, which may retain the same membership for several days or weeks. The ways in which long-term groups are set up, and the ways in which their tasks are defined and evaluated differ significantly from the methods used for buzz groups.

If a group is to work together for very long, the task assigned must be worth the effort. A class may meet daily for the eighteen or so weeks of a semester, which appears in prospect to be a very long time indeed. In actual practice, the eighteen weeks typically provide just enough time to encompass the most important material to be learned. It is therefore similarly important that the task for group work be an essential aspect of the course, and worth the kind of time devoted to establishing and conducting the group process.

It is also possible to organize all of one's instruction around group work. A home economics teacher assigns students to "kitchens" made up of four students. Then the task for each kitchen is to solve, as a group, the problems which relate to the units of instruction. For example, each kitchen must devise a series of balanced meals, following the guidelines for nutrition which had been studied. In a mathematics class, the teacher organizes small work groups. After a brief introduction of the new problem, a short question and answer period, practice problems are passed out. Each group then proceeds to solve the problems as a group. In the last part of the period, each group, with a rotating reporter, explains the solution to a given problem until all problems have been presented and solved. The practice and review possible by this method results in significant achievement by the whole class.

Obviously, even more than with buzz groups, meticulous preplanning is crucial. The teacher must first think through the facets of the problem and, second, guide the class in planning:

- feasible dimensions for the project
- equitable division of labor
- accessible resources and materials for study
- explicit goals of immediate appeal and lasting significance

Since the problems attacked by long-term groups are of some scope and depth, they have many facets to be investigated. Long-term groups, therefore, can undertake more differentiated and specialized jobs than buzz groups. A business education class, for example, might set up its groups according to the divisions of a large office and work through a problem in office management. Because of the longer period allowed, work that demands a fair amount of skill and coordinated team effort can be attempted with these groups; such projects are not feasible with buzz groups.

Some classes have traditionally been organized in this way, although they are often not recognized as such. Journalism classes, for instance, where the class is also the editorial and news gathering group for the schools newspaper, is in fact a long-term group. Differential assignments to students, the leadership role of the editor, evaluation and critique meetings after the publication of the paper, are all aspects of group process. Using this model, other classes can likewise develop an internal structure which provides for different students to contribute, either alone or with a few others, to a common product. Or subgroups of the class can each become working units in which members perform different functions to enable a final product to emerge.

The science experiments were organized so that they could be carried out by small groups of four or five. One student was responsible for getting the required supplies and equipment. One student arranged the material. A third carried out the experiment. The other four kept records of what occurred. They compared notes at the end and wrote up the results as a group. A fifth member then cleaned up the area and put the equipment away. These tasks were rotated every time an experiment was to be conducted. Students developed a roster for each group with task assignments identified so there was no confusion about who did what.

Group membership may be determined by a number of factors, such as interest, ability, student background, interpersonal relationships. An example of each is given below:

INTEREST GROUPS

A world history class was studying Egypt. The students became interested in the kind of schools that children went to in ancient times and expressed interest in various phases of the subject. Mr. Stein listed on the board some of the things they suggested that might be worth investigating: what the students wore to school; what subjects they studied; what a typical school looked like; what kinds of children went to school. Some were interested in whether there were special kinds of schools for the nobility; whether there were separate schools for boys and girls; whether those schools were better or worse than contemporary ones. The students were asked to indicate which topic interested them most. Mr. Stein pointed out that some topics might be illustrated by models or drawings and that some might be dramatically portrayed to the class. One or two topics, which were obscure, demanded research in the main town library.

As Mr. Stein looked over the names of the students who had signed up for the various topics, the teacher could easily see how the natural interests of the students had determined the group they chose. Johnny, who liked to carve wood and was interested in very little else, had chosen to work on what a typical school looked like. Polly, who designed her own dresses, chose the group on clothing. Alicia, with a high IQ, chose the topic of the subjects studied in ancient schools, which might require work at the main library—where she practically lived anyway. And so on around the class.

ABILITY GROUPS

The senior English class was very much concerned about passing the English entrance examinations for the state university. Much emphasis was therefore being placed on gaining competence in grammatical usage, reading comprehension, and facility in composition. Miss O'Neil gave the class several achievement tests in English and clearly saw the major weaknesses of each student in these three areas. She suggested to the class that she might arrange groups for them in which they could work together on these weaknesses. The class accepted the idea, and it was agreed that Tuesday and Thursday would be the days when the "problem" groups, as they were to be called, would meet together. Workbooks and special exercises would be provided by Miss O'Neil. The other days of the week would be devoted to regular class instruction.

After this plan had been operating for several weeks, the students suggested a revision. It was clear that some students were very good in one area where others were weak. It was also clear that the teacher could not get around to all the groups each period to work with them on their problems. They asked whether every other time one of the better students might be assigned to the groups as a sort of teacher's aide. This meant that a number of the students did not meet with their own groups, but worked as experts with slower or less capable students. Then the situation would be reversed; a student who was skillful in grammar might be poor in reading or in understanding poetry; he would then be given assistance by another student.

As the semester progressed, many shifts in groupings occurred. The teacher kept a record of the problem groups and their membership; she also noted those students who acted as teacher's aides. She found that almost every student had worked on at least one aspect of each skill area, and, in addition, all but five students had been able to develop sufficient proficiency in some special topic to be asked to work with a given group for one or more periods.

GROUPS BASED ON BACKGROUND

A biology class was studying communicable diseases. A question arose about which parts of town were the most sanitary. The students at this union high school came from over half the county. By a show of hands, it was found that most of the students fell into natural groupings according to their home addresses. A map of the school district was obtained from the principal, and rough districts were drawn. All those living in a given district agreed to explore sanitation conditions in their section. By planning with the students, the teacher was able to set up five groups of four to six members for each section of the map. The groups were then given the remainder of the hour to list the things they thought they should look for. The next day, each group submitted its list. A master list was then compiled. The teacher suggested further reading in the text and some additional references so that the students would know how to recognize danger areas. Thus a group project was launched.

GROUPS BASED ON SOCIAL RELATIONSHIPS

A second-year Spanish class planned a fiesta for "Back-to-School Night," a night on which parents visited various classes. Each student was asked to name three students with whom he or she would like to work. Miss Esperanza discovered some facts about her class that she had never suspected. Albert was widely chosen, whereas she had believed he had few friends. Deborah was selected by only one girl, and she had been certain that everyone liked her. The only two Spanish-American girls in the class did not indicate each other as preferred workmates. Henry, easily her worst student and certainly the most irritating, was chosen more widely than any other person in the class.

As a result of these discoveries, Miss Esperanza had some doubts about the wisdom of student selection, but she decided to balance the groups to the best of her ability. Some of those who were widely accepted she placed with others rarely chosen. It was Miss Esperanza's first attempt to use this means of forming groups, and she soon found that she had made some mistakes, but within a week, with some judicious shifting, the groups functioned surprisingly well.

Advance scheduling of the work of long-term groups is mandatory if a secure sense of progress is to be maintained. Each group should know where it is to be each day (classroom, library, or other location), what it is to be doing (discussing, researching, and so forth), which materials and supplies are required (periodicals, pamphlets, and the like), when tasks are to be completed (day, week, etc.), who has the various responsibilities (typing, illustrating, and similar tasks). It is usually good strategy to place on a bulletin board a summary of the essential elements of scheduling.

Almost all students need their time sense sharpened. Before they know it, deadlines are upon them. Group morale deteriorates and the project collapses. A few minutes spent regularly in a review of group progress, with specific discussion of what remains to be done, prevents these catastrophes.

The teacher will want to help the groups realize that different members may make good leaders for different kinds of work. Some are good pre-planners and assigners of responsibility. Others are good at expediting matters. Still others are adept at compiling final reports and summarizing group opinion.

Sometimes it is feasible to run brief leadership clinics to show group leaders just what responsibilities their job entails. Problems encountered by the different groups can be discussed, and next steps proposed by the several leaders.

EVALUATING GROUP OUTCOMES

How effectively the group functions as a group is at least as important as the products of its efforts. The group should become conscious of what helps it to operate well and what obstructs its functioning. This means a good hard look at both individual members and the group as a whole.

It will require some practice before students can look at themselves with any degree of objectivity. Discussion has to be focused on *what* was done to help or hinder, rather than on *who* did it. The list of do's and don'ts will grow gradually. One class developed this list:

Helps	Hinders
Willing to work	Ducks responsibility
Willing to try something else	Wants to play it safe
Cheerful and helpful	Cross and selfish
Has a sense of humor	Always expecting the worst
Suggests another way when people disagree	Insists on having own way
Wants to do things well	Likes to find the easy way out
Gets things done on time	Has a lot of excuses

Each class should develop its own list. Some classes have found it worthwhile to make posters generously decorated with caricatures of the various group roles. With a little help, the groups themselves can use these guides to recognize group members' strengths and weaknesses.

EVALUATION OF GROUP PROCESS

Evaluation of the way a group works is as valuable, in the long run, as evaluating the outcomes of the work of the group. Since we will be living in groups all of our lives, it can be a significant contribution to lifelong learning if young people are helped to become competent in this essential area. Too often a teacher uses an approach to instruction without assessing the ways in which students are utilizing that approach. When group work is first introduced to students, they should be told that there will be continuous evaluation so that it does not come as a surprise or as something extraneous. It is indeed appropriate for the teacher to give some background regarding the role of groups in everyday life, to show students the importance of the group skills they can learn. Such an introduction to the group process may help make students more aware of what they are doing, and thus better participants in the whole endeavor.

Groups are sustained in their efforts when they have specific guides for appraisal. Several are described below as illustrations of types classes will wish to adopt or adapt for themselves.

At the end of a period, when the groups have been meeting for some time, the teacher may use a very simple form in order to get a quick check on group members' satisfaction with their meeting:

HOW GOOD WAS OUR MEETING?

Name (or group number or group topic)
_____

1. Check the line below at the point which best indicates your feeling about your group meeting:

_____

  Very Good   Good   All Right   Not Very Good   No Good

2. What was the best thing about the meeting?

3. What was the main weakness of the meeting?

4. Comments and suggestions.

Records of group participation may be filled in either by the teacher as he or she observes the groups, or by a member of the group. An example of a form that may be used is given below. This will help the teacher, as well as the group, to see to what extent certain individuals are doing either too much or too little. Various kinds of observation forms may be devised by the class itself for special purposes.

GROUP-PARTICIPATION FORM

Leader

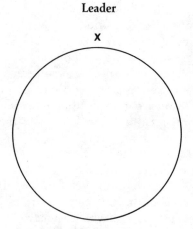

The names of group members are written around the circle. Whenever a person makes a contribution, that name is checked. The group participation pattern may be recorded in any one of three different ways:

Quantity participation record: A tally mark is recorded after each person's name every time he or she makes a contribution. This gives a sum of contributions.

Quality participation record: As each person makes a contribution, an evaluative mark is put after the name. These marks are:

Plus = a contribution that aids group thinking.
Minus = a contribution that delays or interferes with group progress in think-
      ing.
Zero = a remark that neither aids nor hinders: a "blah" remark.
  ? = individual asks a question.

In using this scoring method, it is often difficult for observers to put down many minus marks, since it is likely to hurt the feelings of those evaluated. However, if the discussion about the scoring is objective, and everyone sees that a minus score may simply mean lack of skill in group participation, then the negative factors may be recorded without damage to morale.

Group interaction record: An arrow is used to join the names of individuals whenever they talk to one another. When an individual addresses a remark to the group as a whole, the arrow should point out toward the edge of the paper. The pattern recorded is apt to be very interesting; it is possible to note how the leader or chairman is leading the discussion, or whether two people are carrying on a personal argument.

USE OF GROUP OBSERVERS

It may be helpful to use group observers in evaluation, assigning one student to each group. These observers can then report to the whole class on how well the group was able to work together. The role of the observer provides excellent training; and the task of observing often helps students who have particular difficulty in working with a group.

USE OF GROUP RECORDERS

The function of the group recorder may be to report the group's progress both to the group and to the teacher or class. The recorder is more than a secretary and should be an assigned role for boys as well as girls. The recorder helps the group to think toward its goal. The leader of the group can help balance the discussion and include those who are least verbal, while the recorder asks such questions as, "Now what is the issue we are discussing?" "Is this an accurate statement of what we decided to do?"

"I am not sure that we covered the point raised by John a while back regarding————." From the record made in this fashion, the teacher as well as the group has a sense of where it is going, and how.

METHODS OF APPRAISING
INDIVIDUAL PARTICIPATION

Often the class, as well as the teacher, may be dissatisfied with giving a whole group the same grade for the group report or group product, whatever that may be. As a method of helping to assess the individual efforts, the teacher may ask the members of the group to evaluate one another. Each student may also evaluate his or her own progress. A form similar to the one below may be used.

Members of the Group	Effort	Leadership	Quality of Work	Cooperation
1.				
2.				
3.				
4.				
5.				

Directions: In the spaces after each name, put a letter grade to indicate how well, in your opinion, each member of your group demonstrated the particular item listed. Include a grade for yourself in each category.

Invitations to self-evaluation help some students to face up to their responsibilities. They can be phrased quite directly (see following page).

The teacher will find it very useful to develop such a rating form with the assistance of the entire class. When the students aid in building such evaluative tools, they are learning some very important social skills. In addition, they are learning to discriminate among ideas, to establish values regarding interpersonal behavior, and to view behavior—their own and that of others—objectively. It is easier for students in the class to fill in such a rating form intelligently if the items and the form itself have been phrased and designed by them.

	Yes	No	Sometimes
I do my part of the group's work.			
I get my work done on time.			
I accept leadership seriously.			
I offer any ideas I have.			
I assist others.			
I am uncomfortable in my group.			
Group members don't like me.			

REPORTING THE FINAL PRODUCT

While some long-term groups will not need to report to the rest of the class, others should share with their classmates the results of their research. Experience with group reports has been gratifying wherever the groups have been enouraged to try new ways of educating their classmates. The following steps should be taken with the class prior to group reporting:

Set a deadline for groups to report. Some groups may report earlier than others, or all groups may be asked to be ready for reporting by a certain date. This date may be shifted forward or backward depending on the progress of the groups in obtaining the needed information or performing the assigned tasks.

A schedule for reporting once agreed upon should be posted on the bulletin board or placed on the chalkboard where it will not be erased. The posting of deadlines becomes a continual reminder; no one can then say, "Oh, we didn't know we were supposed to report on Tuesday!" when the day and date have been prominently displayed for several weeks.

Agree on the function of the group report. If the report is to inform, then the group must emphasize facts; must seek ways of discriminating between important and unimportant facts; must find media for presenting factual material so that all can see it at once—such as graphs, charts, slides. If the report is to stimulate discussion, then a panel, a debate, a dramatic introduction of some sort is required.

Discuss what it means to educate others. The class will often need to analyze the difference between that which is educational and that which is

EXAMPLE OF EVALUATION SHEET FOR INDIVIDUAL
OR GROUP REPORT TO CLASS

Delivery

_____Too formal	_____Relaxed; at ease
_____Rambling	_____Well-organized
_____Read from notes	_____Put in own words
_____No visual aids	_____Used appropriate visual aids
_____Insufficient detail	_____Sufficient detail; used examples
_____Poor eye contact	_____Good eye contact
_____Uninterested in subject	_____Enthusiastic, interested
_____Poor posture	_____Good posture
_____Didn't ask for questions	_____Asked for questions
_____Too informal; disorganized	

Informational Content

_____Few sources used	_____Variety of sources used
_____Errors in information	_____Information sound
_____Needs more research	_____Good research

Total Evaluation

Generally poor   Fair   Good   Excellent

---

merely novel, entertaining, or startling. Turn the thinking of the class upon what their classmates need and want to know.

Encourage originality. Point out the poor effects of a dull, boring, and confused presentation. Suggest some things that groups can do to enliven their report and attract the interest of the class.

Some tenth-grade students who were reporting on their vocational choice, elementary school teaching, recognized that they were shy and fearful about facing their classmates. They therefore borrowed the school tape recorder and, in the privacy of a quiet room, merely conversed about their findings. The next day in class the recorded report had a freshness and vitality that pleased everyone.

Review the material on good oral reporting. Since the success of many group reports will depend on the skill of its members in oral presentation, some class discussion of oral report forms is very useful.

Arrange for responsibility for evaluating the information contained in the report. It should be clear just what the class audience will be asked to recall as a result of the presentation. The teacher may announce that the group will make up exam questions on the basis of its reports, that the teacher will take this responsibility, or that designated members of the class will be asked to make up the questions for a later quiz. Or, the class may be directed to take notes on the presentation, or to summarize the main points presented by the group. This is a vital aspect of assuring class attention to the report, but the teacher will want to be careful not to make the audience so anxious about every minor fact that it interferes with communication.

Designate clearly the teacher's role during the group effort. Sometimes the teacher may request a few moments at the end of the report to add, summarize, or emphasize some point the group may have overlooked, or give a brief evaluation of the report. Once in a while a discussion is so lively or a report is so amusing that the class gets somewhat out of hand; the teacher should then step in. If a group member freezes completely with stage fright, the teacher may want to come to the rescue rather than leaving it up to a chairperson.

OUTREACH

The outcomes of group work take on added significance when the report goes to a person or agency outside the classroom.

The students in Mr. Perloff's introductory graphic arts class conducted a survey of businesses in the employment area of their middle-sized city. Each group was assigned one area, which was marked off on a huge map that hung in the classroom. They phoned many of the stores or workplaces; others they visited. They found out a great deal about the need for persons trained in graphics, and the level of training and experience different employers expected or required. When the groups were ready to report, the school counselors from the three high schools in the city were asked to visit so they could learn about the work needs in this career area. Not all could come, but there were several from each school. They found the data interesting, and commented on how helpful it was to them as none had any background in graphics.

When there is this kind of outside reporting, group members find the work more significant. In addition, they are no longer working for a grade, yet their work will be of higher quality than if a grade were the only goal.

Remember that it is not always necessary for a group to report directly to the class. Sometimes too much class time is taken for student reports. The group report should be a significant activity, and each report must be carefully worked out. Sometimes using bulletin board displays or circulating a written report is a satisfactory substitute for the oral report. Too frequent group reports can become monotonous and may be as inefficient as too few.

PROBLEMS TO WATCH FOR

As all teachers know, the best made plans for an exciting instructional period can evaporate like so much fog in a hot sun. A fine plan may not work because the students just cannot be stimulated to effort. At other times, students wade into a project with the best will in the world but soon flounder and get bogged down.

Group work, with its considerable stress on initiative and independence, has its share of success and failure. Some of the mistakes that make failure more likely are listed below.

Starting a group or committee project without preparation of the class by the teacher. What is the group to do? Who is to do it? How are leaders to be chosen? What is the responsibility of group members? These and similar questions should be explored early and fully.

Setting up a research job but failing to provide adequate materials for the groups. Having insufficient materials may cause many students to be idle while a few do the work.

Confusing individual goals with group goals. Because students are so used to individual grades and individual work situations, it is often difficult for them to learn how to be responsible and cooperative group members. The teacher must assess the level of group skills of the entire class as well as of individual students in order to provide needed guidance along the way. The problem chosen for group work should be one that requires or rewards group effort, rather than a problem that could more easily be done alone.

Making projects either too complicated or too simple for the time available. If the project cannot be accomplished, a group will soon give up the task. If the problem is so easy that it can be solved in far less time than provided, then members are going to find something else to occupy their time, and may possibly harass the teacher.

Putting the wrong people together. Sometimes certain combinations of students are explosive. The teacher should always announce to the class, particularly when setting up long-term groups, that, if necessary, members may be shifted around. The use of sociometric procedures, described later, helps establish good group "mixes." The next section of this chapter will provide procedures to help the teacher identify appropriate groupings.

THE TEACHER LEARNS, TOO

Yes, there can be too much of a good thing. Although group work is one of the most significant techniques for raising the efficiency of learning as well as solving many of the disciplinary problems of the classroom, there is such a thing as too much group work. Students also need ample time to develop their own skills and interests, to learn to pace themselves at their own speed, and to work alone at tasks which are uniquely suitable for individual achievement.

It is a truism of education that the closer teachers can get to knowing each student as a person, the better able they will be to provide each student with an education. One of the special dividends of group work is the large fund of observations about learning needs and potentials that the teacher accumulates: Susie surprises you by coming up with good compromises; Loudmouthed Jack injects a needed bit of humor when discussion verges on argument; Joe is particularly sensitive to those who have not yet had a chance to say anything; Nancy is so intent on hard work that she drives the other members of the group too hard.

When groups are effectively at work, the teacher does not settle back at the desk with a sigh of relief for a needed rest. Rather, this is a rare opportunity to see students as a whole. Many teachers have come to a new appreciation of some students by observing the adequacy with which they can operate with their peers. These may be the same students who try and often succeed in making life miserable for teachers. But equally significant, the teacher has a chance to observe and become acquainted with all the students.

Most of the problems associated with group work listed above are easily and quickly remedied when the teacher is alert to what is going on: This means that the teacher is circulating around the room continually while the class is in groups. The role of the teacher is to provide support, to give a word of advice where needed, to assist when a real impasse is reached, to challenge a group that gets a solution too easily, and to suggest other alternatives the group has not considered. It is true that, after a class has settled into a group project, the teacher may then be free to hold individual conferences with students and even to leave the room for a few minutes on an errand. But most of the time the teacher must be visible and in communication with all the groups. Just by being present and observant, the teacher communicates to the students a concern for what they are doing, which provides the kind of support students need in order to flourish.

UNDERSTANDING THE CLASS SOCIAL STRUCTURE

To be successful, group work procedures may depend on a careful analysis of the subgroups already existing, or the groups may be of such short duration that it does not really matter who works with whom. However, whether the teacher uses groups for extended study purposes, or for only short buzz-group sessions, it is valuable to have insight into the network of interpersonal relationships that exist. Some group work situations, whether or not of short duration, do not succeed because the teacher has put the wrong "mix" of students together.

Some classrooms seem to have a good atmosphere, others do not:

A student teacher was struggling with a difficult eighth-grade class. Few things he tried met with much success. They were sullen, antagonistic, refused to do homework, and did a minimum in class. It was suggested that perhaps group work might be tried. The supervising teacher, who often used group work herself, said that it would probably not work with this class. She explained that the class members literally hated one another. They were a group of relatively slow learners, plus some adolescents with very difficult behavior problems. They were "block scheduled": That is, they had to take most of their classes together, although they moved from teacher to teacher. So these students, among whom such animosity existed, were forced to be together for most of their school day. No wonder group work was impossible! However, with some perseverance, the student teacher was able to identify some pairs of students who could work together, although there were some with whom no one could, or would, work. The students enjoyed working in pairs; the student teacher finally overcame their antagonism; and most of these class members eventually were able to increase their achievement, as well as to gain more success in learning.

In addition to being hindered by inadequate class groupings, teachers are often puzzled to observe that some students appear to "fit in" while others do not.

When Tony entered the eleventh-grade physical education class in the middle of November, the teacher, Mr. Papadoro, observed that the other boys didn't seem interested in him. Often, when a new boy came, the other students came around, chatting about where he had come from, giving him a few helpful hints about the school. But Tony was ignored. On the surface he seemed like any other kid: average height, regular features. But he was quiet, almost sullen. Sitting behind him on the bench, Mr. Papadoro saw Bill come up and sit next to Tony. Bill didn't say anything, just sat. Bill was another lonely boy. The other students ignored him too. Mr. Papadoro was interested to see a rather silent friendship evolve. Thereafter, Bill and Tony sat on the sidelines together, two "outsiders." Mr. Papadoro was still puzzled, though. He had no idea what it was that made these two boys seem so isolated. What did they do that made the others shy away from them, leave them alone? Mr. Papadoro tried putting each of the boys on a different team, but they still didn't mix with the others. The only playfulness he ever saw them exhibit was when the two of them tossed a ball back and forth together. Then there was much typical kidding and running commentary on each other's skill. But with the other boys, they were silent. Why?

Many teachers often feel just as puzzled as Mr. Papadoro. Here is Jane —pretty, well-dressed, nice manners—and yet no one seems to claim her as a friend; on the other hand, Jill—sloppy, not too bright, giggly—seems to be the center of a whole group of girls and boys. Thelen[4] and his associates have studied classroom groups and have come to the conclusion that with appropriate diagnosis, "teachable" groups can be identified and students who worked well together and who worked well with a given teacher can then be placed in the same classroom situations, thus enhancing the learning of all.

A network of likes and dislikes, prejudices and tolerances, crushes and hatreds, is always present in every classroom. The judicious use of a rather simple technique can give the teacher some hints as to the social structure and social valuations of a class.

SOCIOMETRIC TESTS

As the name implies, the sociometric test measures social relationships.[5] This device is so simple that its real significance is sometimes overlooked. Typically it consists of the following. The teacher states:

> Tomorrow we had planned to set up the groups for our review of the unit we have just finished. It doesn't matter which group you are in, because we will all be doing the same thing. However, I know that students work best with those they like. So I am going to ask you to indicate on this slip of paper the three other members of this class that you would like to work with in this group.
>
> Put a number 1 to indicate your first choice, a number 2 for your second choice, and a number 3 for your third choice.
>
> Now, in case there is someone you would not like to work with, draw a dividing line and write the name of that person.
>
> You probably can't all have your first choice, but I will do my best to see that you work with one or more of the persons that you have listed.

Note that the teacher wanted a work group choice. For other situations, she might have asked for a team-mate choice, for a party group choice, for a bus seat companion, a fire drill companion, a seat pratner in class, a laboratory table partner, a problem-solving team choice, an assembly-program group choice.

The teacher studies the results of the choices very carefully. A chart such as the following one on p. 266 helps in plotting the total number of choices a student obtains.

It is important to obtain another view of the social pattern, however. A sociometric test can be translated into a sociogram, which reveals mutual choices, cliques, isolates, and those who are rejected. The illustration on page 267 is a sociogram of twelfth-grade class.

---

[4] Herbert A. Thelen, *Classroom Grouping for Teachability.* (New York: Wiley, 1967).
[5] The earliest discussion of this technique will be found in J. L. Moreno, *Who Shall Survive?* (Washington, D.C.: Nervous and Mental Disease Publishing Company, 1934).

A SAMPLE OF SOCIOMETRIC CHART
Chosen

Chooser	1 John	2 George	3 Jane	4 Mary	5 Henry	6 Bud	7 Phillip	8 Joe	Etc.
1. John					3	R	2	1	
2. George									
3. Jane									
4. Mary									
5. Henry									
6. Bud									
7. Phillip									
8. Joe									
9. Etc.									

John Dodge

The three people I would like to work with in a group are:

      Henry—1st
      Phillip—2d
      Joe—3rd

I would not like to work with:
      Bud

No. of times chosen

Total score

Directions: To enter the choices made by John Dodge, one reverses the weight: a first choice gets a weight of 3; a second choice, 2; a third choice 1. Then, when all choices have been entered, adding them up gives a quick measure of relative popularity; a high score indicates an individual with first and second choices.

ANALYZING A SAMPLE SOCIOGRAM

There are several points of immediate interest in the sociogram. First, the large numbers inside each circle refer in code to a student in the class. This helps retain anonymity of the sociogram just in case any outsider happens to see it. Second, the small numbers on the edge of the circle indicate what choice was made: a 3 means that that student was given third choice as a friend. The arrows indicate who did the choosing. A double line, with double arrowhead, indicates reciprocal choice. Third, the sociogram is drawn to indicate relative popularity; the larger the circle, the more choices, and the more first and second choices. Immediately we notice student 10, a boy who is markedly superior not only in total number of choices but also in first and second choices. Student 5 is also chosen often but all are second choices. Fourth, the cleavage between boys and girls is worthy of note. Only girls 18 and 19 chose boys. No boys chose girls. Boys 5, 10, and 15 have close reciprocal friendships, with 13 attached on the fringe as a friend of 10. Among the girls, 17 is on the edge of the clique made up of 18, 19, and 20.

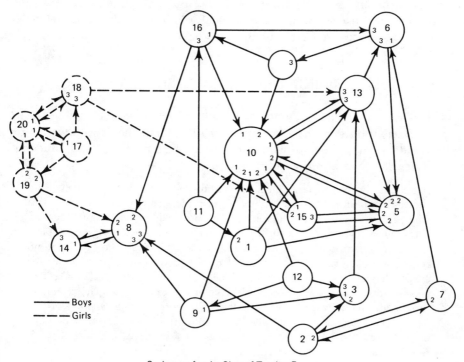

Sociogram for the Class of Teacher E

SOCIOGRAM FOR THE CLASS OF TEACHER E

In any sociogram we can see all these: direction of choice, intensity of choice, reciprocation of choice, accumulation of choice around individuals, and pattern of choices. The class we diagramed is unusual in some ways and typical in others. Since it is a twelfth-grade physics class, we would not expect to find many girls, nor do we. All the students are college-bound, and the girls are known as "brains." The two girls chose boys with whom they had worked. Often even the closest of boy–girl couples may not choose each other unless the class has had considerable group work already.

Why is boy 10 so popular? In this instance, he is the student-body president and a genuine student leader. He attracts the choices of the other students, although, again, no girl chooses him despite his high prestige. Student 8 is a foreign student, shy, with a language handicap. A girl chooses him: so do a number of others. This may be a protective role that the students are taking toward him, since he is so quiet and shy. The teacher was not aware that he had any friends.

Before this test was given, the teacher indicated his idea of the class structure. He picked student 12 as a popular student; but 12 received no votes at all from his fellow students. The teacher felt that no student was disliked; yet student 7 was actively rejected by three students (this is not indicated on the sociogram). Handicapped by these and other errors of judgment, this teacher would have difficulty improving the social relationships in his classroom. Certainly he would have a hard time setting up work groups.[6]

GIVING THE SOCIOMETRIC TEST

It is clear that this technique is a great aid to the teacher. It is easy to administer; it does not seek more information about the private worlds of the students than they are willing to reveal. As a matter of fact, students welcome the chance to choose!

In a Senior Problems class, the class had finished one project in which group choices had been based on a sociometric test. Mr. Landowsky asked the class whether they wanted to choose their group members the way they had before. The class was very enthusiastic in response, since the group experience before had been highly successful. Several students who had made no contribution before had, in a group of close friends, been able to do a very creditable job. The second time the choices were made, the teacher also had a list of topics for group projects. He asked them to indicate a choice among these and, finally, to state whether they felt more strongly about working on a given topic or working with the friends they had chosen. This gave more leeway for individual interests to assert themselves and met the different needs of the group as well.

[6] Sociogram and data adapted from material supplied by Dr. Fred Pinkham.

The importance of the secret vote must be emphasized. Often, voting that is done in class is by show of hands; students see whom others choose and are swayed or silenced by the will of the dominant members of the class. By allowing students to write down individual choices and having the teacher act as the repository of this confidence, more valid data may be obtained.

It is very important that the teacher respect the privacy of the choices. The teacher must use this kind of information with great discretion, since it has the power to hurt infinitely more than a single judgment by a teacher.

> Mr. Cecil was setting up a group situation for a quiz and asked the class to indicate in what group they would like to be for the test. In the class was a star athlete, a boy whose reputation extended far beyond the town. He seemed a nice fellow, although irregular in attendance and very quiet and unresponsive in class. He always sat with a group of boys who were also athletes, and the teacher had assumed they were buddies. But he was astonished to find that the star athlete was not liked by his "friends." Not one of his supposed buddies had chosen him. Mr. Cecil sought out the coach and asked him about the student. Both worked to help this boy handle more adequately his fabulous reputation, which was hindering, rather than helping, his long-term adjustment.

It is possible that some students, particularly those who fear that they will not be chosen, will develop great anxiety over the process of choosing. "Choosing sides" is used in some elementary schools, and there are always those who are chosen last. For some, this may be a traumatic experience.

> We were observing a beginning teacher in one of his first efforts to set up small groups for working on a series of science problems. It was an experimental setup in which classes were divided into groups of boys and girls on the hypothesis that girls often did not do so well in science because it was a "boy" subject. The teacher selected (on some basis which we never found out) five girls as team leaders. He asked them to select members of their "teams" in rotation. Each girl chose her best friend, who in turn strongly suggested whom to choose next. The horrible truth soon dawned on us: The least liked girls would be very obviously sitting in the nearly empty classroom while the team captains reluctantly selected among the unwanted. The most painful incident of all was the very last girl: All five captains simply refused to choose her. Her face was a picture of adolescent tragedy; our hearts broke for her. As the groups moved over to designated spots in the classroom we heard a number of angry mutters about the method of choosing. Later the teacher told us, with some surprise, that for some reason the method he had used in setting up the teams just had not seemed to work with the girls at all. In the boys' class (which we had not observed) he said the method had worked out very well. He complained that he just was not getting along well with the all-girl class at all.

It is important to emphasize the timing of the sociometric test. Teachers who have followed the suggestions given here have reported that, if they plan carefully, and have a very interesting and involving activity immediately after giving the sociometric test, then students rarely if ever ask questions about it, because their attention has been drawn into something of competing intrinsic interest.

The first sociogram that a teacher makes is bound to be difficult. It is not easy to see the relationships indicated by the choices, and manipulating the circles and triangles around the paper so that the lines of choice are as direct as possible seems very difficult, particularly with thirty-five to forty students. By making a sociograph first (the chart previously referred to on page 266), the teacher can see some of the patterns. It may be useful to pick out only two or three students and see the friendship pattern that exists around them. A magnetic board[7] may be very helpful in setting up a sociometric pattern easily, since it is an aid to moving the symbols around. A felt board[8] may also be used.

USING THE RESULTS OF THE SOCIOMETRIC TEST

After a sociometric test has been administered, the teacher is often amazed at the individuals who emerge as leaders or those who are not chosen. How reliable are the students' choices? It must be remembered that these choice patterns often shift. The grouping one week may differ considerably from that of the following week, and the grouping that occurs for one situation will be different from that of another.

The teacher may want to use sociometric information in order to deliberately influence the groupings in a classroom. Thus, one use of the technique can be as a check on the effectiveness of developing good human relations. Have the isolates acquired friends? There are some dramatic stories of changing social structures affected by utilizing sociometric insights. Of course, it must be remembered that to understand the many factors that go into sociometric choice requires years of working with young people. A beginning teacher cannot immediately see the dynamics of choice: why Mary gets ten first choices to Andy's one, or why tenth-graders refuse to cross sex lines in choices. Used judiciously, the teacher is provided with some insights into the hidden world of the adolescent.

Another very important function a sociogram can perform is indicating to the teacher which students are the indigenous leaders of the class. Knowing this can spell the difference between survival and disaster in some

---

[7] A magnetic board is simply a sheet of metal. Sociogram symbols are attached to small magnets and may be moved about the sheet of metal at will.
[8] A felt board is made of felt attached to a sheet of cardboard or a strip of wood. The sociogram symbols are glued to strips of felt or coarse sandpaper. The figures then will cling to the felt panel.

secondary schools. Wise teachers locate such leaders and carefully cultivate them so that these students support the goals the teacher has in mind. Often such students are not themselves aware of their own power; others do know and use it negatively and destructively. If the class leaders are against you, teaching is a struggle. If they are on your side, you can get the class to move as you want. Too many teachers are totally naive and uninformed about who the class leaders are, and also ignore the power and influence of such individuals. It is not a matter of catering to such individuals, but recognizing that they are an important factor in the response of the class, and as such should be given special attention.

SOME OTHER SMALL GROUP PROCEDURES

The human relations literature in the bibliography for this chapter includes references in which there are many different kinds of group procedures. Most of them are primarily for use in situations where the deliberate and accepted focus is better human relations. Some secondary schools provide classes in which the goal is to develop better human relations, but in most instances this can only be a by-product of techniques whose main purpose is academic instruction. Several techniques are useful, however, for both purposes.

Fish bowl

Fish bowl is a technique which lends itself readily to group decision making and conflict resolution. The class is divided into subgroups of five or six. One individual is designated as group representative. The groups are given four or five minutes to come to a decision about a problem. They instruct their representative as to the position the group will take. The representative then joins the other group representatives in the middle of the room—in the fish bowl. The group representatives then debate the issue, with all of the class as observers. No one but the group representatives can talk. The group members may communicate with their representative by sending notes. A representative can ask for "time out" if the need is felt to consult with the group for further instructions. A group can ask for "time out" to instruct its representative. When "time out" is called, all representatives return to their home group. After a set period, or when the problem or conflict is resolved to the satisfaction of the class, the activity ends.

Anita was undoubtedly the most persuasive person in class. She was able to sway others, even though her logic and information were sometimes dubious. This time the class faced a dilemma. A field trip was being planned. One plan called for making the trip all in one day, and the other called for an overnight stay. Anita wanted to stay overnight. There were obvious cost problems, but most of the class could manage it. However, for a few it would be a hardship. Also I had been told that some parents might not allow their darlings to stay overnight in the city. But Anita was bound to have her way. I decided to use fish bowl as a way to get the arguments in the open, and also to reduce Anita's power to sway the group. She was not the representative of her subgroup. Without her vociferous arguments, the fish bowl discussion proceeded amicably to weigh the pros and cons, and finally agreed to make the trip in one day, and then later in the spring to have an overnight trip, invite some parents as chaperones, and go to a site they regarded as less objectionable. The class was pleased with the decision, though Anita muttered about it for days.

An adaptation of fish bowl is to divide the class into two sides, as for a debate. One side is "affirmative" and the other "negative." Each side is then subdivided further into subgroups. The subgroups prepare full statements on the issues. After enough time is given for researching their position—which can take two or more periods if the issue is complex and worth intensive study—the group representatives meet as in a formal debate, with each side represented by two or three speakers. Prior to the formal debate, each side has its own preparatory fish bowl, listening to the arguments that the other groups on their side are preparing, and helping to determine the best set of arguments they can.

Both of these procedures involve all the students in a class discussion. If the topic is also an academic one, then all students are involved in thinking through the issues. In traditional debate, for example, only the team members really care about the outcomes, or have done any research into the topic. By making the whole class participants in the development of the debate issues, everyone knows the issues, and everyone cares about the outcome.

> A local battle divided the community. The major industry in town was under orders to reduce pollution. The managers were resisting, saying it would raise costs so much they would have to leave town, or go out of business. Many suspected this was bluffing. The science teacher decided this was excellent material for a class debate, and used the modified fish-bowl approach. The industrial arts teacher, who often felt that his classes were considered nonintellectual, also launched a student debate, with an entirely different set of students. When the two teachers heard that each was undertaking a study, they agreed to have a joint class meeting after school and let each class debate selected representatives of the other class. It was a roaring success!

Triad Interviews

The "triad interview" is a method of structuring exchange so that each person has a specific task in the group, and this task is rotated among the three members. The class is assigned to groups of three. These triads may be set up beforehand by the teacher or organized on the spot, depending on the purpose of the triad interview. The interview consists of one student interviewing a second student, while the third one records the contents of the interview. When the first interview is completed, the task rotates, with the second student interviewing the third one, and the first one recording. Round three is completed with the third student interviewing the first student, and the second recording it. One easy method of identifying who will do what is to have the group array itself in alphabetical order. Then they are designated A, B, and C. The following chart shows the interview progression, and should be placed on the board:

1. A interviews B; C records
2. B interviews C; A records
3. C interviews A; B records

After each round the teacher should collect each record. By collecting the records, the teacher indicates a genuine interest in the interviews. Depending on the topic, student names may or may not be required.

The subject matter for the interviews can vary widely. Topics which have been successfully used are: getting acquainted (favorite hobbies, music, TV stars, school activities); individual educational autobiographies; the history of one's family name; likes and dislikes about a school subject; plans for ten years hence; suggestions for dealing with school vandalism.

Following the completion of the interviews, the teacher can ask the group what has been learned. The teacher may report back to the class the next day what the major emphases of the group were or may ask a committee of volunteers to summarize the reports.

The triad is especially valuable as an ice-breaker, to help students get acquainted, to open up channels of communication. Because of its focus on individual opinion, students respond to it well; there is no one we like to talk about more than ourselves—when we have an interested audience!

SUMMARY

A class is more than a collection of individuals. A class is a group with many subgroups. The typical class is too large for actual group interaction. By using a variety of small group procedures, a teacher has at hand a very powerful, yet easily used tool for instruction. In addition, the sociometric test enables a teacher to identify some of the potent informal social groupings which occur in any collection of people and which have a significant impact on how well a class will respond to instruction.

SELECTED READINGS

Berkovitz, Irving H. (Ed.), *When Schools Care: Creative Use of Groups in Secondary Schools.* La Jolla, Calif.: Learning Resources Corporation, 1975. Emphasis on groups used for guidance, and also useful for understanding group processes in other settings.

Greer, Mary, and Bonnie Rubinstein (Eds.), *Will the Real Teacher Please Stand Up? A Primer in Humanistic Education.* Pacific Palisades, Calif.: Goodyear Publishing Company, 1972. See Chapter 6, "The Group as a Way of Exploring Ideas," pp. 129–156. Interesting and varied short readings which illustrate the many ways in which groups enter into the instructional process. See also Chapter 7, "The Group as a Way of Exploring Feelings," pp. 157–172.

Lifton, Walter M., *Groups: Facilitating Individual Growth and Societal Change.* New York: Wiley, 1972. Reviews the research to date and suggests implications for educational practice.

McGrath, Joseph E., and Irwin Altman, *Small Group Research.* New York: Holt, Rinehart and Winston, 1966. Reviews the research which supports the educational outcomes of small group work.

Nelson, Murry R., and H. Wells Singleton, "Small Group Decision Making for Social Action," in Dana G. Kurfman (Ed.), *Developing Decision Making Skills,* Washington, D.C.: Forty-Seventh Yearbook of the National Council for Social Studies, 1977, pp. 141–176. Useful and practical guide to establishing small groups and assisting them in problem solving.

Pfeiffer, J. William, and John E. Jones (Eds.), *A Handbook for Structured Experiences for Human Relations Training,* vols. I, II, III, IV, and V. La Jolla, Calif.: University Associates, 1974–1976. These handbooks are among the most useful for teaching, and provide many varied approaches to small group activities. Easily adapted for many subject areas.

Pfeiffer, J. Wiliam, and John E. Jones (Eds.), *The 1978 Annual Handbook for Group Facilitators.* La Jolla, Calif.: University Associates, 1978. These annual handbooks are invaluable resources for creative teaching. Included are practical applications, short statements on theory, instruments, and additional resources for group process experiences.

Schmuck, Richard A., and Patricia A. Schmuck, *Group Processes in the Classroom.* Dubuque, Iowa: Wm. C. Brown Co., 1975. Practical guide with many suggestions for small group activities.

Shaw, Marvin E., *Group Dynamics: The Psychology of Small Group Behavior* (2d ed.). La Jolla, Calif.: Learning Resources Corporation, 1976. Covers the many facets of group development and change needed to understand how groups function in the classroom situation.

FOCUS ON CHAPTER 11

When learning is active, teachers employ a variety of different teaching methods. Each subject area has, of course, specific approaches which are unique to that content: laboratory experiments in science, work with power tools in machine shop, batik designing in art class. However, there are some methods which all teachers can use, regardless of subject matter. Among the most useful are the three which are presented in this chapter.

Significant ideas presented in this chapter include:
- Discussion is important in the secondary classroom, but learning how to develop good discussion is not easy.
- Some questions are far better than others in sparking genuine discussion.
- Teachers play several key roles when leading discussions, some of which are acting as a backboard, traffic officer, and guide.
- The personal attributes of the discussion leader contribute to the success of class discussion.
- The technique of role playing contributes significantly to student involvement.
- Games and simulations provide unique and interesting ways of involving students in active learning.

chapter 11

Places Please!:
discussion,
role play, games,
and simulations

earning is a uniquely individual activity. No one can
L learn for someone else any more than one individual
can digest food for another. Learning takes place within the learner, and it
occurs in each individual idiosyncratically. No two learners learn anything
the same way, to the same degree, and retain it for the same length of time.
What learning "is" remains one of the mysteries of behavior. Dogs and
horses can learn many specific behaviors; cats are resistent to learning.
Frogs and elephants have widely variant capacities for learning. As for
human beings, we do not know the ultimate potential of learning for the
human animal. As teachers, we hold tremendous power as we select those
instructional approaches which promote learning, or those which erect
barriers to learning. Teachers are in the business of making learning as
available to as many students as possible. As most teachers have learned,
some methods are more likely to induce learning in students than others,
just as some foods are more nutritious than others.

This chapter describes some classroom techniques which are powerful
methods for engaging most students in learning: problem-centered discussion, role playing, and learning games.

THE CENTRAL FUNCTION OF DISCUSSION

When we observe classes and talk with experienced teachers we find
that a great deal of their time is spent in leading a class in discussion. Skill
in discussion leadership is one of the key resources of the good teacher.

Good, problem-centered discussion is effective classroom technique; poor discussion is boring, wasteful, and frustrating.

WHAT IS DISCUSSION?

The teacher's role in the development of good discussion is tremendously important; it is all too easy to prevent any real thinking. Here is a verbatim report of one history class.

Teacher: We have a real problem to discuss today. I wonder how many of you thought about why we have an electoral college.

Rodney: Because people in those days hadn't done much voting.

Teacher: Well, that is not exactly right.

Bob: Because someone suggested the idea, and no one could think of a better reason.

Teacher: No. Can anyone give us the real reason?

Jennifer: Did it have anything to do with transportation?

Teacher: Now let's not guess. This is a real problem. Can't we discuss it?

Linda: I think it was because the leaders didn't want the people to vote for the president.

Teacher: Now you're getting on the right track; any other good reasons?

Despite the teacher's disclaimer, this exchange is little more than a guessing game. What did the teacher above do that killed discussion?

The behavior of the teacher showed that he or she already had a notion of what the right answer ought to be and the student's task was to guess what the teacher had in mind. Good discussion begins when the teacher recognizes that a problem has several plausible solutions, each of which deserves careful examination in order to find the most fitting one.

Much classroom dialogue, traditionally called "recitation" is not discussion, and it is educationally sterile. Teachers drag out of students a miscellany of uncertainly memorized, unrelated facts that the students barely understand. Of course facts are needed to discuss an issue. But in discussion, *the issue comes first*, and facts are then assessed for their relevance to the issue. Judgment, not merely memory, is vital.

- Discussion is *not* recitation.
- Discussion is *not* just talking by people who know little and care less about the subject being discussed.
- It is *not* a debate in which different factions try to win.
- It is *not* a chance for two or three students to show off their verbal acrobatics.
- It is *not* a bull session, where individuals exchange prejudices or feelings.

What is problem-centered classroom discussion? Here is an example of how another teacher presented the problem of the electoral college:

Teacher: We have a real problem to talk about today. There has been much discussion recently about abolishing the electoral college. What would you think about abolishing it?

George: Well, I think it has outlived its usefulness.

Teacher: That's a good point; but John, would you agree with George?

John: No—not entirely—uh—after all, the electoral college is part of our tradition, and in these times I think we should keep to our traditions instead of doing away with them.

Susan: Well, but John, if something isn't useful anymore, why should we keep on doing it? After all, if you had a car, you wouldn't keep on riding a horse and buggy just because your grandfather did it!

Mary: But the people must have had some good reasons for putting in the electoral college.

George: Except the only trouble is those reasons never worked. Don't you remember when we were reading about the—what was it?—Convention? Constitutional Convention, I think . . .

Teacher: Let's see, John, there seem to be two sides here. Will you have a try at saying what they are?

At this first stage in any discussion, the thinking is muddled, opinions are offered without supporting evidence; the teacher is careful to keep in the background so that differences in point of view can be freely expressed. Such freedom is a fragile thing, and teachers must take care not to nip it in the bud by intervening too early.

DEVELOPING ORAL FACILITY

The current concern over the educational deficits of students has prompted a call for "back to basics." Although most people believe this means reading, writing, and arithmetic, we also know that improved skills in reading and writing occur when students have developed adequate verbal facility; such facility is developed most effectively through practice in oral exchange. Ideas and the words to express them, as well as understanding of the ideas of others, comes from *use*. There is ample documentation that relates oral facility to other fundamental skills of learning.[1]

But who does most of the talking in the typical classroom? The teacher, of course. Studies of verbal interaction in schools have shown over and over again that the person who least needs to develop skill in oral speaking—the teacher—is the one who does most of it.[2] Why do teachers do so much

[1] R. B. Ruddell, "Oral Language and the Development of Other Language Skills," in R. L. Cayer, J. Green, and E. E. Baker, Jr. (Eds.), *Listening and Speaking in the English Classroom* (London: Macmillan, 1971).

[2] Arno Bellack, et al., *The Language of the Classroom* (New York: Teachers College, 1966).

talking? In many instances they are imparting information otherwise not available. But it has been suggested that some of the reasons that teachers talk so much and that there is *recitation* rather than *discussion* in the classrooms is that teachers do not know how to motivate students for genuine discussion; they are afraid of the outcomes of a true discussion (students may arrive at conclusions different from those espoused by the teacher); or that they do not believe that students have any intrinsic interest in the subject.[3] A teacher with skill in discussion leadership will soon learn that not only is it a highly motivating exercise, but that the novelty of possible outcomes is in itself highly motivating, that students do indeed have an intrinsic interest in most of the intellectual issues presented, if given a chance to explore them, and finally, that the problem-centered discussion controls or limits classroom disruption.

THE CONTROVERSY OVER CONTROVERSIAL ISSUES

It is possible to list almost instantly a number of questions that are bound to bring any group of teenagers immediately to life—questions they would love to argue, debate, and research—but which would cause many communities to call for a teacher's dismissal. Schools have always been sensitive to controversial issues. Topics that are considered appropriate for classroom discussion today would have been severely restricted in times past. The liberal atmosphere of the 1960s opened up many classrooms to discussions of topics which earlier were considered taboo. Then, in the mid-1970s, there were increasing reports of community displeasure when students engaged in classroom discussion of sensitive topics, a backlash phenomena according to some observers. In one community a teacher had trouble because he invited a spokesman for gay rights to come to class as part of an extensive study of civil rights for minority groups.[4] A student teacher was told she could not prepare a unit on the population explosion because it would entail a discussion of birth control. Such discussion would involve discussing contraception, and contraception was an inadmissible topic for twelfth graders in that community. Evolution is still a suspect topic in some school systems in the country.

There are controversial issues in every subject field, although many teachers appear unaware of this fact. In the complexity of today's society, adolescents must learn to negotiate in many areas. It seems obvious that they should be given every possible chance to analyze controversial subjects, to obtain facts regarding the issues involved, and to be allowed to evaluate the consequences of different actions and solutions. Unless young

[3] Robert Dreeben, "The School as Workplace," in Robert M. W. Travers (Ed.), *Second Handbook of Research on Teaching* (Skokie, Ill.: Rand McNally, 1973), p. 466.
[4] Charles Kocheiser, "What Happened When a Speaker for Gay Liberation Addressed High School Students," *Social Education*, 39 (April 1975), pp. 219–222.

people are assisted in this task, they will move into an adult world they barely perceive and whose problems they are not equipped to analyze or to understand.

HOW TO ASK QUESTIONS

The teacher, by presenting provocative situations, is posing not one, but many questions. Yet each series of explorations involves a quest, which in turn implies selection of questions that require student responses above the level of recall or "giving back teacher what he wants."

The following criteria help decide what questions are, or are not, worth asking:

- *The question implies a genuine interest in divergent points of view.* It suggests the existence of differences of opinion and indicates that such differences are respectable.
- *The question probes an area of experience which is of immediate, as well as more remote, concern to young people.* A question including some present-day reference, but also by implication embracing more general aspects of the problem, will encourage discussion.
- *Discussion questions imply values and the process of evaluating known facts.* They should not merely promote a memory search for right as opposed to wrong facts.
- *Questions should ask for most, least, best, worst*—which would you rather do?; is it better to?; and the like, encourage a sorting and evaluating process that promotes an exchange of knowledge as well as ideas. Those that ask for facts, pure and simple, are hardly likely to stir much interest. The students who have the facts will smugly wave their hands, while those who did not read the assignment will sit silently, barely aware of the topic suggested.

Examples of some questions requiring mere factual answers are:

- Why did some fish feel compelled to come out of the water and become amphibian? How did it happen? What caused it?
- Who was the world's first chemist? What do you think he did?
- Why do rats have no gall bladder?
- What is the name of Hamlet's stepfather?
- What color is produced when you mix red and blue?
- What is the first safety rule when using the parallel bars?

Other questions require a reporting back of a series of concepts that are not really debatable. Such questions are:

- Should initial cost or wearability be the chief factor in selecting a coat?
- Is violence on television excessive?
- When does a piece of music become a classic?
- What alternative strategies could Nixon have used to protect his presidency after his tape recordings were revealed?

Some questions invite undesirable or irrelevant student responses:
For example:

- Why should anyone take algebra?
- Are women more intelligent than men?

Questions of this sort are too inviting for the classroom clown. Unless the teacher desires a light touch, as a preamble into a serious discussion of the significant aspects of the question, then these topics are best avoided as stated.

A genuine discussion is more apt to emerge when questions such as the following are posed:

- Which policy would you support? Federal assistance to individual artists or grants to museums to buy the works of artists?
- Would a high tax on automobiles or a high tax on gasoline be more likely to reduce automobile use?
- In choosing a career, are abilities, interests, or amount of additional education the major considerations?
- What is the responsibility of a scientist who makes a discovery which is potentially very dangerous?
- If your boss tells you to do something which you know is unethical, what should you do?

For additional information about questioning, see pages 206–211.

GETTING DISCUSSION STARTED

The teacher is not the only initiator of discussions: Students may also bring in ideas or topics which they wish to consider in class.

Although Ms. Grant teaches ninth-grade algebra, she is interested in the ideas of her students, and also has found that a brief "open talk" time at the beginning of class helps the students to settle down as well as to get their work started by tapping their ever-present kinetic energy. She may bring a news item herself to class, make a comment, and ask for student response. Or she may have a picture, or report on some item from a TV show the night before—anything to spark student interest. Classes have discussed the high accident rate of teenagers, whether the president should veto the latest tax bill, why the cafeteria can't serve more hamburgers, the high cost of popcorn at the movies. After about five minutes of spirited give and take, she turns to the lesson for the day, the assignment is on the board, and algebra instruction begins.

Other discussion starters include open-ended films; role-playing (to be discussed later in this chapter); current events items; bulletin board displays developed by either teacher or student groups; odd or unusual objects; resource visitors, pictures that are deliberately selected as ambiguous or provocative. Commemorative days such as United Nations Day, Valentine's Day, Martin Luther King's birthday, may be well used to analyze why the day is important, the historical background of an event commemorated, or what meaning the day may have for different people. Local events in the community which have aroused student interest—or which *should* arouse student interest—are good for discussion starters.

The medium used to promote discussion may itself take all the available time. This is particularly apt to be true of films, resource visitors, and recordings. To capture for later discussion the controversial aspects of these media, the teacher can direct the students to take notes on the presentation. Half the class, for example, can be directed to note down all the things they agree with in a speaker's lecture; the other half of the class can take notes on all the things they disagree with. The next day a lively exchange of items can take place. Similarly, when watching a film which is presented to evoke discussion as much as to inform, the instructions to the class prior to watching are tremendously important (see Chapter 8).

With any medium—in fact, any good controversial issue which is worth class time to discuss—a teacher may find that more questions are raised than there is really time to pursue. Then, with class cooperation, a decision is made to focus on *key* issues only and to put aside interesting, but peripheral, side issues. However, many teachers have found groups persisting in their interest which, in the eyes of the teacher, is not the most significant one. Generational differences may be the cause of the disagreement. The good discussion leader does not impose a predetermined course on a discussion, knowing that much can be learned about the world of adolescents by encouraging them to discuss issues as *they* see them. Out of such discussion can then come a better understanding of the educational needs of a group of students.

> I was appalled at the ghoulish way my students were discussing a particularly distressing murder which had upset the local community. The students showed little insight into the motivating behavior. Also they seemed more curious about how upset the victim's family was than expressing sympathy or empathy. I didn't see how to relate this to anything I was teaching in first- and second-year French, but I spoke to the psychology teacher and asked if she could use the material on aggression, which she typically presented late in the year, somewhat earlier so that it could be related to this local event. I also made a search through some of the French selections which might have some commentary on why humans are motivated toward violence.

A final warning about discussion: Be prepared for the unexpected and the embarrassing moment. Since well-run discussion means that many minds will be engaged in pursuit of a solution to a problem, it is always possible that some creative and original mind will come up with an unusual or unexpected comment or solution. It is essential that the teacher accept such unusual contributions, even if they may be very far from anything the teacher may have had in mind. Many students are more creative and original than their teachers. Relax and appreciate this fact. It is true that some of the unusual contributions may be embarrassing or disturbing, and the teacher may be put on the spot:

> Mr. Slone was finishing a unit on racial tolerance. There had been much lively discussion, and his students had been very interested. I felt that it had been a highly constructive experience all around. The film "Americans All," from the "March of Time" series, had been chosen to help summarize the unit. There were a few moments of class time left after the motion picture, and discussion was somewhat desultory. The group was pretty well "talked out" on the subject. Then Philip, who could usually be counted on to provide a jolt to the group, raised his hand: "Mr. Slone, would you marry someone who wasn't of your race?"

What happens next? This is the kind of question that teachers fear, some of them so much that they will not risk raising the issues at all. Yet there are always ways to handle these questions. Here are two ways in which Mr. Slone might have replied:

> "Well, Philip, I think that's a very important question. Frankly, I don't have an answer to it. I'd like to give you a good answer, and not just the first thing that pops into my head. Let me think about the problem, will you? And then perhaps we can come to an understanding of it."

> "That's a serious question you raise, Philip. It is asked by many people whenever this subject is discussed. I think I know what I would do, but before I give my opinion, I would be interested in hearing what other members of the class think."

Oh, you say, the teacher is just stalling for time. Yes, indeed the teacher is asking for more time. Mr. Slone knows that he must arrange his own thoughts so he can give a reasonable answer, and one that will not be misinterpreted. The motives of students who ask questions like this one may be suspect, but the issue must be faced. You cannot allow yourself to get upset, to retort angrily to the student that it is none of his or her business, or loftily ignore the question as though it would fade away if not answered. The teacher finds useful phrases that provide time to sort out various thoughts, and then turns the question back to the class so that there is a sharing in seeking a reasonable answer. There is indeed great wisdom in not answering immediately. Admitting that a pat answer is not at hand may be the most convincing evidence of honesty, which is essential in creating and maintaining an attitude of trust.

ROLES OF THE DISCUSSION LEADER

Once the discussion has been started, it is the job of the leader to keep it moving forward toward possible consensus. A discussion may, it is true, have so much vitality that it will continue regardless of anything the leader may or may not do. When students have become accustomed to talking together about live issues in the classroom, there may seem to be no leader at all. In fact, after the class is over, the discussion will rage on; in the hall, the lunchroom, the library, or on the stairs. Certainly it is a sign of good education when students are so consumed with a desire to talk together about important things that discussion continues whether or not a teacher is present.

The discussion leader has three roles: *First, the leader acts as a "backboard,"* tossing questions back to the group much as a backboard bounces the ball back to a person practicing a tennis stroke. *Second, the leader acts as a traffic officer,* directing the flow of questions and making certain that individuals take their turn in debating the issue. *Third, the leader acts like a guide with a road map,* stopping from time to time to show the group the road they have taken, the branches that have been noticed but abandoned, the wrong turns, the fork in the road that now approaches—and pointing toward the goal of the journey.

THE LEADER AS BACKBOARD

The first activity of the leader needs constant emphasis. A good leader rarely, if ever, answers a question unless it is a minor one which would retard good discussion. Rather, the leader sees to it that members of the group answer the important questions. Many would-be discussion leaders cannot resist the temptation to answer, to explain, to clarify. That is what the group must do for itself. When a student says, "Isn't it better to spend our tax money on hospitals than on schools?" the teacher should answer, "That's a good question. What do you think about it, Henry?"; "Sue, what is your opinion?"; "We haven't heard Jim on this problem yet"; or "Donald's mother is manager for a local hospital; what do you think, Donald?" A simple matter-of-fact question may be answered by the teacher if it is not so important that the group should take time to get the needed data by itself. A minor question of semantics or a quibble over whether a report is in error should not be allowed to impede the process of group thinking.

A cardinal principle of good discussion leadership, and the one which is probably most often ignored, is to *toss all important and vital questions back to the group.* Otherwise, the discussion becomes a series of little conversations between the teacher and members of the class.

The discussion pattern that is merely dialogue would look like this:

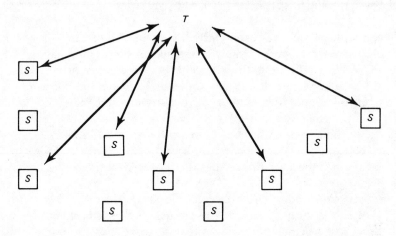

A picture of participation in a segment of a discussion where real group thinking was going on would look more like this:

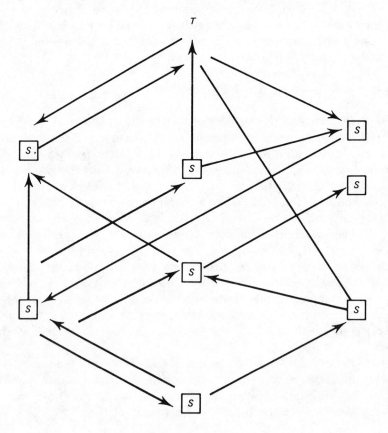

As noted earlier, *most teachers talk too much*. We cannot emphasize too strongly the need for teachers to toss questions back to the class when leading a discussion. It is *so* tempting to make a comment, express an opinion, or introduce an additional clarifying word or two! Resist!

One of the very hardest lessons for teachers to learn is to keep still. When a provocative issue has been posed, one of the most dramatic strategies a teacher can use is just to be silent, look around the room expectantly, and say nothing. Then, there will be nonverbal clues that Jack or Jean is ready to say something, and a nod in their direction will provide all the permission needed to break the silence. Additional nods or gestures from the teacher can encourage others to join in. If a discussion just stops, and there is silence, it is not necessary for the teacher to leap in nervously with a comment. Wait. Watch. Most people do not tolerate social silences easily. Someone is bound to say something, and it is better the students do rather than the teacher! It will be gratifying to you as a teacher-leader to feel how responsive a class will become when they realize the discussion is theirs, not yours.

THE LEADER AS TRAFFIC OFFICER

The second role of the leader is that of traffic officer. The leadership prerogative is used to direct questions to specific members of the class, to see to it that the more verbose do not dominate the discussion, to keep voices down to a reasonable level, and, finally, to see to it that only one person is speaking at a time. These disciplinary functions are highly important, but must be exercised with care. A leader who pounces on a class as soon as a slight rise in temperature is noted, the moment a voice becomes a bit shrill in argument, or when small bits of conversation spring up in answer to someone's statement, will soon thwart student interest in discussion.

A really good discussion is bound to generate some heat. The leader must see to it that this rise in interest does not interfere with logical and productive group thinking, but the restraining hand should be lightly applied. A word of caution, such as "Now, let's not get too excited, yet!" can ease mounting tension and remind the students that after all they are in a classroom and engaged in an intellectual discussion. Similarly, the leader must be alert to guide the discussion toward students who have not yet contributed, to interrupt—judiciously—those students who tend toward speechmaking, and must use every bit of knowledge he or she may have about students as a method of helping them make their best contributions. Knowledge of a given student's interests, out-of-class activities, father's or mother's occupations, and travel experiences is very useful when the leader seeks a strand, no matter how tenuous, to weave the interest of students into the discussion going on around them.

This policing function, therefore, is not only one of keeping the traffic of ideas flowing, but also seeing that all contributors get their full share of attention and opportunity to express themselves—no matter how shy or inarticulate. Student observers, keeping checks on how many times individuals make contributions, and the type of contribution each makes, are invaluable assistants to the new teacher. The class also becomes interested in charts of its own discussion. Such reports, treated with objectivity, are among the most effective devices to keep loquacious students in check. They can for the first time see themselves in perspective and realize without too much ego-damage how much more time they have taken of the total allowed the class than they deserve. A participation record, used to encourage those who do not participate and keep in check those who tried to talk too much, is one of those indirect, group-centered disciplinary devices that will help the new teacher in class control. Such devices will do far more than any teacher's admonition or the even less relevant prod of a grade. Grading on "participation" is a dismal way to subvert genuine student participation in discussion.

THE LEADER AS DISCUSSION GUIDE

The third major function of the leader is to act as overall guide for the direction of group discussion. Thinking of a discussion as an unfolding map may clarify the nature of the process. After the first experience of trying to keep thirty or forty lively minds focused on a single problem, one sees how rough the going can be. Many ideas are suggested, and for every idea there may be at least three objections, complaints, asides, personal comments, or amendments. How does the question asked by Dave relate to the remark made by Joan three minutes earlier? Such problems arise every other moment during the course of a lively discussion. Thus, the leader as guide is involved in helping the class perform the various steps in problem solving. Briefly, these steps are as follows:

What is the problem? At this stage, the leader may have recourse to the chalkboard. It is useful to get agreement from the whole class at the very outset about the limits of the topic that has sparked the discussion. Then, if an irrelevant comment is offered, the teacher—or other students as they gain in facility—may point to the statement on the board and say, "Is that part of our problem?"

What are the major issues? Here, again, leader and students should use the chalkboard to list the things about which there is significant disagreement. Matters of fact need to be listed in a separate column as topics for further research. It may be—and this often occurs—that a discussion must be temporarily suspended at this stage. Perhaps what has appeared to be a disagreement is merely a difference of opinion about the facts on a given problem. The teacher may then utilize student interest in solving the problem to motivate the class to find answers to the questions where apparent disagreement occurs.

What are the possible solutions? As the issues are clarified and as the more important ones are separated from the less important ones, the focus of the discussion is on solutions for each major issue. Suggested solutions are then posted on the chalkboard. Again, additional research may be called for to determine whether a given solution is feasible.

What are the consequences of possible solutions? The test of feasibility must be applied. Can the proposed solutions work? Are they in accord with what is known about human beings and society and the physical world? At this stage, some lines of action or syntheses of arguments are discarded, and those the class as a whole find agreeable are chosen.

What consensus is reached? In a real discussion it is usually both unnecessary and undesirable to have a vote. With sufficient participation by the group, the leader can usually tell when general agreement has been reached. Constant voting on each point would be both a waste of time and a useless interruption. In this last stage of discussion, where the sense of the group is finally attained, there is a feeling of satisfaction and relief. The leader may step in to summarize and point out where the group has traveled in its thinking.

What action is planned? This stage is not always reached. Where a discussion involves merely an intellectual exchange of somewhat abstract ideas or general principles, no action is likely to occur. However, if a discussion starts on a topic such as "What play should the seniors choose for the first school assembly?" then some plans for action should result. Sometimes committees are selected to carry out the plan. Other outcomes may be writing a letter to the local member of Congress, preparing a skit for a PTA meeting, preparing a plan of study for the succeeding six weeks, or agreeing on the strategies to be used in the next basketball game.

DISCUSSION LEADERSHIP: THE OVERALL STRATEGY

These steps in the process of group thinking described above constitute the fundamental structure of problem solving. As the leader becomes accustomed to this sequence it also becomes relatively easy to help others to do so. As an aid to logical thinking the leader can make explicit which step the class is approaching. For example, as the class approaches the first step in problem solving the leader might say, "We must define our problem before we go on to discuss where and how we disagree," or, as the class edges around the second step in problem solving, "Now are we all agreed on the definition of our problem?" and then, "Now, let's be sure what the issues are in this problem before we try to find out what a good solution might be."

The leader also assists in the appraisal of contributions. When a student makes a suggestion that is supposed to be pertinent, the leader will want to ask, "Joe, is that your opinion, or is that a fact?" The source of information is significant. Developing a critical use of standard sources of information is a major result of learning. Did the newspaper report the event accurately? Why does this paper's report differ from the one in this magazine? How did radio and television report the same event? If two students report on an interview, do they both report the same data? Such questions will develop out of discussion when the leader directs attention to the quality of individual contributions. As students gain facility in discussions, they will learn to discriminate among authorities, to think objectively rather than emotionally about facts, and to modify opinions on the basis of logic.

Finally, the leader of a discussion is interested in keeping the group moving toward its goal. "Needling" the group to sharpen its thinking, getting it back on the right track, challenging it to new ideas when the discussion seems to be bogging down, are all part of the art of leadership. To serve these purposes, a series of questions or queries may sometimes be formulated prior to the discussion by the leader. Obviously, these stimulants should be judiciously administered lest the leader get too far ahead of group thinking. It is important to check frequently with the group by means of such remarks as, "Do we all know what the point under discussion is?" or "Was that last issue clear to everyone?" before moving on to newer fields. The leader may find that while the interest and vitality of a few keep a discussion moving swiftly forward, a good portion of the class has lost the thread of the argument several twists back. A group with widely differing intellectual abilities is likely to make the faster students impatient, or move too quickly for the slower ones. A teacher may want to use some of the small group techniques outlined in Chapter 10 in order to raise the skill level of the whole group, particularly impressing upon those who think most quickly that waiting until the slower ones catch up is essential to democratic group thinking. This does not mean, however, that creative thinking is to be discouraged.

PERSONAL ATTRIBUTES OF DISCUSSION LEADERS

Wishing won't make a teacher a good discussion leader. Some particular qualities needed are discussed in the following paragraphs:

A personal and lively interest in the subject under discussion. Good leaders do not try to promote a discussion about topics they themselves find boring or dull. Excitement generated by the leader is contagious and will help enliven a classroom group.

An open mind about the outcomes or the pattern to be taken by the discussion. Group thinking changes as groups change. When choices are to be made, it is unwise to have too great a personal–emotional stake in any one choice; this is likely to spoil the quality of leadership. Students soon descend to the guessing game level of participation under this kind of leadership.

A sense of the humorous as well as a sense of the serious. Being able to shift from low gear to high, from the light to the heavy and back again, is essential to the art of leadership. Ability to laugh at the unexpected remark or retort will keep young people in tune with the leader in more serious areas.

A genuine interest in the opinions of young people. Some adults enjoy discussions with other adults, but become bored when youngsters express naive, bigoted, rigid, or ignorant opinions. Discussion does not flower in this sort of atmosphere.

An ability to suppress the expression of one's own opinion most of the time. Students are quick to sense what the leader considers to be the correct point of view unless the leader is skillful at summarizing both sides of an issue impartially. As rapport is established, the leader may use the assertion of an opinion to encourage disagreement. However, this technique should be used carefully.

The teacher will seek to develop skill in leading discussions, but all that has been said here should be passed on to students in order that they too may become more skilled in thinking through problems cooperatively and giving leadership to such endeavors. The more the teacher is able to let student leaders preside during appropriate discussion periods, the greater will be the students' opportunity to gain in poise, responsibility, and maturity of reflective thinking.

STRUCTURED DISCUSSION

The use of debate as a way of structuring discussion has a long educational history. However, one sees somewhat less use of formal debate in today's classrooms, and interscholastic debating is not as common as it was some time ago. Formal debate, with an affirmative and negative team, following the rules of argument and rebuttal, may be a useful way to put some of the loquacious and intellectually able students into a situation that requires discipline, clear organization of ideas, awareness of both sides of a proposition, and quick utilization of data for rebuttal purposes. The preparation for a formal debate can take many days of independent and team research; it provides a way to motivate students to use many resources, including the library, and adds the drama of confrontation plus the social glue of working as a member of a team. Typically, debate has been limited to social studies, English and speech classes. Yet the value issues in many other areas can just as well be used for debate if the teacher sees the issues.

For example:

> **Resolved:** "Artists are born, not made."
> **Resolved:** "Scientists should not work on research that goes against their beliefs."

The limitation of formal debate is that, typically, a team consists of only two, or at most three, members. The rest of the class, who may be the ultimate judge of "who wins," does not get to participate in the research and intellectual activity. A class as audience can, of course, become very involved in a well-presented formal debate. In one classroom observed the whole class found the material so interesting that they asked for additional time so that everyone could express an opinion.

An adaptation of the debate technique can be utilized so that the whole class will have the experience of taking a position, finding supporting evidence, identifying the points the opposition may make and being ready with data to refute them, by combining small group work with a debate panel. (See Chapter 10 for a guide to setting up groups.) If the class has thirty-six members, six groups can be organized of six members each. Three groups will choose, or be assigned, the "pro" position on an issue; three groups the "con" position. Each group, after some preliminary research and getting to know one another, selects a representative who will represent that group on the debate panel. After sufficient time has been allowed for the groups to assemble their data, the representatives take their places, on the panel, with three pro members on one side, three con members on the other. Rules may be established by the class governing the order in which the panel presentations are made: alternating one from each side, for instance; limiting presentations to three minutes each; and so forth. When all the arguments for each side have been formally presented, the representatives then return to their home group members, for instructions· for rebuttal. Each group then must think with its representative about what the weaknesses are of the other side's position, how to counter their most telling points, and similar issues. Again, the representatives return to the debate panel, and the rebuttal takes place. When each side has had its two minutes per member, the teacher may open the question up to the whole class so that team members who may have felt their representative did not cover the group position, or omitted a point, can have a chance to participate in an informal way.

The procedure described has the advantage of getting everyone involved in the "debate." It also provides group support for the speakers, who can turn to their classmates on their team for ammunition and ideas. This procedure is also helpful with groups who are not used to oral discussion or who shy away from public speaking. The formal debate is useful with students already full (sometime too full) of independent initiative. The structured discussion-debate using teams and representatives, provides support for those less skilled and less motivated to express opinions before others.

ROLE PLAYING: WHAT IT IS AND WHAT IT IS NOT

The tenth-grade English class was struggling with Romeo and Juliet. The Shakespearean language baffled them, or seemed to. After reading and discussing each day's assignment, Mrs. Bukowski had different student volunteers role play, in their own words, the particular episode that had been read. This device helped her ascertain the degree of understanding achieved, and helped those who were most confused by the archaic and complex language. By the end of the unit, almost everyone in the class had participated in role play, and Mrs. Bukowski believed each one had gained personal insight into the play.

In a United States history class, the material being studied concerned George Washington's selection as the first president. After reading the text and having a brief discussion about it, the teacher asked one student to be George Washington and two students to be the committee who called upon him to ask his acceptance of the nomination. At first the students were unable to portray the roles, but after further class discussion as to how George Washington actually would have felt and would have answered, after consideration of the appropriate arguments that might have worked, the little drama was reenacted to the satisfaction of the class.

A journalism class was discussing interview techniques. In order to make the lesson clear, the class described various kinds of persons one might interview: the high-handed celebrity, the sobbing mother, the tough politician, the frightened child, the garrulous gossip. Then members of the class practiced different interview approaches to each situation. The discussions after each presentation often resulted in a replaying of the interview, with different performers trying different techniques. The teacher discovered that some students had more insight than others into how real people act, and that those with less insight learned a great deal by having to think through the problems presented.

In an inner-city economics class the teacher utilized a series of newspaper reports on high credit charges to slum residents, with particular emphasis on the shoddy practices of high-pressure, door-to-door salesmen. She developed with her classes incidents in which the girls played the role of the housewife visited by a home repair salesman, an encyclopedia salesman, a TV salesman. Each class focused on some aspect of the problem which differed from the interest of other classes. Each however, via role playing, was able to see how gullible one can be when approached by "smooth-talkers."

These examples of role playing illustrate the key element in this versatile teaching method, spontaneity. *Role playing is unprepared, unrehearsed dramatization.* The material to be role played may come from any source: history, literature, student experience, imaginary or fantasy worlds. Because of its spontaneous nature, role playing is one of the simplest devices to use, yet it is one of the most telling in terms of impact on individuals and classes. The very act of having to think oneself into a character in a role play demands tremendous psychic energy and concentration. Experience indicates that few persons who engage in a role play forget the experience, even though it might last only two or three minutes. Role playing is a technique used with great success in management training and business, industry, and government. By role-playing situations the participants are able to "rehearse the future." Individuals can try out various ways of dealing with predicted conflict or problem situations.

Role playing has not been as widely used in educational settings because of lack of skill on the part of teachers and because of some confusion about what is learned from role playing. True, some of the outcomes of role playing are difficult, if not impossible, to measure. Like many techniques which depend on interpersonal interaction the long-term consequences are more apt to be acknowledged by individuals some time after the event. For those who have themselves been participants in effective role playing, no convincing is necessary.

A caution: role playing is not therapy. Although a form of role playing (psychodrama) is utilized in treating mental patients, the focus in teaching is different. Teachers are not trying to reach the hidden psyches of individuals. They are trying to help them reach more appropriate, more insightful intellectual understandings of human behavior, including their own. They are trying to give individuals a wider range of behavior skills for dealing with daily life. For these purposes, role playing is useful. Because of the increased sensitivity of the public to invasions of student privacy, the teacher would be well advised to use role playing for nonpersonal problems. If a student overidentifies with a role play and begins a confessional regarding personal situations, or about family, then the teacher should adroitly shift the discussion to "people in general."

ROLE PLAYING: HOW TO DO IT

The specific steps to be taken in initiating role playing are described below. These steps are merely suggested. After one or two tries, the teachers will probably want to alter or adapt them to suit their own situations.

SELECTING THE SITUATION. The situation should, first, be a fairly simple one, involving one main idea or issue. *Second, the situation should be one involving personalities.* The issues should be those which arise because people have different desires, hopes, and aspirations; or they should be problems that arise from the inability of people to understand the viewpoint of others.

When introducing this technique for the first time, the teacher should have an idea for a role-playing situation clearly in mind. Open-ended scripts or stories can be used as role-play starters.[5] Later, the class members will be able to describe situations of their own choosing and select the roles that should be taken. It is easiest to begin with situations that require from two to four characters. Large numbers are confusing until students know more about what they are supposed to do.

The teacher, with the help of the class, should describe each of the roles to be taken. As an illustration, suppose the role playing concerns the problem of incorporation of an agricultural community. Opinion is divided; to some residents the increased services do not seem sufficient to counterbalance the increased tax load; to other residents, incorporation offers distinct advantages. A petition is being circulated. The role playing then revolves around the various characters who might be concerned with such a problem. Farmer Jones is selected as one role to be portrayed. The essential details of his role are sketched in: He is married, has lived in the area about fifteen years, and has never made very much money—just enough to live nicely. Other details may be added as appropriate: He is stubborn; or he is a sharp bargainer; or he is very slow and ignorant. After one portrayal, the teacher and the class will learn how much description of each role is necessary. Then the teacher and the class should set the situation: Farmer Jones is visiting Farmer Smith in order to get his signature on the petition, or Farmer Jones has come to ask Farmer Smith's advice about the local controversy.

CHOOSING PARTICIPANTS. When first trying out role playing, the teacher should select students who are fairly well informed about the issues to be presented and who are imaginative, articulate, and self-assured. The show-off often freezes up or clowns absurdly; the shy student feels insecure and inadequate. Both types can be assisted in their own personality adjustment by first being given minor prop roles, such as that of secretary or doorman, and later being allowed to take larger roles. It will also be found that those with dramatic training are not necessarily the best participants in spontaneous dramatics, since role playing draws upon the individual's own resources of feeling and imagination.

[5] Jean Dresden Grambs, *Intergroup Education: Methods and Materials* (Englewood Cliffs, N.J.: Prentice-Hall, 1968), pp. 59–86. See also Fannie Shaftel and George Shaftel, *Role-Playing for Social Values* (Englewood Cliffs, N.J.: Prentice-Hall, 1967).

Some teachers call for volunteers for role playing. Although those who first volunteer are often the most articulate and the least self-conscious, they may also be show-offs and use the situation to get attention through "hamming it up." So care must be taken when choosing volunteers. One hard and fast rule; no one is ever allowed to volunteer someone else. Either the person volunteers, or the teacher makes the selection. After a few role plays, the teacher can make it clear that everyone will be asked to take part, so that selection will be made on the basis of giving each person a chance. Once students have watched and then participated in role playing, they see what fun it is, and also how much they gain from the experience.

SETTING THE STAGE. When the participants have been selected, they should be sent out of the room or to some quiet corner for about two minutes. They should be instructed to "think themselves into" the role they are to take. The participants may want to decide together how the scene will look, where the furniture will be, who will enter first, and other details of staging. Later, the class as a whole may describe the complete setting before the participants are selected.

Although many times one can conduct a role play without this warm-up period, experience indicates that individuals are more apt to have a better repertoire of ideas and behaviors if given a short period of time to think. It also provides a chance for the teacher to do the essential task of preparing the audience. The quality of role playing is usually enhanced by this kind of "warm up."

PREPARING THE AUDIENCE. While the participants are out of the room for their two minutes of thinking, the teacher should direct the class to observe the action as though each one were acting in it. The students should ask themselves: Is this the way these people act and feel in real life? The students should be concerned with how a housewife would act and what she would say when defending her interest in sentimental TV "soaps" rather than how Harriet Smith acted as the housewife.

The exploratory nature of role playing should be clear to both the participants and the audience. It should be understood that no finished product is expected, but that, in fact, everyone will learn more if the participants are considerably less than perfect.

ACTING OUT THE SITUATION. When directing role playing the teacher becomes a cross between director and audience. When a role player appears to be slipping out of his or her role, the teacher should remind the player of what is being enacted. When the students seem to reach a dead end, the teacher should cut the situation short. However, the teacher should otherwise allow the action to follow its own pattern as completely as possible, since this very naturalness, the feeling of freedom to become wholly involved in the situation, contributes immeasurably to the reality and the success of the experience. Few role-playing episodes will last more than five minutes, unless the situation is very complicated or the students have a great deal of information.

FOLLOW-UP. When the situation is finished, the class will be eager to comment. This stimulation of discussion, centering on how people feel and why they act as they do, is the basic contribution of role playing. The students may have so many ideas for a reenactment of the situation that it may be appropriate to go through it again with new actors. On the other hand, the students may feel that more knowledge is necessary before trying again and may want to do more reading and study about the personalities involved. This outcome, of course, is most desirable; and the alert teacher will make the most of the opportunity.

The participants may also report how they felt as they acted through the role playing. Their feelings will provide the teacher with a clue to the students' insight into the wellsprings of human emotion.

In the follow up, as in the preparatory period, the teacher should always stress that no one is expected to do a perfect job in role playing. The teacher makes a point of expressing pleasure at how well the students have succeeded in the task. Role playing can, in this manner, be an effective learning medium, which provides both students and teachers an opportunity for joint creative experience.

Here is an example of a complete role-playing activity:

There had been much concern in this school about intergroup relations. Some covert conflict seemed to exist between the Mexican-American group and the other students. The English teacher, Mrs. Morgan, felt that some dramatic enactment of a related situation might help clarify the immediate school problem. At the start of one class she announced that they were going to try a new kind of dramatics; they would make up a play as they went along and see how it worked. She then presented the "plot" to the class:

> The son of one of the leading ranchers in the area, Sidney Stuart, had been killed in Vietnam while serving as a Marine. In memory of his son, Mr. Stuart said he would like to make an annual ward of $50 to the student in the school considered the best citizen by a student committee. The first year the award was made, the committee, composed of George Green, Doris Bacigalupi, and Tony Nevin, chose Bill Thompson. Bill did very good school-work; was one of the track stars of the school; and just the previous semester had, at great personal risk, saved a whole family from disaster. Bill was black. When Mr. Stuart heard who had been given the first award he was furious. He told the principal that under no circumstances could he agree to the award being given only to a black student. "Isn't there a white student who is a good citizen?" he asked. He said he would even give another $50

award and let Bill keep the one for which he was selected. The principal, Mr. Jenkins, agreed to call the student committee back together again and explain Mr. Stuart's position.

The role playing took up at this point. Students were selected for the various roles, and the "committee" met with the "principal." The members of the first committee were assigned specific roles by Mrs. Morgan. The student to play George Green was told to take the position that Mr. Stuart was right, that another award should be selected and then they could have two awards. The student who played Doris felt that this was absolutely wrong and was opposed to a second award. The student who played Tony carried the burden of the committee decision. The class listened to the description of the situation and then, after the role assignments had been given, there was a marked rise in interest and alertness. This problem assumed reality, and everyone leaned forward to see what the "committee" would work out.

The committee carried on a rather extensive argument with the principal. The students playing the roles found it difficult to reach agreement. The principal seemed to favor Mr. Stuart's proposal. The meeting finally was called to a close by the principal, who suggested that they think it over until the next day, since they obviously were having difficulty in reaching a decision.

At this point, when Mrs. Morgan turned to the rest of the class for their reaction, there was an immediate hubbub of comment. Mrs. Morgan merely waited, without saying a word. One by one students started to voice their opinion of what they had seen. One student finally stated that he knew what he would have done if he had been the principal. This sounded like a good idea to Mrs. Morgan, so she called him up to be the principal, quickly picked a new committee from the class members, and they went through a new sequence. As the new principal worked toward his solution, which was not a very ethical one, the teacher turned herself into a secretary and announced that Mr. Stuart was waiting to see him. Without warning she called one of the class members up to be Mr. Stuart. Then a new situation evolved, with Mr. Stuart reacting to the proposal of the principal. This discussion grew quite heated as the student playing Mr. Stuart flung himself into the role of a highly prejudiced person. The teacher felt enough had been said and, again being the secretary, told the principal that he was wanted on the telephone. Then the role playing ended for the time being.

A lively discussion ensued. The students by this time were very deeply involved in the problem. Two major ethical points had emerged, one regarding attitudes of tolerance, and one regarding the justification of a lie. The lie had been the last principal's solution, which then became the focus of class discussion. By the end of the period, the teacher felt that the groundwork had been laid for a follow-up discussion the next day regarding tolerance and understanding of others. Eventually she hoped to open up the immediate school problem of understanding and working with the Spanish-American students in the school.[6]

If a teacher is alert to student reactions, there can be a very rich role playing experience. In the example, the teacher captured a student idea regarding a solution and "tried it out." By seeing their suggestions in practice, the students gained a deeper insight into reality.

The use of open-ended stories or scripts, or films, as the starters for role playing is a helpful device for the teacher who is not ready to develop a role play "from scratch." For example, one brief short story has four characters: a teacher and three students. The teacher selects students to play these roles. They are seated in the front of the room. As the teacher reads the story[7] she points to each of the role players, identifying who they are. The story provides the plot and the characterizations of each person and the position each person in the situation takes regarding the problem at hand. When the climax is reached—that is, when the problem appears insoluble—the story or script ends. The student role players then go to teams of their classmates who have been assigned to them as helpers. There is a "teacher team" and a team for each of the three students in the problem situation. The object of each helping team is to give the role players advice in figuring out a strategy to solve the problem when the role-playing situation begins. This kind of group support (described also on page 291 in reference to structured discussion) makes the ad-lib part of role playing much easier and, also, of course involves the whole class in what is going on.

The use of role playing has been found particularly effective when the role has immediate carry-over into real-life situations. For example, when developing the idea of working in a group, the teacher can use role playing to show the class how different people assist or impede the process of group thinking.

Miss Hood had been concerned about some of the group projects in her class. Several of the groups were working very well together, but in two groups there was discussion because of dominating leadership, as well as disagreement over what the group was trying to do. Therefore, at the beginning of one class hour, the teacher said that she was going to ask several members of the class to be a "pretend" group. She called up five students and gave each a separate slip of paper, cautioning them not to tell anyone what was on the paper. The slips read as follows:
1. You are very eager to be chairman of the group.
2. You don't like anything that is suggested.
3. You are very enthusiastic about almost any project suggested.

[6] Adapted from Shaftel and Shaftel, pp. 368–374.
[7] See Grambs, *Intergroup Education: Methods and Materials*, pp. 60–62, for an example of an open-ended story.

4. You refuse to take sides in the discussion.

5. You are eager to see the group working together on almost anything.

She then asked the students to pretend that they were a group similar to one in class and gave them a project to plan that paralleled those being worked on. The students threw themselves into the roles with great vigor, to the amusement and chagrin of various class members who saw their own group roles being portrayed. After about ten minutes, when it was obvious the group wasn't getting very far, the teacher called the group to a halt and then threw the problem open to the class to discuss. She started by asking them to identify the roles each person had taken.

This situation may well arise in science, home economics, business education classes, and often in team sports. If individuals have developed inadequate or difficult personal roles for themselves, role playing may help them find a more adequate pattern of behavior.

Role playing is especially useful in any situation where various kinds of leadership are being evaluated. A teacher who is the adviser to the student council may have to aid the president of the student body in appropriate behavior. The president may need help in developing the ability to be fairly assertive and poised, in being able to interrupt long-winded speeches, turn aside provocative comments, encourage, and praise. By acting out some of the typical experiences in presiding, the president may become better equipped to carry out the responsibilities of the office. Similarly, a team captain may be able to work out appropriate ways of encouraging the members of the team. In sessions of role playing, a sympathetic audience can say, "Alan, you shouldn't be so sharp when you tell Joe about his mistakes." Or, "I think, La Barbara, you might try another kind of comment when Nancy hogs the ball." Then Alan and La Barbara can try out a few different ways of working with the team members.

Role playing can often be used in guidance. Role-playing situations can be developed around such personal problems as shyness or being a newcomer, around family communication difficulties, or conflict with a teacher or administrator.[8]

Teachers who have made use of role playing find it improves if evaluation periods are held as a matter of course. One history teacher used role playing to help students visualize history, and also to help them identify the key conflicts or issues in a particular historical period. Groups of students were assigned to each chapter and selected significant episodes to role play. After the enactments, following the discussion of appropriateness and significance, as well as the interpretation of the event—all of which provided excellent discussions of *history*—improvements were suggested for the next time: "Don't turn your back on the audience"; "Don't giggle or act silly"; "Talk clearly so you can be heard"; "Have your

[8] Mary G. Ligon and Sarah W. McDaniel, *The Teacher's Role in Counseling* (Englewood Cliffs, N.J.: Prentice Hall, 1970), pp. 81–86.

role clearly in mind when you start." Such comments helped guide later role playing.

There are a number of variations on the technique of role playing, which the teacher will soon discover. Teachers who are interested in trying this method might do well to form a small group and run through some role playing of their own in order to know how it feels. Teacher–principal, teacher–parent, and teacher–student problems are fitting subjects for such practice. An experience in role playing is the best way of discovering what this method accomplishes for the participants.

WRITING SKITS, RADIO OR VIDEO SCRIPTS, AND PLAYS

In role playing, the classroom teacher has a very simple but effective tool with which to build some original and dramatic presentations. Such presentations require carefully planned and detailed scripts. Informal role playing is one way to get a first draft of a script.

An assignment had been given to try to write a simple one-act play. One student chose the scene in which Anne Boleyn, just before being beheaded, said farewell to her daughter. The student asked various class members to take the few roles needed and to ad-lib the parts. The students, after a quick briefing, excitedly took part in the scene. The conversation that ensued had the breath of real life in it. As a result, the student playwright had the basic structure of her play set up and also obtained some important clues about how people might interact in a crisis like this.

This technique is applicable in almost any situation where a script or playlet is to be written. Radio scripts provide good motivation for writing in classes where writing is not the primary aim. They can be easily tape-recorded and played back to the class, and local radio stations can sometimes be persuaded to use the better efforts.

A print-shop teacher had taken his class on a field trip to a newspaper plant. When they returned, the teacher suggested a follow-up activity involving the preparation and recording of a script describing the field trip and what was learned. The class divided into groups: one group were the experts, who checked the script written by the writers for accuracy of facts and scientific soundness; another group, the sound engineers, arranged for the recording equipment and studio; another provided background music and sound effects; and still another became the critics to see that the whole thing was an effective presentation and could be used for PTA, assembly, and other industrial arts classrooms.

An increasing number of schools have videotape facilities. The procedure for videotaping is an excellent device for allowing students—players and viewers—to focus on specific issues (see Chapter 8).

Students may develop "living newspaper" presentations, either on stage or through audio or videotape. These can be presented at assembly meetings, or used as a service activity in elementary schools. It must be clearly kept in mind that this kind of activity is not solely the province of drama or English classes, or even social studies classes. There are significant current events in science, in foreign affairs (of interest to foreign language classes), industry, the arts, sports, and home economics. Role playing is a flexible technique which provides a creative educational experience for both teacher and students.

GAMES AND SIMULATIONS

One of the liveliest innovations of recent years has been the development of instructional games and the use of simulations for learning. In Chapter 12 games used for drill and review are discussed. The instructional games referred to here are designed to teach a new skill, develop an insight into a process or event, or provide new knowledge. *Games* involve some kind of competition, either of player against player, or player against chance or luck. Checkers is a pure game; when adapted to war-games, one can see how the game strategies of checkers can also be used with opposing armies. Board games, like *Monopoly*, have moves regulated by the drawing of cards (chance) and/or the roll of dice (luck). The players have some choices to make; by clever assessment of the degrees of freedom involved as against the probability of a bad stroke of luck, a player or team can win. *Simulations* are abstractions of a real situation, in streamline or miniature versions. Role playing is of course a simulation of the purest kind, where the least structure is provided for those participating. Most simulations provide roles and rules, after which the players construct their own reality. It is probable that most instructional games fall into a category of simulations in which elements of both competition, luck, and real world situations have been mixed. You will find the terms used interchangeably.[9]

A large literature has developed around games and simulations. Teachers have found them to be a valuable adjunct to direct instruction. Students enjoy them, and because most games and simulations are commercially produced, they have been pretested on large numbers of students. One can usually expect that the "bugs" in a game will have been resolved so that it will work as expected.

Mr. Martin describes a game he uses very successfully with twelve- and thirteen-year-olds. The game is called "Dump." Students are given a map of a mythical town, and each is assigned a lot. The problem is where to put the new incinerator for the town. The map includes areas marked town

[9] Don H. Coombs, "Games? They're a Serious Approach to Learning," *Planning for Higher Education*, 4 (October 1975), p. 23–28.

forest, abandoned quarry, church, school, town land, cemetery, lumber yard, pond, and industrial area. The students not only own land, but they have an interest in the various activities or businesses in the town. They are to prepare for a town meeting, where a decision is to be made, on the basis of the votes of four-fifths of the members (of the class). Discussion has included such issues as zoning, ecology, and community rights versus individual property rights. Sometimes the debates and discussion, with related research, take over a week of class time. A day is spent discussing the process of decision making when the final decision had been reached.[10]

Since many adolescents really do not have much facility with thinking about how present decisions will affect their future, the game of *Adventure* provides them with an opportunity to experience such decision making.[11] Where drug abuse needs to be considered by students, the simulation game, *Community at the Crossroads*, has been developed, published, and distributed by the federal government.[12]

When studying the impact of misleading advertising or distortion of scientific findings, it might be well to use *The Propoganda Game* which shows students dramatically how various devices are used to influence opinion. It is designed for two to four players, and can be used by a small group while others are engaged in another activity.[13] As part of the national curriculum program in geography, the High School Geography Project developed a game having to do with industrial location in relation to resources and trade. The simulation game, *Metfab*, is complex and involves many intellectual tasks. To make a decision as to where to locate a new plant, students must draw on considerations of the environment, their own preferences, and specific areas of expertise that were allocated to them via a role card. A team of five, composed of a factory president, sales manager, production manager, personnel manager, and treasurer, are given a set of data regarding the plant, and national statistics showing the relative activities of major cities. Each team of five have the same data, and one objective of the simulation is to see how each team resolves the problem.[14] An advanced business law class or economic class might want to use *Mr. Banker*. It teaches many of the basic concepts of our banking system through a mixture of role playing and decision making. The students become community bankers who must decide whether or not to make specific loan requests, as well as to build up community resources. The complexity of banking decisions is thus revealed.[15] Accident simulation has been

[10] Edward C. Martin, "Reflections on the Early Adolescent in School," *Daedalus*, 100 (Fall 1971), pp. 1090–1092.
[11] Abt Associates, Cambridge, Mass., or Educational Manpower, Madison, Wisconsin.
[12] Government Printing Office, HE 20.2408/2:C 73 S/1724-0161, 1972, $13.75 per kit.
[13] Available from Wff'n Proof, Ann Arbor, Michiagn.
[14] High School Geography Project, "Using Simulation To Involve Students" by Dana G. Kurfman and Ina M. Phillips, Association of American Geographers, 1970.
[15] *Mr. Banker*, Federal Reserve Bank, Minneapolis, Minnesota.

effectively used to develop more understanding of and response to shop safety where students use small power tools. Groups trained with the simulations, had fewer "accidents" than groups not exposed to the simulation.[16] A number of home amusement games have developed around sports. The games require knowledge and ability to do strategic thinking.[17]

The popularity of simulation games is apparent from any reading of the current professional literature of education. It would be useful to look through several issues of the journals in your field, particularly looking at the ads, to pick up leads to games and simulations in your area of interest. In the bibliography at the end of this chapter are some of the key resources for obtaining more information about these excellent additions to a teacher's repertoire.

SUMMARY

There are many methods which teachers can use to involve the whole class in learning. One of the most widely used, and misused, is class discussion. All teachers need to develop skill in leading discussions. Stimulators to discussion, such as role playing, require no costly materials or special aids. Role playing can be a dramatic device for bringing subject matter to life. The recent developments in simulation games for instructional use provide the teacher with superb materials for learning and promoting individual involvement.

[16] Stanley Rubinsky and Nelson F. Smith, "Evaluation of Accident Simulation as a Technique for Teaching Safety Procedures in the Use of Small Power Tools," DHEW, Public Health Service, #ICRL-RR-70-4, 1971.
[17] Produced by 3M, Tudor Games, and Avalon Hill.

SELECTED READINGS

Gall, Meredith D., and Joyce P. Gall, "The Discussion Method" in N. L. Gage (Ed.), *The Psychology of Teaching Methods*, Seventy-Fifth Yearbook of the National Society for the Study of Education. Chicago: University of Chicago Press, 1977, pp. 166–216. Provides the psychological rationale for the utilization of discussion to promote learning.

Greenhaven Press, 1611 Polk Street N.E., Minneapolis, Minn. 55413. This publisher has developed excellent materials, in pamphlet and audiovisual form, on controversial issues, which can be used in a variety of subject areas.

Horn, Robert E., *The Guide to Simulations/Games for Education and Training* (3rd ed.). Didactic Systems, Inc., P.O. Box 457, Cranford, N.J. 07016, 1977. Invaluable resource for listing and descriptions of games and simulations in all subject matter areas.

Kiley, Margaret, *Personal and Interpersonal Appraisal Techniques for Counselors, Teachers, Students.* Springfield, Ill.: Charles C Thomas, 1975. "Role-Playing–Sociodrama and Psychodrama," pp. 190–201. Shows how to develop and utilize role playing as a technique for guidance and developing insight into student problems.

Kohl, Herbert R., *Math, Writing and Games.* New York: New York Review Book/Vintage Books, 1974. Innovative ideas for assisting students in learning through imaginative exercises.

McGuire, Christine, Lawrence M. Solomon, and Philip G. Bascook, *Construction and Use of Written Simulations.* New York: The Psychological Corporation, 1976. You can write your own simulation by following the how-to-do-it instructions in this manual. An exciting activity for the creative teacher.

Sanders, Morris M., *Classroom Questions: What Kinds?* New York: Harper & Row, 1966. Excellent presentation of questioning process related to a taxonomy of questioning. Many useful examples at each level.

Seidner, Constance J., "Teaching with Simulations and Games," in N. L. Gage (Ed.), *The Psychology of Teaching Methods,* Seventy-Fifth Yearbook of the National Society for the Study of Education. Chicago: University of Chicago Press, 1977, pp. 217–251. Why is play a significant aspect of learning? When are games and simulations appropriate for the classroom?

Shaftel, Fannie, and George Shaftel, *Role-Playing for Social Values.* Englewood Cliffs, N.J.: Prentice-Hall, 1968. The best description of role-playing techniques. Includes a number of open-ended stories selected to illustrate recurring moral issues in democratic society.

Social Studies School Service, 10,000 Culver Blvd., P.O. Box 802, Culver City, Calif. 90230. The annual catalog distributed free from this source provides a listing and annotation of materials in many fields: guidance, career education, skills development, women's studies, and includes many hard-to-find games and simulations.

Stoll, Clarice, "Games Students Play," *Media and Methods* 7 (October 1970), pp. 37–44. The major reasons that games and simulations are of special value in involving students actively in learning.

Weil, Marsha, and Bruce Joyce, *Social Models of Teaching: Expanding Your Teaching Repertoire.* Englewood Cliffs, N.J.: Prentice-Hall, 1978. "Role Playing Model," pp. 25–108. Detailed report of ways to utilize role playing in teaching. Shows the essentials of this model in action.

World Future Society, 4916 St. Elmo Ave., Washington, D.C. A resource for several particularly interesting games: "Futuribles," "The Game of Future Shock," "New Town."

Yanes, Samuel (Ed.), *The No More Gym Shorts, Built-it-Yourself, Self-Discovery, Free School Talkin' Blues.* New York: Harper & Row, 1972. These activities, including games, have been developed from the alternative schools movement.

FOCUS ON CHAPTER 12

Changes in schooling during the last generation have unfortunately led to the notion that drill and review are not necessary in the learning process. In fact, all learning requires some kind of repetition and reinforcement. Many ways exist for making drill and review pertinent and enjoyable. In addition to learning classroom techniques for drill and review, students also require habits for drill and review which can be applied in their homework and independent study.

Significant ideas presented in this chapter include:
- Drill is intensive repetition for the purpose of ensuring swift, accurate responses.
- Review is a reconsideration of learning for the purpose of deepening understandings and relationships.
- Games lend themselves particularly well to drill exercises.
- Students can learn review techniques directly, but they can also learn them indirectly—through organizational procedures of classroom activity.
- Learning to study is a "survival skill" which cannot be left to chance.
- Independent study and homework procedures require specific attention as part of classroom concern with study skills.

chapter 12

One More Time: teaching for learning and retention

I was in an alternative high school during the early
1970s when it was popular for kids to do their
"own thing." I was always on independent study
or in a rap group . . . or skipping. I don't
remember anybody ever making us drill anything.
Consequently, I still have trouble with certain
verb forms, my vocabulary is an embarrassment
to me, and don't even ask me about math.

Exposure to subject matter is one thing; retention of it is quite another. The learning process that is essential to retention of information and to use of mechanical skills is called drill. Another essential process for synthesizing what is retained is called review.

DEFINING DRILL AND REVIEW

Drill provides intensive repetition to ensure swift, accurate responses; it is intended to establish associations that are available without "thinking-through" each time the associations are needed. Review may be defined as reconsideration of learning in order to deepen understanding. The separate elements of these relationships may require drill. Many times, therefore, drill and review work together to increase retention.

Obviously not everything studied is a fit subject for drill, but once it has proved to be appropriate, the learning established is retained best when it becomes part of the larger pattern of understanding that is furnished by review. For example, it is necessary to drill some words in spelling. But these ought to be the words needed by students for written expression or for instant recognition. Even those words on which drill seems justified will be retained correctly only if they are reused in further writing. It is rewriting, in this case, that becomes the best kind of review. Many long hours are wasted in secondary school classrooms drilling materials that are never needed as automatic responses. Still more hours are spent unprofitably drilling materials, however much needed, in a setting that is without meaning for students.

In the following discussion the distinctive procedures for drill and review have been generalized so they may apply to most secondary school situations.

USING CLASSROOM DRILL

One repeated criticism of "back-to-basics" advocates is that drill has been abandoned. Hence, the argument runs, learning is not as solid as it used to be: Reading is poor, spelling is weak; arithmetic is deficient; handwriting is not legible.

Actually, drill in its proper place is as strongly recommended as it ever was. The "proper place," however, is better defined than it used to be. It is now recognized that drill is profitable when it is restricted to skill learning, such as motor skills (e.g. the use of tools and machines); intellectual skills (e.g. the use of an index or the correct pronunciation of foreign languages). Drill is wasted on principles, such as Gresham's law; on attitudes, such as a feeling of responsibility toward one's community; and on appreciations, such as responsiveness to music. In addition, four other more specific limitations on drill are:

1. All students may not need repetition of the same material. Only rarely should the whole class be engaged in identical drill.
2. Unless great care is exercised, repetition quickly becomes monotonous and breeds misbehavior.
3. Only a few skills can be drilled at a time; otherwise, retention is poor.
4. Unless the information or activity is clearly understood at the beginning, drill may only reinforce misunderstanding or mishandling.

There are a number of helpful considerations to be absorbed by the teacher before he or she can use drill successfully:

1. Make certain that students realize why they need the skill that is being drilled. People do not gain much from repetition unless they can see a need for it.
2. Take time to see that students understand how to perform the skill. It is quite possible to instill an erroneous, awkward, or confused procedure.
3. Supervise initial practice closely. There are so many variations in the way learning proceeds that diagnosis and adaptation of practice are of great

importance. Students must capitalize on their strengths and consciously avoid their weaknesses.

4. Introduce variety to retain good morale. The next section of this chapter suggests games as one means of minimizing monotony.

5. Keep adjusting both the amount and the kind of practice to individual students. Spelling bees are good examples of drills that do not help those who need it most. Poor spellers "go down" fast while "natural" spellers battle to the finish. In addition, those in need of spelling help would benefit more from written rather than oral repetition.

6. Use shorter periods and space them over some time. Long drill periods tend to suffer from students "going through the motions." Effective drill requires continuing effort to improve.

7. Offer regular opportunities to apply what has been learned. This provides reassurance that the labor of drill is worth it.

8. Resist the temptation to keep adding items for drill. Unfortunately, so many practice exercises are available that it is all too easy to use one more to "keep them busy."

9. Provide a number of ways to get help. Since good drill is individualized, assistance must be, too. The teacher should meet with individual students as fast and as often as possible. Aid can also be furnished by other students; sometimes, teams of two students can act as "coach and pupil," aiding each other and reversing roles at regular intervals. Self-checking exercises also give responsible students a chance to develop their own insights.

10. Devise graphic ways of recording progress. Individual charts, score cards, and rating sheets make improvement concrete and apparent. They become a silent challenge to push a little higher, showing students where they started and how far they have climbed. These charts should not be posted for public display. Laggards are humiliated further and those ahead can become insufferable snobs.

GAMES FOR DRILL

In all classes, there is a certain amount of material that is, in itself, not interesting to learn: connecting a name with a date or an incident in history; spelling new words; memorizing names of objects; remembering sequences of events or processes; learning terminology. These, and similar kinds of material, are easily adapted to games. Students learn this kind of material more readily through games since the atmosphere of the classroom is one of friendly competition, encouragement, and reward.

Teachers in the elementary grades have found games to be essential, not only to the learning of skills, but also in helping children work together as members of a group. The technique is not used as much in secondary school. There is an unfortunate impression that using games is "kid stuff" or "sugar coating." The attitude that learning, to be genuine, must have a "no nonsense" approach is longstanding. Yet, such an attitude is a denial of what is known about how people learn: namely, that they learn when they wish to learn, that more is learned from success than from failure, that more is learned from pleasant than from unpleasant experiences. It must also be remembered that adolescence is not far removed from childhood. Secondary school students enjoy many activities common to both stages of development.

Games are useful to students and teachers because:

- They break classroom routines in a pleasant way.
- They provide an opportunity to see familiar material in a new relationship.
- They are excellent motivation for all students for the kind of learning that requires drill. The fact that students become interested and competitive in the game acts to balance their reaction against drill.

Games help the uninterested to take part in the class. One of the most important contributions of games is that students who have not done the work because of lack of interest, ability, or some other reason become engrossed in the competitive situation and find themselves arguing about right or wrong answers as vociferously as those who have done the work. The class, caught up in a game, can spend energy and time debating subject matter that under standard routines is dismissed as "boring" or "dumb."

Imaginative teachers design some of their own games, but here are some examples that can be adapted to many classes.

"WHO AM I?"

A world history class, after a study of Greek and Roman history, can be divided into two teams, one taking Greek historical figures and the other Roman. Each team decides on the figures to present, one for each student. A student gives to the other team one or two clues about his identity; the other team is allowed a certain number of questions to help them guess. If they fail to guess in a stated time after using up all their questions, they do not earn a point. The teams alternate in asking each other to guess the essential characteristics of an individual. The following adaptations can be made.

Science: Identify different chemicals, insects, diseases, germs, plants.
English: Identify characters in a book, parts of speech, authors, books or poems.
Music: Identify musicians, instruments, selections from recordings.
Art: Identify artists, paintings.
Film: Identify major films, directors, actors.
Health: Identify diseases by symptoms.

"Twenty Questions" is a variation of "Who Am I?" A "host" and four "experts" seat themselves at the front of the room. The host starts the game by announcing the subject chosen—animal, vegetable, or mineral; person, place, or idea, according to the particular class and subject. On the board, hidden from the experts, the exact item is written. The object of the game is to see whether the experts can guess the identity of the host using only a total of twenty questions that can be directly answered "yes" or "no" by the host. The class is in on the secret, since they can see the host's "identification." Using only four students as the questioners and a different host each time lessens the possibility of confusion in the class. It is true that few students actually participate since most of them make up the audience. The level of interest can be raised by having the host and the experts represent two different teams previously set up in the class. Score can be kept on how often each group of four is able to guess correctly within the specified number of questions.

BASEBALL AND FOOTBALL

These games are similar and may be alternated according to the sport in season. Basketball and track rules may also be used. The class is divided into two teams, and a captain is chosen either by the team or by the teacher. The teacher or the students (or both) have previously composed a series of questions on class material. The questions are sorted into three groups by the teacher or by a committee of students: easy, hard, very hard. In baseball, a correct answer to any easy question gives the team a one-base hit; a hard question, two bases; very hard, three bases; and some especially difficult questions can be added for home runs. Each side gets its innings; three wrong answers are equal to three outs. Then the other side is "at bat." The role of the captain is to decide the "batting order" and what kind of hit the student is going to try, although often the decision on the level of question can be left to each team member.

A diamond placed on the board and a scorekeeper will assist in keeping track of the progress of the game. The teacher acts as umpire, otherwise, student squabbling over a right or wrong answer can spoil the game. Since the students invariably know the rules of these games well, it is not difficult to clear up the possible points of controversy. In baseball, it is important to decide whether, if a man is on first base and the next student answers a two-base question, that puts the first man on third base or gets him home, thus scoring a run for his team. The class can decide this issue quickly before the game starts.

In football, the questions are ranked by number of yards according to their difficulty. Each team gets four questions (four "downs") to make the necessary ten yards; or the ball is handed over to the other team. The farther down the field one team gets toward the goal line, the farther the other team has to carry the ball back down the field in the opposite direction.

As a variation, the two teams could have a chance to prepare the questions to be asked beforehand; thus, the drill is made doubly effective, since if students must know the material in order to ask the questions to begin with, they must know it in order to answer. Teachers or students may decide the degree of difficulty of the questions; the teams may get only the questions asked by the other team, or the questions may be mixed, giving each team a 50–50 chance of getting its own questions.

Evaluation may be carried on by the teams or by selected members if the questions are submitted prior to playing the game and are reviewed for pertinence, clarity, and significance. The teacher may choose to review questions and give added points to the team that submitted better ones.

Answers to the questions may also be provided in advance by each team for the teacher to check; this ensures even more review.

Instead of having the teacher give the questions, each team may do so; one person acts as pitcher and tosses the ball (question) to the batter on the other team; then the next person in line takes the floor as pitcher, and so on.

Each team may be penalized for infractions of the rules, such as getting too noisy, illegal coaching, asking questions that had previously been ruled out, and similar faults. The teacher may also choose to penalize a team for poorly thought-out or superficial questions. One further word: Penalties should usually not be invoked until the class has become used to playing the game.

> Two eleventh-grade Business Law classes, one slow and one average in ability, played "baseball" as part of their review before a quiz. Both classes enjoyed the game greatly; the slower class was easier to control and did not get as excited or full of "team spirit" as the other class. When the game was halted for another activity (hearing a recording), the two classes were reluctant to stop, even though the material had been relatively uninteresting and remote in time. The students paid close attention to both the questions and the answers in order to be sure that their team's plays were being called correctly.

"IT'S ACADEMIC"

In this variation of the popular regional television program, an "expert" introduces the contestants. These students may be representatives of teams, or groups in the class may volunteer for the game or may be chosen by lot by the teacher so that everyone has a chance and obligation to participate. The contestants are replaced at regular intervals during the game. From a box, the "expert" draws a question that has previously been prepared by a committee or by class groups or teams. Any one of the contestants may answer the question. The one who raises a hand first is usually the one chosen to do so. Once a student raises a hand, withdrawal is not possible. For each correct answer, the contestant gets a tally, which may be a personal score or part of a team score. If none of the contestants can answer, audience volunteers may try, getting a chance to add to their team score. However, if the questions have been prepared by the teams, they should be marked so that team members do not try to answer questions they have prepared.

CARD GAMES

The game of "Authors" is an old and popular game. In it a set of cards is made up with the names of famous books and plays and their authors. The cards are shuffled and passed out to four or six players so that all have six or eight cards. The rest of the cards are put face down on the table. Each person tries to match author and book. Each such pair is placed in front of the player and gives one score point. Each person must draw one card and discard one card. The player has an option of drawing from the discard pile (those left face up) or from the pile that is face down. However, when drawing from the discard pile, the player must take either the top card—or if another card is desired—all those preceding it. The student who correctly matches all cards held first, wins. This kind of game works best for one or more small groups functioning on their own, while the rest of the class is engaged in other kinds of drill or in some other activity.

There are many variations of this game applicable to other fields. Names, dates, events can be matched in history and social studies classes. In science, matching names and properties of materials can be arranged. In English and foreign language classes, such a game can assist in vocabulary drill, in learning the parts of speech, and in practicing good usage. Other variations can be used in shorthand, bookkeeping, drama, journalism, psychology, mathematics, vocational education, and art and music appreciation courses, among others. Certain commercially prepared games, such as "Al Pha Bet,"[1] designed for vocabulary and spelling improvement, and "Euro Card," which develops knowledge of Europe through map orientation, are worthy of attention.[2]

When using homemade materials, the teacher probably should prepare the first few cards, but completion of the rest would be a worthwhile student project. Thus both the students who make, and those who use, the cards are gaining practice in review, with a special kind of recognition for talent in making neat cards for the game. In fact, some students may select the items for the test; others may check the items for accuracy, relevance,

---

[1] Richard Higgins, "Al Pha Bet" (Miami, Fla.: Solar Products Corporation, 1966).
[2] Robert W. Allen, "Euro Card" (Ft. Lauderdale, Fla.: The Maret Company, 1967).

and coverage; and, finally, a group may elect to cut and letter the cards. In this way, many talents are used at many levels of intellectual competence and cooperative effort.

Card games may also be used to learn sequences or chronology. Thus, some of the cards may be a number series and the others a set of historical events. The student's objective then is to put the cards in the right sequential order. This variation might best be played by one student alone, then checked by another for accuracy as a quick method of individual practice and review.

LIMITATIONS OF CLASSROOM GAMES FOR DRILL

The teacher should select the members of each team on some basis that protects the feelings of the students. Under no circumstance should a student select team members.

The spelling bee model of a game is not recommended. As pointed out, those who are least successful, those who are least adept at the type of problem presented, are those who are dropped first. Those who know the most get all the practice.

One other comment: The games described here all assume that the content or skills selected for drill are carefully chosen. Games are an effective method of making drill interesting and enjoyable, but it is important that the drill be directed toward genuine learning.

STEPS FOR REVIEW: SOME GENERALIZATIONS

Review furnishes the overall structure for retaining learning. Both the learning of skills developed through drill and the learning of concepts, attitudes, and appreciations are joined in a framework of concrete relationships. The culmination of a unit in science, for example, might well demonstrate some skills with laboratory equipment and materials besides some ideas, feelings, and sensitivities about the need to conserve energy. When students see how all these learnings belong together, they have an organizing structure that helps them hang on to what has been studied. Some part of each day's work should be devoted to review. Students should not begin or leave a class with loose ends of learning dangling; they need a chance every day to tie things together.

Review may begin the work of the day. This is particularly valuable for those who learn more slowly, precisely because they do not "tie things together" well. Review may encompass a brief statement by a student, or several students, on: (a) the material covered yesterday; (b) today's assignment; or (c) the plans made for today's work. Since yesterday's class, each student has been taught in four or five other classes. The work of each class is usually unrelated to that of the others. If the student has the work of any special class clearly in mind, it is that of the class just left and not, in all likelihood, the class now beginning.

Some fields of instruction probably do provide a more immediate sense of organization than others. Mathematics, for example, is often taught so that each day's work progresses rather inevitably from that of the previous day. In a problems of democracy or drama class, on the other hand, the sequence may depend on long-range understandings, with some elements playing a part one day but not necessarily entering the picture again for some time. For example, in problems of democracy, an understanding of propaganda techniques contributes in some measure to understanding advertising and consumer buying but may soon drop out of consideration as other aspects of the course are viewed. As the study of political ideologies is approached, the earlier study of propaganda may be pertinent again. In drama, pantomime technique returns repeatedly in the development of the course. Consider with other majors in your subject some of those understandings. Share them with students in other subject areas in order to see comparisons and contrasts that exist among disciplines.

Review may also end the work of the day. The few minutes before the bell rings are not the time to introduce material: Students are much too aware that the end is near. It is wiser to do work clearly labeled "The End for Today," which strengthens the student's sense of having accomplished something. The review may center in such queries as:

- How would you summarize what we did today?
- How does this relate to what we have been studying?
- What next steps do you see?

Review procedures allow excellent opportunities for students to integrate and apply knowledge from all areas of their experience to the material at hand.

The review at the end of the unit is, of course, a larger undertaking. Perhaps most difficult of all in this kind of review is the task of involving all students in the review. It is essential that slower students be given an opportunity to participate in this important task.

Probably the least effective review procedure is the recitation, the teacher-student response situation, or the oral quiz. In such a situation only the student being quizzed is actively involved; the others are nervously or angrily wondering what question will hit them!

In order to help students develop review techniques, it is important in class to develop a review system. The major divisions of study can be established by discussing basic questions with small groups and with the entire class:

1. What were the major things we learned in this unit? Students should be encouraged to try to add personal touches as they look back on their work. Standardized summaries should be avoided. "Put it into your own words" is good advice. Students should always paraphrase in their own words when making charts, card files, writing examples and reports, or stating generalizations or principles.

2. How did we arrive at what we know? A renewed sense of the sequence of development lends clarity to the review: "First we did this and that led to something else, which developed into some further study." It may help to think again of the specific activities: the survey, the role playing, the group work. How did they contribute? Or it may be useful to recall some materials: a motion picture, a tape recording, a series of pamphlets. With what content or skill were they associated? Sometimes it is even worthwhile to repeat an activity (such as an especially rich role-playing experience), or to use a resource again (perhaps an unusually stimulating motion picture).

3. Where can we apply what we have learned? Students should know the uses of knowledge and skills in a world where they face adult responsibilities. Where can they use the results of their study of "Color and Texture" in art, of "Weather" in science, of "Percentage and Interest" in mathematics, of "Personal Hygiene" in physical education?

4. How does this unit relate to what we have previously learned—this semester, last year, in elementary school? Articulation of learning both within the secondary school and with the elementary school is tenuous at best. It can be improved only when each secondary school teacher learns what students have been taught before, uses this knowledge in the planning of new units, and reinforces and reconsiders the old learning with the new.

Review procedures should, of course, be related to evaluation procedures. In part, evaluation will include paper-and-pencil examinations. If an examination is to appraise broad concepts, then the review should concentrate on broad concepts and should examine them in the same way that the test itself will. It is frustrating for students to have a review on one level and then to be quizzed on another. One way to ensure a common understanding about emphasis is to ask the students themselves to prepare examination questions, discussion of which can then clarify the remaining problems. It is advisable when this is done to include some of the better questions in an examination.

SUPERVISED STUDY

Many secondary school teachers in the academic subject fields plan supervised study for each period. Out-of-school competition for students' time means that often homework is either not accomplished at all or is done rapidly and carelessly. In addition, if students do not know how to study, teachers can provide needed guidance only when they are able to observe students' habits. In-class study time, however, does not mean the last three minutes of the period; who could even start to study in so short a time? Sample assignments carried on in the classroom, under the teacher's watchful eye and helping hand, assist in translating theory into practice. As the year passes, concerned teachers will continue to allow time for supervised study so that students can develop greater sophistication and so that assignments may increase in depth as students reveal their proficiency.

Supervised study naturally helps students work more effectively out of school as well as in. Moreover, once they have been helped to transfer their improved techniques to other subjects and to at-home assignments, a cumulative effect will be generated that results in widespread and continuing success.

Whether study is to be in or out of class, the importance of teacher supervision must be emphasized. Supervision begins with preparing the students to use study time in class to advantage. Such preparation includes:

- Agreeing with the class on objectives for the study period. Often motivation for using in-class study time is on the low level of, "If you don't do this in class, you'll just have to do it at home." This implies that learning is a distasteful enterprise best terminated at the earliest possible moment. A better approach is to help students to see the importance and relevance of the material being studied. Then the study time in class becomes an opportunity rather than a chore.
- Providing specific objectives to be attained. The questions to be answered, concepts to be understood, problems to be solved, and information to be collected should all be understood by the class before the assignment is undertaken.
- Identifying clearly the reasons for study. List questions either on the chalkboard or in a study-guide worksheet. For a teacher to say, "Read the next chapter and be ready to answer questions on it" is, for almost any student, a vague and useless kind of direction.
- Helping students set goals regarding the time needed to accomplish the study task. Suggest, for instance, "Try to get the first five problems solved in class, and then you can finish the rest at home." Remember, however, that variation in student ability will mean that much more will be accomplished by some than others. Nevertheless, all students can be taught to make efficient use of the study time provided.

When study time is offered in class, individual supervision should be provided. While the students are studying in class, the teacher should:

1. Walk around the room to observe study habits.
2. Discuss with individual students any study problems that arise.
3. Watch how student work is progressing. The teacher may find it advisable to call the attention of the whole class to some particularly difficult passage or interesting point that should not be missed. See that full advantage is being taken of the resources that are available in school but not at home, such as a room reference or the instructional facilities of a laboratory or media center.

4. Ask students about their progress. The teacher should not wait for unfinished or poor work to indicate a trouble spot.
5. Note different ability levels. All students do not need, and should not have, the same home-study assignments.
6. Be alert to class activity. By anticipating difficulties, observing behavior and providing a sense of "positive momentum," the teacher contributes to a working atmosphere. Be careful to observe your own behavior. Do not create disturbances when there is an orderly atmosphere. Do not expect students to have materials unless you announce their need beforehand.

Time for study should be carefully provided for in the overall plan, but it is important to vary the daily schedule enough so that students remain alert and interested. Establishing a weekly planning session will aid the class in allocating needed class time for study; remember that the result of these joint planning sessions should be a program that allows for the different rates of progress that will be made by different classes over similar material and that permits adjustments to varying student interests and abilities. It is unwise to have an inflexible rule of "twenty minutes every period for in-class study" as it is to have no plan at all for helping students to develop study skills.

OUT-OF-CLASS STUDY

All school learning experiences have as their purpose the transference of behavior to life outside the classroom. If there is to be a transference, what happens in the classroom must have genuine meaning for students. If students are asked to work outside the classroom on assignments, then that homework will "pay off" only when it is an outgrowth of something relevant, vital, or exciting. Countless experienced teachers avow that homework has meaning only when it is an extension of something that makes sense in the classroom.

HOMEWORK FOR LEARNING

Busywork—in or out of the classroom—is destructive; it develops animosity toward schoolwork in general and destroys student confidence in the teacher's values. The only homework that is of any worth, then, is homework that genuinely involves learning—work that extends meaning and offers reward on its own merits.

Homework can function effectively as review, and parts of it will frequently call for drill. Therefore, it is all the more important that students experience practical, helpful approaches to review and drill in the classroom. They cannot implement at home those things they do not know.

At its best, homework should be tailor-made for the student, the class, the subject, and the occasion. Realistically, such an accomplishment is impossible when teachers deal with groups of thirty or more students. To do so would involve countless hours of planning and preparation. It is possible, though, to arrange homework assignments that are sufficiently flexible for students to adapt study and materials to their own needs and interests. Choice of approach, opportunity to practice a needed skill, or review an area of weakness, and the possibility of selecting an alternate assignment can encourage self-awareness and direction as well as creative solutions. Homework that can be accomplished in a reasonable amount of time will allow students a sense of proportion and assure them that the teacher is aware that out-of-class work is assigned in other subjects as well.

Homework of worth is also that which allows the teacher to maintain a gauge of student development. Out-of-class work that will indicate how successfully students are perfecting study skills and to what extent they are able to make relationships, locate and utilize materials, and work without supervision will all enable the teacher to provide individualized instruction and allow maximum personal development.

ASSIGNMENTS THAT STUDENTS WILL DO

If students see worth in an assignment, they will do it. It is that simple. Certainly, most students will "complete" assignments—whether mechanically, or by copying or by sharing in a division of labor with others—in order to stay within the bounds of safety. But the assignment in which students become involved and from which they learn is the one for which they see a reason. The teacher can help students find a reason for out-of-class work by the nature of the assignments and through discussion that helps them to understand the nature and purpose of those assignments. Group or committee assignments; interviews; community resources; observing ecological patterns; attendance at public hearings; interviewing community leaders and workers, all these possess endless opportunities for assignments that are rich in meaning. All avoid the standard, lackluster approach of simply reading, or answering, questions from a textbook.

In addition to short-term homework, long-range assignments can be beneficial and challenging because they demand planning and budgeting of time and allow an opportunity for reflective thinking. With this type of assignment, in-class study time permits the teacher to assist students in planning and allotting time out of class to do most of the work. This planning will help minimize home situations such as these:

- "I have to turn in my two-week journal in psychology tomorrow. Do we have any extra notebooks?"

- "I have to read *Moby Dick* by tomorrow. Where's that book called *100 Best Plots?*"
- "I have to write 500 words on being the sole survivor after a nuclear explosion. What'll I say, Mom?"
- "I have to get my Science Fair project in by tomorrow. Any ideas?"
- "I have to build a model of the Parthenon by tomorrow. Do we have any sugar cubes?"

When homework is assigned, it is extremely important that it be examined or checked in some way by the teacher.

> There were many things about the worst teacher I ever had that make him stick out in my mind. Among the most hateful was the way class was conducted. Every day he put us through a new lesson from the textbook, told us to begin the exercises at the end and be ready to hand them in the next day. He never corrected that homework and never made any remark about it, but we still had to turn the junk in every day.

Students quickly resent homework that is ignored in class; eventually, they either stop doing such work, correctly assuming it isn't important, or they resort to cheating in order to have something to hand in.

For both in- and out-of-class assignments, it is necessary for teachers to consider beforehand what weight they will give to content and form. Should a student be judged on the ability to conform to a teacher's predetermined style of presentation or on the substance of the work? Do teachers foster unreasonable conformity when they say, "Do it this way"? Is creativity and perceptive thinking stifled by such tactics? How would form-minded teachers have evaluated the work of James Joyce, e.e.cummings, or Albert Einstein?

JUNIOR AND MIDDLE SCHOOL VERSUS SENIOR-HIGH-SCHOOL HOMEWORK

Homework assignments, as all others, must alter with the ability, interest, maturity, and achievement of students. Therefore, tasks set for students must undergo change—in breadth and depth—from junior to senior high school. For many students there is genuine "culture shock" in going to middle school or junior high school—with change of classes, many teachers, and the emphasis on grades in many school systems. Therefore, whatever younger students are asked to do at home should be planned with extreme care and should be introduced gradually. Emphasis on study skills is essential and all outside assignments must capitalize on such skills if they are to be effective. Variety is also important; most students in the electronic age have short attention spans, middle school and junior-high-school students especially so. Alternations of tasks, new approaches, change of emphasis, and the involvement of hands as well as brains will do much to encourage interest and learning.

Unquestionably, homework must be as interesting and relevant to senior-high-school students as it is to younger ones. But as students mature—intellectually as well as emotionally—they should be confronted with tasks that go deeper and broader in their demands. Increasingly, assignments should allow students to consider the problems of daily existence which many of them already face or will confront in all too short a time. While certain skills of study and performance will need repeated practice, consideration of the controversial and universal aspects of all subject areas is essential if high school students are to become enlightened, active citizens. Studying the French or American revolutions is important, of course, but can we afford to overlook the fact that we are living in what may be regarded as one of the great revolutionary periods in history? Discussing the honesty of Jean Valjean in *Les Miserables* is necessary, but how about being honest when taking exams, completing income tax returns, and adhering to traffic regulations? Knowing the functions of the body is important, but can the ethics and morality of organ transplants be ignored?

HOMEWORK: HOW MUCH, HOW OFTEN?

Teachers should think twice about the nature and amount of homework and about coordinating their assignments with other teachers.

With the exception of long-range assignments, it is educational suicide to give homework over weekends, holidays, or on nights of, or before, important school activities. The assignment will be done hurriedly (if at all), in which case the entire exercise is pointless. Regardless of its meaning, homework in these circumstances has the same effect as busywork.

LEARNING TO USE HOME-STUDY SKILLS

Circumstances of the classroom largely control students' use of time while they are there; guidance in out-of-class study is needed. Discussion of how students utilize their time may help dramatize its importance. Asking students to keep a time record of their activities for a week, translated into a graph, will illustrate what percentage of time is given to recreation, employment, "loafing," and study. When relationships are drawn between what the graph relates and individuals' success in school and goals beyond, they may be able to determine that, as application to study increases, probably so will learning. It is to be hoped, as well, that students will see clearly from their own experiences the necessity of budgeting time. Encouraging college-bound high-school students to recognize that wise use of time is essential to college success should benefit them immediately as well as ultimately. Other students need assistance in this skill, also. Using time well is a lifelong personal and job-related necessity.

Teachers should discuss with students other conditions that are essential for efficient home study. These are:

- Reviewing work in class to see what, if any, difficulties may be encountered at home, and checking with the teacher for help in these areas.
- Arranging a specific time and place at home for uninterrupted study. This is often not easy and may even be impossible for young people who live in crowded or disorganized homes. It is not infrequent to find young people who, of necessity, are employed for many hours a week, or whose responsibilities in the home are physically exhausting. Others live in situations of emotional havoc. These students simply may not be able to do home assignments. To penalize them is not simply petty, but inhumane.
- Reviewing the importance of learning habits, of individual concentration and responsibility for one's own learning tasks, and relating this to later vocational needs.
- Providing time in class to exchange experiences about the methods of study students finds most helpful, so that they can help one another. Advice from a peer is often more acceptable than advice from a teacher or other adult.

HOME ENVIRONMENT AND STUDY SKILLS

Home environment plays a significant role in the success students have with homework. Generally speaking, parents in comfortable suburban communities will favor, and even insist on homework, usually because they mistakenly believe that a great deal of it is a sign of true teaching and that mastery of content thus obtained will aid in college admission. There is no evidence to prove this. There is evidence, however, that parents in these situations are so eager for their children's success that they will actually do partial or entire assignments for them.

Members of poor socioeconomic communities also usually take homework as an indication of good teaching. In fact, they may resent it if students are not given homework, interpreting this as a sign that the teacher believes their children are incapable of doing it. Disadvantaged parents are just as eager for their children to succeed as are affluent ones. However, in some cases, they simply do not know how to help their children. They may not understand that study space and materials are essential and they may be financially unable to provide them; they do not know how to help their children perfect study skills; and they may not be able to do the assignments themselves. Whether serving affluent or disadvantaged students a teacher will want to work with parents to help them understand the goals and procedures of the classroom, homework included. The teacher's task will be to help parents see that homework for the sake of homework is destructive and that an absence of homework does not mean "nothing is going on in that school." Some avenues for this communication between teacher and parents might include PTA meetings, letters to parents, telephone and in-school conferences, and home visits.

READING STUDY SKILLS FOR RETENTION

Without the ability to study effectively on one's own, the opportunities for self-learning and for review and drill are severely limited. In addition to the reading suggestions in Chapter 5, it is important to the development of study skills that each subject teacher assist students in how to use printed materials appropriate to the particular discipline. The significance and value of the other parts of a book—title page, copyright, table of contents, preface, appendix, glossary, and index—in addition to, and in relation to, the main body of the book are essential. Practical exercises in using and evaluating these sections can make the use of text and reference books effective learning tools. Review or instruction in the use of subject-related resources will ensure some familiarity with content and use of important aids that students will be expected to employ on their own. Scanning materials with an eye to unit headings, chapter headings, and subheadings will encourage students to see a framework in material. Training is necessary, also, in helping students learn how to get clues from italics, bold-face printings, and color markings as well as in being alert to such words as "Review," "Summary," and "Conclusion."

THE SQ3R TECHNIQUE

The SQ3R technique of reading is helpful for focusing students' attention on developmental steps in studying. The SQ3R technique uses the following approach:

Survey: Glance through the assignment, observing main headings, illustrated material and captions, and any editorial techniques, such as italics. Skim the content of the first and last paragraphs in each section.

Question: Turn each heading and subheading into a question. For example, the heading, "Use of the Carriage Return Lever" in a typing manual can be rephrased to "What are the uses of the carriage return lever?" or "How may I use the carriage return lever?"

Read: Keeping the purposes established in the questions in mind, read to obtain the desired information.

Recite and Review: When reading is completed, demonstrate in some way that understanding has taken place. This may mean performing a skill, restating the material as it is, or putting the material into one's own words. Paraphrasing is especially helpful in certain situations where one is reading for information. Making brief notes as each section is read may be helpful.

It is necessary to review in an expanded way when an entire chapter, section, or work is completed. Look again at the major divisions and think about them, trying to see a connection between them and the major topic under which they fall. Continue this process through minor divisions. Use whatever notes have been made, checking to be sure that they are in order of development.

Not only is the SQ3R technique effective, but it is also timesaving and orderly.

OTHER STUDY TECHNIQUES

Other techniques that need attention in each subject area are outlining (but do not assign students the stultifying job of outlining chapters in a book!), organizing and presenting oral reports, finding the specific form for written assignments, and using the library for obtaining and using subject-related materials.

Notetaking is an important skill that can be practiced in all subject areas. Whether the notes are made from written or oral sources (the classroom included), students should be encouraged to record only significant information—in their own words and in capsule form. Students should also be helped to see the importance of a consistent form of notetaking in all their classes and study work. If direct quotation is made, it is necessary to be exact, to use quotation marks for the excerpt, and to record the source completely. All notes should be dated, and when information comes from a written source, it should include the author's name, the title, publisher, copyright date, and page number.

Exercises in this skill, as well as in the skill of translating note material into spoken and written reports, should also be handled according to the specific needs of the subject and the particular operation of the class.

PREPARING FOR TEST TAKING

Considering the number of tests which individuals are required to take during their schooling—and sometimes beyond that—the importance of learning skills of preparing for and taking tests seems obvious. If tests are seen as educational, that will help students to be "test wise" and they will be viewed as important. In addition to helping students develop appropriate procedures for test preparation, it is important to assist them in developing sophistication with regard to the kinds of tests that are offered within a subject area; it is also important to acquaint them with teacher-made and standardized tests and the variety of format and content each may contain.

The following is an outline of how one teacher develops skill in test-taking:

1. Before the test:
   a. Review
   b. Reread
   c. Relax
   d. Rest
2. Take the test with a calm, realistic attitude. Be on time. Take the proper materials with you.
3. Survey the entire test before you begin. Make notes if permitted.
4. Do the easiest questions first. Skip anything that is difficult until you have completed all other items.
5. During the test, stop periodically (if it is long) and relax: Close your eyes, breathe deeply, and consciously work to relieve tension.

Students will develop trust in the teacher and skill in testing if, at the beginning of the year, they are provided with a sample test or two prior to the first one that counts. They should also understand the teacher's approach to marking and grading before they are exposed to a test "for keeps." Chapter 13 contains additional information on approaches to testing.

SUMMARY

Drill and review, in many forms, are essential in all subjects if students are to master essential information and skills and to remember to use what they have mastered. Games are particularly useful in drill exercises, and so is a sense of humor. Specific procedures for review, as well as specific procedures for out-of-class study, are essential for students to know. These procedures can be learned from direct instruction and also from the indirect organization of the classroom.

SELECTED READINGS

Annis, L., and J. K. Davis, "Study Techniques: Comparing Their Effectiveness," *American Biology Teacher*, 40 (February 1978), pp. 108–110. Some study skills methods may be more appropriate for some students than other approaches.

Bruner, Jerome S. (Ed.), *Learning about Learning.* Washington, D.C.: US Department of Health, Education, and Welfare, Office of Education, 1966. Reports on the research on learning relevant to secondary teachers.

Doll, Ronald C., "How Can Learning be Fostered?" in William Van Til (Ed.), *Issues in Secondary Education,* Seventy-Fifth Yearbook of the National Society for the Study of Education, Part II. Chicago: University of Chicago Press, 1976, pp. 269–294. Given the modern climate of society, how can a teacher organize teaching assignments so that adolescents are motivated and supported in their learning endeavors?

Kotnour, J. F., "No Homework—a Student's Right," *Clearing House,* 51 (February 1978), pp. 180–181. One side of the homework argument.

Kranyik, Robert, *How to Teach Study Skills.* New York: Atherton, 1968. Presentation of study-skill basics. Guide for both teachers and students.

Mattleman, M. S., and H. E. Blake, "Study Skills: Prescription for Survival," *Language Arts,* 54 (November–December 1977), pp. 925–927. Useful guidelines for helping students develop adequate study skills.

McGaugh, James L., "Learning and Memory," *NEA Journal,* 57 (April 1968), pp. 8–9. Presents changing concepts of how memory and learning are associated with new insights gained from the biological sciences.

Shavelson, Richard J., "Teachers' Decision Making," in N. L. Gage (Ed.), *The Psychology of Teaching Methods,* Seventy-Fifth Yearbook of the National Society for the Study of Education, Part I. Chicago: University of Chicago Press, 1976, pp. 372–414. Discusses the factors which may influence a teacher in deciding when to utilize a particular task in the classroom.

Shockley, Robert J., *Using Homework as a Teaching Tool: Extending Classroom Activities through Guided Home Study.* Englewood Cliffs, N.J.: Prentice-Hall, 1964. This brief pamphlet shows effective ways to lift homework out of the "busy-work" category.

Strang, Ruth, *What Research Says to the Teacher: Guided Study and Homework.* Washington, D.C.: National Education Association, 1968. Reviews the research relevant to study and homework, with recommendations for best practices.

Thompson, M., "You Think Politics and Religion Are Touchy Topics? Just Mention Mandatory Homework," *American School Board Journal,* 165 (March 1978), pp. 37–39. Another side to the homework controversy.

part V

EVALUATION:
tests
and
grades

EVALUATION helps the teacher and student answer the question: "How well are we doing?" Although there is much agony—and mythology—surrounding tests, test making, and test taking, gaining skill in evaluation is not difficult, if the teacher observes some simple and clear guidelines. More difficult is selecting material worthy of evaluation, and probably most difficult of all is assigning grades. Grades are so important in the lives of teachers and students that clarity concerning what grades tell us about learning is essential.

FOCUS ON CHAPTER 13

Although no one has ever claimed to like taking tests, such measures provide both test maker and test taker with valuable information. When tests are used for diagnosis they are important aids to the teacher and the student for planning remedial action. Making good classroom tests is not easy; developing a good test is a time-consuming occupation. Teachers have found, too, that using a variety of approaches to testing, subjective as well as objective tests, performance and observation, oral and written, will allow different kinds of students to demonstrate proficiency.

Significant ideas presented in this chapter include:

- Although testing and evaluation are often considered to be synonymous, an evaluation program is far more than mere testing; it includes a whole range of activities and measures which tell student and teacher what has been accomplished, and how well it has been accomplished.
- The teacher-made test is the most common kind of test utilized. There are a wide variety of types of tests which teachers can develop, each of which is particularly useful to assess a particular type of learning or skill.
- There are some practical guides which teachers need to observe in administering and supervising testing, and which will reduce the amount of confusion or cheating which seems to accompany test making in many instances.
- Increasingly, standardized tests are being utilized to determine the achievement of specified competences; some of these are norm-referenced and some are criterion-referenced. With the emphasis on accountability, teachers will be expected increasingly to use and understand these tests.

chapter 13

"Testing, Testing . . .": tests and measurements for learning

Is there anyone who likes to take tests? Tests, quizzes, and examinations are almost unique to school life, although there are other times in one's life when tests have to be taken: to get a driver's license, to obtain a civil service rating, to get into graduate school. Once these tests are taken, there may be years before another test situation occurs. Or, for some lucky people, once the test is over, there will never again be the need to prepare for testing. Not so in school, where students are subjected to testing almost continuously. In one form or another their behavior and achievement is appraised, measured, judged, tested, sorted, and graded.

Since teachers are responsible for most student evaluations, it is important that teachers do a good job. But, sadly, one must admit that one of the weakest areas of teacher preparation and performance is in the development of adequate evaluation tools. This chapter introduces some of the possibilities and some of the pitfalls in testing and evaluation; it is strongly suggested that you practice developing tests in your own subject field in conjunction with the reading and discussion of this chapter.

THE SCOPE OF EVALUATION

Testing is only one aspect of the activities referred to as "evaluation." As a teacher, one is constantly making judgments about what a particular student is doing; comparing what a student does in relation to others in the class or to previous students; considering one's idea of what ought to be done by any one student at a particular moment, and judging the quality of a student's performance. It is obvious that no teacher can give an accurate report on this range of activities for all of the 100 or so students that stream in and out of class in a single day. For this purpose teachers utilize a range of tools: short quizzes, long tests, objective tests, essay tests, homework assignments, laboratory performance, product evaluation, performance measures, rating scales, student self-assessments. Each subject field requires some specific kind of evaluation device. In physical education there is the measurement of skill progress. In art, there is the final product showing how well the student uses color, space, perspective. In typing, there is concern with how many errors are made per minute on a timed test on new material. (What are some considerations in your subject area?) In addition, each subject field includes knowledge which can be measured through recall on a written test.

Evaluation:

- lets students know how well they are performing in relation to others, and in relation to their own goals
- shows students where they need to improve
- helps teachers know how well they have taught a given area of information or imparted a skill
- shows the teacher which students need special help in a given area
- provides data on which to base a grade
- informs the community regarding the level of achievement of students.

Many school systems are being criticized by parents and other community members because students appear to drift through their education without much appreciable learning taking place. Increasingly, one hears about "competency-based education," the demonstration that achievement of a given skill or area of content is achieved before one is allowed to move into the next level of learning. In addition, "competency-based evaluation" means that having gone from 8th grade to 9th grade the student is *competent* to undertake learning at the higher level. Also involved is the determination that students who do not have a minimum level of skills will not graduate. If an individual student manages to stay in school for 12 years and yet is only able to read at the second or third grade level, then there will be documentation that this is due to a genuine inability to learn, rather than an unwillingness to learn, or incapacity of teachers to teach.

There are many controversies swirling around "competency-based education" which will continue to be debated in professional forums for some time to come. But it is clear that sloppy procedures which allowed thousands of uneducated or undereducated students to pass through the schools in the balmy days of the 1960s and early 1970s can no longer be tolerated. And, the teacher is, of course, central to the process of identifying levels of student competency.

WHAT EVALUATION TELLS THE TEACHER

There is apt to be some confusion about what data mean in a discussion of evaluation as well as what evaluative data may be used for.

As part of an assignment for a course, Ms. Andesto gave a surprise examination to her third period French class. She included material on the vocabulary and grammar that had been covered, and also some questions about French culture and government. She told the class that the material was not going to count on their grade as she did not believe in "pop quizzes." As part of her task, she had to analyze results determining what students did not know as compared to what she thought she had taught. When she made a record of missed items, she found a distinct pattern: Few of the students did well on the idiomatic phrases she had included; there were gaps in vocabulary which seemed to be shared by most of the class; and they did poorly on knowledge about France. Her analysis told her where she needed to strengthen her teaching.

Indeed, diagnostic testing can be most revealing *for the teacher.* Any test can tell the teacher what the class does or does not understand about a given assignment. Typically, teachers assert that what students have not learned is the students' fault. Another way of looking at the circumstances is that *a test shows what the teacher was unable to teach.* Ideally, every test situation should be considered an opportunity for the teacher to find out just what the weaknesses may be in a particular teaching presentation. When grading projects, for instance, if most of them are weak in one particular area, it is probable that this is a teaching fault, not a student fault. If the test is an objective-type test, it is relatively easy to do an item count, simply recording how many students failed to answer a particular question correctly. Then one has to ask: "Is this failure due to lack of understanding of the concept or poor wording of the question?" For example:

Which of these has been used to obtain accurate estimates of the age of the oldest known rock strata?

Percent Answering Correctly

22	Radiocarbon dating
2	*Uranium-lead dating
3	Potassium-argon dating
5	Estimation of sedimentation rates
22	Correlation of age of fossils contained in the strata
43	I don't know
1	No response

* correct answer

The skewed distribution clearly shows that the respondents don't know the material. But it has also been suggested that part of the problem was the poor wording of the question.[1]

Diagnostic testing is also extremely helpful for individual students. Such testing lets them in on the secret of how well they are doing. Instead of focusing exclusively on a total number of answers right or wrong, or a single letter grade on a test or paper, the teacher can emphasize the individual *items* which were missed. Each student can then be given an opportunity to examine the item and see how to correct it.

One of Mr. Harvey's regular practices was having us correct our own tests. He knew we would not cheat because most of the tests were used to find out what we did or did not know. Then he would collect the tests and look them over himself. I guess he did something with the results, because we would have some special drills after each test on things which I guess most of us hadn't learned very well. Sometimes he would tell us to redo each question we got wrong, or explain what it was about the question we did not understand. Once in a while he corrected the tests and then we had to redo the items we failed. Anyway, we got a good idea of what we were doing wrong, and it sure helped because then we could go to him for special help when we really didn't know what the problem was all about. Most of us made pretty good grades in his course, too, though I don't think we liked the subject all that well nor were we particularly smart.

Some school systems are even using tests to diagnose how well teachers are teaching—part of the move toward teacher accountability. It is understandable that if a teacher is supposed to be teaching chemistry, yet very few students can pass a first-level examination in chemistry after a year in class, then something is seriously wrong. Equally, something is amiss if a teacher instructs students in punctuation and capitalization and after six months the students are as foggy about proper procedures as they were at the beginning. The teachers may claim that students were so deficient to begin with that it requires more than six months for remediation. So, too, the chemistry students may be said to be so lacking in basic reading and computation skills that they cannot grasp the concepts of chemistry. Indeed, these arguments may be true and, as such, may be part of the problem. There may also be a few teachers who are not teaching as effectively as they should be. In these situations, diagnostic methods which clearly relate to what a given teacher is doing are useful. There are major political and personal implications for such a use of diagnostic measures, however. Most teachers' groups are opposed to any assessment which focuses on the individual teacher. The public is demanding some

---

[1] National Assessment of Educational Progress, Report 1 "1969–1970 Science: National Results and Illustrations of Group Comparisons" (Denver: National Commission of the States, 1970), p. 130.

accountability, however, so that in some instances scores are published school by school. This practice is replete with political significance, though, since test scores so often reflect educational deficits that students bring to a situation as much, if not more, than they demonstrate teacher ineffectiveness.[2]

WHEN TEACHERS MAKE TESTS

Many hours of teacher time is spent constructing tests. Most of the testing done in schools is done by teachers, in their own classrooms, with "instruments" they have devised themselves. Most of us have experienced every form of testing by the end of high school. And most of us have clear ideas about our feelings about teachers' tests. Most readers probably recall tests with feelings of distaste. Is there any way that tests and test taking can be made pleasant? There are some ways in which the process can be improved, but there is probably no way to make anyone love tests. However, a well-constructed test, whose objectives are clear, whose format is readable, and which is corrected and returned expeditiously, will help diminish the resentment of students toward test taking.

In the following sections various kinds of tests typically used by teachers are described. Helpful hints, designed to guide development and use of each kind of test, are provided. Following this section, there is a summary table giving the good points and limitations of each type of test.

PERFORMANCE TESTS

For some areas of the school curriculum, performance tests are appropriate. In this kind of test the student is required to perform the necessary act much as he or she would in a real-life situation as, for example, in student teaching. Such subjects as driver education, music, art, foreign languages, home economics, industrial arts, and physical education lend themselves to testing by performance.

In the performance test it is especially important that the criteria by which the student will be evaluated be made clear to him or her. Checklists and rating scales are often used. Some subject areas, such as art and home economics, may require projects as part of a test.

The following is a rating scale designed by a home economics teacher, in which students learn to evaluate their own work.

---

[2] Frank J. Sciara and Richard K. Jantz, *Accountability in American Education* (Boston: Allyn and Bacon, 1972); Don T. Martin, George E. Overholt and Wayne J. Urban, *Accountability in American Education: A Critique* (Princeton: Princeton Book Company, 1976).

Evaluation Sheet for Jumper Project

Directions for scoring: Circle one number in each group which best describes the quality of work done. Pupil uses regular pencil. Teacher uses pencil of a different color. Key: 4 = excellent, 3 = good, 2 = fair, 1 = poor.

1. Selection of fabric	4	3	2	1
a. Fabric suitable for jumper	4	3	2	1
b. Color appropriate for jumper	4	3	2	1
2. Cutting and marking				
a. Clean-cut edges, not jagged	4	3	2	1
b. Fabric straightened	4	3	2	1
c. Marking made clearly	4	3	2	1
3. Stay-stitching				
a. Done ¼ to ½ inch from edge	4	3	2	1
b. Done in matching thread	4	3	2	1
c. Done in regular stitching	4	3	2	1

Teacher's Total Score _____. Student's Total Score _____.

A rating scale provides a valuable guide for students showing the criteria used for a given product. In an art class, for example, students were working on designs for posters. Since a community home fire safety campaign was to be launched shortly, the local fire department asked if students could prepare posters to be used in store fronts and other public places. The assignment therefore had practical as well as educational value. Students and teacher devised a rating scale to evaluate the final work. However, it took a great deal of discussion. They agreed that the poster should be "dramatic." How can that quality be measured? Finally their rating scale was devised:

1	5	10
dull, hard to read, couldn't tell what it was about	ordinary, message clear	eye-catching, irresistible

But this scale seemed ambiguous. Aren't the judgments of "ordinary" and "irresistible" subjective? More discussion followed. One suggestion was to have everyone in the class rate every poster, and then determine the extent of agreement. Another was to bring in other teachers, both from the art department and outside the department, to determine the concensus of their opinions. Another idea was to rate previous poster work and see how they would rate. For a low rating, for instance, they would use a poster rated as poor. For a high rating, they would show one that all agreed was outstanding. These "models" would then be used for the fire safety poster rating.

Other items on the scale were easier to decide: They agreed that the poster should be neat, the lettering clear, and there should be "good use of color." "Good use of color" posed some problems, and here the class referred to principles of color use which had been previously illustrated in class. "Good design" posed another problem, and again the class reviewed principles of good design which had been part of preceding lessons. In the end, although the discussion of the rating scale for the poster had taken considerable class time, the teacher realized that there had been a great deal of review of other lessons, and the students were clear about the objectives of the new assignment. Furthermore, there was agreement on what would constitute good performance. Class motivation was high, as well, since there was a general structure for the final evaluation.

Rating scales or performance measures can be used in many situations. When students give oral reports, for example, in a science, social studies, home economics, or English class, a rating scale of the presentation is a useful way to upgrade final performance. When students know what is to be evaluated, they will try to include those items. The best rating scales are those cooperatively developed by teacher and class, so that specifics can be discussed and ambiguities clarified. Even if the teacher is relatively sure what items will be included on a scale for oral presentations, it is invariably a better procedure to build the scale with suggestions from the class.

Rating scales also show students what standard of competency is expected. In programs developed around behavioral objectives, students are often provided with a list of those items which they are expected to achieve at the end of a given unit of instruction:

After six weeks of instruction in tennis fundamentals you will be able to:
* state the rules of tennis regarding scoring and line faults
* return 70% of correctly played balls
* place 50% of first serves
* use proper form in serving 75% of time
* hold racket properly
* play a full set

As noted, such rating scales or checklists are particularly well suited to situations where behavioral objectives have been developed for learning. The typical statement of a behavioral objective provides the measure of evaluation of achievement of that objective:

Given a series of misspelled common words, the student will be able to provide correct spelling for 90 percent of them.

A series of such statements can be provided to students at the beginning of a unit of work so that they know clearly the expectations for achievement. As has been indicated, however, many objectives for instruction are elusive and subjective and do not clearly lend themselves to the specification of behavioral objectives.[3]

[3] Joseph F. Callahan and Leonard H. Clark, *Teaching the Secondary School* (New York: Macmillan, 1977), pp. 15–41, "Planning: Behavioral Objectives."

ESSAY TESTS

Essay tests are considered "subjective" while contrasted with "objective" tests. It must be clear that objective tests are, in some ways, just as subjective as essay tests. Both types represent the subjective judgment of the teacher as to what shall be tested. Both depend on the ability of the teacher to write adequate questions; a poor essay test question is no better or worse than a poor objective test question. Scoring either question can be subjective. Who is to say that ten items wrong out of a hundred equals a "B" grade, any more than one can for sure say that one essay answer was good and another mediocre. Both decisions are dependent on teacher judgment, and in that respect are subjective. The major difference, of course, is that the subjectivity of the objective test is obscured by the visibility of the measurement itself. A question can usually be "seen" as clearly right or wrong. When several readers look at an essay test, however, they may come up with different judgments about rightness or wrongness.

Despite obvious problems, essay examinations are an important part of a teacher's evaluation repertoire. For one thing, essay examinations give students needed practice in writing. The writing skills of Americans are generally regarded as poor in quality. Lack of practice in writing is probably the cause. Writing answers to essay questions, if the questions are well phrased, provides students with an opportunity to organize ideas, express them in logical sequence, employ appropriate vocabulary, and, thus, communicate understanding of concepts. Because they are important skills, they deserve the time and thought for their frequent practice.

Essay questions also allow a teacher to see how students formulate ideas in their own words. One thing known about learning is that learners who can recreate concepts in their own minds, in their own words, as well as in writing, have learned the concepts. If they are unable to do so, it is very probable that the concept is not fully learned or understood. Persons can repeat bits of data and information by rote memory and recall, but unless they can also use such information in a written exercise it is difficult to be sure they have incorporated the information fully. The essay question provides the opportunity for students to inform the teacher about the depth of understanding.

The limitations, alas, of essay questions often seem to outweigh their usefulness. Essay tests are difficult to grade. Teachers are almost without exception influenced by handwriting and the appearance of the paper. Poor spelling and grammatical errors may be a heavy influence on a score, even though the student may have shown adequate grasp of ideas. Grading papers is very much affected too by the fatigue of the scorer. After reading twenty-five test papers, one is just not as clear and careful with number twenty-six as with number five. On the other hand, the first students graded may suffer from too critical a reading, while those at the end may benefit from cursory reading. The "halo effect" may interfere with one's judgment. Here is Donald's paper. His work is always good; therefore, one is predisposed to view his test with favor. David, however, who rarely seems to have any notion of what is going on, is unlikely to do any better on this test than on previous ones, and thus his work is read with bias. What if Donald did not study for this exam? Would he get the benefit of the doubt and receive a spuriously good grade? Or if, by some miracle, David did see the light, would the biased reader detect the "new David" and give him the grade he deserves?

Essay questions take time to answer, and thus relatively few areas which have been studied can be tapped by an essay test. Undoubtedly you have had the experience of being prepared for a test only to find that the questions related only in part to the material you knew well. Thus the result is that the rest measured only part of your understanding. It is hard to "cover the waterfront" with essay tests.

Overcoming the handicaps of essay tests is relatively easy. Since this kind of testing should be used by all teachers, it is important to observe some guides which will insure better results for both teacher and student:

1. *Write clear, relevant questions.* Formulating good essay questions is as tricky as writing good objective questions.

   Poor: List three causes for malnutrition.

   Better: If a child is supposedly malnourished, what are the things you would want to know about to make sure?

   Or: Some controversy exists over the chief causes of malnutrition in the United States. Which appear to you to be the main causes? Defend your choices.

   Terrible: Describe B. F. Skinner's theory of psychology.

   Poor: What is the major psychological theory associated with B. F. Skinner? (Can be answered in two words; not an essay.)

   Better: Why is the psychological theory associated with B. F. Skinner so controversial?

   Poor: What was the message Salinger was trying to convey in *Catcher in the Rye?*

   Better: Why do many adolescents find the chief character in *Catcher in the Rye* sympathetic?

   Terrible: Despite opposition, Roosevelt was determined to get his way in New Deal legislation which the Supreme Court, as it was then constituted, was obstructing by declaring it unconstitutional, so he decided to take a new tack which caused a tremendous uproar from business and other parts of the country. What was this new plan and why was it not adopted and what do you think might have happened if it had been accepted?

Better: Roosevelt, furious because the Supreme Court declared key New Deal legislation unconstitutional, decided to act. What did he decide to do? Did he get his way? Explain.

2. *Develop scoring guides for each question.* When you write an essay question, you should have in mind what you think would be included in a satisfactory answer. Jot down some of the key points which you think should be included. Occasionally, and more times than one might expect, bright and creative students offer ideas for answering a question which go beyond the teacher's thinking. One needs to be ready—and open—for unexpected responses. Having a guide helps keep one from variance in scoring because of fatigue. A guide also helps prevent bias for or against individual students. But a guide should not exclude the unanticipated and also correct answer.

3. *Indicate all the factors which will be considered in grading.* If you care about handwriting, spelling, and grammar then it is essential that you tell students that these will contribute to the examination grade. If these factors are considered, then it is wisest to give two grades: one on content and one on the other factors. A student could get an "A" on content and a "D" on handwriting. Or "C" on spelling. Both grades could be entered in one's grade book, but clearly the one on content would be regarded as more important, unless it is an English class. Other subject matter teachers, however, do have an obligation to help raise the level of student work in writing; to ignore poor spelling and grammar is to do students a disservice.

   Other factors which may enter into grading should be communicated to students. These can include:
   * organization of material
   * validity and clarity of statements
   * use of appropriate supporting facts or specific instances
   * use of relevant authority
   * clear presentation of all steps in problem solving

4. *Guard against bias in grading and the "halo" effect.* One procedure which helps to offset the "halo" effect is to have students, from the very beginning, use a number rather than a name on their test papers. Although one may, after a few months, get a fair notion of who students are because of their unique handwriting, or the fact that Barbara uses purple ink and Stanley uses a black italic lettering pen, grading papers without names on them helps reduce some element of bias. Other ways of achieving greater fairness in grading is being sure that papers are not read in the same order every time. The papers read first on one set of tests should be read last on another. Random shuffling of papers achieves this. Although some teachers like to alphabetize papers so that it is easier to enter grades, this can be done after papers are graded, not before.

   Another procedure to eliminate bias is to grade all the papers one question at a time. If there are five questions, grade all the first questions at once, then the second, and so forth. Do some spot-checking; after having read ten or so papers, go back and reread the first one or two and see if you would still grade them the same.

   Since failure is frequently devastating, it is important to reread all papers which are marked failure. Are there any redeeming features? Are the "failures" as bad as when first seen? What about the border-line papers? Should some of them be reclassified?

5. *Provide a range of options.* As noted, essay tests sometimes ask questions which do not tap the individual's area of knowledge. If one of the objects of a test is to find out what students *know*, then it is wise to give them options. Every essay examination should include choices from which students can pick. If there are four questions, the student can select a given number of the four. A few teachers occasionally state, "Here are questions that I want you to answer. However, there may be something I have left out about which you want to demonstrate your knowledge. Write your own question and answer it." The teacher and student may, of course, disagree as to the relevance or quality of the student initiated question, but why should the teacher be the only one who decides in what area a question is significant? Yes, this does pose problems of differences for the basis of appraisal. Yet, if there are enough testing situations, and enough other ways for evaluating student progress, test situations which are more open to identifying what students know and volunteer to share can establish a more amiable classroom climate of evaluation.

6. *Avoid being taken in by the glib and highly verbal.* Students who are highly verbal like essay tests and they sometimes boast about the "snow job" answers they provided. Studies indicate that almost always longer answers to essay tests get higher grades. True, the longer answer often does mean the student included more facts and data, or analyzed ideas in greater depth. But this may not always be true. We can recall vividly writing at great length about something only vaguely recognized, but using most of the large words in our vocabulary, and passing with high marks. Many less verbally facile students do get the main idea and do know the important facts but express themselves tersely and succinctly. It is useful to have at hand the guide you prepared for grading each question which will help guard against overgrading the glib or undergrading the terse.

7. *Help students in taking essay tests.* As in all test situations, practice improves performance. Essay tests are no different. Students can be given some practice questions to try out. These can be graded in class, with small groups evaluating one another's answers. They can compare notes and report to the class; in this way everyone can see and hear how variable good answers can be. Students also gain a sense of why some people do not do well on essay tests.

The precise wording of essay questions is important, and students need to have this pointed out to them. Such words as "compare," "discuss," "give your opinion about," or other specific directions need to be identified when the student prepares to answer. Many students are confused by one or two key words in a question and rush into the answer without considering what the question as a whole is about. By reading practice questions in class, similar to ones which may appear on a test, and by getting students to indicate what they understand a question to mean, will clear up this problem.

8. *The test setting should be appropriate.* Of course, desks should be cleared so students have an open writing surface; left-handed students should be at desks that allow them to write freely. If students lack materials, do not

penalize them by refusing to let them take the test; as noted in Chapter 16, this is a student ploy which may mean fear of the situation. Do not let the student evade the test through lack of materials, but also do not make a fuss over it. Be matter-of-fact and businesslike, and provide the needed materials.

When an essay test is being given it is often difficult to gauge the time needed. It is always better to provide more rather than less time. Remind students that it is helpful to reread and proofread their answers when they have finished. Those who do finish early should be asked to be sure they have reread their questions. They may want to amend or change them at this time, and of course, this should be permitted. Periodically, the teacher should call out the time, to alert students to the time remaining. As papers are completed, it is probably best that the teacher collect them. Also, while the test is being given, the teacher should be available to answer individual questions, quietly, at the desk of the individual student. However, if a student asks a question which shows that something in the test is not clear, the teacher may wish to stop all students to point out an error in the question, or to make a clarifying statement. Since few of us ever pretest a question, it is only after a number of years of teaching that we can come up with a test in which all questions are error-free.

9. *The essay question as communication.* Since the essay test allows for freedom of student response, teachers should use the opportunity to react to these responses. Typically, insufficient avenues exist for feedback to students regarding the quality of their work. The teacher has responsibility for too many students to give individuals close attention on a daily basis. But on a test, a teacher does have a rare chance to write the word of comment and commendation. A "good idea" or "well stated," or "this is really good" or "nice comment" or "good grasp of facts" are statements which can be put on student tests to provide much needed recognition.

OBJECTIVE TESTS

Objective tests come in many shapes and sizes. With the development of automatic scoring methods over the past thirty years their popularity has grown. While few teachers have use of an electronic scorer, they can, through careful development of their own tests, take advantage of many of the benefits of objective tests.

First, it is important to be clear what objective tests can and cannot do. They are not objective in the sense of being without bias. An objective test can be designed to fail anyone simply by the way in which test items are selected, phrased, and scored. As noted earlier, the selection of what knowledge to sample via testing is a subjective judgment. Objective tests, whose scores can be provided in numerical terms, lend an air of immutable truth to the final sum. Because it can be quantified does not make a test result better or more accurate. A test score is only as good as the test in telling what a student knows or does not know.

Objective tests are good to use because they are, when properly written, a clear communication between student and teacher as to what has been learned and what has not been learned. Objective tests are easy to score and thus require relatively little of the teacher's time.

- *Directions should be clear and unambiguous.* Even when directions seem very straightforward, it is sometimes helpful to read them aloud and discuss them. If there is to be some kind of special scoring, such as a penalty for guessing in a true/false test, then this should be explained at the beginning.
- *The test should be neat and uncluttered.* All of the blanks to be filled in should be on one margin or the other. If a blank is to be filled in, in the middle of a sentence, then the blank for the work should be on the side of the page, so it can be easily found by the scorer.
- *Be sure the test is at the reading level of the class.* Using big words when little ones will do is no help, unless one is grading on vocabulary. If you are grading on knowledge be sure your test is not also a reading test.
- *Use the right test question for the material.* If you want to know whether students can define "chlorophyll" do not turn the question into a test of whether they can spell it.
- *Be sure the material is worth a test.* Is it important to know whether Abraham Lincoln was the third, fifth, or sixteenth president, or is it more important to know that he was president during the Civil War?
- *Inform students of the area to be covered before they prepare for the test.*
- *Proofread a test before handing it out.* If there are errors, and it is too late to correct all the test papers, put a list of these errors on the board and tell the students where they are. Do not interrupt test taking to tell the class about errors, unless they are ones found by students after testing has started.

EXAMPLES OF OBJECTIVE TEST ITEMS

Below are some examples of acceptable test items for each type of test in a number of different fields. Sample directions are given for each type. Note that answer spaces are provided uniformly at one side of the test paper, which makes it possible to use simple answer sheets, for example, an IBM test sheet, to be placed beside the answer spaces.

True-False

Below is a series of statements. Some are true and some are false. If you believe a statement to be true exactly as it is stated, circle T; if not, circle F. Do not guess.

T   F   *The Citadel* and *Arrowsmith* are both novels about college professors.

T   F   The "Cross of Gold" in William Jennings Bryan's famous speech referred to income taxes.

T   F   Eye color is determined entirely by heredity.

Multiple-Choice

For each question or statement that appears below, place the letter of the item which best answers, or completes, that question or statement in the blank.

_____ 1. A type of speech which is found largely in a certain geographical area is called
    a. a dialogue
    b. an anachronism
    c. a colloquialism
    d. a dialect

_____ 2. Why do legislators often prefer an "Aye" or "No" vote, a rising vote, or a vote by tellers, rather than a roll-call vote?
    a. There is less confusion and the voting is more orderly.
    b. There is less possibility of error in the count.
    c. The minority party has a better chance to be heard.
    d. There is no record kept of how the individual voted.

_____ 3. A dacron and cotton blouse which will be both comfortable and easy to care for should have at least:
    a. 15% dacron
    b. 35% dacron
    c. 65% dacron
    d. 50% dacron

Matching

In the left column is a series of words; in the right column is another series of words. For each word in the left column, select from the right column the word which is most nearly the same in meaning. In the spaces at the left of the numbers, insert the letters of the words selected.

_____ 1. arena	a. amphitheater
_____ 2. assassination	b. chopper
_____ 3. cleaver	c. contest
_____ 4. consternation	d. dismay
	e. murder
	f. militant

In the left column below is a series of statements; in the right column is a series of names. Select the name that is correctly associated with each statement and place the number of the correct name in the space at the left of the statement.

_____ His revolt against the Church probably would have been unsuccessful had the Emperor not been engaged in foreign warfare.	1. Henry VIII 2. John Huss 3. Martin Luther
_____ His conflict with the Church netted him great economic advantages	

For each group of items below, place in the blank before each word or phrase in the left-hand list the letter of the word or phrase in the right-hand list with which it is most directly associated.

_____ 1. anopheles mosquito	a. bubonic plague
_____ 2. rat	b. influenza
_____ 3. tsetse fly	c. malaria
	d. smallpox
	e. sleeping sickness

Completion

Each statement below has a blank where a word or number is missing. Write the missing word or number in the space provided:

The author who is credited with writing the first detective story in American literature was   _____

One way to represent the world is by a map, but a more accurate way is by a   _____

Car engines should not be run in a garage with doors closed because the engine's exhaust contains   _____

Any test can (and probably should) be made up of a variety of test items. However, care must be taken that items in one part of a test do not provide information which can be used to answer questions on another part of the test.

DETERMINING TEST QUALITY

One way of determining the quality of a test is to utilize a procedure called "item analysis." Suppose you have a class of forty students. When they have finished taking a thirty-item objective test, you are interested in finding out how the students scored on the different items, and thus how good a test it was for discriminating among well-prepared and poorly prepared students. You select the test papers of the top 25 percent of the class and the lowest 25 percent and tally the responses for each test. For one item the tally was this:

	High	Low
a.	0	0
b.	3	2
*c.	6	3
d.	1	5

* is the correct response

On this question, six of the top ten students chose the correct answer and three of the bottom 25 percent of the class. To find out whether the question really discriminates between the two groups the following formula is applied:

$$\frac{\text{Number right by high group} \quad - \quad \text{Number right by low group}}{\text{number of high group}}$$

or:

$$d = \frac{RH - LH}{NH}$$

For the question we are examining, the discrimination index (d) comes to .03. It is suggested that an index of this magnitude or higher is adequate. The test item then will usually discriminate fairly well among the best students and the least prepared students.

How difficult is the item? That is, will most or few of the students answer the question correctly? The following formula is used:

$$\text{Difficulty} = \frac{\text{Number right of high group} \quad + \quad \text{Number right of low group}}{\text{Number high students} + \text{number low students}}$$

or:

$$D = \frac{RH + RL}{NH + NL}$$

Since nine of the twenty students in the sample used (25 percent of 40 students) answered the question correctly, then the difficulty level of this question is .45. Probably the best level of difficulty sought is around .50. That is, half of the students answer the question correctly.

The discrimination index is better when it is higher. That is, a .50 discrimination figure is better than a .20. A discrimination figure of —.20 would show poor discrimination indeed. The reverse is true of a score for difficulty. Here, the higher the score, the less difficult an item is.[4]

Few teachers do item analyses of their tests usually because of lack of time. It is useful to have the check of a simple numerical calculation to check against one's own hunches. In this way, one may develop more educated hunches for the years ahead. A test item file can be a teacher's best friend. It should of course be kept in a secure place, preferably at home. Here all test items are placed on file cards with dates when used on the back. Any item analysis data can be added. Students' reactions to the items provide guidance for changes and improvements. It becomes a relatively easy job to mix and match items each year for a new test by keeping such a file.

Involving students in developing test items is a wise strategy. It helps

[4] "Short-Cut Statistics for Teacher-Made Tests" (Princeton, N.J.: Educational Testing Service, 1960).

focus students' attention on what is worth learning, and sharpens students' ability to read test items later. At the end of a chapter or unit of work, students can be placed in small groups (see Chapter 10) and asked to write three or five test items on the material that has been studied. The teacher can promise that the best items will be used in a test. Criteria for good test items can be developed by teacher and students. Such things as the following should be guides:

- covers material worth remembering
- is not ambiguous
- can be understood by most students
- can be answered in the time available
- can only be answered correctly if answer is known; not subject to guessing

These are criteria which should guide the teacher, too, in test construction! The practice of making up test questions involves the students in an intense review of the material which they otherwise might not undertake on their own. Making up test questions can also be a homework assignment. The teacher will be pleasantly surprised to receive good test items which can be incorporated into a test. Another strategy includes the test items developed by an individual or group and then, when the test is returned, having that person or group explain the rationale behind the question as well as the correct answer. This is valuable review experience which helps students retain the material.

TESTS AND CLASS ROUTINES

Many teachers find that tests and examinations pose some special problems in classroom routines. Will the examination be put on the chalkboard? Will the examination be duplicated? How will the examinations be returned?

Consideration of some of these problems should be helpful. Where schools have insufficient duplicating equipment, the teacher may have to rely primarily on the chalkboard or on oral tests. If test questions are read, students who complete the question quickly must wait until slower students finish, thus providing prime time for mischief and other distracting behavior. However, for some kinds of tests, such as true-false, fill-in, or those requiring very short answers, reading the questions may be an adequate procedure. In a room with poor acoustics, of course, this procedure may be a severe trial for students in badly located seats. A teacher who reads a test aloud must be sure to enunciate clearly, speak slowly, and pronounce words so that they are understood by the students. The teacher can pretape the test questions and while the tape is playing, draw student response. Teachers with strong accents should avoid giving tests orally. Students may

	Completion	True-False	Multiple-Choice	Matching
Situations for Which Effective	Information: who when, what, where, how many	Beliefs, attitudes, superstitions, information	Most generally applicable in all subjects	Information: who, what, when, where
Advantages	Easy to construct	Easy to construct	Easy to score	Compact
	Requires adequate basis for response (difficult to guess)	Wide sampling	Many adaptations available	Reduces guessing
			Easy to give	Easy to construct
Limitations	Subjective scoring	Ambiguities	Laborious to construct quality test items that really tell student and teacher what has been learned	Necessity for using single words or very brief phrases
	Inconvenient to score	Guessing		
	Emphasizes role response	Apt to deal with trivial items		Probability of clues
				Probability of related errors
Precautions in Constructing	Use brief response	Provide convenient arrangement for scoring	Provide choices at end of statement	Keep numbers small (10 to 15 items)
	Use direct question if possible			
	Avoid textbook language	Use approximately equal T and F items	Remember that question form is sometimes better than incomplete sentence	Provide extra responses (especially if less than 10)
	Avoid grammatical clues	See that crucial element stands out in item	Avoid textbook or standardized language	Provide consistency in classification: "most men," "most battles"

Provide blank near end, if incomplete type	Avoid traps	Avoid negatives
Assure scoring convenience	Avoid textbook language	Avoid making the longer response always the correct one or vice versa
Avoid too many blanks	Avoid clues	Avoid grammatical clues
Avoid indefinite statements	Do not use subordinate clauses	Use plausible distractors
		If there is more than one correct match for each item, be sure to be aware of this in scoring and alert students to this possibility in test instructions
Only key words should be used for blank items	Do not use negatives Focus on important data	Avoid ambiguity
Make response lines of same and of adequate length	Remember longer statement is more likely to be true	Avoid pattern, as in having third response consistently the correct response
Give credit to any correct response (even if not the expected one)	Make test long enough —10 or 20 items at least	Provide at least four choices
	Avoid partly true statements	Study published tests for good models

mistake a word or phrase and therefore make an error which is obviously not their fault.

If the chalkboard is to be used, the teacher will want to have the test ready so that no time is wasted waiting for it to be written on the board. Some teachers put the test on before school, then lower a map or chart to cover it until time for the test. Other teachers put a long question on first, then, while the students are answering that one, put the remainder of the test on the board. This means, however, that the teacher is not able to observe the class while it is taking the first part of the test. In a class where the test is crucial to success, the teacher must be alert to prevent cheating. The teacher should be available to explain anything that is confusing so that students do not turn to each other and create an impression of exchanging information. The wise teacher, of course, will avoid creating any provocation or temptation that encourages cheating, a topic discussed at length later.

WHEN HAVE YOU TESTED ENOUGH?

There are some demon teachers who will give students a test every other day. Perhaps those teachers believe that this is the only way to keep students working. It is probably more accurate to think of this technique as overkill. However, as noted later in discussing cheating on tests, many good teachers will have numerous testing or evaluation activities every semester. Some teachers announce ahead of time their testing/evaluation schedule so that students are clearly informed of the fact that their performance and achievement will be subject to regular assessment. Many subject areas do not lend themselves to such a format. It is useful for the teacher to keep in mind, however, that frequent assessment is critical to adequate student progress. How can students know what to study, how to study, what to practice or what to attempt if there is no feedback? Testing is one of the main ways in which students receive a report back which tells how well they are doing. And, as noted later, it is unwise to make any one test so significant, so crucial, that most of a semester's grade depends on it. To do so produces incredible anxiety in students and is unfair to those who may have achieved adequately but who fall apart in test situations.

Another area of controversy surrounds "pop quizzes." Reports from many college students indicate that "pop quizzes" were a frequent adjunct of their high school experience. Most students felt that such quizzes were unfair. Some felt that their teachers used them punitively, to get back at a class which had misbehaved or had fallen below expectations. No quiz should be used for punishment. Any use of subject matter as punishment indicates to students that the worst thing in the world is to understand or study history, English, Spanish, or algebra.

Some teachers do find that the possibility of a "pop quiz" is one way of keeping students current with their assignments. The announcement ahead of time that they should always be prepared for such a quiz may be motivating to some students. The motivation of the teacher in using this device should be clear; it is to help the students learn, not to catch them unprepared. Then, by having the "pop quiz" also graded in class, on the spot, the students are given immediate feedback on their performance. In this way the "pop quiz" is being used effectively and for educational ends. But the teacher should be wary of this device to be sure there is no build-up of student resentment. If resentment occurs, it is a case of the means not justifying the ends, and the practice should be dropped.

TEST CONSTRUCTION: SOME GUIDELINES

Teachers have a number of options regarding the ways in which tests are to be administered to students. Many times the teacher will duplicate the test, either on ditto masters or on stencils, and have enough copies for all students. In the typical school, teachers will find that they are the ones doing this clerical chore. Whoever does the test should double check it for such obvious things as grammatical errors or misspellings. It is time-consuming to have to go through an exam before the students take it to correct mechanical errors. Yet time after time students are penalized or are confused (and thus do less well) because of carelessness in the simple mechanics of test duplication.

An assumption here is that the test will be typed. Most tests are better if they are typed because they remove the problem of reading handwriting. The handwriting of most teachers is either bad or terrible. In some schools typing can be done through arrangements with the typing instructor; some student clerks are paid to do typing for teachers. If it is a very important test, it is also necessary to be sure that no word leaks out regarding the test.

Teachers with many slow readers or who suspect that their students have reading difficulties that interfere with adequate performance may find a combination of written test questions and oral reading of the questions to be valuable. For instance, the test questions can be put on a transparency and projected on a screen. At the same time, while the students are reading them in order to determine what is involved, the teacher reads them aloud. This is an aid to poor readers whose oral vocabulary may be adequate; they can understand the question when read aloud even if they have trouble reading it. They thus have a better chance to show competence in understanding material.

The teacher should always ascertain that the directions for the test are clear. The teacher should take ample time to go over directions and special instructions before anyone starts the test proper. Once the test is underway, the teacher can go around the class to answer individual problems a student may have in understanding directions or the meaning of a word or phrase. Obviously, the teacher, in providing such individual help, does it in a manner that will not disturb or interfere with the quiet and concentration expected of the class.

HOW LONG SHOULD A TEST BE?

High school classes still are typically forty-five to fifty-five minutes long. Few traditionally organized schools allow longer periods for examinations; thus a main consideration must be the length of the period. If a test is to be an equally valid measure of the performance of each student taking it, every student should have an opportunity to consider each item on the examination. In a class with a wide range of abilities, all but the slower students will finish early and may become bored; therefore, work assignments that can be done quietly should be given in advance. By putting a humorous question three-fourths of the way through a test the teacher can tell, by the laughter, how much time the fastest and slowest students require.

ITEM TYPES AND SEQUENCES

Tests containing a variety of item types typically have the objective-type items first. Essay items are usually at the end so that it is possible to attach additional blank sheets for the answers. The problem with such an arrangement is that some students will inevitably fail to note the passing time and not allow themselves ample time for writing a coherent answer to the essay questions. If such an arrangement is used, the teacher should set specific time allotments for each section of the test and notify the students when they should be moving on to the next section. A well-constructed multiple-choice item should require a minimum of one minute for consideration, assuming that the students are average or better-than-average readers. Other types of objective items, which demand recall of information, will require less time. Some teachers choose to utilize two days for testing, giving essay questions one day and objective items the next.

CHEATING AND TEST ADMINISTRATION

Pressure on students to get good grades is often a real factor in promoting cheating: Getting the grade by any means becomes more important than being virtuous or acquiring genuine knowledge. Thus, if there is widespread cheating, the teacher will first want to see whether undue pressure is being put on students to get grades, no matter how. But even when this pressure is not severe, cheating continues. Objective tests are a "natural" for cheating; by glancing at a neighbor's paper, a student can quickly find an answer. It is difficult to cheat on an essay test. Since essay tests are not always appropriate and since it is difficult to use other approaches—seating in alternate seats, for example, or having several versions of the same test— the teacher must devise other means to minimize cheating.

One of the best guarantees against cheating is the teacher's behavior during a test. Mr. Duval, for example, observes those who are having trouble with the material and is ready to help an individual who does not understand the directions. At the same time, he is also watching to see that students work on their own papers. During a test, the teacher who is concerned about cheating can find a spot strategically at the back of the room. The students, with their backs to the teacher, cannot tell whether or not they are being watched and potential cheating is thwarted. The teacher can also walk around the room, observing students' performance on test items. A test—if it is important, and if cheating is a problem—is not the time for the teacher to become buried at a desk behind a stack of homework papers.

There are two very good ways to avoid cheating. One is by getting to know students and their work so well that there is no point in cheating: any drastic deviation from previous levels of work will be an instant flag for the teacher's attention and concerned inquiry. Of course slow students have been known to "catch on" suddenly to what was going on, and make a genuine spurt in performance, or a lethargic student or one with massive home problems may be released from these constraints and become an avid and effective student. It would be a tragedy if the unknowing teacher then called such students in and accused them of cheating.

The second way to avoid cheating is to have so many ways of showing how well one performs that students are not tempted to cheat. When no single test or exam "counts" for a major portion of a term grade, then there is little need to cheat. When tests are considered ways of improving, of showing where help is needed, then there is little temptation to cheat.

Where there is cheating, and it is indeed endemic if not epidemic in secondary schools and colleges, the practices of teachers are often to blame.

RETURNING TESTS: AN OPPORTUNITY FOR INCREASING LEARNING

No test should be given unless ample class time is given to a discussion of the questions when it is returned, to providing correct answers, to reviewing ambiguous areas, and to making sure that students know what was to have been reported in the test. Some teachers have students redo those parts of the test which were missed, although this method may not always be the most profitable use of students' time. Of course, sometimes the material is fundamental and requires mastery by every student: Then the teacher would do well to have some additional, different exercises for the students to complete.

A test should be returned as soon as possible after the students have taken it, so that the material is still alive and important. The day the test is to be returned, the teacher should plan to use the first ten minutes or so for supervised individual study. Then, while the students are reading or working out problems at their desks, the teacher moves around and quietly returns each paper This gives him or her an invaluable contact with each student. To Alice, who unexpectedly achieved a superior grade, the teacher can give a word of warm approval; to Harry, who turned in another poor test, the teacher can suggest the need for some special help, perhaps an after-school conference. As the papers are returned, the teacher should have some personal comment, no matter how slight, which shows awareness of, and interest in, each individual's progress. The rewards of this rather simple device of personalizing the return of papers will be great for teacher and students alike.

After all papers have been returned, the teacher should call the class to order and make some general comments on the level of achievement. Then the class can ask about puzzling items. A rapid review of the particularly difficult questions is appropriate, to be sure that everyone understands what the answers are. After this session, the class might return to supervised study, so that students with individual problems on the test may talk privately with the teacher. It is important for the teacher to avoid public bickering over an answer. A student who thinks an incorrect grade has been given should have time to talk individually with the teacher. Of course, the teacher should always be ready to admit when a real mistake has been made and adjust the student's grade accordingly. This kind of fairness is prized highly by students.

Tests should be considered not only a means of evaluating progress, but moreover a particularly valuable learning experience. Post-test discussions are often tremendously fruitful in developing new insights by students who were previously puzzled or confused.

STANDARDIZED TESTS

Everyone who has arrived at college has experienced standardized testing. In most school systems in the country, students are given standardized tests many times as they progress through the grades. The power and influence of such measures grows yearly. In addition, the National Assessment of Educational Progress (see p. 355) provides a "standardized" clue as to what a stratified sample of American school students have gained through schooling and life experience.

Most secondary teachers will have little direct contact with standardized tests. Special personnel, typically school counselors, will take charge of the testing program. Teachers may be trained in how to give such tests and monitor test taking, but otherwise they are rarely involved in any subsequent work with the tests. In many schools the central office will issue a "test profile" for individual students indicating their progress to date in basic skills. Then the teacher will be called upon to interpret these profiles so that students in turn can interpret them to parents.[5]

Since standardized tests are so prevalent, it is important to understand the term "standardized."

1. The process of standardizing a test begins when the test maker tries to find out what attitudes, understandings, and skills should be represented in ninth-grade arithmetic, or tenth-grade English literature, or twelfth-grade physics. This information may be obtained from textbook analysis, examination of courses of study, or the judgment of experts.
2. Various test items are tried on large numbers of students, who represent many geographical areas and many kinds of schools. Those combinations of questions which are able to measure a range of achievement are retained. Usually several combinations of items are culled so that more than one form of the test can be constructed.
3. Specific methods for administering the test (directions, time limits) are established.
4. Scoring rules and keys are developed.
5. Norms are prepared, which make possible the comparison of individual scores with national average scores.

Standardization is intended to secure validity, reliability, objectivity, and ease of administration. But the process of standardization does not guarantee that a published test is appropriate. It is instructive to check any published "standardized" test in the most recent edition of Buros' *Mental Measurements Yearbook*.[6] Here each test is critiqued by a number of experts.

The tentativeness with which the results of these tests must be viewed is increased when local conditions are considered in detail. A specific teacher and class may have focused attention on objectives not encompassed by the test. This may be especially true in the development of attitudes. Further, the national norms lump together all manner of students in all kinds of schools under all kinds of teachers. A class of superior capacity and environment would be expected to produce scores exceeding the performance of the national average. Classes with many students of limited educational capacity, or from deprived environments, reflect these condi-

---

[5] One effort to educate parents and students about standardized tests and their significance is "A Handbook of Standardized School Testing," published by the D.C. Citizens for Better Public Education, Inc., 95 M Street, S.W., Washington, D.C. 20024.
[6] O. K. Buros, *Mental Measurements Yearbooks* (Highland Park, N.J.: The Gryphon Press). Periodically updated; look for latest edition.

tions and should not receive censure for falling below that average. It is important to keep reminding oneself that in any kind of national average—whether of height, weight, physical dexterity, or achievement in academic matters—local differences, as well as individual differences, are deliberately screened out.

This is not to say that standardized achievement tests do not have their place in a modern evaluation program. Within the limitations noted, the tests indicate where a class stands in relation to other classes. The tests help to diagnose weaknesses in class and individual achievement and in teacher instruction and thus can guide future instruction. In short, used with many other means of evaluation, standardized tests serve a useful purpose. Only when they are considered the sole gauge of learning is there serious damage to good education.

Many teachers find it useful to check test publishers' catalogs annually and send for the new instruments in their teaching field. In this way, through sample tests purchased at nominal cost, they keep informed of the new techniques in testing.

What criteria can guide the teacher in selecting appropriate standardized tests? The following checklist should assist teachers in examining tests and their accompanying manuals:

Validity. What is the test supposed to measure? On what basis were these test goals chosen? Was it on the basis of meeting both individual and social needs? What research was used to determine how these needs might be met through this test content? A validity coefficient of $+.65$ is considered a criteria for the acceptability of a test.

Reliability. Most standardized tests are available in at least two versions. What evidence is presented to show that this test consistently yields a similar score, regardless of which version is used? Test experts usually say that for individual students a test should show a reliability coefficient of about .80. This coefficient indicates the degree of correlation between scores on the various versions of the test. The higher the decimal fraction, the closer the test comes to yielding the same score on its various versions.

A "standardized" test for which no validity and reliability coefficients are provided should be avoided.

Objectivity. Good tests ensure that identical scores will be secured with equally competent scorers. Is the test key precise throughout, so that no doubt exists about the correct response?

Ease of administration and scoring. The directions in the manual should be so clear and easily read by at least 99 percent of the students that the test can be given with ease, and under comparable circumstances, each time it is used. Does the manual tell exactly how to give and score the test?

Norms. The manual or a supplement should list average or median scores earned by students who have taken the test. There should be an indication that these norms have been regularly revised and are currently applicable; the character of the school populations from which the norms were derived should be indicated. Preferably, the norms should be given for each tenth of the school year, since achievement obviously varies from September to June.

Standardized tests, besides showing achievement in relation to other large groups of students, can provide teachers with good suggestions to apply to their own homemade tests. The teacher can find out, for example, how best to word certain kinds of test items. The standardized test has been tried on many students, and the teacher can therefore assume that the average middle-class student will understand the test items as constructed. If the school population is deviant from middle-class suburbia, however, the teacher should be very careful about test use and generalizations about test questions.

A teacher could select from a standardized test some items to use as models, but modify them to suit one's own class. Standardized tests are copyrighted so a teacher cannot just "lift" an item and use it.

There is discussion in the professional literature about *criterion-referenced tests* and *norm-referenced tests*. The first kind are tests of mastery, assessing how much an individual has achieved toward an absolute goal. A *criterion*-referenced test in spelling, for instance, would be based on an assumption that by the end of the tenth grade all students should be able to spell correctly a given number of common words.

A test criterion is established by those who construct the test and who state in absolute terms what is meant by achieving proficiency in a given task. Since many items are typically developed to measure a given area of learning, the criterion-referenced test is a valuable aid in assessing a pupil's strengths and weaknesses. A *norm*-referenced test indicates how well individuals do in respect to other individuals of the same age or who have had the same instruction. In this kind of test, items are constructed so that answers have to discriminate between good and poor students.

The score of an individual is understood in relation to the scores obtained by other members of the group on which the test was normed. A particular student can be identified as someone who performed better than 75 percent of those in the norm group. Typically, norm-referenced tests have fewer items in any one area of the content being assessed and spread over a wider range of topics in that subject area.

The differences between these two types of tests are important. They reflect the different purposes such tests serve in informing teachers, students, and parents how well an individual student is performing. The terms norm-referenced and criterion-referenced are found increasingly in test reporting; teachers should keep this in mind when they are given student scores or when they report test results to students or parents.

The National Assessment of Educational Progress provides a very valuable bank of test items. The National Assessment repeats the test process on a stated cycle, every three to five years, for the different subjects assessed. The Assessment, with expert help, develops test items for nine-year-olds, thirteen-year-olds, seventeen-year-olds, and adults. Each test is described in terms of expectations of correct responses for different age levels. For each cycle, a certain number of test items are "released," that is, they are made available for teachers and school systems to use with their own students. Such items are very helpful in diagnosing the learning needs of one's own students. The subject areas in which the National Assessment has developed test items are Reading, Writing, Literature, Science, Citizenship, Math Fundamentals, Consumer Math, Career and Occupational Development, Music, and Design and Drawing Skills. Details of these tests, test results, and analysis of the assessment in general can be obtained from: National Assessment of Educational Progress, Suite 700, 1860 Lincoln Street, Denver, Colorado, 80295.

Teachers help students in the area of standardized testing by helping them understand how to take such tests. When students are given practice, in taking such tests, their test scores usually improve. Sometimes the instructions for taking such a test are confusing. Students are often nervous, anxious, and insecure in the strange surroundings of the standardized test. When they open the test booklet they face a task which is strange to them. Even the supposedly helpful explanations may not be helpful. Without impugning the integrity of the test, the teacher can obtain copies of old tests, or of the instructions for old tests, and go over such instructions with students. Taking a standardized test as a practice exercise can be a very enlightening experience. After taking the test, all students score their answers. Next, each question is examined in detail. Why was item "b" correct? Why did so many then give item "c" as correct? Did some students misread a key word or transpose the numbers in a problem? Such practice will be of great help for the many students who will take SATs, LSATs, Civil Service tests, and all the other tests that are part of educational and career advancement.

SUMMARY

Test construction and test grading and reporting will take up many hours of the teacher's time. Well-developed tests, administered in a relaxed and quiet environment, are appreciated by students. Well-developed tests are also an essential aid in student progress. There are many kinds of test models available in every subject field. Students are provided ample information about their progress by using a variety of testing procedures. Tests also provide the teacher with valuable information about areas of teaching strength and weakness.

SELECTED READINGS

Brown, Donald J., *Appraisal Procedures in the Secondary Schools.* Englewood Cliffs, N.J.: Prentice-Hall, 1970. One of the clearest, briefest and most well written introductions to the development of test items by the classroom teacher. Highly recommended.

Bushway, Ann, and William R. Nash, "School Cheating Behavior," *Review of Educational Research,* 47 (Fall 1977), pp. 623–632. What research shows about incidence of cheating and factors which contribute to it.

Ebel, Robert L. *Essentials of Educational Measurement.* Englewood Cliffs, N.J.: Prentice-Hall, 1972. An excellent resource for anyone wanting to gain mastery of the field of measurement. Well written, comprehensive.

Findley, Warren G. (Ed.), *The Impact and Improvement of School Testing Programs.* Sixty-Second Yearbook of the National Society for the Study of Education, Part II. Chicago: University of Chicago Press, 1963. Includes a significant analysis of the major criticism made about testing programs and valuable ideas for improvement.

Greenbaum, William, *Measuring Educational Progress: A Study of the National Assessment.* New York: McGraw-Hill, 1977. A valuable examination of the first effort in the United States to obtain national data on how much young people know.

Martuza, Victor R., *Applying Norm-Referenced and Criterion-Referenced Measurement in Education.* Boston: Allyn and Bacon, 1977. A practical guide to teachers in identifying and using these two kinds of testing practices.

McDonald, James B., and Bernice J. Wolfson, "A Case against Behavioral Objectives," *The Elementary School Journal,* 71 (December 1970), pp. 119–128. The ongoing argument about how educational objectives should be stated is well analyzed in this brief article.

Test Service Notebook. Occasional papers distributed free of charge from the Test Department, Harcourt Brace Jovanovich, Inc., New York, N.Y.

Weigane, James E., *Developing Teacher Competencies.* Englewood Cliffs, N.J.: Prentice-Hall, 1971. See Chapter 2, "Formulating Performance Objectives," pp. 43–80. Arranged in programmed text format, this provides a clear presentation of how to develop such objectives as the basis for evaluation.

FOCUS ON CHAPTER 14

No one likes to be judged continually; no one enjoys continually being a judge. Yet giving and receiving grades places students and teachers in this uncomfortable situation. Grades are a fact of life for everyone in the secondary school. The way in which teachers grade can make the difference in how students respond to learning tasks.

Significant ideas presented in this chapter include:

- The grading system is complicated by the mystique which surrounds it in the mind of both student and teacher. The myths regarding the existence of an absolute standard and about grading on "the curve," contribute to further complications.
- Achieving objectivity in grading is a task which can only be accomplished when teachers identify their own biases, as well as the hidden biases which pervade the system.
- Although grades should reflect student achievement, they may be misused often to serve as extraneous rewards or punishments.
- Grading can be made more humane, and can be used by teachers to extend their communication with students as well as to reflect student performance more accurately.

chapter 14

"A Grade by Any Other Name":
grades and
the educational
process

There is undoubtedly no task associated with teaching that is more universally disliked by teachers than grading. Yet it is something that every teacher must do, every day, every semester, every year. Few are satisfied with the current system of grading; many would like some kind of change. But hardly anybody knows what kind of change is needed. Beginning teachers are often shocked by the reality of having to grade students. Learning to cope with the personal conflicts and educational issues presented by the grading system is not an easy task for any teacher.

HOW THE GRADING SYSTEM WORKS

Having to grade students makes me feel like a judge. In fact, sometimes I feel like an executioner. I have such a dread of grading that I somtimes even dream about my grade book. It isn't just that it gives me so much power, but my fear that I may be wrong, that I may think someone is doing poorly when in fact it was my fault for not explaining things very well. Or someone is doing well who really is a skilled manipulator and can sling the bull in an exam. I love teaching—but I hate grading!

That is the complaint of one beginning teacher. And it is echoed many times by others as they encounter the reality of the classroom. As a judge, the teacher hands down a sentence of "success" or "failure." Students are apt to develop feelings of helplessness if not hopelessness in a system in which the judges seem so arbitrary and unreliable. "I did ok with Ms. Smith in English last year; how come I seem to do so badly with Mr. Jones this year? The English is the same; so am I. It must be the teacher." So go student complaints.

Grades dominate students' lives in school. For college-bound students, grades are their major medium of exchange: good grades mean a good college. That all is not well with grades as the key factor in college admissions has been recognized by the increased dependence on achievement test scores—the SATs which haunt high-school juniors and seniors. In recent years there has been a great deal of comment about "grade inflation," which occurs when teachers tend to give unearned high grades to students. Therefore teacher grades are no longer trusted as a reliable measure of how well students will do, especially when it comes to predicting college success.

The process of dividing students into tracks or levels of ability groupings affects the grading system. Since competition for grades—preferably an A, but definitely not lower than a B— is the main concern, and since presumably the "best students" are all together and the average or below average are all together, then it follows that the average and below average should not get As, nor should the "best students" get Cs, because this would confuse the system. How could a "best student" explain a C to a college admissions officer? In some schools, the students in the lower tracks or levels are not permitted to receive anything more than a C, or passing grade. "After all, a grade has to stand for something!"

What are the psychological implications of such a system? Some of the "best students" may not be college bound, but they must pretend to be going to college in order to keep up with their social peers. Being in a section labeled "academically talented" or "accelerated" or "honors" tells students they can learn, but it does not guarantee them anything. Admittance to such a section is only the beginning. A course load of five "solid" subjects a day sets a killing pace for adolescents. They rush from class to class on a schedule that in some schools allows them as few as three minutes between classes. And what is it all for? To get the grade!

Even bright students cannot escape the ever-present prod of possible failure. After all, any lapse from continued production of outstanding work may result in being reclassified out of a top section or class. Such expectation of possible public failure creates a mental health hazard which infects even the most able students.

The pressure for grades has moral consequences. To do well on an examination, to have a good term paper, to produce a well-sewn dress, students will do almost anything—cheat, plagiarize, and have parents help. Many teachers do not allow student projects to be worked on at home since there is this ever-present danger that parents or an older brother or sister will do the student's work. One junior-high teacher has a rule that no student papers can be typed. In her mind, only a parent would know how to type and therefore the work would not be that of the student. Apparently she has never bothered to check whether some of the students do know how to type. Teachers go to great lengths to be sure students do not cheat; and students go to great lengths to try to outwit teachers. Many teachers' days are spent poisoned by a miasma of paranoia, fear of what the students will invent to circumvent doing their own work. Students' days are poisioned by trying to figure out how to get a good mark without really learning the material.

Some students refuse to play the game. What happens to them? There are students for whom getting the grade is not motivating. Many of these are students who have already been told that they are not intellectually able by having been placed in low or slow sections in elementary school or junior high. They know little is expected of them, and they do not respond to the threat of an F. The sky did not fall in when they got an "F" before so why worry now? Such students may cause no one any trouble, but they also do not learn. Some are troublesome because they are bored and angry. They do not see any reason to work for a grade. The teacher who uses grades for motivation is not perceived as very pursuasive. Such students are potential dropouts.

Many students want to remain in school even if they are unsuccessful—perhaps because they want to be with their friends, because there is nothing to do outside of school, because a diploma is necessary for a job, or because they want to participate in extracurricular activities. But all of these (except perhaps being with friends) depend upon the student *getting the grade*. There is documentation that participating in athletics has kept many young men in school who otherwise would have dropped out. The value of this participation has resulted in keeping many on the road to responsible adulthood. But of course, only if they have *made the grade*. The reasoning here is that only if the boy has worked hard enough in his regular classes is it possible for him to do "extra" work in athletics. One can see the irony of this in schools with track systems where low sections are doomed to low grades, no matter what the efforts of the students or the caliber of their work. Often such students are excluded automatically from the type of adolescent activity which might be positively motivating. The carrot of athletic activity is held out, but then it is withdrawn from those who most need it.

THE MYTH OF THE ABSOLUTE STANDARD

In some never-never land teachers may be able to judge absolutely whether students merit 40 percent or 57 percent or 100 percent—or D or C—, or B+. It would be most convenient if teachers could be that confident about the meaning of a grade. But research and experience show that an A to one teacher may be a C to another. Consider some of the sources of variation in student grades: Aside from the fact that all students, even in the same track or level, do not take the same courses, teachers use different criteria in assigning grades. There are variations in the examinations themselves; some teachers will use objective tests, some will use essay tests, others will use a combination of the two. Furthermore, some teachers grade on class participation, while others require term papers as a major part of the grade. Students will vary in their ability to perform in different areas, and thus their grade will be higher or lower according to their ability or lack of it in the areas that count. Then, some teachers like to be considered "tough" graders. New teachers are especially prone to employ "tough" grading procedures. Part of this stems from their idealism—a desire to upgrade the whole system—but part of it is an attempt to gain their colleagues' respect. Peer pressure on the teacher is a fact of the teacher's life which new teachers are likely to underestimate.

> Correcting a set of math papers, Mr. Francis did not find many perfect ones. However, there were a few students who had managed to get all the answers. "I don't grade them on neatness—after all, I'm not a nursemaid," he said.
>
> Mrs. O'Leary was burning the midnight oil. The math papers before her were a real problem. Here was Bill: All his answers were correct. She expected this; his father was an engineer and drilled Bill nightly on mathematics. But what a mess his paper was! Someone should tell him mere ability to get the right answer was not the only thing to be sought. She marked his examples as correct, but took off a half grade because his paper was so untidy.
>
> Mr. Black was grading math papers in which he required the students to show every process by which they arrived at the answer. Here was Jane. She never seemed to get the right answer, but she did know the right process. It was always a matter of simple arithmetic. Actually, she was skilled in solving problems; but somewhere she had been deficient in the simple combinations. How could he grade her down? Someday she would surpass all of them. He felt he must put an A after her name because she had shown a real flash of brilliance in working out an original solution to a complex equation. But what was he going to do about her arithmetic?

Thus even in mathematics, the most "exact" of all subjects, we find considerable variation among teachers. Where the teacher is absorbed in obtaining the right answer, there is little opportunity for students to experience the right process. If mathematics can develop logical methods of problem solving and science can develop a reliance on scientific method for arriving at solutions, then teachers must focus on the way to get in and out of a problem. Too often, the overemphasis on the one correct answer encourages lazy thinking, cheating, and merely mechanical manipulation of arbitrary and meaningless symbols. Accuracy should be rewarded, but this one skill should not be exalted above the real and important other skills that science and mathematics can develop.

THE "NORMAL CURVE"— ANOTHER GRADING MYTH

As an attempt to get away from the absolute standard of assigning grades, many teachers have used the "normal curve." Indiscriminate use of the curve system of grading, however, is as unfair to students and as arbitrary as the absolute standard. The curve referred to is what statisticians term the "normal curve" or the curve into which measurements of any natural phenomenon, if there is an infinite and random sample, would fall. Within one standard deviation each side of the mean would fall about 68 percent of a normal group. Within two standard deviations of the mean would fall about 95 percent of the population, and 99 percent of the population would fall within three standard deviations of the mean. In actual practice the curve is modified for the purpose of assigning grades so that scores 1.5 standard deviations above the mean receive a grade of A while scores 1.5 standard deviations below the mean receive a grade of F. Scores between $+.5$ and $+1.5$ receive the grade of B, while those $-.5$ to -1.5 receive Ds. Scores $+.5$ to $-.5$ receive Cs. It is, of course, at the premise of having a random and infinite sample that the concept of the normal curve breaks down for classroom use. Few, if any, secondary school classrooms are large enough, or random enough, in their population to represent a true "normal curve" of ability or achievement. With the widespread use of grouping by design or self-selection in electives the likelihood of finding such a truly random population is further reduced. Yet grading on the curve is a practice found in the typical school. The real problem with grading on the curve is that there is an assumption that a certain percentage of students *must* fail. Even before anyone does any work at all, some students are doomed. But if teachers try to differentiate instruction to meet the varying needs of students, whole classes may result where no students fail.

Mrs. B. was one of the best teachers in school, and also one of the most independent. She also had one of the most interesting rooms, full of artifacts and books. She taught English, but her specialty was creative writing. She was able to develop rapport with the most unlikely students, and induce them to write—not brilliantly perhaps, but they wrote. And many wrote very well indeed under her tutelage. One summer when school had been out about a month she had a call from the high school. The principal wanted to see her. When she came to see Dr. S. she had an unnerving interview. He had been going over the grade distributions and she had "given too many A grades." "How," she asked, "could one give too many As! If students did A work, then shouldn't they get As?" The principal acknowledged as much, but said that it was the policy of the school not to give too many A grades. She should watch her grading in the future. He didn't threaten her, but she felt intimidated. "I should have told him," she recounted later, "that the kids got As because I was such a good teacher. Do you think that would have made any difference?"

In Chapter 13, there is a discussion about a procedure to evaluate whether a test item "discriminates" between high and low students. The problem with this procedure is that it results in a test which *forces* some students to fail. Although it is useful to know if a test is made up of items which will show which are the high and low students, we should ask whether we want most of our tests made up of such items. Or, if we would rather have tests which show how much *all* students know.

Serious questions have been raised about the use of this concept of forced failure in grading because it is based on the erroneous assumption that educational achievement is distributed according to a normal distribution. The very process of education is an effort to achieve commonality and if we are successful in some key areas students may very well be more alike than they are different. Certainly, the burden of failure is one that we must examine carefully since it is the source of much of the personal misery that bothers so many youth in school.

GRADING AND BIAS

No teacher deliberately sets out to give biased grades. Yet study after study shows that teachers are in fact influenced by factors other than the actual achievement of a student. As we noted in Chapter 4, the teacher has a great deal of power to determine the future fate of individual students. Much of this power derives from the responsibility of the teacher to give grades. A student with good grades has a future; a student with poor grades has a limited one. The basis for making the decision which will mean a green light for one student and a caution for another student is thus very powerful. The decision should be made on the most objective basis possible.

However, there are a number of biases which creep into teachers' grading. Girls, for example, get higher school marks than boys, although boys have IQ and achievement scores similar to, if not higher, than those girls who out-score them on grades. In one school system, for example, boys had to be in the ninety-second percentile in chemistry as measured by an achievement test to receive an A grade, while girls needed only to make the eighty-sixth percentile. A comparison of achievement on a standardized test in other subjects also showed a large discrepancy, with girls in almost every instance getting higher marks from the teacher than their actual achievement might have warranted. The teachers, of course, were not grading on the basis of the achievement tests, but on the basis of in-class work.[1] For over sixty years there has been documentation of the grading bias against boys. At one suburban high school there were eighty-four students inducted into the honor society, and only eight of them were boys. The American College Testing Program studied the test scores and the grades received by boys and girls. Boys had higher mean scores on the standardized tests in mathematics, social studies, and natural sciences. Girls had higher mean scores in English. The composite scores gave boys a mean 20.3 and girls a mean of 19.7. Teachers' grades, however, were consistently higher for girls. The average mathematics grade for girls was 2.51 (on a four point scale, with 4=A), boys 2.34; girls had an average grade of 2.98 in social studies as against boys' 2.76. The average for all high-school grades for girls was 2.80 and for boys it was 2.53.[2] Obviously, such a pattern of bias cannot be attributed to the influence of bias of teachers of one sex or another. In fact, there are more male secondary teachers than female. So teachers of both sexes seem to give girls higher grades than their achievement warrants.

Interestingly enough, despite this bias against boys in the grading system, boys' achievement is consistently rated as higher or better. That is, when teachers are asked whom they think will achieve in later life, they almost always pick outstanding boys. Girls are not thought of as being expected to aspire or achieve as high as boys. However, the consistent impact on boys of getting lower marks from teachers cannot help but have an impact on their view of schooling and their view of their own potential.[3]

A similar invidious discrimination operates against students of lower socioeconomic status and from minority groups. There is ample data to support the contention that many secondary school teachers show bias against lower class students, and students who are black or have Spanish surnames, as well as native American students. Although there have been numerous well-publicized studies of this effect for decades, the situation has not perceptibly changed.[4]

In a devastating research study it was found that teachers responded to behavior clues that resulted in their overgrading some students and undergrading others. A group of flunking students were given special laboratory tutoring via programmed learning and other instructional aids in English

[1] Fairfax County, Virginia, Public Schools, Department of Instruction, Office of Psychological Services, "A Study of the Relations between Grades and Standardized Tests, July 1970," unpublished report.
[2] The National Commission on the Reform of Secondary Education, *The Reform of Secondary Education* (New York: McGraw-Hill, 1973), p. 151.
[3] Jean D. Grambs and Walter B. Waetjen, *Sex: Does It Make a Difference?* (Scituate, Mass.: Duxbury Press, 1975), pp. 125–129.
[4] Christopher Jencks, et al., *Inequality: A Reassessment of the Effect of Family and Schooling in America* (New York: Basic Books, 1972).

and mathematics. These boys, typical of many disadvantaged, were able, within a few months, to gain a whole year in these subjects. However, back in the regular classrooms, these students were still barely passing. The researchers visited the classrooms. They observed the behavior of the students who were passing and that of their own group. They found that there were three groups of students. We'll call them: Bright-Eyes, "Scaredy-Cats," and Dummies.

Bright-Eyes had perfected the trick of:

1. "Eyeballing" the instructor at all times, from the minute he or she entered the room.
2. Never ducking their eyes away when the instructor glanced at them.
3. Getting the instructor to call on them when they wanted, without raising their hands.
4. Even making the instructor go out of his or her way to call on someone else to "give others a chance" (especially useful when bright-eyes themselves are uncertain of the answer).
5. Readily admitting ignorance so as not to bluff—but in such a way that it sounds as though ignorance is rare.
6. Asking many questions.

Scaredy-Cats (the middle group):

1. Looked toward the instructor, but were afraid to let him or her "catch their eyes."
2. Asked few questions and gave the impression of being "underachievers."
3. Appeared uninvolved and had to be "drawn out," hence were likely to be criticized for "inadequate participation."

Dummies. (no matter how much they really knew):

1. Never looked at the instructor.
2. Never asked questions.
3. Were intransigent about volunteering information of any kind in class.

To make matters worse, the tests in school were not standardized and not given nearly as frequently as those given in the laboratory. School test scores were open to teacher bias. The classroom behavior of students counted a lot toward their class grades. There was no doubt that teachers were biased against the Dummies. The researcher concluded that no matter how much knowledge a Dummy gained on his own, his grades in school were unlikely to improve unless he could somehow change his image to a Bright-Eyes.

The researchers then worked with the failing students to teach them the tricks of response learned by the Bright-Eyes. As they learned to raise their hands and to "eyeball" the teacher their grades went up. In summary, one student commented:

Don't try to do it all at once. You'll shock the teacher and make it tough for yourself. Begin slowly. Work with a friend and help each other. Do it like a game. Like exercising with weights—it takes practice but it's worth it.[5]

The teacher will want to ask, "Is the poor grade associated with actual lack of achievement in the subject; or are the students being penalized for being boys, or for being poor, or for being from a minority group, or for not having the skills to manipulate the teacher?"

WHY STUDENTS DO NOT LIKE TEACHERS—AND GRADES

Teachers, by and large, would like to be friendly with their students since it is more pleasant to teach those whom one likes and who return the affection. One of the prime requisites for teaching has always been a liking for young people. This presupposes that the liking will be reciprocated: that the students will in turn like the teacher. Does this mutual liking occur? If it does, it may be distorted when the teacher assigns grades. A study of the fantasy life of adolescents showed that "teachers who were almost always stern, threatening, and avenging figures—seldom was any affection shown by or for them."[6] When the basis on which grades are awarded is one that the students neither understand nor accept, it is difficult indeed for them to develop positive attitudes toward the grade-giver.

The whole elaborate cultural pattern of "apple-polishing" is most revealing. Sometimes students make quite a game of this, comparing notes on the appropriate technique to try on the teacher: "If you tell old so-and-so you think frogs are fascinating, he'll give you a good grade." Or, "Never argue with that teacher about *Hamlet* because she flunks students who think *Hamlet* is dull." Everyone remembers how the pretty blonde who giggled so appreciatively at the professor seemed to get a grade completely out of proportion to what she seemed to know.

How can Dave who really likes English or who really thinks the math teacher is great express his true feelings? Dave's peer group might very well obstracize him if Dave seemed to ally himself with the enemy— teachers. A study of gifted adolescents showed that many of them, because of their obvious talent and interest in school learning, wandered alone throughout their secondary school careers.[7] It is such students that teachers

[5] Charles W. Slack, "If I'm So Smart, How Come I Flunk All the Time.?" *Eye*, 2 (January 1969), p. 69.
[6] Percival M. Aymonds, *Adolescent Fantasy* (New York: Columbia University Press, 1949), p. 223.
[7] Kenneth A. Kurtzman, "A Study of School Attitudes, Peer Acceptance, and Personality of the Creative Adolescent," *Exceptional Children*, 34 (November 1967), pp. 157–162.

may find turning to them for companionship since they have been left out of the social world of their peers. Anyone who actually likes learning, whether gifted or not, is apt to be isolated. Exceptions do exist, particularly if the class is action oriented, or practical, as in physical education or industrial arts classes. Then it is acceptable to like the coach or the teacher who helps one master the skills needed for a job. But for most academic teachers, the grading system introduces an element which makes anyone suspect who is interested in the importance of ideas.

The whole blame for anti-intellectualism cannot be laid at the door of the grading process. Yet clearly grades do displace the goal of learning from achieving knowledge to achieving a mark. Although the grade is supposed to be a measure of knowledge, all too often it is only a pleasant coincidence if it is. And because a teacher gives grades, the whole relationship to students is distorted.

HOW GRADING AFFECTS TEACHERS

Teachers are deeply affected by the grading process. They are likely to develop a fear of students' motives and to distrust students who seem appreciative or interested. It is the rare teacher who does not at some time overhear a cynical remark and realize with chagrin and anger that the teacher has been "played for a sucker." What happens then? Teachers build barriers between themselves and students by freezing with suspicion whenever students make friendly overtures. After all, the teacher's main function in the life of the students is to induce them to work hard at learning. When the principal emphasis is on grades, and not on learning, the student's main function in life becomes one of seeming to learn without having to go through all the agony—to escape failure at all costs. The battle over grades, then, becomes a fierce and unyielding struggle in which students attempt to outwit the teacher and the teacher constantly seeks to anticipate students.

When students do have successful and important experiences in a classroom, they will of course develop considerable attachment for the teacher. Yet nothing can destroy a long and rewarding friendship more quickly than a poor report-card grade from a "friend." In fact, when teachers know their students well, it becomes even harder to give them low grades: Teachers feel guilty, feel they have betrayed a trust, and feel that they have done something behind the back of a friend who believed in them. This kind of situation produces great ambivalence in both student and teacher. Some teachers escape the problem entirely. Teachers may insist that any student who attends class regularly and is not too unruly will get a B because they cannot stand to hurt, through grades, students they genuinely like. Other teachers may become so cold, distant, and unapproachable that students are barely more than names and faces. With such a frame of reference, it does not hurt to flunk anyone.

Beginning teachers find themselves in situations where the pressures are fierce and contradictory. On the one hand, they need to grade "hard" enough so that students will not be tempted to "take advantage" of them and think they are too "easy." And, of course, one's grading reputation soon reaches the ears of colleagues, who look with scorn on the "easy grader." Respect is gained among other teachers for being a hard grader, able to resist parent and student blandishments.

The beginner may observe that the school system may look with disfavor on the person who is too easy, but there are also pressures on those who are "too hard." Teachers who may feel they are on solid ground and give failing grades to many students may find themselves called upon to explain to unsympathetic administrators. Colleagues may also judge a teacher who gives out too many low or failing grades as a poor teacher. After all, if too many students do not seem able to learn the material, is it not the teacher's fault?

Beginning teachers know full well that students respond to rewards for achievement and that low grades produce discouraged and sometimes hostile students. There is also the knowledge that some students are just not equipped to do well in meeting the intellectual demands of some subjects despite putting prodigious effort into the attempt. Should such students deserve only D and F grades? What about those at the other end of the spectrum, the A students who achieve grades without seeming to tax their intellectual capacities? How can one honestly evaluate both groups of students using the grading system employed in most secondary schools?

GRADES AND PEER RELATIONS

The competition for a limited number of rewards divides students. Since it is clear that, in the usual class, only a few will get the top grades, students may develop strong hostilities; after all, their neighbor might win the coveted award from them. Some students develop a great selfishness regarding their own knowledge, hesitating to help a fellow student because that would reduce their own chances at the top grade. Among the students at the bottom of the heap, the reverse is true. Since they are sure that they will not get anything but a low grade, they have no moral compunctions about cheating; to them, this is merely sharing and helping a fellow unfortunate escape the ultimate disaster of failure.

In commenting about an able student in an inner-city classroom, a classmate said:

> The questions he would answer! It's not so wrong to answer some of them, but we would never answer all, tell all the answers, because we wanted to

leave something for the next day. If you answer all of them, the teacher would give you homework, you know. This boy was killing us and he was proud of it.

You know how it works. The teacher says to himself, "Well, you know this, I might as well give you some more." And we would never want more homework. So even if we know, we don't say, so as to have something else for the next day. Sometimes a little left over. If you answer all of them, you're cooked. You get new work the next day and you might not know it and then you are really stuck. Stuck for the weekend!

Like that kid, he proved he had brains for the answers, but he didn't even make friends with anybody first. He was bothering everyone. All he had to do was make one snooty remark to anybody. Man!

He got beat up outside the school; practically every day for months it happened. As far as that goes, he didn't have to do anything. Just go along minding his own business. Otherwise he'll have a lot of trouble.[8]

The amount of work done, as well as the quality, is affected by the students' view of what constitutes success or failure, and this view in turn becomes a grinding source of conflict and despair.

THE PROBLEM OF FAILURE

When am I justified in failing a student? During my student teaching, I encountered a girl in a home economics class who just couldn't learn to thread a sewing machine. It isn't really a very difficult task, but all the evidence we had showed that she just didn't have the mental capacity to learn this simple mechanical operation. She tried; she tried very hard. But someone always had to untangle it for her. She could sew a little once the machine was threaded. I gave her a D for the unit of work I was teaching, which included this aspect. But how could she get a passing grade for the course? She certainly had failed the major part of the sewing course. Fortunately, I didn't have to make the decision, since my student teaching was over before the final grade were determined.

How should this student be graded? First, of course, a teacher would have to ascertain the school policy on failing students. In some schools a student may get a failing grade in a single course and not have to repeat the course. If the course is required for graduation, then failure may well involve repeating the same course. If this is true, does the student have to repeat it with the same teacher? If failure is a direct result of actual lack of ability, certainly little or nothing is gained by repeating the course. In rare instances, failure may bring an otherwise irresponsible adolescent face to face with reality.

Research and observation indicate, however, that often neither the threat

[8] Charlotte Mayerson (ed.), *Two Blocks Apart.* (New York: Holt, Rinehart and Winston, Inc., 1965), p. 74.

of failure nor actual failure makes much difference. Repeating a course does not always promote learning that did not take place the first time. It may, however, result in a feeling of complete incompetence and a lively hatred of school and all it signifies.

Unfortunately, many adults seem to think that they were motivated to success in school through fear of failure. Perhaps. But at what cost? A far more reliable motivation toward further success is success in the first place.

But shouldn't individuals face failure sooner or later? Isn't this what "real life" is all about? Yes—and no. Security in the self is so basic to adequacy in all endeavors that schools must foster it. Certainly such a sense of competence must be honestly won; that is, Fred cannot be convinced that he is as good a baseball player as Bill when he can see himself outdistanced by every available measure. But the concomitant of "not a good baseball player" is not that Fred is not a good person. He may indeed be very able, but not in baseball. Yet, in many classrooms, the Freds are subjected to competition with the Bills in all kinds of situations. Is it fair to force Bill, the good baseball player, to compete with Fred, the genius in the automechanics course, where Bill is all thumbs? Certainly "real life" is kinder than the classroom. In "real life" individuals compete almost wholly with their peers, with those who have some degree of skill in the same areas in which they are working. People usually do not continue to compete in fields where they know they are not at all able. A young man would be considered very foolish if he tried to be a professional athlete when he had no obvious talent, or an auto mechanic if he were extremely awkward. Yet schools often put students of diverse talents into many of the same courses and set essentially the same tasks for all of them. This seems a far cry from the competition to be faced in later life and is really poor preparation for it. Isn't it the teacher's task to minimize the potentially hazardous impact of unfair competition and to allow students to compete with those who are their peers? Shouldn't the school engender a genuine respect among all kinds of students for all kinds of talent?

OVERCOMING THE GRADING COMPLEX

The beginning teacher has a responsibility to try to extend the conventional grade to a more adequate appraisal. One place where some changes have been made is the elementary school. There is, traditionally, a wide gulf between secondary and elementary school. Yet practices that are sensible at the lower level may also make sense when adapted for an older group. The traditional report card is less likely to be used at earlier grade levels. Frequently "narrative" report cards are used which allow the teacher several opportunities during the year to write at length about the progress of the individual child. The parent may be asked to make a written reply, instead of simply supplying a signature. Teacher-parent conferences, in which parents sit down with the teacher and go over their child's work, are also an essential part of this reporting system.

The junior and senior high schools have not yet reached such an understanding in reporting to parents. The problem is admittedly more difficult because each teacher has so many students—sometimes as many as 200—and thus can hardly write narrative accounts about each one. But perhaps the hard fact is that the problem itself has never been scrutinized closely. There is no "built-in" system of regular and extensive communication with their children; when these young people are telling them least about the significant things that are occurring, the school is also least helpful.

The problem cannot be resolved here. It can be pointed out, however, that practices are changing in other parts of the school system. The beginning teacher can experiment with some modest changes in the system. Here are a few suggestions:

Discuss the grading–marking system with students. The teacher will find that class time spent in discussing grades with every new class will aid immeasurably in bridging the gap between teacher and student. The teacher will want to state carefully the limits under which he or she works: For example, in college preparatory courses grade requirements for college admissions which influence high-school grading practices should be explained.

Provide a variety of avenues to achievement. Every course of instruction has a multitude of possible and important purposes. After being in a mathematics class for a semester, a student should not only have attained some skill in solving problems, but should also have developed an ability to draw graphs and charts, write neatly, discuss intelligently, work cooperatively, be responsible for aspects of class management, and so forth. Thus, a student may have more than one avenue to classroom success.

Develop self-evaluation tools. The teacher can give students a technique for looking at their own achievement through a report form developed jointly by the teacher and the class or by a class committee for the various phases or units of work.

When this form is completed by the student, it should be kept by the teacher to check his or her own judgment of the student and—where teacher and student disagree drastically—to use as a basis for a personal conference. If the student indicates significant problems and weaknesses, the teacher can easily discuss these with him or her.

Utilize many evaluation techniques. When a teacher gives the same kind of test all the time—objective, essay, matching items, problem solving—then only students proficient in that kind of skill or in learning material that can be fitted into such a test will be able to do well on the test. This will discourage those who are unable to do that kind of task well and will not challenge those who always succeed. Furthermore, it will encourage cheating, since the student is given only one way to success. Therefore, in fairness, the teacher must use many evaluation techniques.

Plan for a conference period with all students to appraise their progress. Such conferences are highly valuable if held early enough in the semester so that the student may have time to improve. And a conference at the end of the semester regarding the final semester grade will help students to accept realistically the teacher's appraisal of their work and to fit it into their own self-appraisal. Keeping folders in which students file their work throughout the semester is very helpful. The student and teacher together can then look over several months' work. This method enables the teacher to base a final grade on growth, rather than on an average of noncomparable periods of work.

CONTRACT LEARNING

In the 1930s the Winnetka, Illinois, School System developed a procedure for individualizing student achievement through a "contract system." Teachers outlined the requirements for a given unit of work and indicated what would be required to achieve a given grade. Then students could indicate what grades they would work toward. A contract was drawn up and filed. Although the contract eventually faded away in Winnetka, a few teachers kept on using it. In recent years it has been resurrected in many places. It has been found to be a useful adjunct in motivating students and in overcoming some of the limitations of the grading system.

A learning contract system is one that is integrated into the planning for a unit. Typically a unit plan will include specific student activities. The teacher will then indicate how many of these activities a student needs to achieve for a specific grade. For example:

A unit will include:

- reading the chapter in the text
- completing three weekly assignments
- passing the unit test
- doing one independent study activity
    1. read a related book and make brief report
    2. give a ten minute oral report on a related topic
    3. participate in bulletin board committee on topic
    4. make a display illustrating one of the concepts in the topic
    5. interview a resource person related to topic
    6. make an original contribution ⸺⸺⸺⸺⸺⸺⸺⸺

A contract is then drawn up by the student and signed by both student and teacher. A contract may include the grade level which the student wishes to reach. For instance, to get an "A", all must be passed with an

"A." The independent study work must be at an "A" level. An extra assignment may be outlined by the student, which would be completed at "A" level quality.

A SAMPLE CONTRACT

I, _____ agree to complete the following

work on the unit _____
topic

at a level of C or better:

    1. Read and review text.
    2. Complete all in and out of class assignments.
    3. Do one library assignment.
    4. Give one class demonstration.

Date _____   Signed _____
Student

_____
Teacher

Another type of contract may be developed on the basis of stated activities for a unit. The teacher (and class) can agree as to how many of these activities, at what level of achievement, should result in a student earning an A, B, C, or D grade. Students, then, are quite clear about what is expected, and it is also apparent that grades will depend in part on how much the student is willing to invest in each class as well as the level of achievement reached. It is possible that a teacher could motivate a class so well that all students wrote A and B contracts, and on an absolute measure accomplish their goals. Grading on the curve would be thrown out.

A few school systems are even experimenting with contracts which include teachers and parents as well as students. The communication which would then be set up could be highly desirable.

A DIFFERENT SOLUTION

There are many suggestions about ways to deal with the problem of grading. So far, none have been adopted because of the practical problems and issues involved. As an interim solution, it is suggested that any teacher can institute practices which might alleviate some of the distress surrounding the giving and receiving of grades.

One proposal involves giving each student three grades: one grade would be a measure of achievement against an absolute standard (criterion-referenced). The student would know how a given skill or accumulation of knowledge measured up to an expected and described standard.

A second grade would be for achievement relative to others in the class or others of that grade level. Jane would be told that she did "B" work when compared to others in her class, though she might have done "C" work when compared to an absolute achievement standard.

Finally, students would be given a grade which reflected the teacher's appraisal of effort and class performance. Many low-achieving students actually put in a great deal more effort than some high-achieving students. It is a useful reminder to glib and clever Andy that the "A" he got was a true measure of what he had learned, and was also an "A" in relation to the achievement of others in his class, but that the teacher was not satisfied that Andy had put forth maximum effort. It might indicate that Andy's in-class behavior left something to be desired. Andy could get a "C" or "D" for effort or behavior.

With three such measures at hand, students could gauge their own work. It would accomplish three useful things: (a) inform students as to how well they did in learning what was expected in that subject area at that grade level; (b) tell them how well they were doing relative to others of their class; and (c) tell them how their performance was judged. It also would help reduce the amount of subjectivity in teachers' grades. Some school systems now are using such double or even triple grading systems. If more of these were adopted it is likely that more students would feel better about school work.

SELECTED READINGS

Cureton, Louise Witmer, "The History of Grading Practices," *Measurement in Education* 2 (May 1971), pp. 1–7. A series of Special Reports of the National Council on Measurement in Education, Office of Evaluation Services, Michigan State University, East Lansing, Mich. An illuminating historical report on the development of current grading policies and practices.

French, Lois, "How Does It Feel To Fail?" in *Mental Health and Achievement,* E. Paul Torrance and Robert D. Strom (Eds.). New York: Wiley, 1965, pp. 377–384. A sympathetic review of the impact failure has upon a student's ability to perform and what teachers can do about it.

Gray, Farnum, with Paul S. Graubard and Harry Rosenberg, "Little Brother Is Changing You," *Psychology Today,* 7 (March 1974), pp. 42–46. A group of junior-high-school students were shown how they could modify the behavior of adults by their own responses.

Holt, John, *How Children Fail.* New York: Pitman, 1964. A critical examination of school practices that make failure the overriding fear and goal for learning. But the author also shows why this process produces only more failure. A controversial book well worth reading and debating.

Kirschenbaum, Howard, Sidney B. Simon, and Rodney W. Napier, *Wad-Ja-Get?: The Grading Game and American Education.* New York: Hart, 1971. A critical look at current grading practices with interesting proposals for reform.

Pinchak, Barbara Moretti, and Hunter M. Breland, *Grading Practices in American High Schools.* Princeton, N.J.: Educational Testing Service, 1973. Reviews current grading practices in a large sample of American secondary schools. Shows how little change there has been since 1920.

Rehberg, Richard A., and Evelyn R. Rosenthal, *Class and Merit in the American High School.* New York: Longmans, 1978. See especially Chapter 5, "Academic Achievement" for stimulating analysis of the role of grades in achievement.

Wrinkle, William L., *Improving Marking and Reporting Practices.* New York: Holt, Rinehart and Winston, 1947. An older book, but its analysis of the fallacies of the grading system has not been superseded, nor have the grading problems pointed out by Wrinkle yet been resolved.

part VI

INTERACTION:
discipline
and
counseling

INTERACTION between teacher and students and among groups of students provides the yeast of learning. Not all interaction is productive; discipline problems do exist. Every beginning teacher—and many experienced teachers as well —find that establishing and maintaining a positive classroom climate requires constant vigilence, plus wisdom, tolerance, and humor. All discipline problems are not caused by "bad" students, nor are all problems the result of teacher ineptitude, but there are ingredients of both in many problem situations. Learning to listen to, and talk with, students provides the teacher with insight into the human dilemmas students face. As a counselor, the teacher also becomes a friend.

FOCUS ON CHAPTER 15

Discipline presents a teacher with more conflict and potential unease than almost any other aspect of teaching. Since most adolescents are approximately the same size and weight as teachers, they cannot simply be dominated, as may be the view taken by the neophyte elementary teacher. How can a teacher maintain order in a classroom in a way which not only promotes learning, but is consistent with assumptions about democratic education?

In this and the following chapter, the major discipline problems which secondary school teachers may face are presented and discussed.

Significant ideas presented in this chapter include:

- While there are often conflicting and confusing definitions of discipline, the concept of democratic discipline will, in the long run, contribute fundamentally to successful teaching.
- Although students are most apt to be blamed when there is classroom disorder, teachers who lack social and/or pedagogical skill are the source of many classroom problems with discipline.
- The secondary school surrounds the student with many rules, some arbitrary and outmoded, and also with many persons other than teachers who may be less than skillful in dealing with volatile adolescents; all of these may trigger discipline situations. When the teacher is alert to these other sources of trouble, action can be taken to head off potential difficulty.
- Although the teacher role can be generalized in most instances, there are some situations which produce tension which pertain specifically to either men or women teachers differentially.
- Since 1954 schools have been moving toward racial integration; some with more success than others. Interracial tension remains a source of conflict particularly when teachers are insensitive or unaware.

chapter 15

Troublemakers I:
discipline problems,
teachers, institutions,
and society

Year after year, when college students preparing to become teachers are asked to name concerns about teaching, the first thing they list is "discipline." Discipline looms so large in the minds of many teachers, throughout their careers, that other important issues are pushed aside. No one can teach in a chaotic classroom where pupils are disruptive. But in many seemingly orderly classrooms there may be little significant learning. Order in the classroom is a *first* step toward teaching, but it is far from the only step.

In this and the next chapter we will consider discipline. First we will examine the teacher's role in developing an orderly classroom which is conducive to learning. And then we will see the role of the student in classroom discipline.

DEFINING DISCIPLINE

I had stopped at the drive-in for a quick hamburger and coke before my evening class when I noticed a group of kids who looked very familiar. After a few moments I recognized some of them; they were in my fifth-period business math class. I had no fond thoughts about these kids; two of them were making my life miserable, constantly disrupting and rarely bothering to get the class work done, in class or out. I watched them as I finished my snack; they were evidently planning something. No rowdy behavior. I overhead a few comments: "Shaddup or get out." "*Everyone* has to do something." There wasn't any of the horsing around that caused me so much woe in class.

When young people are planning their own affairs there is little disruptive behavior. If anyone interferes with the group's work that person is summarily quelled or ousted. The work is analyzed and parceled out, and the group is intolerant of any individual who does not follow through. In this kind of group the members are engaged in an activity which is highly important to them, they have chosen this activity freely, and membership in the group is voluntary.

Now take the typical classroom: The topics of study and the activities for learning are usually not selected by the students. Few of the students are in school of their own free choice. Most students know there is some kind of law that requires them to be in school, and they also realize that most of the forces of society are interested in their staying in school. Students rarely have an opportunity to select the school they will attend. A few school systems have developed "magnet schools" or "target schools" in an effort toward desegregation and also to provide some specialized programs to meet different student needs.[1] Even if the student has a choice of school, which is unlikely in most school systems, there is rarely a choice of teacher. The student must remain with whatever teacher happens to teach that subject at that time slot. There is not much "freedom" in this system. Nor, of course, does the student have much choice about who might be in the same class. Many students do try to arrange class schedules so they will be with their close friends, but the arbitrary processes of the computer may override their wishes. And they certainly cannot foresee that one of their worst enemies might turn up in class. Students are accurately described as prisoners of the system. No wonder their behavior is so different in school from what is often observed out of school.

It is not at all surprising that from time to time students will rebel against alien subject matter, enforced inactivity, involuntary attendance, and tasks that are beyond their capacity. This is what might be called "normal" misbehavior. However, sometimes reactions to the ordinary demands of the school are surprisingly violent; individuals seem unable to adjust, even for short periods, to school expectations. This might be called "abnormal" misbehavior.

The teacher thus has two major tasks in dealing with classroom behavior. The first task is one of diagnosis: What was the probable cause of the misbehavior? Was the disturbance within the range of "normal" problems which arise just because many people are together in the same place, and which can be handled with tact, understanding, and diplomacy? Or is the misbehavior really "abnormal," seemingly an overreaction to the kinds of

[1] Charles B. McMillan, "Magnet Education in Boston," *Phi Beta Kappan*, 59 (November 1977), pp. 158–163; Daniel U. Levine and Nolan Estes, "Desegregation and Educational Reconstruction in the Dallas Public Schools," *Phi Delta Kappan*, 59 (November 1977), pp. 163–167, 221.

daily stresses and strains of education? The second task of the teacher is developing skill in responding to either normal or abnormal discipline situations, having a repertoire of procedures which work when things are getting out of hand; ultimately evolving a psychology of discipline which suits one's own personality and teaching style.

WHAT KIND OF CLASSROOM DISCIPLINE IS WANTED?

Most people carry a mental picture of how teachers in their own experiences managed to discipline their classes. Some teachers were stern, cold, forbidding; others shouted at the class constantly; and still others lost their temper on the average of once a week and frightened everyone in the class. But some seemed calm, approachable, unruffled by misbehavior.

It must be underlined over and over that what "works" for one teacher will be anathema or a disaster for another. Each teacher has to develop an idea of good discipline in his or her own terms. One of the most disturbing things that beginning teachers must deal with is the gratuitous advice, which is offered by experienced teachers, about how to discipline a class. Much of the advice may be helpful, but a great deal of it may be wrong—for you or for your class. There are general guides to good discipline—and we shall provide some here—but the specific responses and strategies used by a particular teacher are those which are unique to that person. The best discipline is that with which teacher and students feel comfortable. As presented in Chapter 1, there are many kinds of teachers and each has something which no other teacher has. Also, and this may be overlooked, every school system, every school, every class, and indeed every student, is a unique complex of history, resources and needs.

It is probable that the teacher's way of dealing with a class will be consistent with other aspects of personality. A person who is gregarious, likes to laugh, enjoys many acquaintances and friends, will have a relaxed and sociable classroom climate. Another person, who has relatively few friends, but establishes deep and permanent relationships with them, who is intensely interested in a particular subject area, who considers life a very serious enterprise, will probably have a classroom that reflects this approach to life. We do not change spots for stripes the minute we get in front of a classroom. Many a quiet mouse of a student turns into a veritable lion of a performer when facing a captive audience. The mouse–lion personality, however, is not as inconsistent as might appear, and this kind of individual usually is both shy and distant in interpersonal relations, yet puts on a great act for an audience. Some introspection, therefore, is called for as one begins to develop skill in classroom discipline.

Like advice from other teachers, one's own recollections of good and bad teachers may be misleading:

> My tenth-grade English teacher has to be the worst. Not only was he strict, but very tedious. The smallest error was like an earthquake. One did it correctly, or received a failing grade. Because of him, I hated to come to school. But after two years of college, I went back to him, and thanked him for his methods. What he taught me, I can never forget.

Will this future teacher, then, make a model of such a teacher? Is it necessary to be a devil in order to get students to learn?

Being true to one's own teaching style does not, however, mean being idiosyncratic to the point of being out of step with everyone else. You can be as different as you like—within limits. One major limit, of course, is that of the professional. One has to accede to the expectations of the teaching role. As such, one strives for a classroom where there is good teaching going on, where students are motivated to do the tasks at hand. In this kind of a climate, discipline is taken care of. A competent professional teacher strives to establish a friendly, relaxed, working atmosphere. Remember, one can be a good group leader, and the group will have good discipline, but group leadership is not all there is to *teaching*. Teaching requires much more, particularly guiding students to new knowledge and skills, and judging the acquisition of such skill or knowledge. Inevitably, these role requirements produce strain in interpersonal relationships, and that is where discipline is required.

Another limitation is the need to establish a classroom which is consistent with democratic principles. Establishing a balance between freedom and security means that rules operate and are respected, but that the individual feels comfortable within the framework of the rules. The rules then are the disciplinary agent; the teacher merely helps students observe them. Students are guided toward increased self-discipline, which means that discipline is something that is not merely for the benefit of the group. The activity itself imposes its own discipline in the same way that the rules of a game of basketball impose a discipline on the team.

The conception outlined above, however, is not all there is to the subject of discipline. Several variables must be taken into account. First, we may encounter the problem of teachers who lack teaching and social skills. They are simply tactless, awkward, or disorganized. Second, we must consider the problem of teacher personality and teacher reaction to the activities and behavior of immature students. The first two may be called teacher-caused discipline problems. Third, we may find discipline situations arising from the nature of the institution. These three problems will be considered in this chapter. Fourth, there is the problem of explosive or provocative personality relations among members of the class. Some students are dynamite only in combination with certain other students. Others, unaided, can agitate the whole class. Fifth, there are the problems that reside in the individual personality of certain students. With these students, disturbances in adjustment at home or school have left their mark, making it more than normally difficult for them to adjust to classroom demands. The latter two variables may be called student-caused discipline problems, and will be discussed in the next chapter.

PROBLEMS TEACHERS CAUSE

Discipline problems that arise from inadequacies in teachers from their own intolerance or lack of insight into youth, will respond only to critical self-analysis. Inadequacies in teachers may be subdivided into lack of social skill and lack of teaching skill.

Teachers Display Lack of Social Skill by:	Teachers Display Lack of Teaching Skill by:
Using sarcasm	Conducting classes in a dull, monotonous way
Failing to answer reasonable questions	Speaking in a rasping, irritating voice
Being insensitive to the special problems of students, such as stuttering	Giving vague assignments
Being inconsistent: for example, telling a student who has come in late to ask a neighbor for help, then scolding the student	Giving assignments too difficult for the students
	Proceeding with oral work when there is noise in or outside the class
Being impolite and inconsiderate	Failing to give attention to light and heat conditions
Making personal remarks about students, their dress, appearance, or manner of speaking	Being confused about classroom routines, such as the distribution of supplies
Being unfair; "playing" favorites	Giving in to student pressure at unpredictable times
Making disparaging remarks about social groups in the community	Failing to make all learning steps clear
Gossiping about students in public places	Giving tests on material not covered in class
	Rewarding only one kind of aptitude

Reflect back on some of the unsatisfactory teachers you have known. Can you place their behavior in either of these categories? What can you add to both lists?

SOME CASE STUDIES OF POOR TEACHING

The following narrative provides an example of a teacher grossly lacking in both social and teaching skill. While it may appear to be too extreme to be real, it is an actual record of a classroom observation. The actions described are not uncommon; they do not always occur in one class hour, as in this case, but such malpractices do reveal themselves—and too often.

Mr. Brown stood by his desk, rifling through a disorderly mass of student papers, books, and folders in search of his grade book. He announced to the class, "While I am taking roll, I want you to fill out these registration cards." He passed out the cards.

Good order, even on the teacher's desk, is basic to good management. The time wasted looking for something is time when the class lacks direction and confusion begins.

No explanation of the cards? What are they for? Even routine forms should be explained to minimize confusion.

While Mr. Brown was passing out the cards, two girls came hurrying in. "You're late, girls," he remarked. "But, Mr. Brown, we've already been here once. We just went down the hall for a drink of water." "You're still late. Go to the office and get a late entry pass." The two girls had no sooner gone than another girl opened the door, dropped her books with a clatter on the first desk, and then went out. "Mr. Brown," came a voice from the back of the room, "do we fill these cards out in ink?" No answer. Mr. Brown was checking the rollbook, but obviously had heard the remark.

Better to complete distributing the cards and then speak to the girls privately.

This kind of lack of respect for the classroom activity seems to be a prevailing note in Mr. Brown's room.

He treats the students with a lack of consideration, and they respond in kind.

An expected reaction, because no directions were given when the cards were passed out. There will always be students who do not know what to do, no matter how often a routine has been gone through.

Mr. Brown, pen or pencil?" "You know better than to ask such a question," Mr. Brown finally retorted angrily. "You always fill things out in ink." "But what if you don't have a pen?" "Then use mine, or borrow one." "Oh, I have one. I was just wondering what someone who didn't

Why should the teacher disregard a request for information? If it is a legitimate request, it deserves an answer. If it is an attempt to annoy, the best way to thwart such an effort is to treat it seriously. Certainly telling the student in an angry tone of voice that he ought to know better makes the situation worse.

have one would do." A snicker passed through the room . . .

"I'm going to hand back your papers from yesterday," announced Mr. Brown. Immediately everyone began to talk.

"You people be quiet! Some of you are going to be sent to the office if you're not careful."

Two girls kept right on talking.

"Have you girls finished your conversation?"

"Yes," they answered, with a smirk to their neighbors.

At this point, the three tardy students returned to class. Mr. Brown began to read the answers to the punctuation exercise. He interrupted himself to ask, "Those of you who came in late, do you know what we are doing?"

"No."

"Well, find out." The students referred to immediately turned to their neighbors, and for a moment disrupted Mr. Brown's procedure.

A discussion arose about one of the exercises. It had to do with the use of a semicolon for a comma. "I don't see what harm there is in using it," one student declared.

"Well, it's wrong, that's all," Mr. Brown said impatiently. "We can't spend much more time on this assignment," he continued, "so I'll hurry through the rest of the answers."

While Mr. Brown was reading the rest of the answers, two students wandered up to the wastepaper basket and the pencil sharpener.

This is the result of disregard for students as human beings. The teacher fell into a very neat trap; now his control over the class is in serious jeopardy.

The use of threats should be carefully weighed. Is "the office" the place to settle minor difficulties? What kind of behavior merits such treatment?

Evidently this threat did not work; the students continued to misbehave.

What if the girls had answered "No"?

Obviously the latecomers could not know what the lesson was, so why ask? The teacher might better have told them briefly what to do or have asked them to wait and told them later or have assigned a student to help them quietly.

He is asking for trouble. Of course, such a remark will only lead to a new source of distraction and confusion. And no one could possibly say that this time the students were at fault.

This is not teaching in any sense of the word. If the subject is worthy of class time, it is worthy of some respect.

A class will show its lack of interest by making use of such disturbing actions as throwing away paper and sharpening pencils. Either interest the class in the activity or have rules about using these facilities so that class work is orderly.

"I'm going to read some of your themes," he announced next. The class broke into whispered conversation.

"You will have to be quiet. You are old enough to know when you are being rude."

He finished reading the first theme. The class broke into talking again. Several of the students asked questions. "If you want me to hear you, you'll have to talk one at a time; I can't hear you at all," he said sharply.

He started to read another theme; the class continued to fuss and whisper. He looked up.

"What did you say, Joan?"

"Nothing."

"Talking to yourself?"

"Uh-huh."

Mr. Brown returned to his reading; Joan turned and smiled at the girl behind her. The class snickered. Mercifully, the bell rang.

Mr. Brown is old enough to know that he has been even ruder himself. Students also have personal feelings.

The class is completely disorganized. The teacher has lost the students' attention. He tells them he cannot hear them, but fails to reestablish some order in the room.

The teacher set his own trap again. He deserved to be caught.

This teacher seemed unable to predict the consequences of his own actions. When asked why his class was so chaotic and disturbed, he could only blame the students. Yet a report of what went on shows clearly that he was at fault.

Below is another example of a teacher whose discipline is faulty.

Mr. Green was organizing supplies in the adjoining room when the art class arrived. The class clustered in little groups and chattered about the election that was being held in the school. Mr. Green entered the room and, in a loud voice, said, "Everyone sit down and be quiet!" He read an announcement of a senior class meeting. The seniors bounced up and started to leave the room. In a stern voice, Mr. Green told them to return to their seats and asked for an assignment due that day. He checked the seniors out one at a time, picking up their assignments as they went out. He continued taking the class roll and checking the assignments. This task took from 9:30 until 9:45; the class, with nothing to do, was restless. There were several private conversations going on and six or seven students ambled to their lockers to find the assignment due.

Mr. Green went into the other room to check out paper for the coming assignment. He prefaced with: "Just ask for the color and size of paper you need, no other questions." This distribution took from 9:45 to 10:05. He returned to the main room, called for order, and announced that the marks for overdue assignments would be lowered by one letter grade for each day they were late. There was time left to help three people individually out of the class of twenty. For most of the students, the hour had been spent in waiting and in various diversionary maneuvers.

Mr. Brown, of the first example, was alternately rude and inept; Mr. Green tries to be stern and forbidding. But Mr. Green, like Mr. Brown, is having little success in motivating his students to learn. Mr. Green obviously needs to examine some basic errors in his teaching methods when only three out of a class of twenty get any help during a fifty-minute period.

Mr. Fields coached wrestling. His coaching consisted of yelling at the guys instead of showing how it should be done. If a guy was sick or just got over an illness he made them wrestle. If overweight, he made them starve and exercise till the guy got down to the proper weight. He never instructed the guys on how to maintain their weight. His knowledge of physical and nutritional well-being was zilch from all points of view.

An interest in an enthusiasm for a subject is no substitute for knowing how to teach it, and certainly yelling at students is a poor way to motivate them.

Failure to assess the impact of one's teaching upon students is illustrated by the following descriptions:

Ms. O'Neil had always taught in parochial schools, and her attempt to transfer her authoritarianism to public schools brought utter chaos. She demanded highly regimented behavior (i.e., standing when she or another adult entered or left the room, absolutely no talking, etc.); she required too much homework; she had no qualms about throwing objects at students who she thought were inattentive; and she delighted in publicly humiliating students who were unprepared or unable to perform for whatever reason. It certainly was not *her* fault if any student had difficulty with the work!

I sat bored through two years of Latin and two years of French with Ms. Long. She was not firm about unruly behavior and did not know how to counteract it by presenting interesting lessons. Paper airplanes and spit-balls were frequently on the scene; voices buzzed during the class; cheating was prevalent. The teacher seemed to want to be buddies with all of us. Although she may have known her languages, she didn't know how to teach them effectively. The teacher took the unruly behavior as long as possible, then blew up. The class would calm down that day—perhaps—and start up the next.

Here are some more descriptions of teacher-made discipline problems:

Out of the many bad teachers I have experienced, Mrs. X would have to be the worst example. She was a new teacher, and her lack of organization and ability to teach the subject matter was apparent to us. This resulted in a lack of respect by the class. We would walk out during class, students were drinking alcohol in the classroom. During tests, blatant cheating was evident. But even though she lacked the knowledge and ability to teach, we students were awfully rough on her. The fact that she was black may have contributed to this dislike. But, when a teacher can't remember student names and constantly doesn't know where her roll book is, what chapter we are studying, it was hard for students to become interested in learning the subject matter.

I observed the work of Ms. Kutoski as a special favor for the head of the department. She was a second-year teacher and she was being considered for tenure. I was appalled by her class. She was a nice person—but so ineffective! Among other things she did wrong while I was there was starting a filmstrip on the circulation of the blood. She announced when she started it that probably there was not time enough to show the whole thing, but they should watch it anyway! The room was not darkened, so half the class couldn't see it; the screen would not pull down all the way, so part of the picture was invisible on the green chalkboard. It was such a hot day the doors of the room were left open and noise from the hall was so great (it was during lunchtime and many students were out in the hall opening and closing lockers) that one could not hear the sound track. Unfortunately, she did not seem aware of all the teaching errors she was making in my conversation with her afterwards. "Pretty restless bunch, aren't they?" was the most she had to say about this dreadful lesson.

Although a parade of horrible examples is not the whole story of discipline, a thoughtful analysis of descriptions of teacher mismanagement will at least underline some mistakes to be avoided.

During my senior year in high school I had a history class where the teacher was an elderly gentleman who had long been a member of the teaching profession. One could not doubt that he knew his history, but that wasn't the problem. During class periods the teacher would go over the previous night's assignment by calling on the students to recite. If a student wasn't called upon, he would usually do anything but listen to the answer. At times the class got a little noisy. In order to combat this, the teacher would find a victim from several of the ringleaders who seemed always to be noisiest and give him what was called "inattentives," which consisted of extra work: either 4, 8, or 12 questions to be answered. By receiving these one would have to do a great deal of extra work to receive a decent grade in the unit.

This example highlights some grievous errors. First, the dry, read-and-answer-questions approach to teaching produces boredom and causes students to look for some way to last out the period. Second, the teacher is picking one "victim" for what is a generalized condition. Third, the teacher is using the subject matter as an instrument of punishment—hardly a way to engender interest in that subject. Fourth, the teacher is using his punishment procedures as a basis for grading the student.

The next example illustrates the effect of poor teaching on the interrelations of students.

After five minutes of calisthenics, the boys separated into prechosen touch football teams. The coach handed out the balls to the teams from a bag carried to the field. There were three or four domineering boys on each team. They monopolized all the playing while the other two or three boys on the team centered the ball or blocked—or did nothing. One big boy, who was wearing football shoes, called the plays and carried the ball in almost every play. The coach explained that the boy was a center on the varsity and that he was allowed to wear cleats when he didn't have his tennis shoes. On the same team, a small boy, wearing glasses, didn't even bother to get into the huddles. He centered the ball every time and just blocked.

The coach observed after class, "Boys today don't seem to have any spirit. None of them seems to be interested in learning to play games or learning fundamentals."

Of course the boys in this class do not play well; the teacher has failed to put them in situations where they would want to play.

Three other pitfalls for the unwary teacher should be mentioned here.

The first is the danger of falling prey to one's own personal problems and anxieties. The teacher who is moody—sunny one day and a thundercloud the next—induces insecurity and anxiety in students.

Here is a student's view of one such teacher:

Miss Stanley was my eighth-grade art teacher; she had neither the rapport with students nor the teaching know-how, nor the knowledge of her subject necessary in teaching. To this day I cannot imagine anyone hiring her—but they did. Her classes were absolutely chaotic. Nothing she planned for us to do ever worked, and it was quite obvious that she didn't really care. What particularly stands out in my memory was her unstable emotional state throughout the year. One day she even started crying for no reason apparent to us in the class—it was obvious that Miss Stanley had some serious personal problems which she could not help displaying in the class. It was at this point that we sympathized with her, and attempted to discipline ourselves; not out of any great respect for her but only because we could not stand to see a teacher cry. So thirty-five students sat day after day learning almost nothing, terrified that our teacher might break down again.

The second pitfall is rudeness. Teachers often talk to and treat students in a way they themselves would not tolerate—even from other adults. Such behavior includes telling students they are "dumb," complaining that they are acting like babies, making personal remarks about their appearance in public ("Well, it looks as though Ted finally got his hair cut"; or "I guess Sue Ann is trying to compete with color television with that dress"), hurrying them with impatience, and interrupting their conversations or reports in a brusque and unnecessary fashion. A rude teacher will be treated rudely by his or her students.

Teachers can show students the ordinary courtesies of social exchange, such as "Please," and "Thank you," and other words and phrases which show respect for other people. It is shocking to note how many teachers are careless if not actually rude in their exchanges with students. This kind of treatment contributes a great deal to the surly and rude behavior of many students.

A third pitfall is so obvious that it is typically overlooked: teachers, like other human beings, are bound to react negatively to anyone who makes life miserable for them. It would require a superperson to react with loving kindness toward a sixteen-year-old who continually makes snide remarks in class. It is only too easy to develop a dislike for such a student. Such dislike is communicated in many ways, both overt and covert, and soon the student is doing much more than making only snide remarks, and a full-scale battle between student and teacher may be launched. Mutual dislike is a major impediment to providing help. Yet *many students most in need of help are often those most difficult to like.* Teachers need to be emotionally prepared to deal with students who are causing trouble and toward whom the teacher's first response is dislike. As pointed out in the next chapter, many students who cause trouble for teachers are really students who are *in* trouble with themselves. Such students need *more* help, *more* kindness, *more* consideration because their progress toward maturity is so much more difficult than for other students. One way to deal with mounting feelings of dislike for a troublemaker is to make that student the subject of a case study (see Chapter 2). Such a procedure helps focus one's attention objectively on exactly what the student is doing (and what you as the teacher may be doing, too), which makes the behavior so obnoxious. Also, by looking behind the scenes, into relations with other teachers, test scores, previous school records, home situations, you may find that the student can be someone you can empathize with and help. In such an atmosphere, dislike is eased and often with it the annoying behavior.

AVOIDING TEACHER-CAUSED DISCIPLINE PROBLEMS

What measures can be suggested in cases where discipline problems seem to result from the teacher's own mistakes in management? First, of course, it is imperative to make a critical analysis of those actions of the teacher which cause trouble. Often, this analysis must be made by an outside observer. Teachers who bring about their own misfortunes are apt to be unable to see just what it is they do which seems to be so provocative. The student–teaching period should be the time during which a beginning teacher is helped to see which of his or her actions contribute to a smoothly operating class and which are disruptive. Second, the quality of instruction should be reviewed. In a surprisingly large number of situations, discipline problems arise, not from anything the teacher does wrong, but merely from the sheer dullness of the class work. Third, it is essential to know the particular methodology appropriate to a given subject. Many teachers are assigned one or more classes outside their major area of preparation. When this happens, it is incumbent upon the teacher to become familiar with the special needs of that subject. As one anecdote pointed out, the wrestling coach not only had inadequate understanding of how to demonstrate the needed skills, he also did not know how to instruct students in the nutritional requirements for proper weight control.

Fourth, the last person who can diagnose difficulties in teaching is, typically, the teacher who is the cause of his or her own troubles. Such a teacher often made mistakes early in teaching and did not go back to diagnose those mistakes and rectify them. Perhaps no one was around to point out the problems caused by such teaching errors. As one embarks on a teaching career, it is wise to develop a continual personal assessment process. For example, "Well, that lesson went well; now why did it work so much better with this class than fourth period?" Or, "Why did Tony give me such an angry glare when I said that? What tender spot did I touch in him?" Or, "What caused all the confusion when the class was going back to their drawing boards to work on the lettering assignment?" A persistent self-consciousness about the process of teaching, and an effort to achieve objectivity in appraising one's own teaching is essential to avoid repeating mistakes and to foster learning from one's successes.

Fifth, you can also learn from other teachers. Not from those who say, "Don't smile until Christmas," or "If you have the Stevens kid you will have trouble, just like I do," or "They only respect you if you yell at them." Such advice is counterproductive. It does not take into account individual styles of relating to students; it is also premised on a view of students which makes them the enemy, that assumes the worst rather than the best of individuals. However, there are many excellent, experienced teachers whose classes are models of order and enthusiastic teaching and learning. If possible, spot these teachers early and ask if you can sit in and observe what they are doing. From observations of many such teachers, and from reports from many students about what good teachers did to maintain adequate discipline, the following can be listed:

- interesting teaching methodology
- enthusiastic about subject
- sense of humor
- good relationships with students; cares about student progress
- fair
- well organized; students know what to expect
- knows all students' names
- flexible when necessary; not rigid

- sophisticated; not easily shocked
- does not allow for disruptions
- polite
- routines for supplies and roll taking, etc. are well organized and unobtrusive

Perhaps, by reflecting on some good teachers you have known, you will find items to add to this list. Basically, the list covers those behaviors which the teacher can control. These items are the substance of the beginning of good discipline, but not the whole story. No matter how wise, efficient, and interesting a teacher may be, things will still go wrong.

INSTITUTIONAL TENSIONS

The school as an institution is not a particularly tranquil place. In most secondary schools there are a thousand or more teenagers crammed into a building, often one that was designed for far fewer, or one that was built to last for centuries and, unfortunately, has. The halls are too crowded between classes, the lavatories are unspeakable, lockers are noisy and in the wrong places, the cafeteria food is nauseating—the litany of complaints could go on and on. There are also many schools, new and old, which are bright, cheerful, clean, and relatively serene places. Students amble rather than rush to class; student products are everywhere visible; teachers sit with students at a palatable lunch; even the lavatories are usable. The latter kind of school will not eradicate all discipline problems, but we can be relatively sure that in the first kind of school there will be many. Problems which individual teachers have with discipline often arise as much from the overall atmosphere of the school as from individual student or teacher difficulties. Although the general direction a school takes depends to a great measure on the leadership provided by the principal, it is also apparent that teachers can contribute a great deal—if they choose to. Teacher complaints about poorly organized and poorly administered schools are often valid, but at the same time teachers do not always assess correctly what role they can play in bringing about change.

For example: One junior high required a sign-up sheet posted at the front of every room. A student who left the room had to enter his or her name, indicating time leaving and time returning and what he or she was doing when out of the room. This lent itself to the extensive use of popular four-letter words, and ingenious descriptions of what was being done while out of the room. Many teachers got upset by this behavior and it was a cause of much student–teacher friction. Such regulations cause more problems than they solve, and a responsible faculty would see that such procedures are changed.

Inconsiderate use of the public address system may also lead to disturbances and disorder. Some administrative personnel seem unaware of the effects of these announcements on the unseen classes.

The student teacher was struggling with a particularly intricate set of instructions for a laboratory experiment. Over the public address system came the words, "Excuse the interruption, but will the following students please report to Miss Collins." Twenty names were read. Ten minutes later, "Please excuse the interruption . . ." and another twenty names were read. This continued at ten-minute intervals during the whole class period. The class was angered, the teacher was rattled, and the instructions were of course not completed. Upon inquiry, it was learned that all the students being called upon were juniors; since this science class was for twelfth graders only, the observer wondered why the intercommunication buttons for all other classes had not been turned off.

The rather continual complaint about poor food in the cafeteria can lead to school problems that inevitably become classroom problems. In one school the din in the cafeteria was deafening, but no one was allowed out until the dismissal bell rang. These students went to their next class half-deaf and sullen. The teachers who received them knew that at least five minutes would be lost because of the effort required of these students simply to become calm and quiet and to recover from the assault on their nerves and stomachs.

The split-lunch period is also difficult for teachers and students. This educational monstrosity takes place when lunch periods must be arranged on three or more shifts. In order to accommodate all the students, some classes meet for thirty minutes, go to lunch for twenty-four minutes, and return to their classroom for the remainder of the time, another twenty-five minutes. Before lunch, the students are of course hungry and know that they have not much time to wait; when they return from lunch they are buoyed up by the release from academic routines and the frenzy of seeing their friends, plus the rush to get to the cafeteria and eat in the minimum time allotted. Although some administrators have been able to work out schedules that eliminate the split-lunch period, some seem unable to do so.

The misuse of lavatories has become an epidemic problem in secondary schools. In many schools they are defaced by graffiti, supplies are usually lacking, the plumbing is out of order, and students report they are favorite places for drug use and drug exchange. According to a national survey, students have been robbed and assaulted in restrooms.[2] These situations do not contribute to the peace of mind needed to comply readily and happily with teachers' requests.

There are other peripheral persons and activities that can contribute to student unrest: a rigid hall monitoring system, for instance, a grim and

[2] National Commission on the Reform of Secondary Education, *The Reform of Secondary Education* (New York: McGraw Hill, 1973), p. 121.

unfriendly school secretary, or an unsympathetic and suspicious school nurse. Or there may be a schedule of activities which is always being changed or shifted without prior notice. Some schools have three or four bell schedules depending on whether there is to be all-school testing, assemblies, ball games, or some mysterious administrative decree. But as teachers and students state, no one knows what the bell schedule will be from day to day. These kinds of unexpected events are likely to trigger undesirable classroom reactions. Where teachers and administrators can work together on routines, regulations, and a minimum of interruptions and sudden changes, there is more apt to be harmony and a relaxed atmosphere. A good administrator, too, is quickly aware of such problems as a bus driver who offends students, or a clerk who is needlessly surly, and takes steps to help these people work with youth.

Imaginative teachers can even use these discipline-causing situations as part of class instruction. A home economics class, for example, could do a study of the cafeteria food to determine its nutritional value. If too many students fail to eat the approved "balanced meal" and eat empty-calorie junk food, then obviously they are not getting a proper diet. The class can then make a presentation to the faculty, the cafeteria supervisor, and if nothing interferes, make their study known to the superintendent and board members. Not only could they learn about diet and nutrition, but they would learn some good lessons in civic responsibility.

A lavatory problem could be studied by a psychology class, and recommendations for a schoolwide attack on the problem, with student involvement, could become a test of their insight into human behavior. Noisy halls could be analyzed by a physics class to see if they can develop and test methods of monitoring sound levels, and also—perhaps with the industrial arts teachers—suggest ways of insulating the halls to reduce the sound levels. As pointed out in Chapter 4 on democratic education, students who feel involved in their own education are students who are learning the behaviors of responsibility which make for democratic citizenship—and also make for good school discipline.

Some discipline problems arise from students' all-too-human reaction to the institutional structure of schools. The crucial school situations that seem to make it more than usually difficult for students to control themselves are:

- The last period of the day on Friday
- The last period of any day
- The last five minutes before lunch
- The whole day just before a big game, rally, or all-school event
- The first part of the period following an exciting rally, school assembly, or fire drill
- The day just before report cards come out; the day report cards are issued; and the following day

- At a time of all-school crisis, such as losing the league championship, conflict between students and administration; arrest of students and consequent school scandal; the death of a popular student; teacher strikes; major national disaster
- Before a holiday and before extended vacations
- Fridays in general; sometimes the first half of Monday
- Appearance of a substitute teacher
- The first few minutes of a period

This list could probably be extended from the experience of every teacher. Students respond in a number of ways to such situations. The major symptom is general restlessness, which communicates itself to all of the class; wriggling, giggling, squirming, inattention, inability to stop whispered conversations, short attention span, unexpected bursts of laughter at minor episodes, unusually loud voices—a kind of minor mass hysteria. After all, the students are part of a group, and group feelings are likely to pervade the classroom. A class can be happy, sullen, gay, silly, excited, voluble, or antagonistic, just as an individual can. This means that most students will react similarly, their faces will hold the same kind of look.

CLASSROOM PROCEDURES

In meeting discipline situations arising from student reaction to school life, the teacher's approach should be to deal with the group as a whole. The following courses of action are suggested:

Accept the feelings of the class. The wise teacher recognizes the contagion of restlessness and tension and does not consider this behavior a personal affront. It is unwise to become aggressive because such action will only bring retaliatory aggression from students. If the teacher gets angry, the class will get angry in turn. Nor does it help to become too worried and let the class observe this insecurity. It does help to note, with the kind of good humor most natural, the temper of the class.

Provide an activity in keeping with the class atmosphere. If a class's reactions are very different from its usual ones, the teacher should not expect to carry on regular class activities. Even if a specific activity has been scheduled, it is sometimes wiser, when a class is really restless or disturbed, to propose instead some active, interesting, and attention-getting device: a drill game (see Chapter 12), group quiz, or some other type of short-term activity (see Chapter 10), or general class discussion of a controversial topic of interest. All these approaches help to release the stored-up steam in students. A repertoire of such fall-back activities is very useful for such emergency situations.

Avoid using repressive or anxiety-producing devices. Some teachers have been known to spring a test on a class when it gets unruly. As a result, the teacher finds the class antagonistic and hostile. Future attempts to win students will be handicapped.

Do not give an assignment the night before a big game, or for the evening of the day when some major school activity is scheduled. The battles over assignments are cruel enough without provoking worse trouble. One teacher who failed to observe this principle was in periodic conflict with his class over delinquent homework. He seemed to go out of his way to give students lengthy themes on the nights of the league basketball games. Needless to say, he received few themes the next day, and had to face a belligerent group of students.

Discuss the problem with the class. The teacher can recognize the feelings and say, "Well, we all feel restless today; but work must go on. There are a number of important things to get done in class; how should we go about doing them so that our high spirits don't get in the way?" Such a statement will do much to establish rapport with the students. Talking things over also permits students to gain an objective view of their own behavior and enables them to modify it toward more adult patterns.

The types of student misbehavior considered in this section are undoubtedly familiar. So many of us, in our school careers, have indulged in such antics—to provoke? irritate? attract?—the teacher. There are some special hazards depending on the sex of the teacher.

MALE TEACHERS: SOME SPECIAL PROBLEMS

At least once a year a male teacher will find some female student who tries to get out of doing the work, to escape from a general application of the rules, by using "feminine wiles." These often involve coyness and pretentions of fragility and feminine incompetence. Another device that girls use on men teachers is "the weeps."

As one teacher remarked, "I'll do almost anything for a student rather than have her cry; when I see the danger signals—shiny eyes, trembling lip, shaking voice—I just want to run; so I say 'yes' before I know it, and am committed to something unfair to the other students."

Of course, some students are perfectly sincere; and since they are especially emotional during adolescence, tears come because of the stress of feelings. It is important to distinguish, however, between the genuine and the pretended emotion.

A handy box of tissues and a note of interested concern will rather quickly turn off the tears, and also provide time to assess the genuineness of the emotion.

Another problem is that young male teachers particularly may find themselves the object of some adolescent girl's displaced affection. Such adolescent crushes should be discouraged—tactfully, but decisively. Meetings or contacts with such a student alone should be avoided. A great deal of discretion must be exercised by male teachers in any situation that could even remotely be misconstrued by those prone to do so.

A few male teachers have found themselves accused of molesting students; this is a devastating charge to meet. In one state there were eighteen such charges in five years, and although all were cleared, many of the men left teaching permanently. One suburban junior-high-school teacher took a course in nonverbal communication. He learned that one can demonstrate caring for others by shaking their hands, patting them on the back, a gentle touch on the shoulder. He was soon accused of sexual abuse. He was, of course, cleared, and he took it with humor. But, as the account reported, "He was psychologically strong enough, one of the rare ones."[3] For men teachers, the rule is: *Never* touch a student, male or female. Harsh as this may sound, and important as one might feel that a friendly touch can often convey far more than any number of words, the unfortunate fact is that a rare student may misconstrue the gesture, for obscure and misguided reasons, and then the teacher is in deep trouble.

The teacher who is the object of a student's affection has to be careful. The poignant and eventually tragic case of a student crush described by Bel Kaufman in *Up the Down Staircase*[4] is an excruciating example of teacher insensitivity. Such situations do not usually result in overt tragedy, but they can be just as painfully cutting and destructive in the long run if not diplomatically handled.

WOMEN TEACHERS: SOME SPECIAL PROBLEMS

Women teachers sometimes feel handicapped because of their inability to use the implied threat of physical force to get the bigger boys to behave. Since many women teachers are actually shorter and slighter than the students they have in class, this fear is understandable. But the woman teacher should not therefore use unfair, or psychologically false, disciplinary methods. It is possible for a woman who is a mere five feet tall and weighs all of 103 pounds to be just as poised, calm, reasonable, and firm as a male teacher who was formerly a football star. Few schools will tolerate a teacher who continually uses physical force, so it is obvious that force is no real threat to the students in most school systems. Inner poise and an intelligent use of good educational practices are a woman teacher's best safeguards. Such a teacher should not be susceptible to the flattery of the mature boys

[3] *Washington Post*, November 8, 1977.
[4] Bel Kaufman, *Up the Down Staircase*. (Englewood Cliffs, N.J.: Prentice-Hall), 1965.

in her classes; they will use many of the wiles of their sisters, but may be more subtle about it.

Boys will get crushes on their female teachers, but they may be inhibited in their expressions of such feelings. Even so, there may be suggestions or intimations of a sexual nature to test the teacher's reaction. Written work may be handed in, containing passages with possible double meanings or—in some rare instances—statements that are clearly suggestive. The teacher's disapproval of such statements should be made clear.

A teacher who makes a federal case out of every lewd or suggestive note or comment she gets—particularly if she is young and attractive—will find life miserable. Instead of such comments being made in part to test the teacher, and in part to express newly found masculinity, the teacher may find herself the object of teasing bordering on the vicious. The best response is to ignore the message or comment completely, or to smile coolly and go on to other business.[5]

Women teachers should also be particularly aware of their dress and appearance. They do not need to dress in shapeless bags, without color or style, but it is the height of carelessness to wear see-through blouses or no bras under clinging sweaters. Unfortunately, both instances have occurred with what were reasonably intelligent student-teachers.

> When I was teaching in the mountains the students had few other diversions besides paying attention to the lives of the teachers. One of their favorite sports were loud comments on one's dress. I well recall monitoring the line of seniors practicing for graduation and having one of the older boys make a loud remark about how cute I looked in my form-fitting dress. It was a nice dress, it did fit me rather tightly. I did not wear it to school again. One day I was waiting to cross the highway that ran through the town with my roommate, the girls' P.E. teacher. A car full of happy students passed us and several gave loud wolf-whistles. I was infuriated. Mary, wiser than I by two years, said, *"Don't let that bother you. It's when they stop whistling that it hurts."*

The use of obscene words or phrases is another favorite device of students to goad women (and some men) teachers. Today's teachers are far more familiar with such words than were teachers a few decades back. In fact, one of the problems some teachers face is keeping their own language appropriate in class. But when students use such language, it is necessary to remind them that these words and phrases are inappropriate in a public place. No big issue need be made of this, or the teacher is asking for a torrent of obscenity.

> The class was furiously writing on the exam. Mrs. Lang was walking around checking their progress. All of a sudden there was a sharp crack, and Bill

[5] For a good example in fiction see: William Inge, *Good Luck, Miss Wyckoff* (Boston: Little, Brown, 1970).

yelled out, "Oh shit!" Everyone's head went up. Bill turned scarlet. Mrs. Lang said, "Back to work, everyone" and went over to find that Bill had broken his pencil. She told him where to get another. Incident over.

WHEN SCHOOLS DESEGREGATE

American schools were ordered to cease separating students by race in 1954. At the end of the 1970s many school systems were still facing acute and complex problems of school desegregation. Because of the pervasive and stubborn nature of prejudice, American society is still far from integrated. Housing and employment patterns keep most blacks in segregated situations. The same thing applies to Puerto Ricans and Chicanos. However, under court order, most school systems are or have faced desegregation so that despite where students live they will go to school in desegregated situations. When adults and community leaders make a major confrontation out of such desegregation practices there are bound to be repercussions within the school. The students bring to class the hostility and fear that they find at home. Interracial conflict is an unfortunate fact of life in a number of schools, with most of it occurring on the secondary school level.[6]

Intergroup conflict is most apt to erupt in school yards, in cafeterias, hallways, at games, outside of the classroom. Teachers can contribute to such conflict by partisan acts and words, or they can contribute to reducing such conflict by skillful and sensitive teaching. The teacher should:

* avoid any racial words or phrases
* be scrupulously fair to all, neither expecting too much nor too little of any group
* provide many opportunities for students of all groups to work closely together so that they get to know each other
* be careful to assume student friction has a base in intergroup hostility
* try to include any relevant content which relates to the minority groups in one's class
* discuss school or community problems, if any, with the class even if it is not part of one's lessons
* demonstrate one's openness by making friends with teachers of all groups
* show that prejudiced or biased remarks are out of place in the classroom
* monitor texts and classroom materials for biased representations

[6] Daniel U. Levine and Robert J. Havighurst (Eds.), *The Future of Big-City Schools* (Berkeley: McCutchan, 1977), pp. 156–160.

SUMMARY

Mr. Warner was the worst teacher I ever had the displeasure to have. He taught eleventh-grade math. First, he was rather old, close to retirement. He was the classic crotchety old man. His was the one and only way. He would come to class with his collar up, cuff or shirt buttons undone and even his pants zipper half-way sometimes. The later in the day it was the more disheveled he looked. He'd teach to the blackboard constantly. Erasers were unheard of. If he made a mistake it was hand or sleeve to smudge it around. On the rare occasions when he faced the class, he'd always lean against the blackboard directly in front of the problem we were discussing. The one redeeming aspect was that when he'd eventually turn back to lecture the board at least we could see the problem on his jacket. Besides his sartorial attire and miserable mannerisms, there was simply no communication between him and the class. No wonder he thought we behaved badly; we had no other alternative.

How many years do you plan to remain in teaching? Five years? Ten years? Thirty years? The chances are that if you stay five years you will stay the next thirty. No one wants to end up like Mr. Warner. The time to start is at the beginning. The development of a valid teaching style, continual consciousness of one's relationships with subject matter and with students, working with others in the school to keep administrative procedures supportive will go a long way to insure a productive and satisfying teaching career. It takes self-discipline to provide good discipline.

The discussion of discipline continues in the next chapter, where we will consider the ways in which students are the sources of discipline problems, and consider what approaches to discipline have the greatest promise for success. Readings on discipline will be found at the end of the next chapter.[7]

---

[7] See pp. 437–438 for Selected Readings for both Chapters 15 and 16.

FOCUS ON CHAPTER 16

Although the research evidence is slim, it is probable that most of the classroom disruptions which bother teachers arise from the normal behavior of adolescents acting like adolescents. Understanding such normal behavior is the best preventive medicine for the teacher who then can judge how seriously to respond. Most classroom misbehavior responds to normal requests to cease and desist. But students, like other human beings, may also have troubles which go deeply into their personality structure, and when these troubles surface in classroom misbehavior then it takes wisdom and restraint to know what to do.

Significant ideas presented in this chapter include:

- Learning how to differentiate between behavior which is normal and behavior which is abnormal requires sensitivity and skill on the part of the teacher; experience is a great help, however.
- One of the most useful behaviors for the teacher to acquire in dealing with normal misbehavior is keeping cool and calm and not overreacting.
- Although there are increasing reports of in-school violence, and use of drugs and alcohol by youth, the seriousness of these problems may be overstated; it is also true that schools are gaining in sophistication of ways to deal with these problems.
- The teacher's best help is to utilize a democratic approach to school discipline and develop a style of discipline consistent with one's own personality and values.

chapter 16

Troublemakers II: discipline problems and students

The secondary school teacher must live with an average of over 100 students a day. For sheer self-preservation, an atmosphere of relaxation, interest, and quiet order should prevail. But adolescents have many life experiences to explore, understand, and absorb. These pressures, both social and personal, make it difficult for many students to accept gracefully the numerous demands of the school and to perform the tasks of learning in a compliant and interested fashion. This chapter will discuss the problems that arise out of students' adjustment as adolescents in American culture and the problems that arise from the deeper personality needs of individuals.

Finally, the overall problem of discipline in terms of a philosophy of discipline will be considered. It is important to establish a frame of reference which will enable teachers to distinguish effective, mature, constructive, democratic discipline from repressive, punitive, and destructive procedures.

WHEN STUDENTS ARE THE CAUSE OF CLASSROOM PROBLEMS

Many acts that disturb orderly classroom learning are merely the result of adolescents acting like adolescents; other kinds of misbehavior arise out of deep, unmet needs of individual personality.

An analysis of the kinds of misbehavior which particularly plague teachers and disrupt classrooms reveals four major categories whose primary cause can be said to lie with the students themselves. These are:

- Discipline situations arising from student–student interaction.
- Discipline situations arising from student reaction to school routines and institutional procedures.

- Discipline situations arising from immediate personality needs: "adolescents acting like adolescents."
- Discipline situations arising from long-term personality needs.

WHEN STUDENT INTERACTION IS DISRUPTIVE

Students cannot be expected to behave if seated day after day beside someone they detest anymore than adults can be expected to control their feelings in a similar situation. A discipline situation may also arise from the reaction of students to others they like very much. The kinds of problems for the teacher that arise in the area of student–student interaction are primarily the following:

1. Continued and disturbing conversations
2. Passing notes
3. One student's dependence on another for his or her work
4. Flirtations
5. Cheating

Below are some typical examples.

1. The sophomore class had just returned from an assembly. Ms. Maxwell realized beforehand that the class would probably be full of energy and would want to discuss the assembly and for approximately fifteen minutes he discussed with them their reactions to the assembly. After ample energy and tension had been released through discussions, she led into the topic for the day. The conversion was neatly done and completely unrecognized by the class as a control measure.

2. Sherman and Gerald were seated one behind the other and were obviously close pals. The two had been assigned, as a joint task, the job of presenting an oral report to the class. Mr. Span asked Gerald to read to the class a portion of a set of printed regulations governing sanitation in restaurants. Gerald didn't reply at once, but his friend Sherman volunteered to do it instead. Mr. Span said that he wanted Gerald to read it. Gerald announced that he "guessed" that he had "left it home." Mr. Span told him to speak extemporaneously, telling the class whatever he could remember. Gerald did so. Actually, the printed matter was on his desk the whole time. Later, Mr. Span discovered that Gerald, a ninth-grade student, was for all practical purposes a "nonreader" and very self-conscious about it. His friend Sherman "carried him along," trying to do all his work for him.

3. One day Miss Swann left the room for a few minutes. Several students began to play "catch" with paper wads. This caused noise, and Miss Swann heard it on her way back to the classroom. Her manner was quiet but firm; she expressed disappointment in the disrupters and said she was sorry that she couldn't trust them. The students respected her and showed obvious shame for causing trouble.

4. A group of ninth-grade girls, including the daughters of two of the most

influential families in the district, accused a group of four Mexican-American boys of saying nasty things to them. The boys denied it. The leader of the group of girls insisted; and since she had never been known to lie, the boys were reprimanded, deprived of participation in the baseball game, and restricted in their activities to a very small portion of the school-yard. The next day one of the boys refused to come to school. The others were sulky and rebellious, especially toward the teacher. Mr. Bell, the principal, asked the pupil personnel worker to talk to them. That afternoon one girl came to Mr. Bell. She told him that the boys had really been speaking Spanish and had said nothing bad. The other girls had not understood and had given the words their own interpretation. Mr. Bell called the boys in and apologized.

5. In the class there were about fifteen boys and ten girls. Mr. Pasqual was lecturing in a monotonous low tone; and while the boys were being noisy, the teacher ignored them. Then one of the boys picked a hammer from the shelf and hit another boy on the knee—apparently to check his reflexes. The teacher jumped up and separated the boys, but the class had broken into laughter. Mr. Pasqual then said very sternly, "Don't anyone laugh without my permission!" The class became quiet again, and the two boys were placed on opposite sides of the room. Mr. Pasqual had just settled back in his chair when one of the boys raised his hand. The teacher recognized him and he asked, "May I laugh?" There was not much order restored for the remainder of the period.

6. The class was supposed to be reading the assigned section of the text. At one point a noticeable din was heard coming from a table toward the rear of the class where six girls were seated. They had been quietly talking and laughing, but it had become rather loud and clearly distracting to both the teacher and the students. Mr. Brzowski jumped to his feet and called to one of the girls. He told her that she had been warned enough in the past and to leave the classroom; he would speak to her later. The girl protested that she hadn't been talking, so why should she leave the room? The teacher said she should leave because he had told her to. Again she said she hadn't been talking and the whole scene repeated itself. Finally, when the teacher didn't back down, the girl left.

The examples above show both poor and good practices in relation to some of the typical disturbances created by student interaction. It should be helpful to summarize the teachers' most effective tactics in dealing with them.

CHATTER, CHATTER

Ignore the conversation if the rest of the class is absorbed in activity. The students who are talking may eventually be drawn into the group activity without requiring a special reprimand.

Walk around the room, making it a point to stand near students who are more likely to talk than others. If a student report is going on, the teacher should quietly take a stand near any place where some trouble may emerge. Thus, control can be inconspicuously exercised.

Call the students for a special conference. Discuss the problems they create with the class; ask them for a solution.

Discuss the problem with the whole class if the disturbance is sufficiently widespread. Ask the class to agree on how to behave and to set up rules that should be observed. Have the rules posted if necessary. Thus the attention of offenders can be called to the rule they themselves made.

Study students who talk continually. Do they have a special problem? They may be completely confused by the work. They may have missed class sessions or be beyond their intellectual depth. Or, they may have finished all their work and need extra assignments. Some talkers are exhibitionists and have to learn how to channel this bid for attention. These are best handled by giving them ample opportunity to talk, not by stifling them.

Separating friends who seem to encourage each other to misbehave works no miracles! Instead of giggling together in the middle of the room, they may communicate across the whole breadth or length of the room and inconvenience that many more students. It is wiser to discuss the matter with the offenders, helping them see the benefits of being allowed to stay together and the possible penalty of separation if they refuse to do some self-disciplining.

PASSING NOTES

Like any other student–student disturbance, note-passing is often a symptom of classwork that is boring and lacks challenge, or of pressing home problems. The main problem then is not the note, but a need to introduce a greater variety of activity into the classroom.

Never read a note aloud to a class; it may be highly embarrassing to you and crucifying for a student:

Carol, I really don't know what to do. I'm really mixed up!!! I really mean it. I don't want to stay here, because all I do is get screamed at, my parents don't trust me, they won't let me go out at night, what's the use of staying? The only reason I have to stay is my friends (YOU) and Tom, but Tom's leaving anyway. Diane wants him and Jeff to go with us. I would really feel safer then, but if I get caught with boys, my mother would never forgive me. EVER.

She'd probably take me to the doctor to get a test to see if I was pregnant. Oh GOD Carol, I don't know what to do. I just feel like leaving and never ever coming back, because this place is really, really messed up. I really mean it!!![1]

[1] Jean D. Grambs, "Youth and Educational Discomfort," *The National Elementary Principal*, 47 (May 1968), pp. 10–19.

A teacher found another note lying on the floor after the class had left. What do you think would have happened had this one been read aloud in class:

What bra size do you think Mrs. Reed wears? I say a 36C but Bob says it's probably a 38B.

Passing notes usually means students are bored. If they have interesting work to do, and are expected to be working on it in class, there is little time for note-passing. Sometimes notes are very serious. One teacher ran across this one:

Can you get the name of the Hot Line for me? I have to find out about an abortion, quick!

FRIENDSHIPS

Leave a dependent friendship alone until a more desirable substitute is ready. The students usually need each other and should not be deprived of help until better relationships with others can be built. Give them joint projects; use group methods to wean them slowly away from each other if it seems desirable. Find some skill on the part of the dependent student and encourage him or her to develop it.

SEX IS HERE TO STAY

Do not try to meet any problems head-on. A person intent on attracting the attention of the opposite sex will do so whether or not permitted to. The problem is best met by permitting more, rather than less, socialization by way of content-centered group work so that students can become acquainted without having to disrupt the class to do so. Then, if the problem continues, the teacher has a firm basis upon which to discuss the actions with the offending person.

Avoid making a public issue of the situation. Students will be quick to laugh at the teacher who tries to shame students into ceasing flirtations. The teacher will only gain the reputation of being stodgy and will have made the problem worse. (A dramatic example of this occurs in the short film *No Reason To Stay.* See film list in Appendix 3.)

Do not make fun of the interpersonal relations of students:

Sarah and David had been going together since junior high school. Everyone in the school knew about their friendship. They were seen together everywhere, but usually were not in the same class. They finally managed to take the same psychology class. Mr. Smith found the situation irresistible. At any opportunity he would ask one or the other a question, and then make a crack about their "love-life" causing Sarah to blush crimson and David to clench his teeth. Neither of them liked the class and did as little work for it as possible.

Remember, the secondary school is the greatest matching game in the country. It is here that many boys and girls find their first romantic and/or sex interest. For many of them the opposite sex is the only important reason to be in school at all; classes are an interference with their chief preoccupation!

> You know, between the ages of sixteen and eighteen I actually counted how many men I went to bed with. I kept a running list. I counted four hundred and twenty-five, and then I stopped counting . . .
> "In school I was always getting into trouble. I'd smoke in the bathroom, I'd ditch classes, I'd try and break all the rules. I required a lot of excitement and a lot of stimulation. . . . Why not? I felt the school was so ridiculous. I'd seen a little more of life. The teachers were so dry.[2]

This kind of girl is beyond the reach of the school. Only with wise counsel, support from parents, maybe even a change of location, can this life-style be changed.

CHEATING

Reorganize test or assignment structure. Cheating occurs when the teacher has made it impossible for students either to learn the right answers or to achieve good grades by acceptable means. See also the discussion of cheating in Chapter 13.

Discuss the problem of cheating with the class. Examine the consequences of cheating and suggest that the class think through the problem.

Lift pressure off individuals who consistently cheat. Provide such students with other ways of gaining recognition for achievement.

Provide the opportunity to do poor work over. In this way, students will not be forced to cheat in order to make good on the one chance provided.

Discuss cooperative learning. In this way students can help one another without being guilty of cheating.

OTHER SITUATIONS

It would be impossible to provide examples of all the ways students can find to create disturbances, or all of the ways teachers have found to deal with them. Here are a few examples of additional situations handled with varying degrees of adequacy:

---

[2] Michael Medved and David Wallechinsky, *What Really Happened to the Class of '65?* (New York: Ballantine Books, 1976), p. 27.

When I entered the room it was too dark to see what was going on. However, when I got used to it, I found the class supposedly watching a film on pollution. The picture was quite small on the distant screen, and as far as I could tell not very many students were paying attention. At least three students were sleeping, two students were whispering on the side, and the rest looked with zombie-like attitude at a not very engrossing film. "What can I do?" the teacher told me later. "This film is the favorite one of the head of the department and he says we have to show it. It bores me and bores the kids, so I don't bother them when they misbehave while it is being shown. I have really good stuff on pollution we work on and they know it."

The class was a tenth-grade English class engaged in poetry reading and oral interpretation. The class was reading such poems as "The Pilgrim Fathers," "Chicago," "Thanatopsis," and "The Road Not Taken." In the midst of all this serious reading, Rocky jumped to the stage and began in his most resonant, solemn voice, "Hickory Dickory Dock. The mouse ran up the clock . . ." The class became hysterical with laughter. So did the teacher.

The class was just getting seated when Joe came in. As he walked past Mike, Mike put out his foot and tripped him. Joe slugged Mike in response. As the fight was getting under way, Ms. Strumlauf, the teacher, walked in, quickly sat down at the piano and sounded a chord; class began. The fight was stopped. The students took their seats and paid close attention. The whole class expected to be reprimanded, but no mention of the incident was made.

A girl in business law class had been absent a few days and had just returned to school. Starting at the beginning of the period, she began talking to the other girls sitting in her immediate vicinity. At first the talking did not disturb the class, but as it prolonged it grew louder. The teacher asked the girl to be quiet but in a few minutes the talking began again. Miss Thomann, a young woman, said to the girl that she realized that she had just come back to school and had a lot of news to catch up on, but couldn't she do it after class? She said this with such obvious good humor that the other members of the class laughed with her, and the girl said she was sorry and stopped talking.

WHEN ADOLESCENTS ACT THEIR AGE

Some discipline situations arise primarily because adolescents are adolescents. It is important to distinguish these normal manifestations of misbehavior from the deeper personality problems and disorders that will be dealt with later in the chapter. How does a teacher know whether student misbehavior is merely surface reaction or something deeper? One psychologist[3] has suggested a way of distinguishing the two: The surface

[3] Roger G. Barker, "On Discipline," Unpublished lecture (August 1950), Stanford University.

misbehavior can be controlled by external means. That is, the surface act of aggression, as an expression of ordinary adolescent reaction to adult authority, can be dealt with by a firm tone, by a brief nod, or by being ignored. The student relinquishes the misbehavior easily when the adult toward whom it is directed acts reasonably and confidently. But discipline problems that arise because adolescents are genuinely troubled, either by basic maladjustment in their whole personality structure or because they must endure impossible home, school, or environmental situations, have the following characteristics:

1. They persist; they do not respond to normal teacher control.
2. They are manifest in many kinds of unruly actions.
3. There seems to be no logical connection between one misbehavior and another.

Personality may be thought of as layers of reaction systems; superficial misbehavior comes from the periphery of the personality; deep behavior problems come from the central core of the personality. Both may have similar manifestations; but, as previously noted, the surface problem can be handled by normal teacher control; the deep one cannot.

The kinds of superficial misbehavior indicated here are the following:

Failure to do homework or an assignment
Refusal to obey a teacher request
Impudence
Student-provoked "accidents" and other minor misbehaviors

Skillful handling of disciplinary problems such as these is a major factor in teacher success.

WHEN ASSIGNMENTS ARE NOT DONE

The basic problem in handling any of the above situations is, of course, the attitude of the teacher toward what appears to be a breach of discipline. If we view failure to do an assignment as a personal affront, then punishment is the only recourse. On the other hand, if failure to do an assignment is a problem that concerns both the teacher and the student, then it is open to mutual discussion. Why do students fail to do assignments? Some possible reasons are:

1. Assignments are unclear.
2. Assignments are dull, irrelevant, or stupid.
3. Assignments are too difficult for an individual.
4. No place at home to do the assignment.

CLASSROOM PROCEDURES

In dealing with failure to do assignments, you will want to check your teaching practices (see section on assignments, Chapter 6) and then consider other causes. When failure to do an assignment results from these other causes, the best policy is to deal with the problem on an individual basis.

Since the area of assignments is one of the major battlegrounds between teacher and student, it may be well to cite a few important strategic errors to avoid:

Do not demand a public explanation from each student who failed to do the assignment. One will be forthcoming. The class clown will quickly rise to the occasion and make a wisecrack that will set the class laughing at the teacher.

Do not argue with one student in front of the entire class regarding what he/she did, or did not do, on an assignment. If it appears that a student is going to start an argument, the teacher should immediately divert the discussion "Well, Sally, perhaps we had better discuss this later, when it won't take time away from the rest of the class. Now . . ." and continue with a comment directing the attention of the class to the work ahead.

Do not let failure to do assignments continue without taking action. The student may need help. Do not assume that the whole process of self-discipline has been fully learned by every class member. Many need support, specific study aid, and basic understanding to get them further along the road to maturity.

The teacher who says, "Well, if they don't get their assignments in, let them suffer the consequences at the end of the semester" is doing a grave disservice to students.

Do not forget the obligation implicit in giving an assignment. Giving an assignment and then forgetting to collect it, or failing to return it, or returning it late are all evidences of poor teaching. Students will not do assignments in such an atmosphere.

Some students refuse to do assignments because they find them a waste of time. One school official complained that some teachers may assign ten problems to illustrate one principle; students who discover this to be so will become bored and not bother to finish. If the assignment is obviously busywork then the battle over doing it becomes a losing war for both students and teachers. *No assignment should be given that does not contribute something visible in learning increments for the student.*

What about collusion on homework assignments? Many teachers have suspected that much individual homework is really a group effort. Indeed, with the ubiquitous telephone, it is a rare student who will not consult friends when stuck on a problem. This kind of cooperation cannot be stopped; threats are futile. The importance and significance of doing the homework individually in order to understand the process must be emphasized, and the fact that having help in doing the work will only cripple the student in the long run must be underlined. In addition, students who find difficulty with the assignment should be assured of help at school, so that if indeed a student does not understand the assignment this does not become a reason for failure to do it.

What punishment should be dealt out for failure to do assignments? The whole procedure should be clearly discussed with the class, and procedures agreed upon. Since the type of assignment varies with each subject, different rules should apply. The main point is that whatever is agreed upon works. If the rules don't work, reexamine them—with the class.

A final word: whenever superficial misbehavior is being dealt with, the teacher must keep in mind one cardinal principle: *Never construe student misbehavior as a personal attack.* As soon as a teacher feels that student misbehavior, of whatever sort, is a personal affront and a challenge to individual authority, then effective response is stifled. The ensuing process becomes a confrontation, which often results in a humiliated student and a hostile and sour teacher. Remember, one has to live all one's life with the style of interpersonal relations one establishes in class. It is not enjoyable to live with an atmosphere of suspicion, resentment, and threat. This is an important principle which also applies to the situations examined below, which usually arise from the periphery of the student's personality.

Refusal To Obey a Request

Mrs. Jerome was conducting an oral reading period. In a friendly manner, she asked Phillip to read, just as she had asked others to read. He refused. The first time this happened she passed over it and went on to another student. "But," she asked a teacher down the hall, "what shall I do the next time it happens?"

The teacher has several ways of dealing with a situation like this. For example:

- Never call on the student again for that activity. The student may never learn how to read orally, but he is also prevented from making a real issue out of it with the teacher.
- Give him an F, tell him you have done so, and continue to call on him when it is his turn.
- Insist that he do his task as the other students have done theirs.

- Wait until it happens again. If it does, accept his refusal. Then check his cumulative record, talk to other teachers, and finally ask him to talk with you about his school work.

It should be obvious that the fourth course of action is most likely to produce some workable solution. Why?

As observed in Chapter 15, beginning teachers usually enter the classroom with expectations that discipline situations will develop. But note what can result from the assumption that students will misbehave.

> It was the day after the first United States spaceship made its orbit of the earth. In art class the teacher instructed the students to express their feelings. I was observing in the class and noticed that one of the students was busily painting a realistic replica of a spacecraft. I strolled over to his desk and watched him work for some time. When he finished, I commented on his fine work and asked him his name. "John Glenn," he replied curtly. "What's yours?"
>
> "Franklin D. Roosevelt," I replied. He looked at me with a very puzzled expression on his face. Later, after class, I asked the teacher what the student's name was who had drawn the spacecraft. "John Glenn," she replied.

Although the circumstances in this instance were unusual, the expectation that students would "smart off" caused the beginning teacher to get off on the wrong foot with at least one student. The expectation of unreasonable or inappropriate behavior can cause the very situation one wishes to avoid. Contrary to this, *the expectation of reasonable behavior*, of good behavior, is a potent tool in the hand of the teacher. It is particularly effective in dealing with incipient refusal to comply with a teacher request. But this expectation can exist only if the teacher has made the basic assumption that the student is not really trying to harass the teacher but is reacting as a growing adolescent to a symbol of adult authority.

Refusal may be reasonable and understandable. It is only the consistent or aggressive refusal that warrants action by the teacher. If the teacher follows up a refusal to obey and finds that a student has a reason that is—at least from point of view of the student—valid, the teacher can express interest or concern, or admit not realizing a problem existed. A bond is established with a student when it is realized that the teacher considers personal problems more important than unquestioning conformity.

> My most embarrassing moment, the one I squirm over even now at the ripe age of 25, took place in chorus. I was 16, and although I had been menstruating since the age of 12 those few days were always times of acute discomfort. I was always sure I would have an "accident." And in chorus, that day, the telltale feeling of unusual wetness forced itself on me. I didn't know if it would show or not. I didn't dare chance it. When Miss Anderson rapped with her stick for us to get up, I just couldn't. She repeated the

rapping. I sat. Everyone looked at me. She gave me a queer look, then ignored me, and went on to the practice. After everyone had left, I was still sitting. She looked at me. "Well," she said. "It's just that time of month, Miss Anderson," I said, trembly. "Sorry," she said, and smiled, and started putting away the music. I rushed out. No, I hadn't any problem, but I really loved Miss A for her willingness to give me the benefit of the doubt when I refused to stand up.

Should the teacher ever force the issue, insisting that the student obey? A teacher should recognize a situation with a disturbing recalcitrant student for what it is—a struggle for power, student against teacher. The teacher may feel a need to win in order to assure any kind of future authority over the class. A public showdown between two personalities can be highly embarrassing for the teacher. Showdowns, when necessary, should always be conducted in private. To test the limits of authority, to see how far one can push authority without getting stopped, is a genuine emotional need for some individuals, particularly young children. They try to find out just how far they can go before Mother or Dad rises in wrath. Similarly, some immature adolescents (and some adults) who have found the authorities in their world somewhat unreliable and inconsistent will continue to try out the limits of any authority situation. They will see just how long they can continue aggressive or annoying behavior. The refusal to obey is one such manifestation.

The teacher who understands this need to defy authority responds to it by saying, in effect. "Eddie, you seem to want to find out how much you can get away with in this class before I will get angry. Well, I don't think that will solve anything. But I suggest that we might talk together later about how I, and the rest of the class, expect you to behave as a member of our group." And the teacher then proceeds to attend to the concern of the rest of the class. Shortly thereafter, a follow-up interview will be needed (see Chapter 17). But the follow-up should take place only after sufficient time has elapsed for the emotional reactions to have passed; then both teacher and student can calmly consider the roots of the rebellion.

IMPUDENCE

A parent who visited a school recently made the following observation:

The trouble with our modern schools is that the kids are just too fresh. Why, I heard a student whistle when Miss Green walked by. Another one saw me, waved his hand, and called out, "Hi, Mr. Jenkins," right in the middle of class. These kids are learning disrespect for adult authority; we need more discipline in our schools.

Parents of teenagers are very vulnerable to adolescent attack. They particularly resent their own inability to make young people cease unpleasant behavior. Therefore, it is quite common to hear parents call upon the school to do the job of disciplining or complain that if the schools had only done a decent job, the young people would not be as they are. It is true that in homes where a good working relationship exists between all members of the family, the impudent remark is rare; in a home in which there is tension and uncertain authority, young people may react to lack of security by being sassy.

Some actual classroom anecdotes are given here:

> Attention was excellent during discussion of four questions. After Mr. Rose caused the wisecracker who said December 20, 1860, was "five days before Christmas" to be expelled from the room, the class paid attention in a subdued manner.

When is the teacher justified in expelling a student? It is highly probable that the teacher in this example was reacting too severely. The remark was funny, not necessarily impudent. The teacher turned the remark into an attack upon himself. Perhaps the class remained docile, but it was coerced by fear of arbitrary punishment. Are these students learning anything about self-discipline? Are they learning to like the subject of the course? Are they developing attitudes of contempt for the wisdom of adults?

> During a question period, one of the students asked a foolish question, which was accompanied by the sudden flash of giggling. This attempt at impudence was nipped in the bud by Miss Arto, who simply said, "Bob knows that is a silly question, so I won't bother to answer it." With this phrase, Bob was halted, and the class returned to the discussion.

In this anecdote, the teacher meets the attack head-on. She feels that the question is foolish; she suspects that the student knows it; she makes it clear that she is not taken in by it. The tone of voice used by the teacher is the vital factor in the success of this procedure. Unfortunately, it is often a tone heavily loaded with sarcasm, hostility, irritation, or anger. In this example, the statement that the teacher "won't be bothered" gives a somewhat faulty emphasis. It is the class whose time should not be taken to discuss a foolish question. The teacher might more wisely say, "Bob, that seems like a question that is somewhat off the point. We are now discussing the important parts of our topic today. Perhaps we can get to your question later."

It is important to remember that the teacher's initial judgment of a question as foolish may be erroneous. The student may genuinely be seeking a point of information. Therefore, Miss Arto might better leave a loophole for the student to rephrase his question; or, if the class reaction differs from that of the teacher, she could quickly assess this by a glance around the room and retract the hasty judgment. She might say, "Well, I can see by your faces that this question is on your minds also. I didn't think it was a serious question, but apparently I was wrong. Now, Joe, what do you think the answer to Bob's question might be?"

> A boy in the class gave an impression of insolence in his replies to Mr. Basle's questions. Mr. Basle pointed him out to me: "Now take that student. He looks like a troublemaker but is really a good student who can do good work and usually does. His surface attitude isn't very encouraging; but if handled right, he works hard. It's very important to avoid starting off on the wrong foot with him."

This example speaks for itself. Here is a teacher recognizing the need of some students to test the limits. This teacher sees that if he, the teacher, can react to the real need of the student and not feel that as a teacher he must be dominant in every relationship, he will be helping the student to outgrow his urge to attack authority.

> Miss Swizzle (not her real name) had an annoying habit of playing "feminine." We boys got really annoyed with her silly giggle and look of helplessness when she wanted one of the big old-fashioned windows open. "Oh, I wonder if I have a big strong man who can open this big old window for me!" she would gush. One day Steve said in a whisper loud enough to be heard at the state capitol, "Why doesn't the old fart do it herself?" Miss Swizzle gasped, and as though to help her out of her own mess, several of the boys nearest her gruntingly got up and opened the window. That was the last time she giggled that silly way with us, though. But my brother who had her the next year told me she was still doing it with them; and how they hated it.

It is clear that no teacher can stand for consistent "fresh" behavior—the insulting, stage-whisper wisecrack; the insolent retort; the deliberate use of vulgar, near-obscene, or actually obscene language; the provocative, needling question. Sometimes this behavior is simply a deliberate baiting of the teacher; youngsters try out on teachers the same devices that, unfortunately, work on parents. Some typical devices of this nature are: contrasting one teacher's methods with another, with a clear implication that one is less successful; drawing a teacher into a futile "tis-'taint" debate or "Yes, I did—No, you didn't" dispute; arguing a point of behavior in front of the class. The student usually gets the better of this kind of argument, since in such a classroom climate the longer the teacher can be kept arguing and away from work, the more fellow students approve. When a teacher senses impudence either in an individual or in a group of students, one goes through some searching self-examination to detect one's own contribution to the situation as in the case of Miss Swizzle:

- Do I expect insulting behavior?
- Do I respond violently to any sign of attack?
- Do I lose my sense of humor as soon as I suspect a student is being fresh?
- Am I consistent in my relations with the class—happy one day and tired or hard or chaotic the next?
- Do I react to the slightest move on the part of a very few students? Are these students to whom I overreact outside my cultural group; that is, are they on a lower socioeconomic level, of a different racial group, of a different ethnic group?
- Am I easy to bait? Do I get trapped by a student inquiry and descend to an argument with one student while the rest of the class listens with delight to the teacher being "taken"?

If the teacher concludes, after a searching self-inquiry, that a real behavior problem exists in the students themselves, the next step is to find which individuals in the class seem to be responsible for most of this type of trouble. An examination of office records and a comparison with other teachers' experiences may give the teacher some explanation of the behavior of these students. Armed with some prior knowledge, special recognition can be provided—a special leadership role or perhaps significant class responsibility—for the students who are most prone to impudence. Then individual conferences should follow. The teacher's role in these conferences should be primarily to help students recognize those feelings about themselves and about school which give rise to outbursts.

"ACCIDENTS" DO OCCUR

Adolescents have an undeniable fondness for the unexpected. These "accidents" illustrate familiar minor behavior problems:

> One day there was a slight disturbance when Jack almost fell into the aisle because his chair leg had given way. The students near him laughed a little. He blushed and giggled. Mr. Abrams looked at him and smiled. The rest of the class didn't appear to notice what had happened at all.

> This was a commercial subject and intended primarily for girls. Of the boys who did enroll, most were there because they thought it was an easy course. This was especially true of the one senior in the class. "Red" seemed to be the ringleader in devising practical jokes. One day he kicked the chair out from under Jeff, who was sitting with his chair tilted back. Mr. Roamer asked Red whether he was the one who had kicked the chair. But before Red could answer, Jeff said he had merely slipped. Mr. Roamer gave Red a look that implied he knew differently. The class continued its work.

Overreacting to a student mishap is usually a weak way of dealing with such occurrences:

Silence had descended on the room. Heads were bowed over test papers, pencils busily scraping over the desks. Each student was a model of concentration. "Ah-ah-ah-ah-choo!" came from the middle of the room. Everyone looked up, startled. A flurry of giggling passed through the class. Miss Henrich stalked up to Dave and snatched his paper from him. "That was completely unnecessary young man," she snapped. "Next time you have to sneeze, be polite enough to use a handkerchief. The rest of you get back to your test. Dave, you see me after school." Angry, annoyed, and puzzled looks could be observed on the faces of the students.

CLASSROOM PROCEDURES

A sense of humor, an ability to keep from overreacting, and an expectation of compliance with a reasonable request are the major requirements for meeting these so-called accidents. For accidents do happen; sometimes just to break the monotony, sometimes out of adolescent deviltry, but often because a book really is too near the edge of the desk, or a chair leg does collapse from overwork, or Susy really does have the hiccups. At any rate, the troublemakers should not be singled out for front-row seats. Teachers sometimes believe that these prominent positions inhibit misbehavior. This is rarely the case. Instead, mischievous students now have the whole class behind them to observe their pranks. Incidentally, when teachers talk in front of a group, note where their eyes fall: not on those in the front row, but rather on the students in the middle seats in the middle rows.

Sometimes students substitute startling behavior for accidents.

Miss Sanchez was correcting sentences on the chalkboard. She had her back turned and just as she turned to the class she saw John, who was sitting next to the side board, write someone else's name plus a nickname under his own work. When she came to John's work, she said nothing but drew a line through the fake name.

When incidents such as these occur, the teacher should ask, "Is this important enough to disturb the process of learning?" Sometimes teachers take so much time in conflict with students over minor disturbances that little time is left for creating a good learning atmosphere. It is often wisest to ignore petty disturbances. An isolated expression of adolescent exuberance is not a sign of poor discipline and should not be treated as such.

One student teacher reported the following:

Several students were at the chalkboard working on problems. One of the students kept "squeaking" his chalk, much to the amusement of the class. I told him that if he would hold the chalk properly, it wouldn't squeak; but he said he wasn't doing it purposely. Finally, in exasperation, I said, "Here, let me show you!" When I grabbed the chalk and drew a line on the board, it squeaked louder than ever. The class roared with laughter—I had to laugh, too.

However, if the disturbance is likely to disrupt the class continually, or is a symptom of a need on the part of the student to attract attention and gain recognition, the teacher must prepare to deal with it in the same way as was suggested for impudent behavior.

To close this section, here are two incidents in which students were given permission to leave the room but returned late.

> Just before the start of the class, Grace asked permission to go to her locker. Mrs. Hope allowed her this privilege, and she departed. Some fifteen minutes later she reentered the room, somewhat hesitantly, to be greeted with these words: "Pardon me, Grace, but just where is your locker? Is it in this building?" The young lady flushed and took her seat and considerable laughter, much of it coming from the left corner of the room, where the boys clustered.

> Every day at 2:30 for a week, Tom, one of the older boys in the class, asked for a restroom excuse. On Friday, when Tom asked at the usual time, Mr. Ruml kidded him and told him that this appeared to be quite a habit. Tom was slightly embarrassed. He did not ask for permission to leave in the days that followed.

The technique of public humiliation used in the first example is very unwise. The best procedure would be to ignore the late return, to treat it as though it had never happened, but to make a point of talking with the girl in private later. At that time, without an audience, the teacher might tactfully suggest that such a prolonged absence should be explained, although she personally is sure Grace must have had a very good reason. The teacher expresses, here, the assumption that the student's motives are acceptable. This kind of assumption is the quickest route toward obtaining acceptable behavior. Suspicion on the part of the teacher breeds distrust and defiance on the part of the student. It is important to remember that there are as many legitimate reasons for a student to be away from class for prolonged periods of time as there are illegitimate reasons. Students may have physical problems which require them to be absent, suddenly, and which they are reluctant to discuss or explain to a teacher. There may be an urgent phone call which was suddenly remembered. Even if the reason is, in the view of the teacher, not acceptable, care should be taken to avoid a confrontation in front of the whole class. The situation should be dealt with when the student is alone and without an audience.

ABSENTEEISM

According to one report, absenteeism is the major discipline problem of the late 1970s.[4] In one school the daily absence rate is 17 percent; in another, one-fourth are reported to miss at least one period of class a day.

[4] *Time*, 110 (November 14, 1977), pp. 62–75.

The assumption is that students absent from class cannot learn the material adequately. Unfortunately, this is not necessarily the case. Absence from class may be due to genuine illness or personal emergency. These are certainly acceptable reasons. Why, then, are students absent so frequently, as school after school report? The main reason may well be that there is nothing worth going to class for. If a student can learn all that is needed to pass the tests or do the homework without coming to class, why go there and be bored? If class attendance really is not necessary in order to learn the material, if it is boring, if the teacher is so unaware of what students are doing that there is no incentive to come, then students will accordingly stay away.

There was a regular pattern to the absences of at least five students in Mr. Glass' first period class. Typically, Monday was missed, and often Friday. He noticed, in checking, that they would often turn up later, so they only missed the first or second period. Thus they got out of having to get excuses from home. After considering the problem, and realizing that these students were not flunking the course—nor doing very brilliantly either— he devised a new procedure. He organized the class into "study groups." He gave each group a set of questions on the topic being studied. Monday was report day. Each study group was expected to report on at least one question. These questions were then included in the unit examination. He appointed four of his five "absent stars" (as he called them in his mind) as chairpersons for the groups. This procedure worked remarkably well—and as proof, the student with no responsibility continued the pattern of absences.

There are three major sources of absenteeism: parental lack of interest; teacher ineptitude; school regulations. A teacher can do a great deal on all three fronts. First, a teacher must analyze the classroom situation. If students can get all the understanding of the subject they need without coming to class, then of course they will stay away. So first and foremost *instruction in class must be made central and vital to mastering the course material.* Second, the class must not be boring. The stupefying dullness and boredom of many classes has been reported over and over. Only the teacher can remedy this. Ask yourself: "Would I like to sit in this class myself hour after hour, day after day?" The remedy for boredom is modification of methods to involve students—using many variations of techniques and strategies described in these chapters. *There is no need for any class in any subject to be boring.*

Third, *involve the students in learning.* If students are aware that they will be noticed by the teacher, seen when they are present, called upon to participate and expected to have a contribution to make, they are much more apt to come to class. The use of all kinds of small groups (see Chapter 10) helps insure such involvement. The group which needs all members present to do its task will put peer pressure on students who do not do their share. A group engaged in making a film, for example, rarely if ever has the problem of absenteeism.

The teacher can also do something about parental indifference. Many parents are totally unaware of the fact that their youngsters are skipping school or absent from classes even when in school. Where absenteeism is a real problem, or a problem with only a few students, the teacher has usually the option of informing parents. A warning to students that their parents will be informed of absences may bring some students back to class. A letter home may be helpful with others. A simple form letter may be all that is needed, though a more personal one is even better.

Finally, teachers need to work with the school administration to develop school rules and regulations regarding absenteeism. A study could be made of the absence patterns of the school. A PTA program could be devoted to it. A task force of parents, teachers, students, and administrators could be established to look at causes and propose remedies: Students should be consulted extensively for their views as to the causes of absenteeism.

A recurrent question is whether grades should be lowered because of excessive absenteeism. Many teachers announce the rule to students that there will be a penalty for unexcused absences. Some schools have such policies. The difficulty with such a rule is that it rarely reduces absenteeism; it only increases students disenchantment with the meaning of grades. A grade should, as pointed out in Chapter 14, indicate how much a student has learned. When grades are lowered because of absenteeism then the grade is an attendance report, not a statement of achievement. If students can achieve satisfactorily without attending class, something is obviously wrong.

During the 1970s there was a trend toward the "open campus" policy in a number of high schools. Students were deemed old enough to be treated more like college students, who do not have to have their every moment monitored. A number of new programs were instituted which allowed students to work or study off campus. Some schools developed programs where students could enroll in nearby community colleges or universities in subjects in which they were especially proficient. These programs were a welcome innovation to a number of students. Other students saw them merely as a way of getting out of class. All such programs need careful supervision and review so that the educational goals are in fact achieved.

One distributive education teacher reported perfect attendance for her group of work-study students. They had all been placed in jobs in the afternoon, and had to come to school for their academic program in the morning. She taught two of the three subjects they had in the morning. These students knew that if their attendance fell off in the morning they risked losing their jobs. Also, for the first time they saw the need for English skills and math skills. Considerable time was also spent on problems of employee–employer relations, on-the-job behavior, and analysis of situations which they might meet as well as career exploration to encourage them to think and work ahead rather than feel they were doomed to dead-end jobs.

PERSONALITY NEEDS OF STUDENTS AS A SOURCE OF CLASSROOM PROBLEMS

There are special problems presented by students whose adjustment to themselves and their world has been so inadequate that they cannot behave as others do, no matter how desperately they may wish to conform. These are students who are socially maladjusted and emotionally disturbed. Often they are not classroom discipline problems at all, but sometimes they are serious threats to good order.

First, of course, diagnosis should occur. Using the results of tests of personal–social adjustment, the teacher may detect a future behavior problem before it arises. But other clues are available. To recapitulate the criteria listed on page 410, serious misbehaviors are those that:

1. persist; and do not respond to normal teacher control
2. are manifest in many kinds of unruly actions
3. seem to have no logical connection to other misbehaviors

To a teacher, every student is like an iceberg. The unrevealed nine-tenths of the student's life—personal history, family constellation, previous successes or failures in school, growth in heterosexual adjustment, fears and anxieties about the future—may produce classroom misbehavior.

The teacher should remember that there are a few definitely deviant personalities among the adolescents he or she teaches. These we term "neurotic," "psychotic," or "psychopathic" personalities. One study of school dropouts reported:

> Our dropouts had serious and multiple school problems that interfered substantially with the educational process. Most of them were either failing in their school courses or working far below their mental capacity, a majority were also truanting or cutting classes, and about half were presenting behavior problems in school. All of the students were unsuccessful in adapting to some school requirements or regulations, and three-fourths were having trouble in more than one area of school life . . . the youngsters and their parents had serious emotional problems and (the) school difficulties . . . resulted from emotional disturbances . . . 76 percent were suffering from character problems—maladaptations of the entire personality—in contrast to neurotic conflicts, which usually are of recent origin and more localized in effect.[5]

[5] Solomon O. Lichter, and others, *The Dropouts* (New York: Free Press, 1962), pp. 247–249. Copyright 1962 by the Free Press of Glencoe, a division of the Macmillan Company.

There are students to whom reality is so terrifying, so brutal, that escape is imperative; but in seeking to escape, the personality structure becomes distorted and abnormal. The ordinary things of life become major hazards, and a normal response to the demands of daily living becomes impossible. The behavior that the teacher observes is symptomatic: The behavior is not the problem; it is, however, a symptom of something that is disturbing the student. For example, a student who lives in a world of dreams, of fantasy, who seems entirely unaware of what is happening, is demonstrating symptomatic behavior of a very serious sort. Another student, who seems to get violently ill before any examination, who turns pale with fright at having to answer a simple question, is also over-reacting to a normal demand of life. Teachers are not diagnosticians or therapists trained to deal with neurotic symptoms. However, they should be sensitive to behavior that may be symptomatic of emotional illness. When suspect behavior is observed, the student should be referred to those trained to help.

Other manifestations of personal maladjustment include the following:

- Extreme aggression: destruction of books, fighting, willful destruction of property, persistent and nonfunctional lying
- Compulsive stealing
- Extreme sexual offenses
- Extreme hostility to peers and adults
- Truancy
- Compulsive behavior: exaggerated fear or anxiety, tics, compulsive arm or leg or bodily movement, inability to sit still

From this list it can be seen that some forms of maladjustment lead to behavior directed against others and against the rules of society; some are directed against the adolescent's own person. Many delinquents have manifested these behavior problems before ever becoming delinquent. Their delinquencies may only be intensified, or even produced, by teachers who deal with their misbehavior as though the students were "bad," instead of as though they were in need of help.

When students demonstrate extreme forms of maladjustment, the teacher must have recourse to trained personnel—psychologists, psychiatrists, psychoanalysts, child guidance workers, social workers. These specialists should be available to the teacher through the immediate school system, the county or state school system, or private and public agencies of the community.

The main object of the teacher's control of such individuals is to prevent the student from injuring others through their behavior and, as much as possible, to prevent them from further self-injury and to keep them coming to school. Rarely is it possible for the teacher to aid the adjustment of such students in any fundamental way. They are probably beyond the help of persons untrained in the field of psychotherapy. A strong effort should be made to make school rewarding and supportive. The teacher can only hope *not* to be one more burden to already overburdened personalities attempting to find a way of surviving.

One aid that lies close at hand, perhaps more readily accessible than any other, is utilization of some of the concepts derived from group therapy. The major emphasis in using the group to aid the individual is on establishing an atmosphere of acceptance and permissiveness. The teacher–leader is not a judge or parent substitute; rather he/she is a stable, accepting, secure individual. The group interactions are the method by which individuals learn to compromise their own needs with those of others.

Many communities have "hot lines" for dealing with personal problems. Teachers of all subject areas should know of these numbers and their services. It is highly recommended, that the numbers be posted in a conspicuous place in every classroom, laboratory, shop, and gymnasium. Students who cannot find help at home or at school will often find the hot line helpful, yet many do not know of this service.

VIOLENCE IN SCHOOL

Screaming headlines: "Teacher Attacked at George Washington High School: in Serious Condition at County Hospital." Violence in schools is increasing, and teachers as well as other students are the victims. According to *Time*,[6] in 1975 there were 63,000 attacks on teachers by students in secondary schools, $200 million of school property was destroyed and there were 270,000 school burglaries. In New York City 132 teachers reported attacks in the first six weeks of the 1977 school year. In Los Angeles the school system has a special "assault and battery" plan which supports unlimited paid leave for any school employee who suffers an attack on school grounds. Average payments of over $1,500 were made to 450 employees in the school year 1972–1973.[7] A recommendation of a National Commission on Reform of Secondary Education states:

All secondary school systems should develop security plans to safeguard students, faculty, equipment, and facilities. Specific procedures must be developed for faculty members to follow in case of disruption.[8]

The Commission goes on to cite the "crisis in school security" with a number of unfortunate and lurid cases. As the Commission puts it, "there is no way teachers can escape involvement in this problem. Classrooms cannot long be safe in a school where the halls and restrooms are danger-

[6] *Time*, 110 (November 14, 1977), p. 63.
[7] *Nation's School Report* 1 (December 22, 1975), p. 5.
[8] The National Commission, *op. cit.*, p. 115.

ous, and students who are concerned about their personal safety after the bell rings are not likely to concentrate on their work in class."[9]

What can be done? Many secondary schools, particularly those in large cities, have uniformed guards on duty. Some schools regularly make inspections of lockers to confiscate dangerous weapons. Special school personnel are detailed to contact students and to identify sources of interstudent conflict. The rise in violence—against other students, against teachers, and against property—can be expected to continue as long as secondary schools are overlarge and students come to school from disorganized homes and communities.

There are no simple or easy answers to the problem of in-school violence. What is evident is that good teachers rarely are the object of attack, but there are some dangerous, disturbed individuals in any collection of several thousand. The alert teacher should notice whether there are any students who appear deeply disturbed or prone to violence in a class and report his or her concern to an administrator and/or counselor. In a high risk area, beginning teachers should obviously consult with other teachers as to procedures which protect them from student assault. It is helpful to have teachers in neighboring rooms alerted so that they will respond to any unusual noise. Keeping classroom doors open at all times makes it less likely that a teacher will be caught alone. Women teachers are particularly cautioned to be wary of any kind of behavior which would suggest aggressive sexual interest.

Property losses can be minimized if normal precautions are taken to keep valuables under lock and key. Money is stolen from purses that are left out on a desk or chair, not ones that are securely locked. Teacher carelessness is one of the leading causes of property loss, according to many principals. Where there is pride in a school and where students care about their own learning environment, vandalism and theft are minimal. Teachers are an essential ingredient in building feelings of loyalty toward an institution. If students are treated punitively, humiliated, made to feel stupid and of no personal worth, then one can expect attacks, vandalism, and violence.

DRUGS AND ALCOHOL

Although there has been some decline in the national concern over drug use by teenagers, the actual facts seem to indicate an increase in the use of marijuana, and at even younger ages. Hard drugs are also found in use among secondary school students, though many students claim to be too sophisticated to get hooked by these substances. The use of pills of all

[9] The National Commission, *op. cit.*, p. 124.

kinds—so-called "downers" and "uppers" is endemic in many schools, though few students actually seem to use these pills more than an experimental time or two.

> Pot, the students say, is "as easy to get as beer." Seventy-eight percent of a national poll say they can buy it at school. They can buy it, they report, "at a school game," "in our smoking lounge," "in gym classes right in front of the teacher" . . .
> Many disapprove: "If the teachers would just wake up and recognize this and do something about it, a lot of pot smoking at school would be discouraged."[10]

It is obviously not possible to teach students who are drunk, on drugs, or "stoned" on marijuana. What do you do? *First, you should be able to recognize the symptoms of drug or alcohol use.* Many school systems issue leaflets explaining what to look for and conduct in-service sessions to help teachers. There are additional guides available from the federal programs on drug abuse. Typically, the student using drugs is sleepy and seems out of touch. The word "spacey" describes the behavior of these students very well. They may giggle, give inappropriate responses to questions or make comments that show they are unaware of what is going on. They may be highly irritable. Observe their behavior carefully, and at the first opportunity report your observations to an administrator or counselor. It is essential to distinguish carefully the behavior of a student who falls asleep in class because of an all-night job, or having watched the late, late show on TV from one who is taking drugs.

Second, make no effort in class to argue with the student or otherwise try to utilize usual methods of discipline; they will not work. It is best to leave the student alone, and then, if you feel you have sufficiently adequate rapport, discuss his or her behavior at the next class meeting, when behavior is back to normal. One can no more reach a person under the influence of drugs than one can argue with a drunk, so avoid it.

Third, whether or not there is a serious problem, make room during the year for a class discussion of the consequences of drug and alcohol abuse. In science, students can do research on what drugs and alcohol do to the nervous system. In social studies there are many good guides to teaching about the social consequences of drugs and alcohol. In English, debates can be conducted on the merits of different programs to control abuse. There is sobering literature on the impact of these substances. One very popular book, *Go Ask Alice*[11] has circulated among teenagers for several years because of its explicit and shocking report of what drugs

---

[10] Gordon A. Sabine, "NASSP and Youthpoll America: When We Listen This Is What We Can Hear," *NASSP Bulletin*, 61 (May 1977), pp. 109–120.
[11] Anonymous, *Go Ask Alice* (New York: Avon, 1972).

meant in the lives of some young people. Although adults in some communities object to the language in the book, and it has been banned in some schools, it does appear to have a message for youth.

BETWEEN STUDENT AND TEACHER

There has been frequent discussion in the educational literature regarding the gap between the middle-class orientation and expectations of teachers, and the view of life of the lower-class student. Although there are problems in all secondary schools, it is clear that schools with large numbers of poverty-level students come in for more than their share. The violence which is discussed above is far more apt to occur in the big city schools situated in run-down, slum areas than in schools in middle-class suburbs or in small cities and towns.

It is a mistake, however, to assume that these troubles arise from lack of belief in education. Numerous surveys have shown that parents in these areas hold education in high esteem; they fully realize that education provides a way out of poverty. What many of these parents lack, however, are the skills and knowledge to help their children. Students in such areas may not lack motivation, but they may leave the school and return to homes where there is no place to study, no place that is quiet, no desk, or adequate lighting for homework, no dictionaries or encyclopedias to help. Many of these youngsters are also working—if they can find work—to help support their families or themselves. Many are already parents.[12] It is understandable if they are less than enamored of class assignments that seem remote and irrelevant.

It is evident that teachers need to understand clearly the educational problems of their students. Where there is no place to study at home, then time must be provided in class for supervised study. It is also clear that students will respond to teachers who expect them to perform as well as they can, who show a faith and belief in their ability to do the work, and help them as much as they can.

> I observed an eleventh grade math class in one of the big old schools in the middle of the worst poverty area of the city. After a few minutes, it was clear what the teacher had done. The class was divided in half, and he taught to only one half—the half which seemed to understand what he was explaining. The other half he neither called on nor paid any attention to. They whispered and slept. Obviously they had no notion of what he was doing. He had "written off" one half of his class.

That teacher was lucky that the half of the class which he no longer taught behaved as well as they did. It is the teacher's obligation to teach

[12] Ronald Corwin, *Education in Crisis* (New York: Wiley, 1974), pp. 123–124.

all the students. If some find greater difficulty than others in grasping what is going on, then the teacher must consider other strategies to communicate the skill or information. What we have observed over the past decade is the phenomenon of many teachers "writing off" whole groups of students as unable to learn. These students are then just passed along in the system, eventually getting a diploma which signifies nothing. Such situations are coming increasingly to public attention. Pressure is being exerted on all teachers to reach and teach all students. Teachers will be increasingly held accountable for their skill in this endeavor.

In every class in even the most desperate areas of our communities, there are more students who want to learn, who care about themselves and their futures than there are students who are unwilling to learn. By showing an interest in each student, and providing many channels for achievement, a teacher can reach even those who are most difficult.

WHAT DISCIPLINE WORKS?

"It may not be the kind of theory they teach you in college, but it works" is a standard comment of many teachers when they defend or describe their methods of obtaining classroom control. Such a comment expresses primarily the view that discipline is for the teacher's peace of mind. It succeeds because the students do what they are told within the four walls of the classroom. But is it successful in a larger sense? Discipline must be related to the purposes that direct the total educational program. Considered in this light, discipline really succeeds only when it contributes to the development of democratic individuals, enabling them to perform satisfactorily the various roles of worker, parent, and citizen.

It should be helpful to look at some of the common measures that "work"—punishment, neglect, and emotional blackmail—and see why they negate the broader education goals. An additional look at one uncommon measure that "works"—democratic group control—will show why it affirms these goals.

PUNISHMENT

Typical punishments are increased assignments, lowered grades, detention after school, public humiliation, dismissal from class, sending to higher disciplinary authority—or threats of all these. Do these punishments create better student–teacher relations? From the point of view of the psychologist, punishment, by and large, is a very ineffectual way of obtaining genuine compliance.

Punishment may act as a deterrent for misbehavior in the short run, but it is usually counterproductive in the long run. Punishment produces acute anxiety in the student, and arouses feelings of resentment and animosity toward the one inflicting the punishment. Out of such feelings is born a need to retaliate.

> Miss Clay was famous for her punishments. Students who broke one of her countless "rules" would find themselves sent to detention, given extra doses of homework, or a tongue-lashing. Although she was a pretty good teacher—she prepared for class and was well organized—her way of punishing made us angry. We worked out many ingenious ways to get even: trashing the room after school when she was out, breaking the lock on the cabinets and strewing the books around, spilling the plants she loved and breaking the pots, and dumping mud on her car.

To the dismay of many educators, corporal punishment has been approved as a fair means of chastising students by a recent Supreme Court decision.[13] Because violence only breeds violence, corporal punishment is considered the least desirable form of dealing with misbehavior. It is unlikely that corporal punishment can or will be used with teenagers, but the fact that some of these young adults have been subject to corporal punishment when younger may produce aggressive and violent responses to secondary school authorities.

The case against punishment is well established. Yet classroom after classroom is dominated by a punitive atmosphere. Detention rooms are common, and individual teachers use many varieties of punishing techniques. Why are these used when they are psychologically unsound? First, because they relieve teachers' feelings of aggression. Second, because they are at hand; that is, they require little effort on the part of the teacher to utilize. Third, because students themselves react toward punishment with a superficial acceptance and subsequent compliance: Such measures "work." The question, though, as with other disciplinary approaches, is; For whom does punishment work? It works for the teacher to the extent that it is an aid in maintaining classroom order and insures a surface acceptance of authority. But, as already noted, punishment works against the student as a developing personality. It must also be remembered that punishment inflicts a subtle injury upon teachers, involving them in a punitive climate during all their working hours. Few people can resist the corrosive effects of such a climate, day after day and year after year.

There is another important explanation for the wide use of punishment. Young people, particularly among lower socioeconomic groups and some culturally less well-integrated ethnic groups, are often conditioned, through early family experiences, to understand and accept punishment. These young people may be less adequate persons because of these conditions; yet they know no other sanction that will command their obedience. For

---

[13] Thomas J. Flygare, "Schools and the Law: The Supreme Court Approves Corporal Punishment," *Phi Delta Kappan*, 59 (January 1978), p. 347–348.

this reason, many lower-class youth are simply amazed at a teacher who expects self-control from them on the basis of other appeals.

It is obvious that what works with some adolescents will not, and should not, work for others. Punishment should therefore be used sparingly and only because it is a part of a larger acculturation process, which must have as its objective the development in students of an understanding of self-discipline and an appreciation of the disciplines of reason, fact, and social order.

ISOLATION

Teachers sometimes discipline students by isolating them in a corner of the room, sending them into the hall for a time, or sending them to the library.

Students may be refused aid: "I'm sorry, but I won't help any student who does not remain in his seat like everyone else." Or, "Stanley, you just don't seem able to resist talking to your neighbors and bothering them; you will have to sit by yourself at the back table." Another method of isolation is to ignore provocative behavior as though it did not exist.

Such refusals of attention as we have just described get results. But the same question regarding how they work, and for whom, must be answered. Provocative behavior is motivated by some need; often it is an effort to gain attention that the individual craves. Isolation reinforces the very craving that induced the behavior in the first place. It is as though we said to a student: "If you once let me know you are hungry, I will refuse to give you food; if you don't show any hunger, then I will feed you." Isolation will probably result in a suppression of the undesirable behavior, but just as probably the cost to the individual will be great. This is not to say that teachers must react on the spot and at the moment when the provocative behavior occurs. Sometimes it is better to wait until there is time for a private conference. When it is evident that the student cannot be reached in private conference, it may be necessary to plan carefully exactly what activities in the classroom can help that student become a more acceptable class member. This technique then involves temporarily ignoring the provocative behavior until more strategic measures can be applied. And this procedure is quite different from failure to react at all.

EMOTIONAL BLACKMAIL

Both love and fear can be part of the emotional blackmail used by the teacher. The teacher who develops the feeling of "Now do this for me, because if you don't you will make me so unhappy," is being unfair.

Discipline was excellent. Mr. Halstead was a young teacher. He allowed the students to "buzz" a little almost whenever they wished. But if the buzzing became too loud, he would suddenly look very grieved and disgusted. After a moment or two of strained silence, he would burst into a mild tantrum in which he would shame the students for not acting their age. He would act hurt that he, who always treated them so well, should be subjected to this ungrateful treatment. His whole method of teaching seemed to be geared to a sort of a "proud but grieved parent" attitude.

Young people should be asked to do things in the classroom primarily because it is to their benefit as learners, because they are part of a group endeavor. They should not be told that misbehavior hurts one who loves them dearly.

INDIVIDUAL VERSUS GROUP DISCIPLINE

Here is an example in which a whole class was punished for the actions of a few:

The art teacher gave her time only to the talented ones in the classroom. She marked us not on the ability we showed or the individual progress made by each student, but on how each of us in our drawings compared with her idea of good art. Her disposition was that of a typical old lady. One day she left the classroom, and one of my daring friends got the idea for us to put a wad of sticky chewing gum in her chair. Unfortunately she looked at the chair before sitting down. We were disappointed. She arranged for the entire class to be detained after school until the guilty party either gave himself up, or someone else turned him in. We sat there from 2:30 until 4:30 that day. Everyone in the class hated this teacher so much that no one dared squeal. Finally she had to let us go as several parents had called the school to find out what had happened to their kids. Although she didn't find out who the guilty one was, our entire class got grades of either C or D that semester.

In the following example, one individual is punished for the entire group:

I was on the high-school football team and the whole team was instructed by the coach to stay away from the pep rally in the park and to stay home and rest. Many of us decided to go to the rally. As fate would have it, there was an accident and names were taken. The coach was fit to be tied by our action and threatened to kick us off the team for the rest of the school year. My closest friend, who was also a member of the team, was chosen as a scapegoat and deprived of his uniform the next day. Since the rest of us were on the first string, the coach just gave us a lecture and told us to be ready to play the game of our life.

Punishing a whole class because the teacher cannot find a culprit is one of the devices most hated and resented by students. Whole class punishment for the misdeeds of one or two should absolutely be avoided by teachers.

The teacher can, and usually should, express the idea: "In this class, we just don't interrupt people when they are talking." Or, "Even if you don't feel like studying, Janet, since everyone else is, let's not annoy them." This approach reminds the individual of an obligation to the group and is effective with normal misbehavior. When there is persistent misbehavior that arises from deep sources within the individual, the group approach can be effective only in a therapy situation. Most of the teacher's efforts should be directed to understanding the individual since the origins of the problem extend far beyond this classroom and this course.

SELECTIVE REWARDS AS A METHOD OF DISCIPLINE

The studies of learning and motivation that underlie some current educational programs are based upon a theory of "reinforcement" that is also applicable to classroom behavioral problems. Simply stated, the teacher responds with approval to that behavior which he or she wishes repeated and ignores behavior that interferes with the task at hand. Several procedures have been found effective with many kinds of students in varying circumstances and to varying degrees.

The "instant feedback" of programmed instruction is one instance of immediate reinforcement. Students know almost as soon as they have given an answer to a question or performed a specific task whether they have done it correctly and can proceed to the next bit of work. In many classrooms, students must wait a long time before they find out if their work has been done correctly. If a test is given on Monday it may be several days, if not weeks, before it is returned. In too many instances students receive papers with items marked wrong and the grade. They may or may not find out what is wrong, and they may or may not have a chance to learn what is right. To implement reinforcement theory, the teacher would plan for almost immediate scoring of such tests and also immediate and helpful procedures for determining the right answer or the proper procedure.

Students who otherwise have failed to do school work often succeed when the curriculum is organized in small units of work and there is immediate and obvious "feedback" on performance. The kinds of discipline situations which arise because students do not do assigned work, or in which they disrupt classes because the work does not mesh with abilities, expectations, or motivations, is thus circumvented because careful attention is given to the principle of immediate feedback for tasks that have face validity for the student. Jack, the presumed nonreader, becomes highly motivated to learn to read when he wants to pass the written portion of the driver's test to obtain a driving license.

Another significant application of the theory of reinforcement has been termed "operant conditioning."[14] "Operant behavior is strengthened or weakened by the events that follow the response. Whereas respondent behavior is controlled by its antecedents, operant behavior is controlled by its consequences."[15] Many teachers who appear to have severe problems of classroom discipline often actually provide reward for the very behavior they are trying to eradicate. Reward, in this sense, is approval by peers since the disrupting student has effectively "gotten the teacher's goat." Or the bad behavior has caused the teacher to focus attention on the misbehaving student, thereby feeding the student's need for attention.

In class after class where students continue to misbehave, observers note that the teacher is, without being aware of it, rewarding such disruptive behavior by paying attention to it. "Behavior modification" is another term for operant conditioning. It means modifying behavior so that individuals will repeat behavior for which they receive satisfaction. When student misbehavior continues, teachers should monitor their conscious and unconscious reward system.

In an experiment with some severely disturbed children, a system used was to "reinforce 'good' behavior and nonpunitively discourage 'bad' behavior."[16] As these experimenters comment, "Study after study has shown that whenever a child persists in behaving badly, some adult has, perhaps inadvertently, been rewarding him for it." Working out a system of reward that produces more good than bad behavior is a difficult task. One teacher, for instance, who was having trouble teaching spelling, as well as almost everything else, to a group of disruptive, disadvantaged eighth graders, found that they would at least attempt the spelling lesson when she promised to read them a story. For these students, being read to was considered a real treat; and they were willing to do something they disliked in order to get the valued reward. In another situation a group of boys in a detention home who would not cooperate in the required educational program, became remarkably motivated learners when each increment of learning was rewarded by tokens. These tokens could be used to "buy" time in the lounge for watching television or for buying a candy bar or soft drink, or, as the token system became increasingly elaborate, even a private room in a special cottage. The system worked so well that many boys who had very poor school records increased their reading and other skills significantly. In turn, their self-images as "bad boys" who were "stupid" were changed into those of boys who could be "good" and who could learn.

[14] Ellen P. Reese, *The Analysis of Human Operant Behavior* (Dubuque, Iowa: W. C. Brown, 1966).
[15] Reese, p. 3.
[16] Robert L. Hamblin and others, "Changing the Game From 'Get the Teacher' to 'Learn'," *Trans-Action*, 6 (January 1969), pp. 20–31.

Many teachers instinctively utilize behavior modification. They have learned that disruptive behavior may often disappear when it is successfully ignored by the teacher. This means that the teacher has some other task at hand so compelling, so interesting, so motivating to most of the class, that the disrupting individual gains neither the teacher's attention nor that of classmates. Lacking an audience the student either must go along with what the rest of the class is doing or be left out completely. Some students may turn disruptive behavior into escape behavior. Instead of being loud and noisy, the student sleeps or becomes apathetic. The teacher's strategy is then to find the reward system that makes sense to that student. Grades are the typical standard reinforcer for the middle-class, college-oriented student. Grades do not have the same motivating force for many other types of students. But personal attention, interest, the evidence of almost immediate "payoff" for doing a task, may all have to be tried in order to tap the motivating springs of students who are not acceding to reasonable educational expectations.

Behavior modification has gained a bad name in some circles because of suspicion of unethical manipulation of individual responses. In fact, all reward systems are a form of behavior modification. When one works in order to get a promotion, one tries to fit into the system's accepted pattern, and to do what that system says is right and proper—otherwise, no promotion. So it is in school. Reward systems exist; students who respond appropriately with the "right" behavior, gain the rewards available. Critics of behavior modification assert that in involuntary settings, such as prisons, a system of rewards is unfair. Schools, like prisons, have a population of involuntary inmates, and yet schools are charged with the task of socializing the young—of modifying the behavior of young people to conform to the expectations of society. Schools are inextricably engaged in modifying behavior.

DEMOCRATIC DISCIPLINE

Democratic discipline involves the same basic attitude toward teaching that was developed in the section on the democratic classroom (see Chapter 4). *Democratic discipline stresses the joint responsibility of the teacher and the student in achieving a classroom atmosphere in which teaching and learning may take place.*

The theory of discipline advanced here is one that conforms to democratic ideals—namely, that discipline is merely the kind of classroom control that is most likely to further the development of democratic personalities. Such democratic discipline avoids reliance upon external controls for maintaining classroom order; and this approach to discipline particularly eschews attacks upon the personality of the student being disciplined and harsh or vindictive measures of any type. The following checklist suggests questions that each teacher may use to evaluate the success of any disciplinary technique:

1. Are students developing the ability to obey rules because they understand what is reasonable?
2. Do students help one another in those situations that demand self-control? Does this helping occur because of concern for one another rather than because of a threatened reward or punishment from the teacher?
3. Does the need for the teacher to exercise control diminish as the group continues to work and learn together?
4. Can the students accept a substitute teacher or the unexpected absence of the teacher during the period without becoming disorganized or having to be held down by teacher threats?
5. Can the students develop their own rules of behavior and follow them fairly well?
6. Can students and teacher talk calmly together about class disturbances not anticipated in the rules and arrive at mutually acceptable compromises?
7. Are students who seem to be the source of major problems of discipline being helped by group acceptance or by outside guidance from teacher or specialist?
8. Does the teacher enter the classroom feeling relaxed and in a mood for work? Does this feeling grow throughout the semester?
9. Do students enter the classroom feeling relaxed and in a mood for work? Does this atmosphere develop during the semester?

TEST YOUR THEORIES

On the following pages are a number of descriptions of discipline situations. Some are well handled; some are poorly handled; some are not resolved at all. It is suggested that readers think through their own line of procedure in each situation. Ask yourself: What is the possible consequence of the line of action taken or proposed? Does it conform with my theory of democratic procedures? Would I feel satisfied if I continued to use such methods day in and day out?

When John talked back to the teacher for the fourth time, the teacher turned on him and told him that if he ever did that again she would have to call the principal. She then sent him into the hall. She followed him out and after a few minutes they returned. The teacher looked smug and well-satisfied, but John looked like a volcano that was about to erupt. He did not repeat his behavior that day.

Alan, an almost sixteen-year-old boy in an eighth-grade class, was sitting with his chair leaning back and his feet on the desk in front of him. Mr. Conroy noticed this but paid no attention for a while. Alan then started making "wise" comments to the boy across the room from him. These comments were loud enough to disturb the class. At this point, Mr. Conroy asked him to please sit in his chair properly and to keep his comments to himself until after class. Alan made a few last remarks, laughed, and straightened out his chair. In a few minutes he shifted the chair again.

We were seniors in high school, and all of us were quite active in many school affairs. My girl friend and I had tried unsuccessfully between classes to the music teacher about a practice. About half-way through our home economics class my friend and I (we were in groups working on projects) decided to walk out of class and go to see the music teacher. Without asking the home economics teacher, we walked out. She just let us walk out, but soon after we returned she came over to our table and asked us if we hadn't known we were doing something wrong. We told her we did and told her our reason. She said, "Okay then. But don't do anything like this again." And it was forgotten.

The principal announced over the public address system that the homeroom period would be extended for five minutes for certain business to be transacted in the senior homerooms. This was met by several comments from the students in the class. The teacher, tapping the desk with a ruler, said, "All right, quiet down! You must not disturb the other classes."

The class continued talking. Two boys in the back of the room began a "swipe-the-pencil" game. A scuffle ensued. The teacher, standing with arms crossed, snapped, "I told you boys to behave. Settle down and cut out that foolishness!"

"Yeah," said one of the onlooking boys, "Yeah boys, settle down and be quiet or the little fairy will send you to the office."

A sudden silence came over the room as the other students looked from one to another to the teacher.

In a ninth-grade art class the students were working on individual projects when the teacher left the room for several minutes. Two boys in the back of the room discovered two long pieces of rope in a cabinet. They tied the rope around the legs of a stool and lowered it out the third-floor window. They then returned to their projects. Very soon the teacher from the room beneath stormed into the room yelling, "Who did that? Who lowered the stool out the window?" Of course we ignored her.

We were discussing an algebra problem with a substitute teacher. Substitutes usually have a hard time of it, but this one was pretty good and most of the class was interested and attentive. Then, bang! One boy's books fell to the floor. The boy muttered he was sorry as he picked them up, but he was smiling and looking at one of his friends. Soon another set fell—then another—and another. When the last set fell the teacher told the boy to just leave them there. She then remarked upon the rather odd sequence of coincidences and said she assumed it was accidental but just to be sure, everyone in class should place his books under his seat. After that there were no more interruptions.

The class was a large science lecture with the teacher lecturing and showing slides about the structure of the earth. Things were moving along quite well as most of the class seemed interested, when rather suddenly the teacher stopped the class. Then we became aware of a noticeable hum in the room. A few of the boys who hadn't been paying attention seemed to be smirking. We all knew what it was—a battery powered vibrator was somewhere in the room—but it was a large room. The teacher then said, "Will whoever brought that thing in here please shut it off?" No one moved. Apparently whoever had it thought that the teacher would run all over the room looking for it. Instead, the teacher said, "Perhaps we can locate it the way earthquakes are located." He then asked six people around the sides of the room to point toward where they thought the sound was coming from. As they did so they ended up pointing at one boy who blushingly reached under his seat and turned it off. The teacher then returned to the front of the room and resumed class. I don't think the triangulation system really worked, but he gave those who wanted to go on with the class a chance to point out the guilty party without anybody being able to say he squealed.

DID IT WORK?

The most difficult of all the questions that must be answered concerning discipline is: Did it work? One of the greatest frustrations of secondary school teaching is the lack of continued contact with students. The teacher has a group for five days a week, an hour a day, for four months or even for nine months; then the students are gone. This contact is very slight indeed compared with the six hours a day, five days a week, for the whole school year, which is the privilege of the elementary teacher. It is not often that a secondary school teacher is in touch with students after they graduate and take their place in the world, and this too makes it difficult to assess the effects of the teacher's methods of control. Did they actually make Douglas more self-directing? Did Jane really learn how to control her explosive temper? After all, it is the long-range effects that concern the teacher who desires to utilize democratic methods of discipline. But the teacher is usually denied knowledge of long-range effects.

SELECTED READINGS

Braddock, Clayton, and David Hearne (Eds.), *The Student Pushout: Victim of Continued Resistance to Desegregation.* Washington, D.C. The Robert F. Kennedy Memorial and the Southern Regional Council, 1973. This damning report shows how biased school policies result in unjustified suspensions and expulsions of black students.

Bullock, Charles S., III, "Contact Theory and Racial Tolerance among High School Students," *School Review*, 86 (February 1978), pp. 187–216. This research report shows that when students have genuine interracial contact, tolerance for racial differences increases, which suggests that merely desegregating a school will not produce racial acceptance.

Clarizio, Harvey F., *Toward Positive Classroom Discipline*. New York: Wiley, 1971. Well-developed ideas for implementing democratic disciplinary methods.

Duke, Daniel L., "How Administrators View the Crisis in School Discipline," *Phi Delta Kappan*, 59 (January 1978), pp. 325–331. Administrators from all over the country were polled to see what were the top discipline problems.

Glasser, William, "Disorders in Our Schools: Causes and Remedies," *Phi Delta Kappan*, 59 (January 1978), pp. 331–333. This psychiatrist has provided consultation to school systems nationwide on building positive school discipline.

Henderson, George, and Robert F. Bibens, *Teachers Should Care: Social Perspectives of Teaching*. New York: Harper & Row, 1970. Emphasis in this book is on the social differences and perceptions between students and teachers which often lead to class disruption and failure to learn.

James, Deborah, *The Taming: A Teacher Speaks*. New York: McGraw-Hill, 1969. A personal account of how a teacher deals with disruptive students and the challenge of teaching volatile youth.

Jessup, Michael H., and Margaret A. Kiley, *Discipline: Positive Attitudes for Learning*. Englewood Cliffs, N.J.: Prentice-Hall, 1971. This well-balanced presentation includes numerous case studies to test one's responses.

National Association of Secondary School Principals. *Disruptive Youth: Causes and Solutions*. Reston, Va.: The Association, 1977. A brief (33 pages) monograph which describes five basic programs used in one state in successful efforts to combat school disruption.

Ruchkin, Judith P., "Does School Crime Need the Attention of Policemen or Educators?" *Teachers College Record*, 79 (December 1977), pp. 225–243. A valuable review of the available data that suggest some of the facts may be overblown.

Spady, William, "The Authority System of the School and Student Unrest: A Theoretical Exploration," in C. W. Gordon (Ed.), *Uses of the Sociology of Education*, Seventy-Third Yearbook of the National Society for the Study of Education. Chicago: University of Chicago Press, 1974. Demonstrates how the social organization and structure of the school and classroom produces many problems of discipline.

FOCUS ON CHAPTER 17

Students do not leave their problems at home, nor do they dump them outside the classroom door. Many problems of growing up interfere with learning, and cause students to do less well with learning tasks than their ability or desires would warrant. Teachers cannot ignore these problems, but neither can teachers solve them. However, the understanding teacher can be a genuine help to the troubled adolescent who may need little more than a sympathetic and concerned adult to listen and to accept his or her difficulties.

Significant ideas presented in this chapter are:

- The counseling approach involves the teacher in understanding the developmental stages of adolescent as they ask: Who am I? Where am I going? What can I believe?
- Using case studies and other techniques the teacher can gain an insight into the possible problems besetting an individual student.
- Learning nondirective counseling is important for the teacher-counselor. This approach requires learning how to listen to feelings and to accept persons as they are.
- There are many specialists in school and community available for referral and assistance with troubled adolescents.
- Teachers also often talk with parents; there are skills to be developed for that kind of interaction and cautions to observe.

chapter 17

"I Have This Problem": counseling

In all ages, those who were called "great teachers" were those who were wise and judicious advisors as well as skillful instructors. Too often the secondary school teacher seems aloof and unsympathetic, a mere giver of assignments and grader of examinations. Few students seek out such a teacher for help and advice. Most schools are fortunate enough to have at least one teacher who is the confidante of many students. Not all teachers can be great counselors, for this requires both special training and special personal qualities; but one can understand at least the obligation of the teacher to strive for insight. It has been said that there would be few, if any, delinquents if each student had one teacher in school each year who gave him or her warm friendship and understanding.

In this chapter some of the tools and techniques the teacher can use in performing the function of counselor to the individual student will be discussed. The special problems of group guidance, vocational and academic counseling, and working with parents on the guidance of students will also be presented.

TEACHER–COUNSELOR

It may be useful to point out the essential differences between the formal teacher and the teacher–counselor.

Formal Teacher	Teacher-Counselor
Evaluation is concerned with subject learning only.	Evaluation reveals many kinds of achievement: intellectual, social, psychological, aesthetic.
Few personal interviews are held with students except about academic problems.	Many individual interviews are held about personal, as well as academic, problems.

Formal Teacher	Teacher-Counselor
The student's counselor or other teachers are seldom consulted about the progress of an individual.	Student problems are often discussed with counselors and other teachers.
No home visits are made, and parent conferences at school are evaded.	Home visits are made when possible and invitations are often issued to parents to come to school for conferences.
The role of emotion in learning is discounted.	Sensitivity to emotional tone in the classroom and with individual students is maintained.
"Business as usual" is the motto for instruction no matter what is going on "outside."	Changes in class "mood" are noted, and teaching is adjusted accordingly.

These two kinds of approaches have been identified as those of the "controllers" and those of the "helpers."[1]

HELP!

We all need all the help we can get. Adolescents especially need all the help available. It has never been easy to grow up in American society; current times appear to be even more difficult than previous decades. Much of the disturbing, disagreeable, upsetting, and even dangerous behavior described in the previous chapters on discipline are, underneath, cries for help. Much of the misbehavior which makes school life miserable for students and teachers is in reality the manifestation of a need for assistance. There are many choices facing youth, and unfortunately, the consequences of many of these choices are undesirable—young people may not always be aware of these consequences. They may, however, suspect that all is not well with their world, and they usually know quite well that not much is clear. They wish someone would give them support, assistance, advice, information. Most of what is wanted is not available in any academic class. The kinds of help that youth require have to come between times—between the laboratory experiments, the controversial debates, the poetry readings, the team games, the business letters.

The concerns of young people revolve around three eternal questions:

WHO AM I?

Each of us needs to achieve an indentity which is ours and ours alone, distinct from all others.[2] Yet our identity is tied up with the many roles we may play, which in turn are derived from our interpersonal relation-

---

[1] Benjamin Sachs, *The Student, the Interview and the Curriculum* (Boston: Houghton Mifflin, 1966), pp. 210–211.
[2] Erik H. Erikson, *Identity, Youth and Crisis* (New York: Norton, 1968).

ships—wife, husband, lover, friend, teammate—or work relations—plumber, teacher, pilot, hairdresser, bartender. Some of these roles may conflict with each other. Alex may be a student from 8:30 to 3:30, but after school he is a best friend, a dishwasher at McDonald's, a son, an older brother, a shortstop on the varsity baseball team. Which one of these is the true Alex? Which one is the most important? In some of these roles, Alex may feel tentative, uncomfortable, perhaps even angry.

WHERE AM I GOING?

Because there are so many alternatives, many young people are unable to decide on lifetime goals and postpone this decision by many devious routes such as going to college, getting married, or dropping out of school. Any of these alternatives may be for some students a way of drifting along with whatever peer pressure seems uppermost at the time, with no clear-cut idea of where this particular road is leading. Only later, often when the decision is irreversible, do they find out that the decision was wrong. The adolescent needs help in knowing the significance of any given decision, and the end toward which that decision may ultimately lead.

Career decisions are particularly crucial. Many adolescents have a limited view of the world of work. Most of them are not aware of the sequence of steps which leads toward a career goal. For instance, since girls typically take a minimum amount of mathematics, they cut themselves off from nearly three-fourths of the majors available in college which lead toward careers in science, business, engineering, and architecture. Individuals may have great difficulty differentiating their own goals from those which their parents may hold for them. Some may have lost faith in the future, seeing a world on the brink of self-destruction, and turn to immediate gratification and self-indulgent thrills. Obviously they need help.[3]

WHAT CAN I BELIEVE?

As Erikson makes clear, there is "evidence in young lives of the search for something and somebody to be true to (which) can be seen in a variety of pursuits more or less sanctioned by society . . . in all youth's seeming shiftiness, a seeking after some durability in change can be detected . . ."[4]

The 1970s saw an interesting religious development: young people were drawn toward religious practices, such as Zen Buddhism, Sun Yung Moon's Unification Church, and toward charismatic Christian churches. Others were equally zealous athiests or pantheists. Some turned to nature and the "natural" life. Although a diversity of beliefs has characterized American culture, the visibility and the proselytizing zeal with which these

[3] Erikson, p. 245.
[4] Erikson, p. 235

different groups appear on the contemporary scene is unprecedented. It is confusing to the teenager who is a target for many of the missionaries from these diverse organizations. But without belief, an individual feels adrift and alienated. There is some evidence that the use of drugs and alcohol is one way confused young people escape the dilemma posed by a world which provides no firm ground.

A CONFLICT IN PRIORITIES

The needs that adolescents have typically break down into lists of student priorities and teacher priorities:

What Students Want	What Teachers Want
Making friends	Students to learn at a reasonable level
Improving appearance	Obedience to class instructions
How to study better	Helping youth keep out of trouble
How to make better grades	Students to choose in light of their
Deciding what course to take	abilities
Overcoming worries about home, the	
future, taking tests	

As can be seen, teacher and student priorities do not "match" very well. Teachers put learning goals first, while students put personal goals first. Inevitably, these differences in priorities will lead at the least to confusion and, at most, to undeclared war.

The teacher-as-counselor is one who realizes that no matter how strongly the school may feel about goals of teaching, many of the student's personal goals and priorities may not be achieved.

Evelyn recalled the first months after the schools were finally desegregated, after ten years of bitter court fights. "Sure, school went on as usual. Classes. Tests. Homework. But for the life of me, I can't remember a thing about that. All that I remember is wondering when the first white kid was going to knock one of my books off my desk, or trip me in the hall, or "accidentally" spill soup on me in the cafeteria. And, yes, all those things did happen. And the teachers—they went right on teaching."

It is not easy to see the differences between the school and the social world of the school as experienced by students, and the world of the school experienced by teachers. A very helpful device is that of the Shadow Study (see Chapter 2).

How can a teacher find out what the concerns of students are in class?

1. Ask the students! When teachers develop rapport with their students, students are quite frank and often eager to talk.
2. Observe them—in the lunch room, in the halls, in the yard before and after school.
3. Utilize published checklists of problems typical of teenagers.[5]

Open-ended sentences such as the following are helpful:

I sometimes wish that school _____.

Other people often _____.

If I had three wishes I would most want _____.

School is _____.

The best thing about school is _____.

Most people my age want _____.

People usually describe me as _____.

Several cautions must be observed in administering any of these tests, and in evaluating and utilizing the data. Some schools and communities are very wary of anything that appears to be an "invasion of privacy" on the part of teachers or other school personnel.[6] If administered in particularly sensitive school areas, diagnostic procedures such as those mentioned above might provoke attack by a few, with claims of brainwashing and Communism, ridiculous as this may seem. The teacher should be sure to consult with counselors or administrative personnel, or both, to assess the local climate before entering what might already be troubled waters. In some systems counselors will assist in selecting the proper diagnostic tools and also administering and scoring them if necessary.

The data themselves must be viewed with care. Typically, girls report more fears, anxieties, and less self-esteem than boys. The question (not yet resolved by research) is whether girls are really that much worse off, or just are less afraid to admit that they do not feel personally adequate and competent. After all, American culture says it is all right for a girl to admit feeling weak and fearful, but it is far from the masculine ideal to admit similar concerns. Thus many boys may mask their true feelings, and some girls may overreport trivial or passing worries. Therefore projective

---

[5] Robert Fox and others, *Diagnosing Classroom Learning Environments* (Chicago: Science Research, 1966).

[6] Ramon Ross, "Uproar in Valley City," *The National Elementary Principal*, 48 (1964), pp. 23–26: and Boris Longstreth, "Behavioral Research Using Students: A Privacy Issue for Schools," *The School Review*, 76 (March 1968), pp. 1–22. See also Robert R. Sears, "In Defense of Privacy: Response to Longstreth," *The School Review*, 76 (March 1968), pp. 23–33; and Robert Schmuck and Mark Chesler, "Superpatriot Opposition to Community Mental Health Programs," *Community Mental Health Journal*, 3 (Winter 1967), pp. 382–388.

devices such as the open-ended test, in which there are no "right answers" or guided answers (as opposed to a multiple-choice situation, for instance), may thus be a more effective way of getting at the boys' feelings.

Finally, the teacher must remember that these data, like any other data about the personal aspects of a student, are confidential. The data are not discussed over the gossip-table in the teachers' lounge, or in any place other than the privacy of an office with a competent fellow professional. The teacher also uses care in interpreting any of these data to students or their parents. It is wiser to gain merely a general picture of students who appear to have some areas of personal concern and then keep a watchful eye upon them. Later, when the time is propitious, talk privately with each student. How this is done will be discussed below.

EVERYONE WAS ONCE AN ADOLESCENT

To get some perspective on the problems of the adolescents you encounter, you would well reflect upon your own adolescence. What were the things that bothered you the most? Where did you find help, if any? How did you go about seeking such help, and what did you do when it was proferred?

There is a caution here, of course. What has happened to oneself in one's own lifetime may be unique. The extent to which one can generalize from personal experience to that of the adolescents one teaches may be small. While all have experienced, or are experiencing the process of growing up, the similarity may end there. For example:

- Today's adolescents are a product of "total exposure" to television. In most American homes they have known the medium since birth.
- The parental generation is that of the Korean conflict and the Vietnam war: characterized by affluence, violence, and racial disturbances.
- He and she are apt to know about the Pill. More than 50 percent are sexually active. They have had some experience with, or heard about, drugs. Most drink occasionally, some to excess.

These and other ventures of this generation often are more risky than those of the teacher's generation.

The "Generation Gap," while it may appear to be small (maybe only a mere three or four years in the case of beginning student teachers), is still there and it increases drastically with every decade of age difference.

Teachers may come from a more restricted, or at least different, environment from their students. Women, particularly middle-class, white women entering teaching, have rarely had an insider's view of genuine poverty, of family disorganization resulting from extreme deprivation. How many teachers know the problems faced by blue-collar families, by marginal groups such as the Cuban, Puerto Rican and Mexican migrants, the

American Indian, the displaced miner of Appalachia, or southern black (or white) farm tenant?

Persons who have in their own lifetimes faced some personal traumatic experience or developed strong negative feelings about others, will need to do some personal assessment if the students they teach remind them of these sensitive areas. One teacher whose father had been an alcoholic and had deserted the family when she was an adolescent had very strong and passionate feelings about drinking, and alcoholics in general. It was hard for her to be objective about such parents when she met them, and she found it difficult not to overidentify with students, particularly girls, who might have a similar problem in their homes. As noted earlier (Chapter 5), feelings about one's religious or ethnic group or about others, can influence the way one perceives the problems, potentials, or limitations of students.

Another very important way in which secondary teachers, and their own adolescences, differ from those whom they will teach, is that teachers and future teachers have all been successful with school tasks. They all have adequate intellectual endowment and most have found school work (particularly high-school work) relatively easy. This will *not* be true of most of the students they teach. In fact, since half the population is below 100 IQ (which is what that score means), then at least one-third or more of students will be below 100 IQ. And it takes considerably more than that to do well through college. Teachers are brighter than many (not all) students. Teachers are more apt to come from homes where parents are also well educated, or prize education; the same will not be true of many of their students. Most teachers will come from intact homes; many of their students will come from homes broken by death, desertion, divorce, delinquency or other forms of social or personal pathology.

While teachers have their own personal memories as guides, they must also realize the limitations of such personal experiences in generalizing to others. It is helpful for teachers always to be students of youth and of youth culture. One of the best ways to observe the forces impinging on youth is to listen to them. Another way of gaining understanding is to read the literature of adolescence, written by and for adults, which provides glimpses into the inner world of growing up in a way that research studies tend to mask. (See Appendix B: Adolescents in fact and fiction: selected, annotated bibliography)

GATHERING DATA ABOUT STUDENTS

The teacher may want to utilize one of the diagnostic tools mentioned earlier; but in addition, a standard procedure for collecting information about students is recommended. It is hard to recall all the data about the 100 or more students a teacher may see every day. It is also important that additional information which may be of help in understanding a particular student be easily recorded and located for quick reference when the need arises.

In a loose-leaf binder or a file drawer not readily accessible to students, the teacher may develop a student file. A simple form such as the following could be filled out for each student; data can be provided by counselors, other teachers, the student's cumulative record, and by questioning students themselves as needed:

Name _____ Age _____

Father's, mother's occupations: _____

Test data: (IQ, Achievement, etc.) _____

School record: _____

Hobbies and extracurricular activities: _____

Special information and comments: _____

Physical handicaps, if any: _____

PREPARING A CASE STUDY

Prior to student teaching many colleges require a student to make a case study of an adolescent, or this may be undertaken in conjunction with student teaching. And that is the last case study a teacher ever makes. This is unfortunate. The case study, as students often report, is very revealing.

A case study need not be an elaborate, intensive analysis of a student. Actually, the kind of case study most helpful may take one or two days of concentrated attention. The significant data may already be available in counselor's records. In addition, the teacher would consult the other teachers who have this same student. A record of their experiences will help clear up a key question: Is that student only a problem in one class, or is the student revealing educational or adjustment problems to others? When the student is in class, observe carefully the behavior manifested. With whom does the student usually talk? What makes the student laugh? Turn sullen? Be rude, insolent, or suddenly shy and evasive? In fact, what are the observable behavior patterns of this student? Look over past work; are there clues to particular difficulties? The very act of paying attention to a difficult student often converts that student into an ally instead of an enemy.

WHO SHOULD COUNSEL WHOM?

Logically, the question of who should counsel whom might have been one of the first raised in this chapter. Actually, only as teachers begin to face the real problems of their students does this nettlesome query arise: "Am I the one who should consider these problems with this student?" There is no clear-cut answer.

Should teachers do any counseling at all? It is almost impossible for good teachers to avoid requests for help, advice, and support in many personal problems. This does not mean that guidance experts, where such are available, might not be able to deal more adequately with many of these problems. Unfortunately, in most secondary schools, these experts have case loads far above their capacity to handle. The great bulk of counseling, if it is to be done, must therefore still be done by the classroom teacher.

Are male teachers generally able to do a better counseling job with boys and women teachers with girls? There are certain sex-linked problems that a boy or a girl would be most reluctant to discuss with an adult of the opposite sex who is a teacher–counselor. A teacher with insight and understanding, however, not only can, but will have to, deal with the personal problems of both boys and girls. Being married often helps a teacher understand the personal problems faced by the opposite sex, which previous experiences have usually blocked out. By and large, boys share few things in the lives of girls, and vice versa. Their experiences have been limited to those that concern their own sex most deeply, with only a limited and censored view of the other sex.

Should teachers counsel primarily those of their own racial or ethnic group? Where there is any racial or ethnic tension, experience indicates that students, in the main, feel more comfortable and secure with persons they can identify with. The increased number of black counselors on college campuses is the direct response to this need and is paralleled by similar trends in secondary schools. Where there are many Spanish-speaking students there should be a counselor fluent in Spanish who is aware of the particular problems of such students.

Should a teacher try to act as a counselor with students whose problems appear to be most acute in his or her own classes? The root of the trouble may be a personality clash between them.

After much trouble with Fred, Mrs. Drake was shocked one day when he suddenly got up, slammed down his books, and stalked out of the room, saying so that all could hear, "I just can't stand this any longer." Later, when Mrs. Drake talked with the principal, she learned that Fred had flung himself into the principal's office, saying he just had to be taken out of her class. The principal, a patient and understanding person, let Fred talk. After much preliminary letting off of steam, during which time the principal did not try to argue with the student or pass any judgments, Fred finally said, "You know, I think it's because Mrs. Drake is so much like my mother, and I'm always in hot water at home. I just hate women teachers." After another half hour or so of talk, Fred had uncovered much of his own problem and had stated a solution of his own; he would like a few days out of class—he would study the assignments and do the work—and then he would return and behave better, since he saw the problem better himself. The principal relayed the substance of the discussion to Mrs. Drake, who was interested and relieved. A later interview and visit with Fred's parents helped to give insight into Fred's situation: a competing sister also made him resent women. The principal told the physical education teacher, who was able to give Fred a job as assistant to the student athletic manager in charge of equipment and shower room. This contact with older men and his own male peers did much to help Fred.

Another case, very similar to this, was reported by a teacher. Here the man teacher had evidently antagonized a girl in his class to such a point that the girl's whole life was being dominated by this one conflict. So critical had this become that the parents finally transferred the girl to another school. Some behavior problems do arise out of this kind of personality clash; the aid of another member of the staff may have to be enlisted to gain insight and help.

"BUT WHO HAS TIME FOR COUNSELING?"

The problem of finding time for counseling must still be faced. Many secondary schools gather their students from a wide radius. Students may arrive by bus just a few moments before the bell and leave just after the last bell has rung. In many schools, from one-half to nine-tenths of the student body are immediately excluded from after- or before-school conference time.

Even if the proper time is found, there is another problem. Students may be suspicious and on the defensive when called for a special interview by a teacher. "I must have done something wrong" is the first reaction. This natural suspicion can be allayed by rather simple devices. First, announce early that you hope, before the first month is over, to have an individual conference with each student, and for that reason you want them to fill out a form, such as the one on the next page.

A scheduled conference with every class member beyond the regular school day would, of course, require many more hours than any teacher has. Two alternatives are suggested:

1. Make an assignment early in the semester that requires library research. Arrange for two-thirds of the class to go at one time, and use the class period to interview the other third.

Name _____

Class schedule: Period   Teacher   Room

                         1.

                         2.

                         3.

                         .

                         .

                         .

Which of the following times would be best for you if we could schedule a
conference at that time?

1. Before school.

2. Lunch hour.

3. Study hall (Hour   Room   )

---

2. Have the class work in groups during the class hour on projects that will
   not necessitate every member's contributing, and then call individual students to one's desk for conferences.
3. Arrange for the last twenty minutes of the class period for work on homework assignments. Call up individual students for a conference. During the
   semester, if such time is used judiciously, the teacher could have an individual conference with every member of the class.

One of the perennial excuses that teachers give for not having individual
conferences with students is that they do not have the time. It is important
to talk individually with each student, and time can be made available. It
is particularly crucial in schools where there is an atmosphere of trouble
and hostility that each teacher become individually acquainted with each
student. The personal touch, this obvious caring about each student, can
make a tremendous difference in student class behavior.

GETTING ACQUAINTED

The get-acquainted interview, as described and recommended here,
should be simple and exploratory in nature. It is aimed at establishing
rapport, indicating the interest of the teacher in the student, and gaining
some insight into the student as a person. The kinds of questions that
might be asked are:

1. Well, John, is typing one of your favorite subjects? What are your favorite subjects? Which ones do you do best in? Do you know why you do better in them than in others?
2. What hobbies do you have?
3. Do you work after school? Have any home chores?
4. What do you like best about school? Are you in any of the clubs, teams, or other groups?
5. What do you want to do after you graduate? What does your family think you should do? (This questions leads to questions about family or guardians if the student is not living with his or her family. The teacher should be careful not to probe; if the student is resistant, then it is wise to go on to the next question.)
6. Have you had any problem so far in the work that we have done in this class?

A well-structured interview, such as the one above, in which certain questions are asked in a certain order, will help, first, to establish rapport and, second, to lead naturally into areas of significance for the teacher. It naturally ends on an impersonal note, so that the student feels that not too much has been revealed.

SEEKING AN UNDERSTANDING OF STUDENT BEHAVIOR

While the individual interview is essential in most cases in order to gain some understanding of a student whose classroom behavior is causing difficulty, one cannot expect in-class miracles to occur just because John talked so freely in a private conversation; John may still be unable to resist the blandishments of his peers who reward his clowning or belligerence in class.

A further special word of caution, too, must be entered: Counselors with long experience with young people from disadvantaged areas find that many of these students, particularly boys, will not respond to an individual interview. Such young people are often not used to individual attention, are threatened by it, do not feel comfortable with an adult in an authority position, and often lack the "language" of the middle-class interview situation. For these reasons teachers in inner-city schools sometimes feel extremely frustrated: "I just can't seem to reach them," is the complaint. "They will say 'Yes, ma'am' and I know they don't mean it, but what do they mean? What do they think?" In such instances, the teacher would be wiser to have two or three of "the gang" come in together to talk things over. The students will reinforce one another, and if one is inarticulate the others may be able to speak for him or her.

With all students, of course, the establishment of trust and confidence is a primary prerequisite to any kind of counseling relationship. One certainly is unlikely to talk about one's problems to an enemy, or to someone who may immediately spread the word to other adults or to authorities. Teachers must make clear and unequivocal their ability to accept a confidential statement as being just that. This does not mean the teacher will not go further for help.

The teacher may find that the problem is rooted in an impossible family relationship, in a physical growth problem, in a neighborhood gang —problems the teacher may not be able to deal with at all. In such a case, what should the teacher do? Obviously, call on those agencies and facilities that can deal with such problems. The important point here is that, although it is a useful tool when skillfully utilized, the interview obviously will not solve all the problems of students.

Another caution for the teacher: In an interview one may find an individual student only too willing to agree with any opinion expressed by the teacher, promising all kinds of changes in behavior—and nothing happens at all. Again, some students have become so accustomed to giving back to the teacher what the teacher wants that they will do so in almost any circumstance.

A WORD OF CAUTION

The interview intended primarily to coerce is bound to fail as an effective counseling instrument. If the teacher is going to "tell the student just where to get off" the atmosphere will be far from conducive to a real understanding of why the student caused the trouble. In order, therefore, for counseling to work, the teacher might very well wait until several days have elapsed after a problem incident has occurred, and then call the student in at a time and place convenient for uninterrupted conversation. By this time both student and teacher have reevaluated their own roles in the problem. If the teacher has used the time wisely, office records about the individual student have been checked thoroughly in order to see whether any light can be thrown on the specific difficulty. Perhaps the most unwise thing a teacher can say, after a student has been particularly difficult and after many warnings, is: "Well, John, you had better stay after school this evening; it seems that you and I should have a little talk." Such "little talks" are usually unpleasant, acrimonious, and lead to increased student–teacher hostility. A better approach might be the following:

Barbara consistently "forgot" her assignments. Whenever any homework was due, she did not turn it in on time and often failed to turn it in at all if no class time was provided for her to do it. Because she had not done the work, she was not informed about the topics the class discussed. She was therefore bored, and in her boredom she constantly tried to distract the attention of her nearest classmates by chattering, sending notes, turning around in her seat. Ms. Cohen tried to help her and often had to reprimand her for interrupting. On Wednesday, Barbara was acting worse than usual and Ms. Cohen, in desperation, asked her to go to the library and complete the last three assignments. For the next several days, Barbara behaved well in class, but still failed to turn in her work.

On the following Monday, Ms. Cohen said: "Barbara, I noticed that you have study period right after lunch, when I have my free period. Could you meet me here so that we could go over some of these long lost assignments?"

Barbara acquiesced. The problem that she faced had not been ignored. The teacher could not pretend that she just wanted to have a "little talk" with Barbara, because they were both aware of the area of trouble. But Ms. Cohen had been careful not to call Barbara in for a conference until the situation between them could be as calm and pleasant as possible.

COUNSELING IN ACTION

What does the teacher do in an interview with a student? There are two schools of thought: One approach is for the counselor to tell the student quickly how he or she understands the student's problem, outline what it is, and give direct instruction about what to do. This kind of directive counseling has an advantage because little time is needed. Furthermore, the student is not uncertain about what is known and what is expected. However, the method has definite limitations, some of which will be discussed below. The other approach, the nondirective, is more subtle. Here the teacher merely expresses to the student a feeling that perhaps the student has a problem. The student is encouraged through interest and relative silence on the part of the teacher to talk about the problem. The teacher gives no judgment regarding what the student says, merely reflects back to the student whatever feeling tone is manifested. This is intended to allow the student to recognize the problem and propose a solution. This type of interviewing will be developed below.

The following pages contain illustrative interview excerpts, showing good and poor techniques in counseling students. These are given in detail, with analytic commentaries, because the interview is central to all counseling. Skill in interviewing must be learned as one learns any other of the skills that contribute to effective teaching.

The descriptions that follow contrast various types of interviewing approaches and indicate throughout the nondirective, client-centered approach to the same problem. The kinds of interviewer attitudes illustrated, which do *not* result in better student adjustment, are:

1. The Disciplinarian
2. The Judge
3. The Moralist

4. The Wishful Thinker
5. The Helper
6. The Prober
7. The Closet Bigot

In reading these descriptions, it is important to note those words and phrases that contribute to rapport and those that interfere with it; those phrases that indicate genuine interest in helping students understand and solve their own problems; and those that make them feel helpless and at fault.[7]

1. The Disciplinarian

Teacher: I don't think you have been working as we expect students to work in this class.

Student: I don't know what you mean.

Teacher: You know very well what I mean; look, here is my rollbook. Let me see: no report for last Friday; last Wednesday, the exam —you were absent that day and didn't make it up. You realize this behavior is not acceptable.

The student is being put on the spot. The teacher is trying to get the student in a corner, with all the advantage on the side of the teacher. If and when the teacher ever gets around to discovering why this series of events occurred, the student will be upset, angry, resentful. Punishment is usually the only outcome of this approach.

Teacher-Counselor

Teacher: I asked you to stay after school for a few minutes because of your work recently.

Student: I know, I haven't done any, have I? (defiant)

Teacher: You know what the problem is . . .

Student: Yeah, I never get my work in. I don't like to do it, it . . .

Teacher: I see . . .

Here the teacher makes the preamble as short as possible, speaks mildly and unemotionally; does not try to interrupt the student, but rather encourages the student to talk about the problem that is of first concern. Later, some other aspects of this problem will appear; but the teacher lets the student talk, following his or her own pattern.

2. The Judge

Student: I just can't do geometry.

Teacher: The real trouble is that you waste all your time.

Student: I really try.

---

[7] Adapted from Dugald S. Arbuckle, *Teacher Counseling* (Reading, Mass.: Addison-Wesley, 1950), pp. 52–68.

Teacher: You might try, but you don't concentrate when you do. I bet you have the radio on all the time. That isn't a good way to study.
Student: But I . . .
Teacher: Now, no buts . . .

No sympathy here. The teacher, like an omnipotent judge, knows far better than the student what the problem is. There is condemnation without listening. The student is clearly made to feel on trial. The student is instantly put on the defensive, and the next step is active hostility. The teacher in only reinforcing a personal need to be all powerful and is of no help to a struggling student.

Teacher-Counselor

Student: I just can't do geometry.
Teacher: You feel you just can't do geometry . . .
Student: I don't know. Sometimes I think I'm just dumb. My mother tells me I'm dumb all the time. I bet she's right.
Teacher: Your mother tells you you are dumb . . .
Student: Yeah . . . but I don't think I am. Anyway, I'm not dumb like old Fatso Grooby—now he's a real stupe. Why, do you know . . .

The teacher reflected back the student's feeling. Ofter this is done in the identical words the student uses, but the inflection indicates no judgment, no feeling on the part of the teacher, merely interest, perhaps slight solicitude. Often, a slightly higher pitch, a slight questioning tone, is an assistance in such an interview situation. Here the student responds well; he is beginning to reveal his feelings about himself, his capacities, his reactions to others. Soon the teacher will have built up a great deal of insight into the problem.

3. The Moralist

Student: What do you think I should do?
Teacher: ' Well, you are the one who really has to make the decision. You have to be able to face these things and decide for yourself. Later in life no one is going to make decisions for you.
Student: Well, I wish you would help me.
Teacher: As I said, you must make your own decisions. Now I think the best thing to do is drop the geometry and take study hall this semester, and then take typing next year.

The Moralist cannot resist telling the student how to behave in life. Such a teacher is ready with aphorisms and value judgments for every decision. So full of moral wisdom is this kind of person that no student would willingly come with a confession of antisocial behavior in order to get help. This teacher would merely make the student's guilt worse without providing any help. The Moralist is compulsive about giving advice.

Teacher-Counselor

Student: What do you think I should do?
Teacher: You feel that you need help in deciding . . .
Student: Yeah, I am sort of uncertain myself, and anyway . . .
Teacher: I see your problem . . .
Student: Now, I could change majors, couldn't I? But my folks would have a fit. I don't know—if I fail geometry it might even be worse. Is it possible to drop a course?
Teacher: Yes.
Student: Now maybe if I do that, by next year I can convince Dad I just can't go to college . . . I just hate the idea of going to college; we fight about it at home all the time. Dad is so stubborn sometimes; sometimes I think if someone from school could tell him what I can do . . .

Notice that the teacher made no judgment about what the student said. The student's feeling of uncertainty is recognized; and yet underneath it the student was about to see possible alternatives. Even more important, an insight has been gained into the real dynamics of the student's problem; it rests with the father in part. An opening has been given for the school to work directly with the parent in solving the student's problem.

4. The Wishful Thinker

Student: I get so worried about not doing well.
Teacher: Now let's not worry about such things. I'm sure everything will turn out all right.
Student: I just feel so blue sometimes and there are so many problems.
Teacher: Now, now, everything will be all right; we can't let ourselves worry about everything, you know; that just makes it worse.

The constant optimist, the Wishful-Thinker type, does not want to admit that things are bad, or cruel, or hopeless, or difficult: "Let's all look at the sunny side." Sometimes this type is the jovial backslapping, booster kind of person. No real counsel is available from anyone who is so aggressively cheery. Such a person sounds patronizing, and usually is. After several such cheery interviews, the student will quickly close up and evade the teacher: "If I feel blue, I don't want someone to tell me I don't or shouldn't.

Teacher-Counselor

Student: I get so worried about not doing well.
Teacher: You are worried about your own success . . .
Student: Well, yes and no. I don't think it is all my fault. It's these darned depressions I get into. I just want to cry and cry.
Teacher: You feel like crying . . .
Student: (Voice shakes) And I do, and I know I'm a big sissy; there isn't anything wrong. (Student starts to sniffle.)

Teacher:	(Hands student a tissue box). You feel ashamed because you cry for no good reason.
Student:	(Takes tissue, blows nose) Yeah . . . Do you think everyone feels this way?
Teacher:	You feel different from other boys and girls.

Again, note the way the teacher resists the impulse to sympathize or reprimand. One of the real possibilities of this kind of counseling, however, is that students will cry or become emotional in another way because this sort of counseling recognizes the real emotions of individuals. The teacher develops skill in meeting these situations, not by getting alarmed or being sympathetic and saying, "Now, now, there isn't anything to cry about," but by merely recognizing that the student has a problem, providing a tissue, and bringing the conversation back into focus.

5. The Super Helper

Teacher:	Now, you just tell me what is bothering you, and I bet I can help you out.
Student:	Oh, I don't think anyone can help me . . .
Teacher:	Now you know we teachers are very happy to do anything we can.
Student:	Well, it's that science class. I don't get along with Mr. Dipple. Would you get me changed?
Teacher:	Well, now . . .

The Helper wants to shoulder everyone's burdens, and, as in this case, if the offer of help is taken seriously, the teacher may be in a very difficult position. Often the teacher can do nothing. The student learns to distrust the offers of help and to suspect that teachers do not mean what they say. Moreover, offering to help leaves the student just as dependent as ever. Teachers need to help young people solve their own problems, not to solve the problems for them.

Teacher-Counselor

Teacher:	You want me to help you, Jane?
Student:	Well, not exactly. I wish I could get out of this mess myself . . .
Teacher:	You feel you are in a mess . . .
Student:	(Bursts out) I just hate Mr. Dipple, and I know he hates me.
Teacher:	I see . . .
Student:	He is pretty nice to me, and all that, but those worms and things just give me the creeps.
Teacher:	You feel Mr. Dipple is really all right.
Student:	Oh, he's okay, I guess. But I get upset every time I see a worm. Do you think he'd let me off if I explained how they made me feel?

Here the teacher does not offer help, but indicates a recognition of the student's need; and, as actually can be seen, the student does not want help but clarification. By the end of the conversation, the student has pinned down the problem to her own feelings; has even outlined a possible action.

6. The Prober

Teacher: Tell me, Agnes, are you sure you are happy at home?

Student: Well, okay, I guess.

Teacher: Now be honest; do you get along well with your parents?

Student: Oh, I don't know.

Teacher: Now we can't get anywhere unless you tell me about yourself. Have you always been moody?

Student: No, just recently, and that is why I guess I seem to mope about in class.

Teacher: Well, now we are getting someplace. You must have some worries you aren't telling me about.

There is great temptation on the part of some teachers to pry personal information out of students. But students, like anyone else, protect their personal lives. This should be respected. The direct attack, as noted here, brings out resistance; this girl is not going to tell anyone anything. The teacher pounces on each new bit of information; even accuses the student of being bad because information is withheld. No information that the student is not freely willing to give should be deliberately sought.

As noted earlier, there is increased wariness on the part of school people to make any kind of inquiries regarding home situations. In some school systems there are community groups ready to pounce on any teacher or counselor who appears to "pry" into what is considered a personal matter. We know that students do not leave their home problems at home when they come to school. But we must respect the wish that all people have for privacy. Where there is true parental abuse, or such outrageous deviance as incest, then of course the appropriate authorities must be contacted and action taken. A nondirective interview with a sympathetic individual may allow these critical and dangerous situations to be aired, whereas the prober may get nothing.

Teacher-Counselor

Teacher: Agnes, I have noticed you have been sort of daydreaming in class . . .

Student: Yes, I guess I have.

Teacher: Do you want to tell me about it?

Student: Gosh, what is there to tell?

Teacher: You feel the daydreaming is your own problem.

Student: Heck, it doesn't bother anyone else.

Teacher: (Just nods thoughtfully)

Student: (Long silence) No one ever noticed before.

Teacher: I see . . .

Student: (Long silence) There are so many things on my mind . . . (Bursts out) You know, my parents are going to get a divorce.

Teacher: You think about your problem in class . . .

Another pattern of counseling can be seen here: The student does not want to talk, but the teacher feels an important problem is present. The teacher allows the student to remain silent, but indicates interest and no impatience. The feeling conveyed by the teacher is that the student doesn't have to talk at all if she doesn't want to, but here is someone interested in her. It is interesting to note that the student shows some surprise that anyone did notice the behavior. And underlying the symptom is the real cause, which the probing teacher above will never uncover.

7. The Closet Bigot

Student: I was wondering about taking fourth year Spanish . . .

Teacher: Well, let's see. You have done pretty well in Spanish, but I can't see how it will help you. You are going into secretarial work, aren't you?

Student: Well, I really was thinking about college . . .

Teacher: Now, now. I like to see an ambitious student. But you people don't have such a good chance in college, you know; the drop-out rate is pretty high. I think you'd be better off with that Business Law course and maybe advanced shorthand . . .

Clearly, this teacher holds a stereotyped view of students from "that group." What right has a teacher to pronounce the future for any student? Certainly, in these days of equal educational opportunity it is imperative that teachers above all should see beyond stereotypes, and should help and support those who have not been helped before.

Teacher-Counselor

Student: I was wondering about taking fourth year Spanish . . .

Teacher: Well, let's see. You want to take more Spanish . . .

Student: Yes, I do real well in Spanish; and with my other grades it would really help me get into the university.

Teacher: You are thinking ahead . . .

Student: Oh yes. I know not many Chicanas have gone to the university, but I know I am a good student and with this language advantage I can really get someplace.

The teacher-counselor is not blinded by stereotypes. Recognition is given to the fact that group identities, although important in many ways, are not limitations. The teacher is a significant gatekeeper in helping young people develop realistic views of their talents and their opportunities. Indeed, teachers are often the key individuals who support and direct a student's ambition, or stifle and kill it.

ERRORS TO AVOID

There are other ways, in addition to those just presented, in which teachers betray the counseling function. Take Mr. Unger, for example: He is always in a great hurry, he fiddles nervously with a pencil while someone talks to him, jumps up as though expecting someone else, looks at his watch in an ostentatious manner, talks briskly with ill-concealed impatience. The student soon gets the message: Mr. Unger has no time for me. Or take the case of Ms. Drew. George appears after school, and Ms. Drew looks up, startled, and says, "Did you want something, George?" "Gosh, didn't you tell me to come in to see you?" he replies. She forgot. But the student will not forget her mistake very soon.

Or what about Linda Walters? She really needed someone to talk to. And Mrs. Martin, who was friendly and interested in class, might just be the person who could help her. What a dash of cold water to turn up after school and find Mrs. Martin greet her appearance with coolness bordering on displeasure and resentment. It is true that some teachers are warm and open when dealing with groups of students and cold and uncomfortable in a one-to-one relationship. If this is one's own personal pattern, it is wise to let students in on the secret, telling them that you like and appreciate them as students of your favorite subject but cannot serve them in a counseling relationship. Or, better yet, one can seek personal professional assistance and find out what in oneself is locking out a significant facet of human interaction.

There are times when an unexpected student drops in and interrupts something that must be attended to. If the teacher is genuinely busy, a simple explanation should be made, "I'll be more than happy to talk to you, Sam, but I just cannot make it this afternoon. Let's set a date when we can get together."

LEARNING THE NONDIRECTIVE APPROACH

The teacher–counselor interviews described above utilized a method described as "nondirective." The student was encouraged to talk, and no attempt was made to impose the teacher's wishes or ideas.

The nondirective approach is contrary to much in one's own experience. Daily life is bound by rules; people are told what and what not to do. It takes a conscious effort when one is in a position of authority not to tell others what to do. Giving orders is a neat and precise way of producing conformist, obedient, automatons who, when actually faced with major decisions to make on their own, either have to run for help or blindly decide—sometimes tragically.

Therefore, despite the temptation to be "tellers" and to give advice and to "lay down the law," teachers, to be consistent with the concept of producing more democratically oriented individuals, must necessarily make determined efforts to be nondirective in their guidance and counseling efforts.

Again, however, it must be noted that young people who have grown up in harsh and punitive environments where behavior and the motives for action have rarely, if ever, been explored, will find the nondirective approach disorienting. They just will not know how to act or react. Teachers may have to learn ways of being flexible to meet the differing personality and environmental patterns of youth. And just as the nondirective method may produce more lasting and significant self-direction on the part of many adolescents, it can be a flop or deterrent for others.

Learning to be nondirective takes time and effort. Beginning teachers need practice and help in developing this special skill up to the point where they feel comfortable in the listening role, are sensitive to underlying emotional content, and are able to suspend the judgmental and authoritarian responses that they are accustomed to.

The essence of this approach includes:

- listening
- reflecting back the feeling of the interviewee's comments
- refraining from making judgmental comments
- withholding advice
- supporting interviewee's line of response
- waiting for comments
- refraining from probing
- asking questions about feelings, not facts
- demonstrating interest and caring by posture
- listening
- listening
- listening

THE SPECIALISTS CAN HELP

This chapter has stressed the role of the teacher in the counseling process and has shown why it is that the counseling burden must inevitably fall on the classroom teacher. It is, however, highly important that the teacher realize there are limitations in working with individuals and know who is available in the immediate school or in the larger community to assist students. In a secondary school with an enrollment of 750 or more students, there probably are full-time counselors on the staff. In schools of smaller enrollment, there may be part-time counselors or none at all. Counselors can provide the teacher with much helpful information about students and can be utilized for referral of difficult cases. The teacher will want to investigate the total guidance program in the school in order to know exactly what kinds of help are provided, since these vary considerably from school to school.

Furthermore, the teacher will want to become familiar with the resources and personnel of the following specialized agencies of school and community:

Welfare and attendance personnel. The attendance office is typically concerned with truancy, dropouts, and the special problems of youngsters that may prevent their regular school attendance.

School social workers. These may also be called pupil personnel workers, home and school visitors, or visiting teachers. The school social worker has the responsibility of linking school and community services, obtaining the help of community agencies where needed, gathering home data for school use, and, in some cases, doing tutorial teaching at home for convalescent students.

Child guidance clinics. Here the teacher will usually find a team composed of a psychiatrist, two or more psychologists, several specially trained social workers, psychometrists, and other special personnel in the field of counseling.

Family agencies and other social agencies. In most medium-sized and all large communities there is an intricate network of social agencies dealing with many facets of family and child needs. Among these are: foster home placement bureaus, detention homes, family service agencies, county welfare departments, welfare agencies organized by local church groups, and shelters for runaways.

Special classes and schools. There are both public and private agencies especially organized to care for the needs of individuals handicapped by physical or emotional problems. Where these are, who can be admitted, and what services are provided should be known by the teacher, who can then pass this information on to those who may need it.

Special poverty programs. During the late 1960s the federal government and state agencies and many private foundations supported a large number of programs aimed directly at ameliorating the worst of the impact of poverty. Many programs lasted for a summer or a year and then vanished. Others have some durability, particularly federally financed ones, but depend on vicissitudes in Congress and priorities in the minds of the public. Such programs as the Job Corps were especially designed to help the young person who has dropped out of high school or who would drop out without some special assistance. Upward Bound is another program designed to reach poor youth who have potential for higher education that is being untapped by standard educational practices. Many young people who could be served are not because responsible adults are unaware of the existence of such new programs.

HOT LINES

In the last decade there has been a proliferation of special services through "hot lines." Many of these developed out of a need to serve youth who were reluctant or afraid to ask for help. Typically, hot lines are prepared to deal with almost any kind of personal emergency, although some are identified as being of particlular help for a special need. Hot lines are useful for young people with drug problems, pregnancy, questions about sex and sexuality, parental abuse, and family problems. Runaways often call on hot lines for help. They have come to fill a vital place in getting help for many desperate and lonely youngsters. It would be helpful if teachers posted in every classroom the phone number of the local hot lines.

SPECIAL PROGRAMS

In this category we would place Alcoholics Anonymous, and their related program for teenagers whose parents are alcoholics, Al-Anon. Alcoholism has become one of the biggest social problems for all ages. Youth whose homes are disrupted by alcoholism need support and assistance. The groups formed of similar individuals are invaluable in giving this support. There are other groups for persons who are overweight, compulsive gamblers and single parents. Lists of such services should be available through the counselor or the local United Givers organization.

GROUP GUIDANCE

The more formal setting for group guidance in many high schools is the "homeroom." This administrative device allows one teacher to take major responsibility for a group of thiry to thirty-five students. The teacher may meet with the group once a day for twenty to thirty minutes, or several times during the week for an hour. During the homeroom period, the teacher is expected to carry out various routines in connection with arranging schedules, to check attendance and absence, to discuss student government and election procedures. In addition, the homeroom may be designated as the guidance period, during which the teacher is encouraged to discuss with students the kinds of group concerns which are not covered by standard curricular offerings. It is a place where the teacher seeks to understand better the problems of each individual.

The kind of classroom atmosphere in which group guidance takes place most effectively is similar to that of the democratic classroom (see Chapter 4). However, certain of its characteristics need further amplification here. To carry on adequate group guidance, the teacher must have a greater-than-average ability to create a permissive atmosphere; that is, an atmosphere in which the teacher actively accepts the way students feel, think, and behave without censure or judgment or disapproval.

> The class was discussing the assignment for the next day. Sidney burst out with: "I think the old windbag who wrote this book must have been a dope." The teacher, instead of chiding him for such an attitude, said instead, "You feel this book isn't very interesting," Susan chimed in: "It is so dull, Ms. Andrews." Other students entered the discussion, many expressing similar opinions, with Ms. Andrews merely nodding, listening, helping those talk who felt they wanted to, until the class had exhausted its comments about the book and the assignment. The group then rather cheerfully went back to the original assignment and carried on a lively and friendly discussion about the major ideas to be sought in the next chapter. The teacher had used the occasion of Sidney's remark to let the students get rid of some of their resentment without scolding for holding undesirable attitudes; as a result, the class was much better able to continue with the expected work.

The principles for leading such a discussion with a group are similar to those for individual nondirective counseling:

1. The leader's comments are basically reflections and clarifications of the expressed feelings of the speaker, or comments indicating an understanding and acceptance of the feeling.
2. If students do not wish to speak, they are not pressed to join the conversation.
3. If the conversation lags, the teacher does not direct the thinking of the students in the "right" channels.
4. The leader at no time criticizes, moralizes, or acts as judge.
5. The atmosphere is permissive, so that each student may say as much, or as little as he or she wants.
6. The leader does not answer questions. Instead he or she may reflect the confusion of the student who is asking the question.

There is danger of overdoing permissiveness, of course. In the hands of an unskilled person, the permissive atmosphere may easily degenerate into chaos. What is emphasized in group guidance or club activity is a greater responsibility on the part of the student for his or her own learning and a greater recognition of the emotional aspects of the learning process.

Group guidance in the classroom may evolve through classroom discussion. Role playing (see Chapter 11) is another technique that is particularly valuable for presenting and analyzing many of the kinds of problems which are apt to emerge when there are implicit guidance goals for teaching. For many guidance purposes teenagers may select their own topics to explore by way of role playing. Parent-adolescent relationships regarding use of money, choice of friends, kinds of clothes to wear, and other typical parental regulations that create family havoc are fruitful focal points of role-playing enactments.

Other types of problems, such as early marriage, leaving school before graduation, racial or ethnic hostility, can be explored through role-playing situations.

EXTRACURRICULAR ACTIVITIES AND THE COUNSELING FUNCTION

Why put extracurricular activities in a chapter on counseling as well as in the chapter on student teaching? (see Chapter 2). It is in such settings that some of the most effective counseling is accomplished. Every secondary school has an extracurricular program, and the larger the school, the larger the program.

The relationship between the students and the teacher—sponsor in the extracurricular activities is very different from that between the classroom teacher and students. As a club sponsor, the teacher is not giving grades, and is therefore not acting as a judge. The teacher is a resource, someone who is around to help, give advice, provide expert assistance where needed.

Essentially, the club should provide a framework within which the students learn independence and have a chance to develop skill in exercising judgment. The teacher must be able to be neutral, to let the young people talk as they wish about subjects that seem significant to them at the moment. Unless the teacher can do this, the club situation, like any other adult-dominated situation, will not enable students to learn responsibility.

ACADEMIC GUIDANCE

The importance of academic guidance should not be underestimated. Encouraging a student to sign up for a college-preparatory course or insisting that a boy take beginning machine shop instead of French may set the pattern of his life.

Studies indicate that students from higher socioeconomic levels and students whose parents have advanced education make up a very high percentage of those enrolled in college-preparatory courses; whereas students from lower social groups, students from minority cultural groups, and students whose parents have had a meager education tend, by and large, to take the commercial, general, home economics, shop, and agricultural courses. Is this a recognition of their ability, is it a response to cultural pressure, or is it out of ignorance? Very often it is true that educated parents understand and pass on to their children a desire for education, while parents with little education themselves may prize schooling for their children but are unable to help their children make competent educational decisions.

Contact can be made with individuals at local colleges or universities, in academic departments, or in the education departments, and ask for a student representative to visit class. Such students can then provide high schoolers with a vivid, and realistic, view of what it means to go to college. There is often a great deal of misinformation about college attendance.

Programs in trade, business, and skilled labor should be identified regarding their academic requirements. The important message for secondary school students is that academic decisions made by them will have a very significant bearing on what they will be doing with their lives later; students need all the help they can get in these critical decisions.

CAREER EDUCATION: VOCATIONAL GUIDANCE

The 1970s saw the culmination of a trend that had been apparent for a number of years: Most young people had very limited career goals, many aspired to relatively few kinds of jobs, and there were stereotyped notions of who could do what. Out of this recognition came a federal emphasis on career education. Conferences throughout the country were held and funds were made available to school systems and groups to encourage education about careers from kindergarten through high school.

Although there is some criticism of the new career education emphasis,[8] it is also evident that understanding the world of work has not been a high priority in education and that something should be done about it.

Individual subject matter teachers have a significant role to play. One thing all teachers can do is to find out the family of careers and jobs which are related to each area of specialty. Does skill in typing lead only to becoming a clerk? Or could typing lead to editing (with appropriate English skills); journalism; international business (with a foreign language); or being self-employed as a free-lance typist. Also, typing skills are as useful for boys as for girls, and the job market for male secretaries is excellent. Anyone going to college is aided by typing skills. The list of ways a particular area of academic instruction relates to careers is limited only by the teacher's imagination. Students will not know about these job relationships if teachers do not spell them out, specifically, concretely, and often.

It is possible for any teacher to help students see the job relevance of the work in his or her course. This does not mean that only concepts that have a specific job application should be taught; but wherever an application is relevant, it should be made.

As a way of motivating students to work on algebra, apparently unrelated to their plans for the future, Mr. Jordan first asked the students to indicate their probable vocational goals. He found that members of the class ex-

[8] David Rogers, "Vocational and Career Education: A Critique and Some New Directions," *Teachers College Record*, 74 (May 1975), pp. 471–512.

pected to enter the usual occupations. A number were going into farming. Many were expecting to enter the skilled trades, such as machine shop and carpentry. Most of the girls were clearly interested in future homemaking. He set up ten groups in the class according to broad occupational categories and then asked each group to interview two or three representatives of that category to see what mathematics they needed in their work.

The reports from the groups were very interesting. Most of the students had no idea that so much mathematics was needed in everyday life.

Another approach to vocational guidance in the academic classroom is exemplified by the following:

One bulletin board in the chemistry laboratory was called "Careers for You in Chemistry." Here Mrs. Grant posted articles about chemists that she found from time to time in *Time, Saturday Review, Fortune, Science,* and *The Reader's Digest.* She had the current report from the government on opportunities for girls in science. There seemed to be a constant stream of articles that illustrated possible kinds of work for a student interested in chemistry and related fields. At least once a semester she would bring in several individuals who used chemical processes in their occupations to talk to the class about the training needed. One was a laboratory technician from a nearby oil refinery. Another was the chemist from the city water department. A third usually was the soil analyst from the state agricultural college, who did extensive traveling around the state. Following this presentation, she would encourage several students to see how many jobs they could discover in which a knowledge of chemistry was important. These activities provided the basis for a discussion about vocations and vocational choices. A number of Mrs. Grant's students found a lifelong interest in careers with a chemistry component because of this introduction.

One high school, with an energetic and imaginative principal and a cooperative and enthusiastic staff found that the parents of the students worked at a wide range of occupations. The parents' jobs represented 90 percent of the jobs in which students had indicated an interest. Parents were invited to visit and tell interested students about their jobs. Then parents were formed into career advisory councils for the twelve academic departments of the school to give advice on curriculum development in relation to careers. And it didn't cost anyone anything.[9]

PARENTS CAN BE ALLIES

In many schools, only the parents of children who are in trouble are well known by the principal, counselors, and teachers. The few parents who are leaders in the PTA are recognized by the teachers; but most parents are vague and unknown quantities. Perhaps on "Back-to-School Night" or dur-

[9] Katherine Clay, "Career Counseling at El Camino," *Phi Delta Kappan,* 59 (November 1977), pp. 203–204.

ing American Education Week, the teacher will neet several parents of students in his or her classes, chat with them for a few brief moments about what a nice boy Johnny is, and that is the end of the teacher–parent contact for another year. Even on these occasions, the parents the secondary school teacher sees are often parents of children who are in serious trouble, parents who are active in PTA and community groups, and parents of the superior children in the school.

An increasing number of secondary schools have "Back-to-School Night" every semester or once a year. And typically, teachers react with dread and distaste. Rarely does one hear teachers speak of "Back-to-School Night" with pleasure. And yet this chore could be one of the most valuable ways to communicate with some parents. Only in small high schools will the turnout be anywhere near 90 percent; usually it is about 10 percent of the potential parent population. But that is an important 10 percent, since they in turn talk with other parents in the community. It is valuable to get your message into the community network.

What message would you want to be delivered to parents in the community? Obviously, that you are a good teacher, that you care about your students, that you will do all you can to help them have a good year in your class. And how do you communicate this? A well-prepared "Back-to-School Night" situation includes:

- your name on the chalkboard.
- illustrative bulletin boards, showing clearly the kind of work students do; if it is an art, shop, or home economics class, projects are on display.
- a brief handout, of no more than one page, indicating the major topics of content which will be covered that semester or year. (Note: Be sure this is the best possible product you can manage: grammatical, no misspelling, and readable!)
- if textbooks are used, one is at each desk where the parents will be sitting. (If there are different textbooks for different classes, try to get a few to pass around each period.)
- a brief statement (or include in another handout) your criteria for adequate performance—what do you base your grades on.
- time allotted for questions. If there are none, indicate you will be happy to talk individually with any parent, and encourage the others to browse in the room.
- a sign-up sheet so you can know which parents came.

Normally, the teacher will not see parents whose children are of low ability, parents who are on the fringe of community social life, parents from minority groups, or parents from the lower socioeconomic levels. There are, of course, always exceptions to the above. Where there are large parent turnouts one can usually assume there are good school–community relations. Once in a while a parent turns up with a gripe which he or she wants to make in public. Accept the comments as gracefully as possible, do not argue, and encourage the parent to take the complaint to the administration; do not assume it is an attack on you.

The failure of the typical secondary school to make contact with parents is not just because school people are reluctant to initiate such contacts, though this is indeed part of the story. Adolescents by and large are often eager to keep their parents as far away from school as possible. This is understandable. Young people are going through the difficult and confusing period of establishing their independence from their families; and one part of their lives which is strictly their own is their life in school. Here they are truly beyond their parent's surveillance; what they report back about their school experiences is a highly edited and censored version. They have no particular wish for others to tell parents anything more.

Undoubtedly, the wishes and needs of the adolescent have acted to reduce the emphasis of the secondary school on teacher-parent contacts. But is the paucity of contact that now exists justified? Would students in the long run grow up better and learn more if parents had a closer contact with the school? Much of the adolescent–parent conflict arises from a lack of understanding of each other's worlds. The school has an obligation to aid the parent, who is still a powerful influence in the life of the adolescent, to gain greater insight into the adolescent's problems, as well as to help the adolescent understand better the world of the parents.

There is increased recognition that without full parental support many youth will fall by the wayside. Some of the most dramatic gains in achievement in inner-city schools have come where parents have been directly involved in their education. The Oakland, California, school system, for example, has instituted a three-way contract between parents, students and teachers of all the students in the system. The contract includes statements of what each will do; one of the things the parents agree to is that there be a quiet place to study at home.[10]

Most secondary school teachers have trouble talking with parents. Teacher training typically omits the personal–social problems of adults in our society, particularly how teachers can understand them. Some of the problems that parents of adolescents face are:

- adolescents challenge the authority of their parents
- adolescents are highly critical of their parents
- parents are entering middle-age, and their own feelings about themselves may be going through a severe period of readjustment
- they are no longer so physically attractive or energetic as before
- realization of the limit to their personal ambitions in terms of job, money, or status.[11]
- mothers in particular may feel less needed; the children are growing up and can take care of themselves; soon they will be out of the home.

[10] "Newsbriefs," *Phi Delta Kappan*, 59 (November 1977), p. 220.
[11] Gail Sheehy, *Passages* (New York: Dutton, 1976).

- parents are fearful of the heterosexual needs of their children; they are particularly anxious that they don't "go bad." The possibility of marriage seems imminent, and many parents feel insecure in the advice and help they have provided their children.
- selection of life goals on the part of adolescents is a pressing problem; the conflict between parent and child about vocational choice becomes crucial for many.
- parents may feel that they have not done as good a job as they should have in raising their children. As parents, they may be highly self-critical and have few feelings of success. Our culture provides so many possible courses of action for the parent that, if one choice is made, there may be the constant feeling that perhaps another might have been better.

There are a number of basic difficulties in communication between parents and teachers; some of them are:

- Teachers may not understand the personal life situations faced by the parent, as noted above.
- Parents are more deeply involved emotionally with the child than the teacher, who can afford to be more matter-of-fact and objective; they speak a different language when discussing the child.
- Parents may approach teachers with stock attitudes; some of these are:
  a. "Teachers are superior and I am inferior; the teacher should tell me what to do."
  b. "Teachers are peculiar people who have never really lived; I don't think they can tell me much about my child."
  c. "Anyone can teach; teaching is merely drilling the child with facts."
  d. "Teachers always made me suffer; I am really afraid of teachers."
  e. "Teachers, especially high-school teachers, are something special; I can't talk to them freely."

Both parents and teachers may be unsure of their values; for example, "Do we or do we not want children of different races to meet socially?" Such differences in values may lead to real difficulties in communication.

Teachers may often be younger than the parents, and themselves may be unmarried or if married, have only young children. Not too many beginning teachers are parents of teenagers.

Additionally, teachers may represent new ideas, a broader world; parents may be more provincial, may not have kept up with new knowledge and discoveries which shake older beliefs.

Teachers, for their part, may fear parents; the parents may be critical, and with reason. After all, teachers know full well no teaching task is ever done perfectly, and no teacher reaches all students. Parents, for their part, may have feelings of guilt or worry since they secretly feel they could have been better parents, and would not want the teacher to judge them.

Teachers are not always sure of why they teach what they teach; they do not want someone coming around who may expect a clear response to "Why teach history in units instead of by dates, the way they did when I went to school?"

Barriers such as these interfere with good communication between parent and teacher. Understanding these barriers is the first step in overcoming them.

"HOW DO YOU TALK WITH PARENTS?"

The individual conference with the parent present additional difficulties that we have yet to discuss. On the one hand, the teacher is a person whose education may be greater than that of the parent; on the other hand, the parent knows a great deal more about the life history of the child than the teacher can ever know. The higher personal stake of the parent in the welfare of the child introduces an element of emotionality that must be recognized. The same principles that operate in the student conference must also prevail in the parent conference. Here are a few warnings.[12]

1. *The teacher should not go on the defensive.*

   Parent: Well, Mary certainly got along better last year when she had Mrs. Dale for her English.
   Teacher: (Wrong) Perhaps Mrs. Dale didn's expect her to work very hard.
   (Better) She seemed to get along better with Mrs. Dale . . .

2. *The parent should not be put on the defensive.*

   Teacher: (Wrong) Of course, some parents see to it that their children have a place to study at home.
   (Better) Mary seems to find it difficult to get some of her work done at home . . .

3. *Do not, by implication, suggest that parents are doing a poor job.*

   Parent: I just don't know what to do with Mary, she is so rude.
   Teacher: (Wrong) You aren't severe enough with her.
   (Better) You feel Mary isn't acting well at home . . .

4. *Do not act omnipotent*

   Teacher: (Wrong) Now, with students in this ability group, we always tell the parents that they should take a vocational course.
   (Better) Mary seems to do better work in vocational courses. What do you think about this?

[12] Adapted from Faith W. Smitter and Bernard J. Donsdale, "Interpreting Education," California State Department of Education, Division of Elementary Education, Sacramento, Calf., April 1, 1947. (Mimeographed)

5. *Do not sound like a social snob.*

    Teacher: (Wrong) Now we have another student—his father is a doctor, you know—who is one of our top students.

6. *Do not pry into other people's affairs.*

    Parent: Oh, I am so mad at my husband.
    Teacher: (Wrong) Now, don't be afraid to tell me your problems; we are here to help you. What did your husband do?
                 (Better) Sometimes parents disagree. Now I think Mary . . .

7. *Be prepared to hear unpleasant, disturbing, unexpected things.*

    Parent: (Weeping) Oh, you just can't imagine the awful things that boy does. Why the other day . . .
    Teacher: (Wrong)   Why, Mrs. Jones, you shouldn't say things like that.
                 (Better)   These things can be very upsetting.

8. *Be discriminating in the information you give.*

    Parent: Now, tell me honestly, is Mary really dumb?
    Teacher: (Wrong) Now, Mrs. Jones, no one is really dumb.
                 (Wrong) Mary has an IQ of 80. That means she is probably subnormal. But there is nothing to worry about, really.
                 (Better) Mary has many assets. She has a good mind for practical and concrete problems, but she does not do so well with vague and abstract things. That's why she is adjusting so well to the new program we planned for her.

9. *Do not become a partisan in family affairs.*

    Parent: To tell the truth, Mary would be all right if her father would only stop nagging at her.
    Teacher: (Wrong) Yes, a lot of fathers really don't understand girls very well.
                 (Better) You feel Mary's father sometimes increases the problem.

10. *Watch your biases.*

    Parent: I've been trying to tell Mary that typing is better than chemistry. Who ever heard of a girl chemist?
    Teacher: (Wrong) Yes, it certainly isn't a good field for a girl. I'll tell her.
                 (Better) Women are entering different fields nowadays; how does Mary feel?

11. *Don't be seduced.*

    Parent: Mary tells me the most wonderful things about you. She really trusts you and so if you would just tell her that she ought to stop seeing that Morris boy I am sure you could influence her.

Teacher: (Wrong) Well, that's very nice of you to say that. I'll see what I can do; the Morris boy is really not a good influence.
(Better) You feel Mary is too involved with this boy?

There are many more pitfalls in parent–teacher conferences. Most of them are avoidable with tact, a clear understanding of the purpose of the conference, and skill in nondirective responses. Despite the problems which have been listed, the overwhelming evidence is that the lives of teachers would be easier if they had closer contact with parents. Working together, teachers and parents can help most adolescents.

Planning for conferences is one way to insure success. It would help to have on hand examples of the work the student has done, and include both good and poor work. If the teacher shows the parent one D paper after another and then says, "See what I am up against in trying to work with Susy," irreparable damage may be done to the parent–child relationship as well as the future school progress of the student. It is important to start with positive material, and with something concrete to show the parent: a report, an examination, a drawing, a comment made by another student. This will give the parent a feeling of security. Of course, to follow this immediately with negative material may make the parent suspicious: "He just showed me that good paper in order to soften the blow." The teacher must realistically express the feeling: "John does both good and poor work; we are interested, both of us, in helping him do more good than poor work. Here, I have some examples of his work. Let's look at this very good quiz he turned in yesterday. See—it is good because it shows grasp of the facts; it is neat, he had obviously studied and thought about the material. But in this paper, he just threw anything at all together."

- Describe a strength, special ability, or interest of the student and discuss the educational implications of this with the parent.
- Describe the student's most immediate need. Do not dwell on a weakness about which nothing can be done (low ability, physical handicap). The kind of weakness that can be helped through education is the major objective: improvement of reading, development of a hobby, finding a vocational objective, and the like. Get the parents' view of this weakness; what do the parents think might be done?
- Discuss both the teacher's and parents' plans for the student. It must be kept in mind that most of the parents whom the teacher meets will be mothers. The mother is more apt to be available; and, during most of the child's school life, has taken the most active interest in his or her schooling. A working mother will probably ask for time off from a job more readily than a working father. The father, although interested in the progress of the child, usually cannot or will not be as active in school affairs or find time for daytime conferences. Thus teachers will want to make a special effort to understand the particular problems of women since they will have to work primarily with wives and mothers.

Although parents have been the focus in this section, the teacher may often find an older brother or sister or grandparent the only responsible adult with whom to talk. Sometimes youth are with guardians or in foster homes. The same general principles of good counseling apply. An increasing number of young people are on their own, some are married, and still in high school. If the student is married, a conference including the spouse would be valuable. Often such married couples are made to feel like pariahs, not wanted by the school, something to be ashamed of and kept out of sight. Nothing should be further from the mind of the teacher. By gaining the cooperation of a spouse, a married student may be helped to complete his or her education, with significant implications for later job needs. Often these young people need help in such basic things as budgeting, dealing with hostile or intrusive in-laws, caring for an infant whose development they do not understand, living in very small quarters with no place to study. A sympathetic ear, even if no immediate solutions are forthcoming, may make a great deal of difference.

SUMMARY

Although the teacher's main function is teaching, the ways in which teachers also provide some personal assistance to students must be recognized. Troubled students have difficulty dealing with school demands. A sympathetic teacher who can learn to listen to students and thus gain some insight into the things that may trouble them, will often be helpful in solving or ameliorating these problems. Learning the skills of counseling takes practice. These skills are valuable when working with individuals, groups, leading extracurricular activities, and dealing with parents.

SELECTED READINGS

Combs, Arthur W., Donald L. Avila, and William W. Purkey, *Helping Relationships: Basic Concepts for the Helping Professions.* Boston: Allyn and Bacon, 1971. This important book shows how professionals who are committed to help others share common tasks and must fulfill common obligations toward those they seek to help.

Grier, William H., and Price M. Cobbs, *Black Rage.* New York: Basic Books, 1968. This book will help readers, both black and white, gain an understanding of black hostility.

Kiley, Margaret, *Personal and Interpersonal Appraisal Techniques for Counselors, Teachers, Students.* Springfield, Ill.: Charles C Thomas, 1975. Excellent compendium of many approaches which will aid the teacher-counselor; well written.

Klagsburn, Francine, *Too Young To Die: Youth and Suicide.* Boston: Houghton Mifflin, 1977. The rising numbers of young people who attempt or succeed in committing suicide is worthy of teacher attention in order to see clues that may identify and suggest appropriate action.

Ligon, Mary G., and Sarah W. McDaniel, *The Teacher's Role in Counseling.* Englewood Cliffs, N.J.: Prentice-Hall, 1970. Well-written introduction to counseling couched in terms useful for the classroom teacher; many excellent case materials.

Rogers, Carl, *Freedom To Learn.* Columbus, Ohio: Merrill, 1969. The originator of the nondirective approach to counseling and teaching.

————, *On Personal Power: Inner Strength and Its Revolutionary Impact.* New York: Delacorte Press, 1977. The most recent statement from the originator of nondirective or client-centered counseling. An affirmative and inspiring report.

Sarason, Seymour, et al., *Human Services and Resource Networks.* San Francisco: Jossey-Bass, 1977. Deft illustration and analysis of the ways in which professionals can obtain support from each other in serving others.

Weil, Marsha, Bruce Joyce, and Bridget Kluwin, *Personal Models of Teaching: Expanding Your Teaching Repertoire.* Englewood Cliffs, N.J.: Prenitce-Hall, 1978. "Nondirective Model," pp. 103–165. Detailed exposition of what it means to use the nondirective approach in both personal interviewing and counseling students and in teaching.

appendix A

bibliography
of teachers
in literature:
fact and fiction

Anderson, Margaret, *The Children of the South*. New York: Farrar, Straus, 1966.

Ashton-Warner, Sylvia, *Spinster*. New York: Bantam, 1961.

——, *Teacher*. New York: Bantam, 1964.

Auchincloss, Lewis, *The Rector of Justin*. Boston: Houghton Mifflin, 1964.

Barzun, Jacques, *Teacher in America*. Boston: Little, Brown, 1945.

Beam, Lura, *He Called Them by the Lightning: A Teacher's Odyssey in the Negro South, 1908–1919*. Indianapolis: Bobbs-Merrill, 1967.

Belfrage, Sylvia, *Freedom Summer*. New York: Viking, 1965.

Braithwaite, R. R., *To Sir, with Love*. Englewood Cliffs, N.J.: Prentice-Hall, 1959.

Brenton, Myron, *What's Happened to Teacher?* New York: Coward McCann, 1970.

Coles, Robert, *Children of Crisis: A Study of Courage and Fear*. Boston: Atlantic Monthly Press, 1967.

Conroy, Pat, *The Water Is Wide*. New York: Signet, 1972.

Craig, Eleanor, *P. S. You're Not Listening*. New York: Signet, 1972.

Dennison, George, *The Lives of Children: The Story of the First Street School*. New York: Random House, 1969.

Ernst, Morris, *The Teacher*. Englewood Cliffs, N.J.: Prentice-Hall, 1968.

Fischer, Louis, and David Schimmel, *The Civil Rights of Teachers*. New York: Harper & Row, 1973.

Forster, Margaret, *Miss Owen-Owen*. New York: Simon & Schuster, 1969.

Gibson, William, *The Miracle Worker*. New York: Knopf, 1957.

Greene, Mary Frances, and Orletta Ryan, *The Schoolchildren: Growing Up in the Slums.* New York: Pantheon, 1965.

Hackett, Allen A., *Quickened Spirit: A Biography of Frank S. Hackett.* New York: Riverdale Country School, Riverdale, N.Y., 1957.

Harris, Mark, *Twenty-One Twice: A Journal.* Boston: Little, Brown, 1966.

Herndon, James, *The Way It Spozed To Be.* New York: Simon & Schuster, 1968.

Hilton, James, *Goodbye, Mr. Chips.* Boston: Little, Brown, 1934.

Hunter, Evan, *The Blackboard Jungle.* New York: Simon & Schuster, 1954.

Inge, William, *Good Luck, Miss Wyckoff.* Boston: Little, Brown, 1970.

Johnson, Bernard (Ed.), *The Literature of Learning: A Teacher's Anthology.* New York: Holt, Rinehart and Winston, 1971.

Jones, Alan, *Students! Do Not Push Your Teacher Down the Stairs on Friday.* Baltimore: Penguin, 1973.

Kaufman, Bel, *Up the Down Staircase.* Englewood Cliffs, N.J.: Prentice-Hall, 1965.

Keller, Helen, *Teacher: Anne Sullivan Macy.* Garden City, N.Y.: Doubleday, 1955.

Kohl, Herbert, *36 Children.* New York: New American Library, 1967.

Kozol, Johnathan, *Death at an Early Age.* Boston: Houghton Mifflin, 1967.

Lortie, Dan C., *Schoolteacher: A Sociological Study.* Chicago: University of Chicago Press, 1967.

Otty, Nicholas, *Learner Teacher.* Baltimore: Penguin Books, 1972.

Patton, Frances, *Good Morning, Miss Dove.* New York: Dodd, Mead, 1954.

Perkins, Virginia C., *The End of the Week.* New York: Crowell-Collier and Macmillan, 1953.

Peterson, Houston (Ed.), *Great Teachers: Portrayed by Those Who Studied under Them.* New York: Vintage Books (Random House), 1946.

Prescott, Peter S., *A World of Our Own: Notes on Life and Learning in a Boys' Preparatory School.* New York: Dell, 1970.

Rasey, Marie I., *It Takes Time: An Autobiography of the Teaching Profession.* New York: Harper & Row, 1953.

Ross, L. O., *The Education of Hyman Kaplan.* New York: Harcourt, 1937.

Rubin, David, *The Rights of Teachers.* New York: Avon, 1973.

Spark, Muriel, *The Prime of Miss Jean Brodie.* Philadelphia: Lippincott, 1962.

Specht, Robert, *Tisha: The Story of a Young Teacher in the Alaskan Wilderness.* New York: St. Martin's, 1976.

Sterling, Philip (Ed.), *The Real Teachers: Thirty Inner City School Teachers.* New York: Random House, 1972.

Stong, Phil, *If School Keeps.* Philadelphia: Frederick A. Stokes Company, (Lippincott), 1940.

Stuart, Jesse, *The Thread That Runs So True.* New York: Scribner, 1949.

Stuart, Jesse, *To Teach, To Love*. New York: Scribner, 1970.

Sutherland, Elizabeth, *Letters from Mississippi*. New York: Signet, 1966.

Updike, John, *The Centaur*. New York: Knopf, 1963.

Van Til, William, *The Making of a Modern Educator*. Indianapolis: Bobbs-Merrill, 1961.

Weber, Julia, *My Country School Diary*. New York: Harper & Row, 1946.

Wilson, Charles H., *A Teacher Is a Person*. New York: Holt, Rinehart and Winston, 1956.

appendix B

bibliography
of adolescents
in literature:
fact and fiction

Anderson, Margaret, *The Children of the South.* New York: Farrar, Straus, 1966. A teacher reports on the impact of school desegregation in one of the first shattering public exposures: Clinton, Tennessee. Particular emphasis on the youths themselves.

Armour, Richard, *Through Darkest Adolescence.* New York: McGraw-Hill, 1963. Humorist Richard Armour's tour of No Man's Land and how to survive the trip.

Bradford, Richard, *Red Sky at Morning.* Philadelphia: Lippincott, 1968. An Anglo adolescent grows up in a Mexican-American mountain community during World War II.

Brannum, Mary, *When I Was 16.* New York: Platt & Munk, 1967. Eighteen women recall what life was like when they were 16, from the turn of the century to the 1960s, with "then" and "now" pictures of the women.

Brown, Claude, *Manchild in the Promised Land.* New York: Crowell-Collier and Macmillan, 1965. An autobiography that tells in frank terms a young man's struggles in the slums, through reform school and finally into law school.

Cather, Willa, *My Antonia.* Boston: Houghton Mifflin, 1924. The hardships of adolescence on the frontier farmland of Nebraska.

Coles, Robert, *Children of Crisis: A Study of Courage and Fear.* Boston: Little, Brown, 1967. Some particularly perceptive chapters on adolescents, black and white, who participated in various aspects of school desegregation.

Crane, Stephen, *The Red Badge of Courage.* New York: Dodd, Mead, 1957. (Other editions available.) The classic American war novel, which although dealing with the Civil War, raises essentially the same questions about war as those confronting contemporary youth.

Cusick, Philip A., *Inside High School: The Student's World.* New York: Holt, Rinehart and Winston, 1973. Based on active observation, this fascinating account attempts to describe the behavior of a number of high-school students and "the way their behavior affects themselves, the teachers, administrators, and the entire school organization."

Deilulio, Anthony M., "Youth Education: A Literary Perspective." In *Youth Education,* Raymond H. Muessig (Ed.). Washington, D.C.: Association for Supervision and Curriculum Development, 1968. (1968 Yearbook). A good bibliography of literature focusing on adolescents.

Dreiser, Theodore, *An American Tragedy.* New York: Liveright, 1925. (Originally published by Boni & Liveright, New York.) In part, a depiction of a young man revolting against the poverty and piety of his midwestern family.

Duncan, Lois, *Killing Mr. Griffin.* Boston: Little, Brown, 1978. High-school seniors kill their English teacher. Melodrama, but offers fascinating insights into expectations and behaviors of contemporary students and teachers.

Farrell, James T., *Studs Lonigan.* New York: Vanguard, 1935. Especially interesting in this trilogy of lower-class American life in the period of 1912 through the 1930s is *Young Lonigan,* which depicts the adolescence of the hero in which he carefully assumes the role demanded by his peers.

Frank, Anne, *The Diary of a Young Girl.* New York: Modern Library, 1958. Now a classic of growing up, in addition to being a revelation of the tragedy of the Jews during World War II.

Gibson, Althea, *I Always Wanted To Be Somebody.* New York: Harper & Row, 1958. Tennis champion Gibson recalls her life—and its turning point in adolescence—from ghetto to fame.

Glynn, Carolyn, *Don't Knock the Corners Off.* New York: Coward McCann, 1963. An adolescent coming to terms with herself in an English free-tuition school. Especially interesting since the novel is the work of a fifteen-year-old girl.

Gordon, Richard E., Katherine Gordon, and Max Gunther, "Children and Adolescents," in *The Split-Level Trap.* New York: Geis, 1961. Growing up absurd in the suburbs, through the eyes of psychiatrists.

Gregory, Dick, *Nigger.* New York: Dutton, 1964. Part of this candid autobiography is concerned with the comedian's adolescent years in the Chicago ghetto.

Griffith, Beatrice, *American Me.* Boston: Houghton Mifflin, 1948. Fictional accounts balanced with a sociological study of Mexican-American teenagers living in Los Angeles during World War II.

Hinton, Susan, *The Outsiders.* New York: Viking, 1967. A book aimed at adolescent readers, it nonetheless reveals adolescent concerns, especially regarding lifestyles. Slum teenagers versus upper-middle-class ones in Tulsa, Oklahoma. Interesting also since it is the work of a seventeen-year-old novelist.

Hulburd, David, *H Is for Heroin.* New York: Popular Library, 1952. Actual account of the experiences of a sixteen-year-old drug addict.

Kayira, Legson, *I Will Try.* New York: Bantam, 1965. The incredible, but true, story of the odyssey of a boy from an African village to an American college.

Keyes, Ralph, *Is There Life After High School?* New York: Warner Books, 1976. An amusing and insightful view of high school "after the fact." Especially helpful in providing documentation for the power of peer pressure and the search for status.

Killiea, Diane, *With Love from Karen.* Englewood Cliffs, N.J.: Prentice-Hall, 1963. Biography of a cerebral palsy victim whose determination and courage enable her and her family to triumph over her handicap.

Kirkwood, James, *Good Times/Bad Times.* New York: Simon & Schuster, 1968. A novel depicting life in a New England boys' prep school. Interrelationships of students and teachers reveal typical as well as atypical adolescent and teacher behaviors.

Knowles, John, *A Separate Peace.* New York: Crowell-Collier and Macmillan, 1959. Life in a New England prep school in which a young man realizes responsibilities of friendship which lead him to a greater awareness of self.

Konecky, Edith, *Allegra Maud Goldman.* New York: Harper & Row, 1978. An amusing account of growing from three to thirteen in an upper-middle-class 1930s Brooklyn-Jewish world.

Larrick, Nancy, and Eve Merriam, *Male and Female under 18, Frank Comments from Young People about Their Sex Roles Today.* New York: Discus Books, Avon, 1973. Prose and poetry written by young people in response to the question, "How does it feel to be a girl or a boy today?"

Malcolm X, *The Autobiography of Malcolm X.* New York: Grove Press, 1965. One of the most moving and significant autobiographies of the martyred leader of the Black Separatist movement.

Mayerson, Charlotte Leon (Ed.), *Two Blocks Apart: Juan Gonzales and Peter Quinn.* New York: Holt, Rinehart and Winston, 1965. Life in the same neighborhood but not in the same community. Graphic and absorbing demonstration of the polarity of ghetto and middle-class lives told by two boys in their own words.

McCall, Dan, *Jack the Bear.* New York: Doubleday, 1974. A thirteen-year-old struggles with family and community problems in Oakland, Calif.

McCullers, Carson, *The Heart Is a Lonely Hunter.* Boston: Houghton Mifflin, 1940. An adolescent girl views the racial and social tensions of her small, southern town.

———, *The Member of the Wedding.* Houghton Mifflin, 1946. Identification and loneliness—and ultimately the beginning of self-acceptance—are the strains of this beautifully written novel of southern small-town life.

Medved, Michael, and David Wallechinsky, *What Really Happened to the Class of '65?* New York: Ballantine, 1976. Fascinating follow-up of high-school seniors ten years later.

Miles, Richard, *Angel Loves Nobody.* New York: Dell, 1967. Describes undercurrent racial crises in a large heterogeneous high school. Somewhat overdramatic, but shows school as minority group students may well perceive it.

Motley, Willard, *Knock on Any Door.* New York: Appleton, 1947. A Chicago slum adolescent is torn between a life of crime and a life that his better instincts encourage. Ultimately he murders and is executed.

Neufeld, John, *Lisa, Bright and Dark.* New York: S. G. Phillips, 1969. The difficult story of an emotionally ill girl whose teachers "don't want to get involved."

O'Neill, Eugene, *Ah, Wilderness.* New York: Random House, 1933. Family life, centered, in this instance, around an adolescent boy who discovers something about the different kinds of love.

Petersen, Len, "Desert Soliloquy," in *Ways of Mankind,* Walter Goldschmidt (Ed.). Boston: Beacon Press, 1954. A Navaho youth reflects on the feeling of being torn between life on the reservation and the pull of the Anglo world.

Portis, Charles, *True Grit.* New York: Simon & Schuster, 1968. A fourteen-year-old girl seeks revenge for her father's death on the frontier of the 1870s and demonstrates her ability to compete at an adult level.

Potok, Chaim, *The Chosen.* Greenwich, Conn.: Fawcett, 1967. Describes the adolescence of two Jewish boys and the religious, as well as personal, crises which they faced. Unusually well written. Also, provides insight into Orthodox Jewish beliefs.

Russell, Ellen, *The Last Fix.* New York: Harcourt Brace Jovanovich, 1971. A melodramatic but gripping story of an adolescent's drug addiction and death.

Salinger, J. D., *Catcher in the Rye.* New York: Little, Brown, 1951. By now *the* book of fiction dealing with the twentieth-century American adolescent.

The Schoolboys of Barbiana (translated by Nora Rossi and Tom Cole.) *Letter to a Teacher.* New York: Random House, 1971. Poignant comments of Italian rural schoolboys expressing their dreams for an education that would allow them to alter their lives.

Shulman, Alix Kates, *Memoirs of an Ex-Prom Queen.* New York: Knopf, 1972. The new versus the old feminism explored through the recollections of a high school "star."

Smith, Betty, *A Tree Grows in Brooklyn.* New York: Harper & Row, 1947. An adolescent view of family life in the early 1900s.

Stegner, Wallace, *Wolf Willow: A History, A Story and a Memory of the Last Plains Frontier.* New York: Viking, 1966. Recollections of life in the 1920s on the Plains.

Strouse, Jean, *Up Against the Law.* New American Library, Signet Books, 1970. A nonjargon introduction to legal concerns for young people. Student rights, parents, marriage, drugs, sex, driving, employment, contracts, the draft, and "getting busted" are included topics.

Van Leeuwen, Jean (Ed.), *A Time of Growing.* New York: Random House, 1967. Eighteen short stories about adolescent girls from authors such as Shirley Jackson, Jessamyn West, Katherine Mansfield, Maureen Daly, and Reynolds Price.

Waterhouse, Keith, *Billy Liar.* New York: Berkeley, 1959. The agonies of growing up presented in hilarious terms by a young man who "comes to grips" by lying.

Wells, Patricia, *Babyhip.* New York: Dutton, 1967. A sixteen-year-old girl, somewhere between teeny-bopper and hippie, verbally overwhelms her parents, teachers, and guidance counselors.

West, Jessmyn, *Cress Delahanty.* New York: Harcourt Brace Jovanovich, 1954. Growing up with a middle-class California girl, who might have been thought of as the typical American adolescent. How different is this picture from today's "typical" adolescent?

Wolfe, Thomas, *Look Homeward, Angel.* New York: Scribner, 1947. A young man grows up observing his family and neighbors in a small town, discovers literature and ideas, and finally leaves home to "discover the world."

Wright, Richard, *Black Boy.* New York: Harper & Row, 1945. The difficulties of growing up in a segregated society, graphically presented.

Yglesias, Rafael, *Hide Fox, and All After.* Garden City, N.Y.: Doubleday, 1974. A gifted ninth-grader confronts the demands placed on him by friends, teachers, parents, and self.

Zindel, Paul, *The Effect of Gamma Rays on Man-in-the-Moon Marigolds.* New York: Harper & Row, 1971. A frustrated mother and her two teenage daughters—each of the three fighting for her own survival.

appendix C

selected filmography:
teaching and learning

Charly—103 min.—Films Incorporated—1968
  Based on the story "Flowers for Algeron," this is a moving account of the struggles of a retarded man's efforts to adjust to confusing changes in himself.

Child of the Future—55 min.—United Church of Christ (distrib.)—1968
  Communications expert Marshall McLuhan examines some possible ways in which tomorrow's children will learn.

Critical Moments in Teaching Film Series—Holt, Rinehart and Winston—1968, 1969, 1970

  Sixteen problem-centered open-ended films which focus on recurrent situations that teachers face. Some are at the elementary level, some at the secondary level. The situations are well developed, and the open-ended nature of the presentation provides an ideal stimulus for classroom discussion and/or role playing of endings. Each film is from 8 to 12 minutes long. A teacher's manual and student guide accompany the set of films.
  Titles in the series especially for secondary schools are:

  Some Courses Don't Count (A student is faced with a decision of desirability versus practicality in choosing an elective.)

  Just a Simple Misunderstanding (A student unthinkingly parrots his teacher's comments on the philosophy of famous writers, causing trouble at home.)

  The Day the Insects Took Over (Restoring order to a classroom discussion that has gone astray.)

  The Poetry in Paul (Handling a case of student plagiarism.)

  Less Far than the Arrow (Motivating a high-school class in poetry.)

  Report Card (How should students be graded: junior high.)

  Tense: Imperfect (The do-gooder teacher in a low socioeconomic area.)

  Walls (Apathy in a secondary school class.)

  I Walk Away in the Rain (High IQ and low effort.)

High School—75 min.—Osti (264 Third Street, Cambridge, Mass.)—1969
   Biting documentary of life in a "typical" middle-class large high school. Shows the many unconscious ways the system dehumanizes adolescents.

If . . .—105 mins.—Paramount Films—1969
   A feature length film about the ultimate destruction of humane education in an English private school ending with the students taking over and gunning down all the adults.

Marked for Failure—60 min.—Indiana University Film Service—1965
   School and on-the-street education in Harlem showing why humans from depressed areas are "kept out" of the cultural and economic mainstream of society.

The Miracle Worker—96 min.—United Artists—1962
   Moving film of William Gibson's play about teacher Annie Sullivan and her deaf-mute pupil Helen Keller.

No Reason To Stay—28 min.—National Film Board of Canada—1966
   Excruciating; part of the day in the life of a high-school student who is cast out by the "system." Highly recommended.

The Prime of Miss Jean Brodie—116 min.—Films Inc.—1969
   An adaptation of Muriel Spark's novel about a most unusual and influential teacher.

Summerhill—28 min.—National Film Board of Canada—1966
   A visit at the famous English educational experimental school with its founder, A. S. Neill. Highly interesting.

Teachers?—13 min.—Franciscan Films—1958
   A provocative and unusual parody of teaching styles which highlights by exaggeration those things which make a teacher good—and bad.

Thursday's Children—22 min.—Contemporary Films—1954
   Deaf children, striving to cope with a hearing world, work to overcome their handicap.

To Sir, with Love—105 min.—Columbia Cinematheque—1967
   Film version of the book by the same name, with Sidney Poitier portraying the problems of a black teacher in an English slum secondary school.

appendix D

bibliography
of fun and games
for learning

The materials suggested here are intended to be used as playful ways of engaging students in learning activities. Some of them involve immediate learning while others can be used as departure points for creative activities.

Armour, Richard, *Twisted Tales from Shakespeare.* New York: McGraw-Hill, 1957.

———, *It All Started with Marx.* New York: McGraw-Hill, 1958.

———, *The Classics Reclassified.* New York: McGraw-Hill, 1960.

———, *It All Started with Columbus.* New York: McGraw-Hill, 1961.

———, *It All Started with Hippocrates.* New York: McGraw-Hill, 1966.

———, *Punctured Poems: Famous First and Infamous Second Lines.* Englewood Cliffs, N.J.: Prentice-Hall, 1966.

Avedon, Elicott, and Brian Sutton Smith, *The Study of Games.* New York: Wiley, 1971.

Borgmann, Dmitri, *Language of Vacation.* New York: Scribner, 1965.

———, *Beyond Language.* New York: Scribner, 1967. Games and Quizzes all based on "playing with language."

Churchill, E. Richard, Linda R. Churchill, and Edward H. Blair, *Fun with American History.* New York: Abingdon, 1966.

———, *Fun with American Literature.* New York: Abingdon, 1968. Games, puzzles, and quizzes that can provide fun and profit in understanding of adults' and children's literature, plays, and movies.

Cook, Earnshaw, and Weldell R. Gardner, *Percentage Baseball.* Boston: Massachusetts Institute of Technology Press, 1968. The application of probability theory to baseball and an attack on conventional baseball strategy.

Databox: Fort Bragg. BFA Educational Media, 2211 Michigan Ave., Santa Monica, Calif. 90404.

Dodge, Lowell, *Creative Approaches to Tutoring.* Durham, N.C.: Youth Educational Services, 1966. Unusual approaches to learning tasks and classroom situations that frequently fail to enlist student interests.

Games and Tournaments for Classroom Earth. San Francisco: Zyphyros Publishing Co., 1201 Stanyan Street, San Francisco, Ca. 94117, 1976.

Games Magazine, 515 Madison Avenue, New York, New York 10022. Issued bi-monthly, the subscription price is $7.00 per year. An interesting—and amusing—collection of puzzles, games, tests, contests, and features.

Game-Sim, Series 1. California Learning Simulations, 750 Lurline Drive, Foster City, Ca. 94404.

Greenburg, Dan, and Marcia Jacobs, *How To Make Yourself Miserable.* New York: Random House, 1966. A how-to book designed to ensure failure, rejection, and misery.

The Insult Dictionary: How To Be Abusive in Five Languages. London: Wolfe, 1966. How to make language study interesting to those who may not ordinarily be interested.

Jaffee, Al, *Snappy Answers to Stupid Questions.* New York: New American Library, 1968. A catalog of humorous responses to questions with obvious answers. Illustrated with cartoons, some with several answers and most with space for additional ones to be supplied by the reader.

Levinson, Leonard Louis, *The Left Handed Dictionary.* New York: Crowell-Collier and Macmillan, 1966. A collection of 5000 "hip definitions" that take a playful second look at word meanings. Many of the definitions included are the work of celebrated humorists.

Lewis, George Q., *The Dictionary of Bloopers and Boners.* New York: Scholastic Book Services, 1967. A compilation of verbal "goofs" from "advertising" to "zoo."

MacDonald, Dwight (Ed.), *Parodies: An Anthology from Chaucer to Beerbohm—and After.* New York: Random House, 1960.

Peck, Matilda, and Morton J. Schultz, *Teaching Ideas that Make Learning Fun.* West Nyack, N.Y.: Parker, 1972.

Pottebaum, Gerard A., and Joyce Winkel, *1,029 Private Prayers for Worldly Christians* (a flip book). Dayton, Ohio: Pflaum Press, 1968.

"Persuasion Box." The Learning Seed Co., 145 Brentwood Drive, Palatin, Ill. 60067.

Price, Roger, and Leonard Stern, *Mad Libs.* Los Angeles: Price, Stern, Sloan, 1960.

————, *Sooper Mad Libs.* Los Angeles: Price, Stern, Sloan, 1962. Stories, songs, and rhymes with blank spaces where key words should appear. Instant success in teaching parts of speech.

————, *Monster Mad Libs.* Los Angeles: Price, Stern, Sloan, 1965.

Quinto, Lingo. Emmaus, Pa. Every issue presents stories in five languages; puzzles; and articles concerned with language development and usage.

Rodale, J. I., and the Staff of *Quinto Lingo, Laugh Your Way to Language Success.* Emmaus, Pa.: Rodale Press, 1965. Fun for language classes in five tongues: English, French, Spanish, Italian, and German. Also contains sections on word origins and other language-related information.

Ramsey, Betty Jo (Ed.), *The Little Book of Famous Insults.* Mount Vernon, N.Y: Peter Pauper Press, 1964.

"Ratrace." House of Games, Inc., 2633 Greenleaf Ave., Elk Grove Village, Ill. 60007.

Sackson, Sid, *A Gamut of Games.* New York: Random House, 1969.

Schatz, Albert, and Vivian Schatz, *Teaching Science with Garbage.* Emmaus, Pa.: Rodale Press, 1971.

Schultz, Charles M., *Snoopy, Vuelve A Casa.* (Snoopy, Come Home) and *Adelante, Charlie Brown* (You Can Do It, Charlie Brown). New York: Holt, Rinehart and Winston, 1969.

Scientific American. Every issue has a department devoted to mathematical puzzles and games.

Williams, Emmett, *An Anthology of Concrete Poetry.* New York: Something Else Press, 1968. Highly creative approaches to verse while making poetry-writing a semantic, visual, and phonetic game.

index